SUPERGIRL
KILLERS OF

writers
MARC ANDREYKO
DAN JURGENS

pencillers
KEVIN MAGUIRE
EMANUELA LUPACCHINO
EVAN "DOC" SHANER
LAN MEDINA
TOM DERENICK
BRAD WALKER
KARL KESEL

inkers
SEAN PARSONS
RAY McCARTHY
EVAN "DOC" SHANER
SCOTT HANNA
WADE VON GRAWBADGER
DREW HENNESSY
KARL KESEL

colorists
FCO PLASCENCIA
NATHAN FAIRBAIRN
CHRIS SOTOMAYOR

letterer
TOM NAPOLITANO

collection cover artists
TERRY and RACHEL DODSON

VOL. **1**

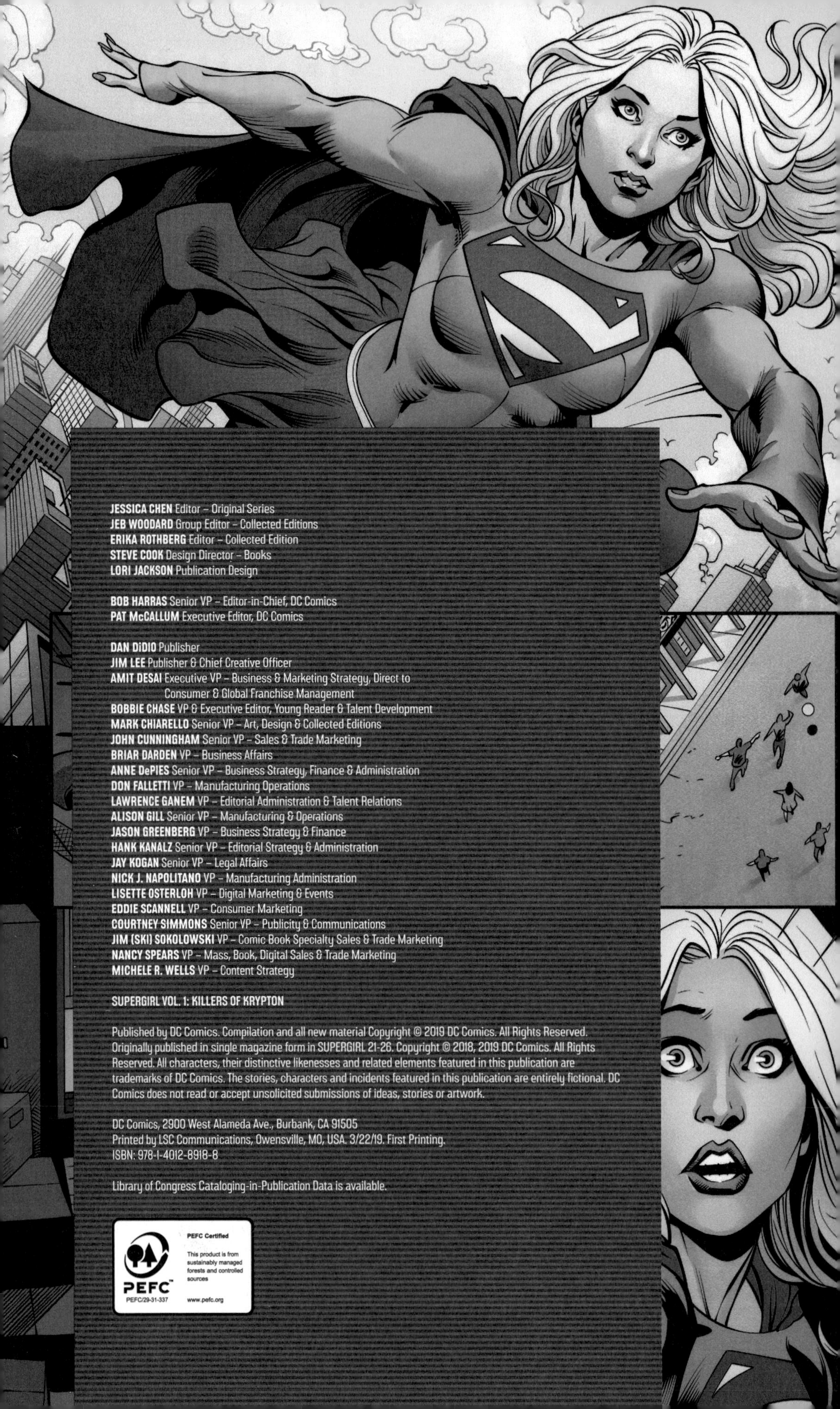

JESSICA CHEN Editor – Original Series
JEB WOODARD Group Editor – Collected Editions
ERIKA ROTHBERG Editor – Collected Edition
STEVE COOK Design Director – Books
LORI JACKSON Publication Design

BOB HARRAS Senior VP – Editor-in-Chief, DC Comics
PAT McCALLUM Executive Editor, DC Comics

DAN DiDIO Publisher
JIM LEE Publisher & Chief Creative Officer
AMIT DESAI Executive VP – Business & Marketing Strategy, Direct to Consumer & Global Franchise Management
BOBBIE CHASE VP & Executive Editor, Young Reader & Talent Development
MARK CHIARELLO Senior VP – Art, Design & Collected Editions
JOHN CUNNINGHAM Senior VP – Sales & Trade Marketing
BRIAR DARDEN VP – Business Affairs
ANNE DePIES Senior VP – Business Strategy, Finance & Administration
DON FALLETTI VP – Manufacturing Operations
LAWRENCE GANEM VP – Editorial Administration & Talent Relations
ALISON GILL Senior VP – Manufacturing & Operations
JASON GREENBERG VP – Business Strategy & Finance
HANK KANALZ Senior VP – Editorial Strategy & Administration
JAY KOGAN Senior VP – Legal Affairs
NICK J. NAPOLITANO VP – Manufacturing Administration
LISETTE OSTERLOH VP – Digital Marketing & Events
EDDIE SCANNELL VP – Consumer Marketing
COURTNEY SIMMONS Senior VP – Publicity & Communications
JIM (SKI) SOKOLOWSKI VP – Comic Book Specialty Sales & Trade Marketing
NANCY SPEARS VP – Mass, Book, Digital Sales & Trade Marketing
MICHELE R. WELLS VP – Content Strategy

SUPERGIRL VOL. 1: KILLERS OF KRYPTON

DC Comics, 2900 West Alameda Ave., Burbank, CA 91505
Printed by LSC Communications, Owensville, MO, USA. 3/22/19. First Printing.
ISBN: 978-1-4012-8918-8

Library of Congress Cataloging-in-Publication Data is available.

PEFC Certified
This product is from sustainably managed forests and controlled sources
PEFC
PEFC/29-31-337
www.pefc.org

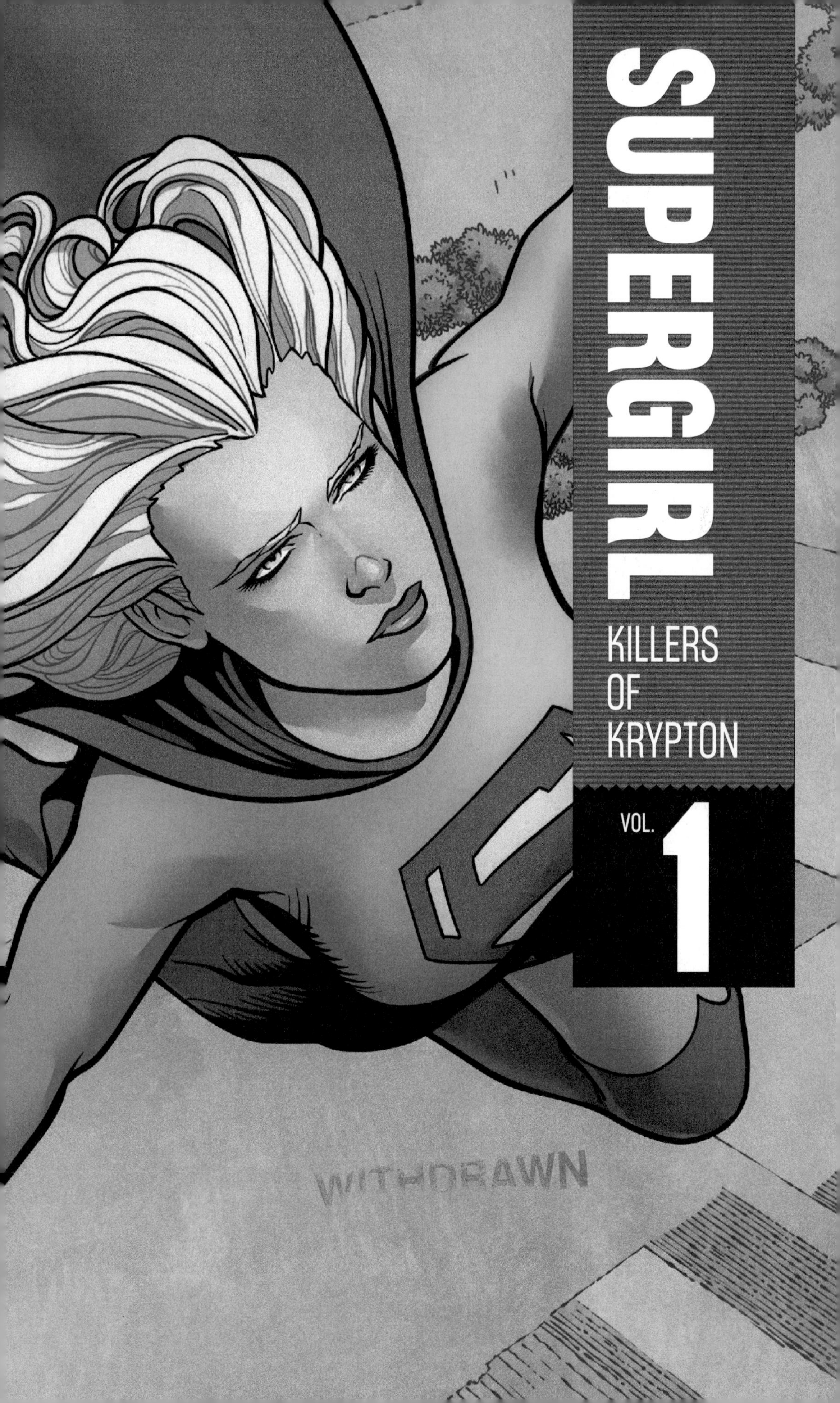
SUPERGIRL
KILLERS OF KRYPTON
VOL. 1

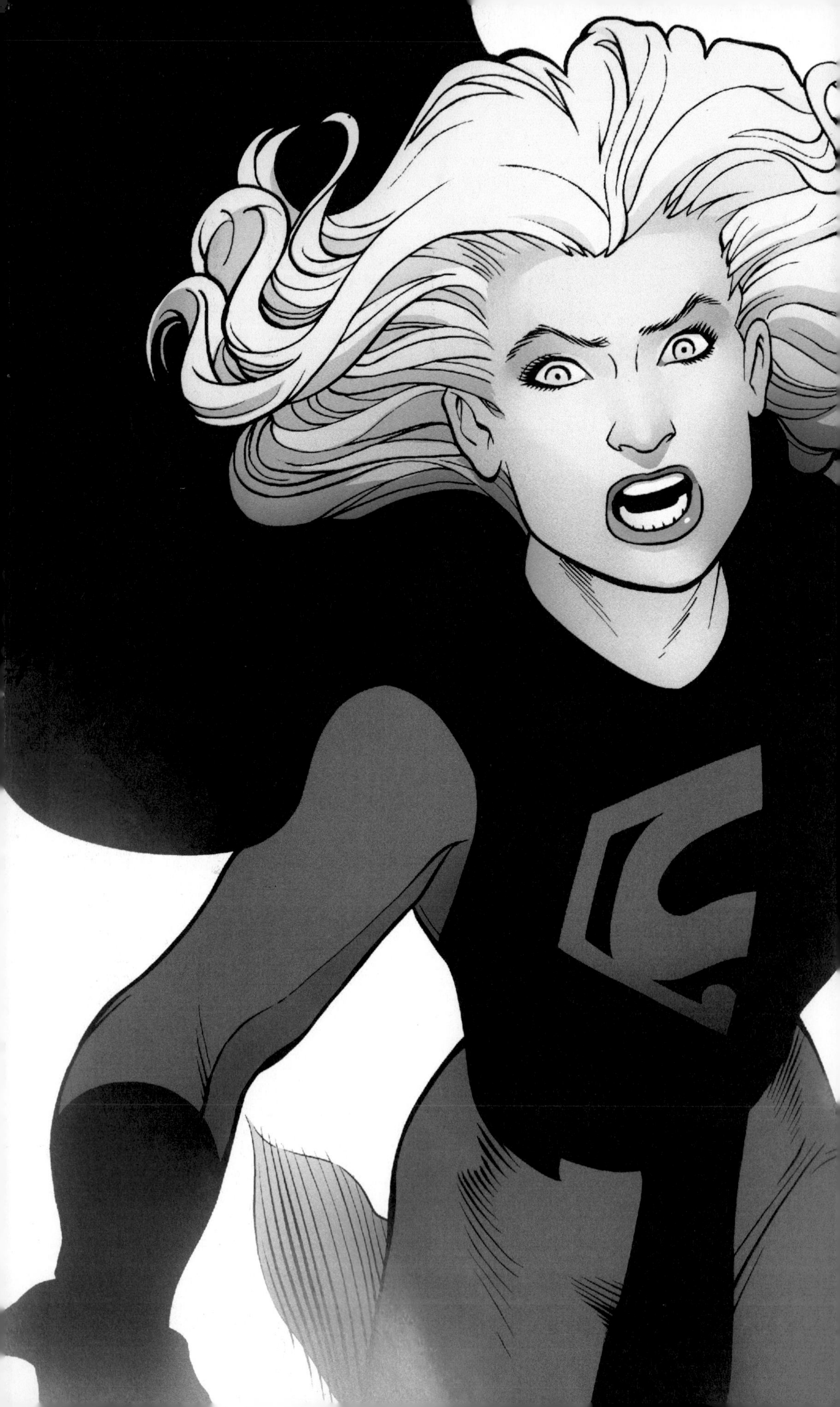

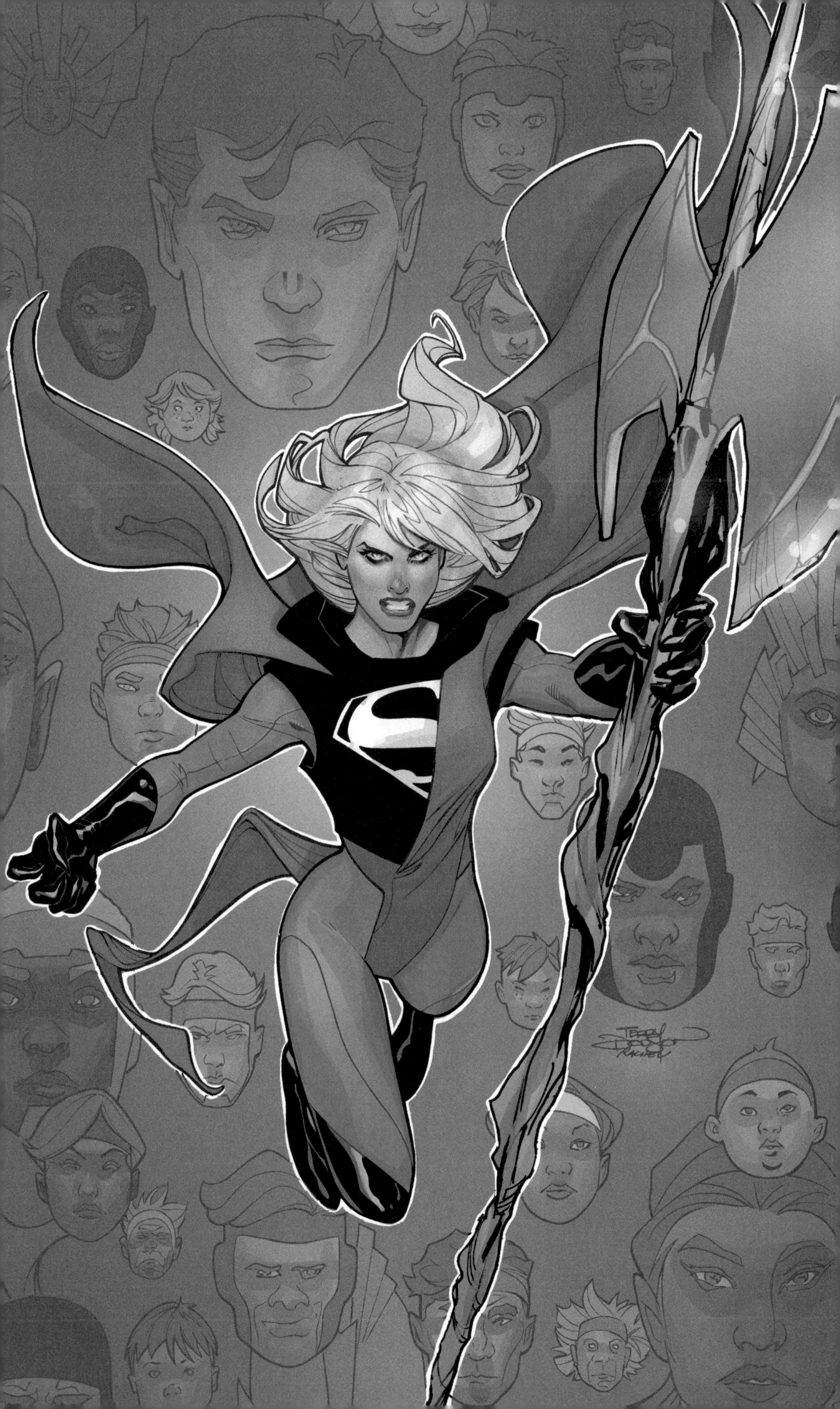

SUPERGIRL
#21

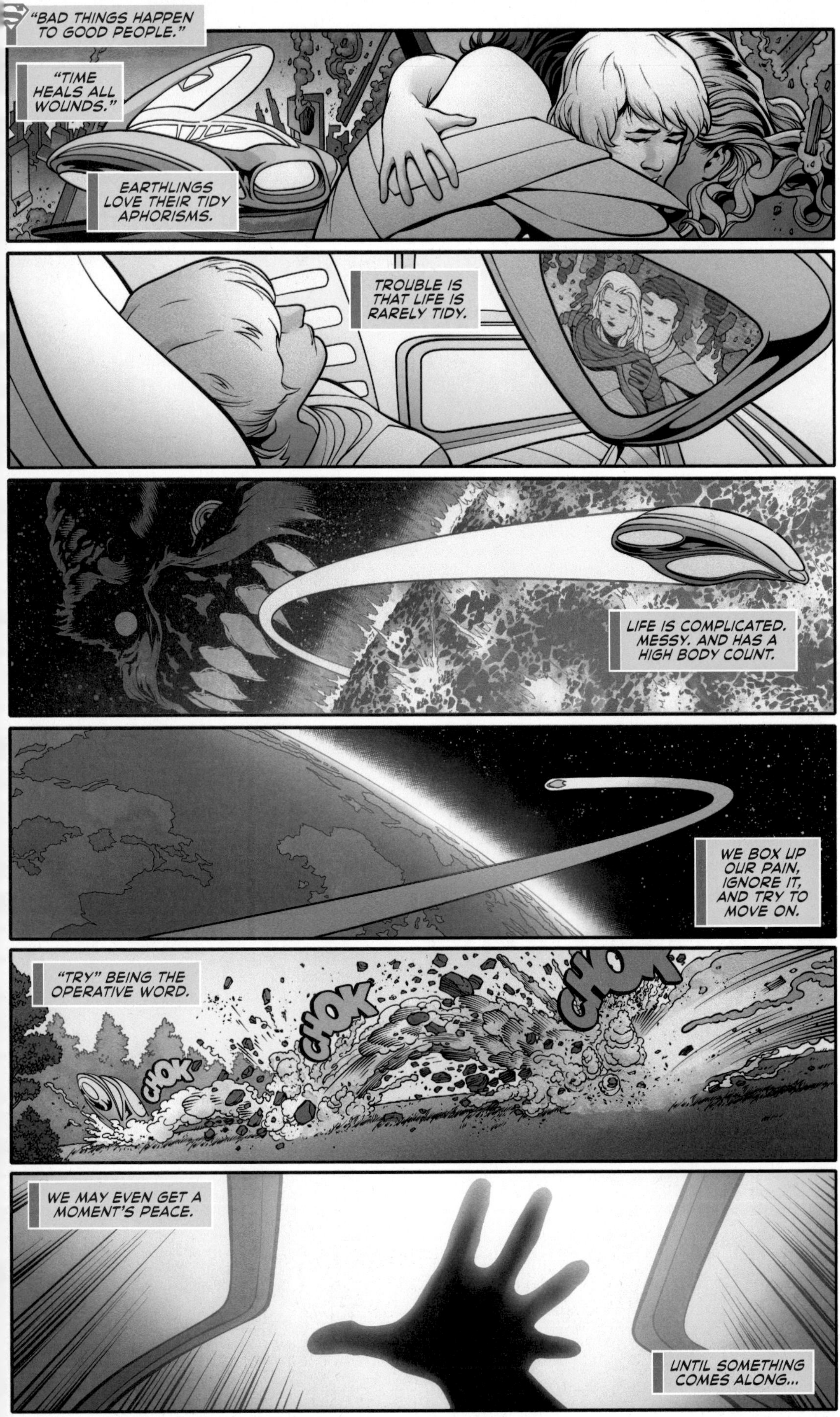
"BAD THINGS HAPPEN TO GOOD PEOPLE."
"TIME HEALS ALL WOUNDS."
EARTHLINGS LOVE THEIR TIDY APHORISMS.
TROUBLE IS THAT LIFE IS RARELY TIDY.
LIFE IS COMPLICATED. MESSY. AND HAS A HIGH BODY COUNT.
WE BOX UP OUR PAIN, IGNORE IT, AND TRY TO MOVE ON.
"TRY" BEING THE OPERATIVE WORD.
CHOK
CHOK
CHOK
CHOK
WE MAY EVEN GET A MOMENT'S PEACE.
UNTIL SOMETHING COMES ALONG...

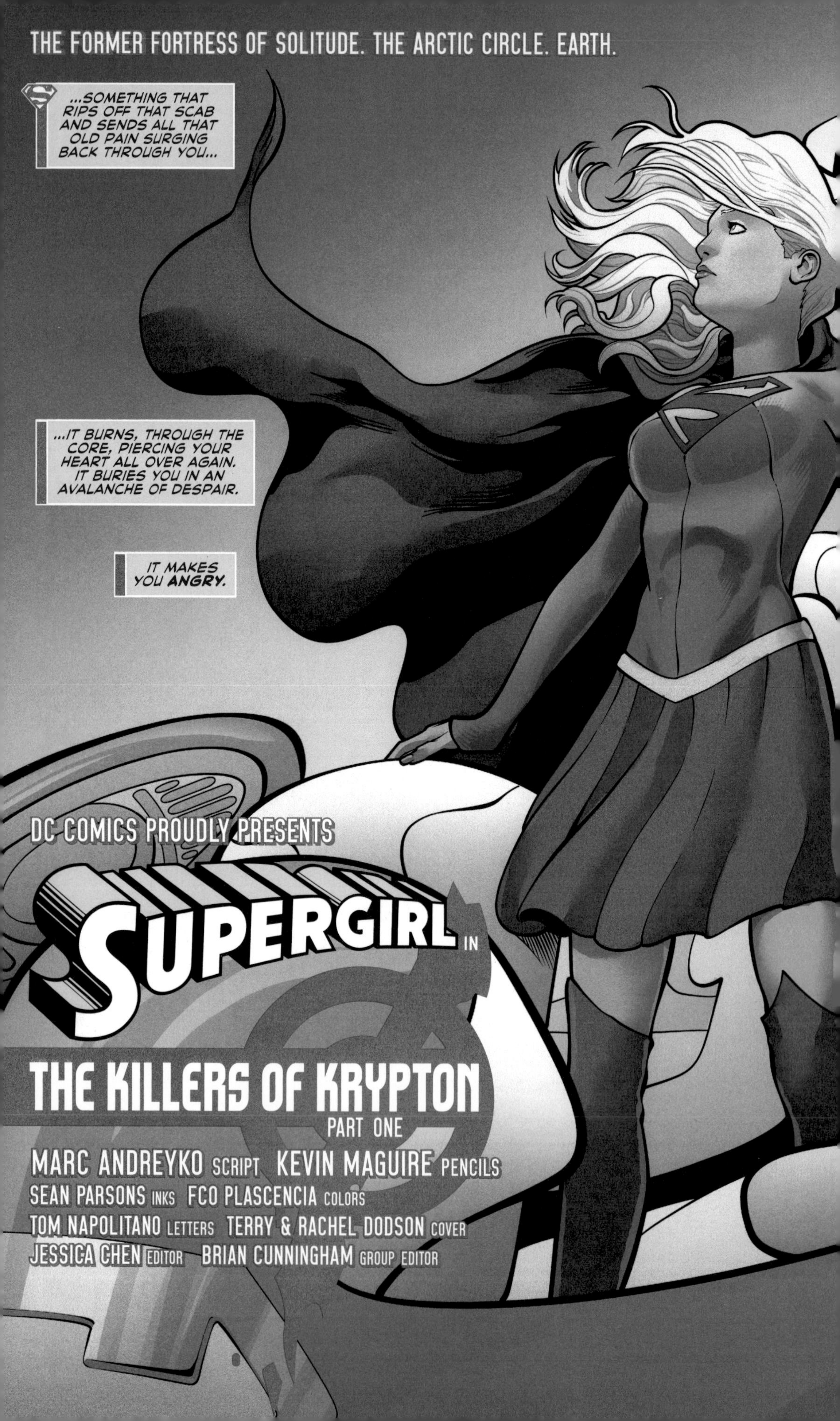
THE FORMER FORTRESS OF SOLITUDE. THE ARCTIC CIRCLE. EARTH.
...SOMETHING THAT RIPS OFF THAT SCAB AND SENDS ALL THAT OLD PAIN SURGING BACK THROUGH YOU...
...IT BURNS, THROUGH THE CORE, PIERCING YOUR HEART ALL OVER AGAIN. IT BURIES YOU IN AN AVALANCHE OF DESPAIR.
IT MAKES YOU ANGRY.
DC COMICS PROUDLY PRESENTS
SUPERGIRL IN
THE KILLERS OF KRYPTON
PART ONE
MARC ANDREYKO SCRIPT KEVIN MAGUIRE PENCILS
SEAN PARSONS INKS FCO PLASCENCIA COLORS
TOM NAPOLITANO LETTERS TERRY & RACHEL DODSON COVER
JESSICA CHEN EDITOR BRIAN CUNNINGHAM GROUP EDITOR

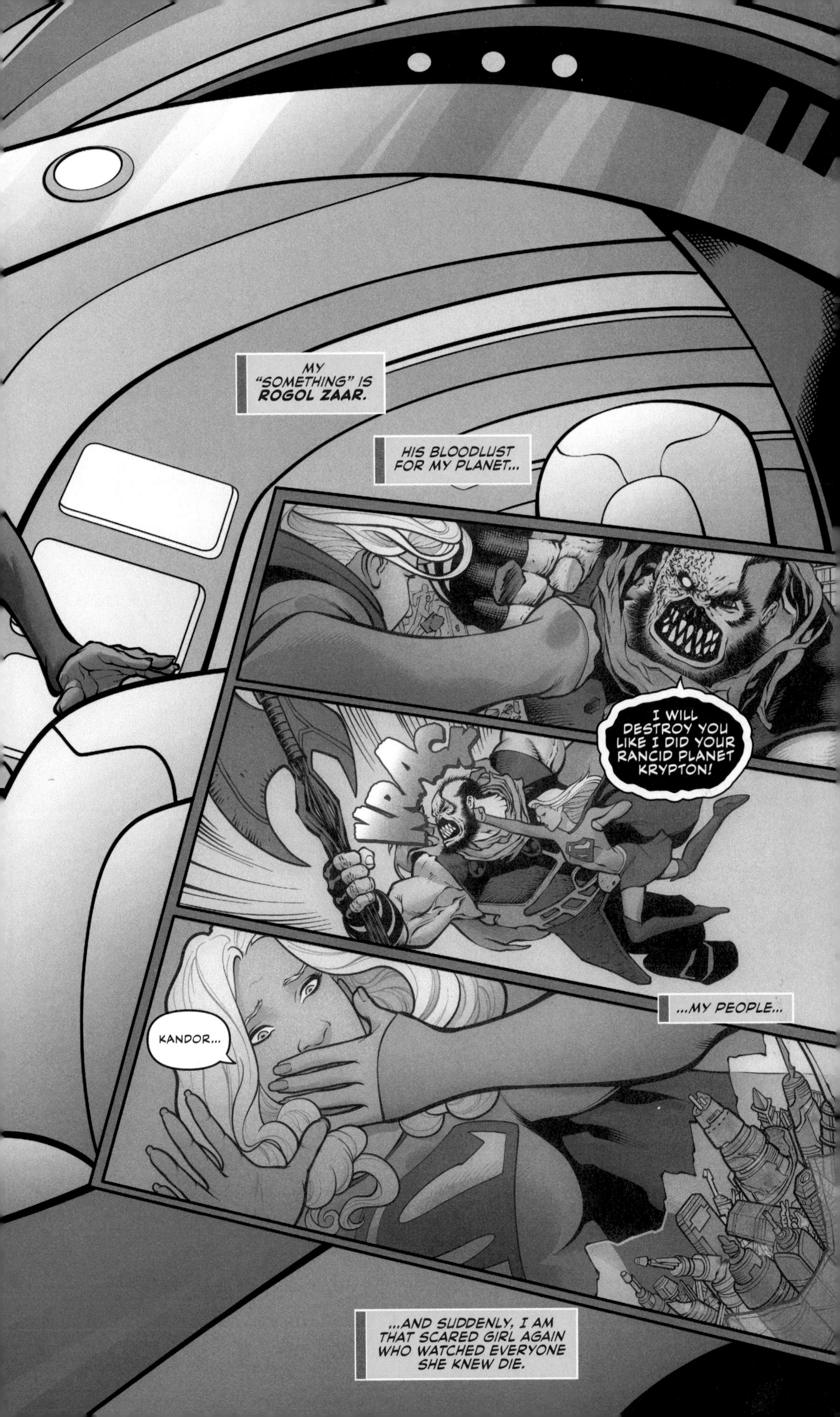
MY "SOMETHING" IS ROGOL ZAAR.
HIS BLOODLUST FOR MY PLANET...
I WILL DESTROY YOU LIKE I DID YOUR RANCID PLANET KRYPTON!
WRACK
...MY PEOPLE...
KANDOR...
...AND SUDDENLY, I AM THAT SCARED GIRL AGAIN WHO WATCHED EVERYONE SHE KNEW DIE.

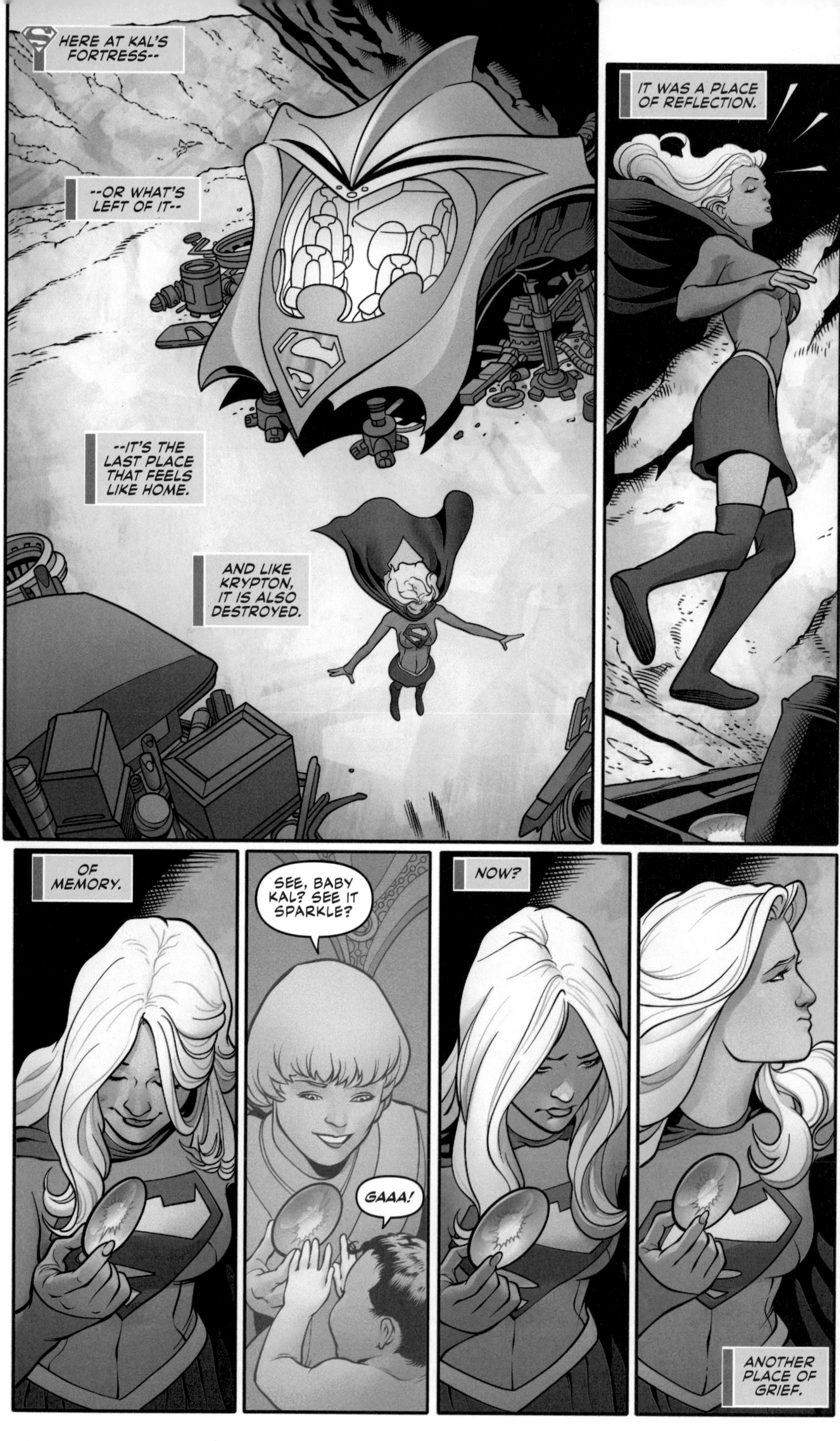
HERE AT KAL'S FORTRESS--
--OR WHAT'S LEFT OF IT--
--IT'S THE LAST PLACE THAT FEELS LIKE HOME.
AND LIKE KRYPTON, IT IS ALSO DESTROYED.
IT WAS A PLACE OF REFLECTION.
OF MEMORY.
SEE, BABY KAL? SEE IT SPARKLE?
GAAA!
NOW?
ANOTHER PLACE OF GRIEF.

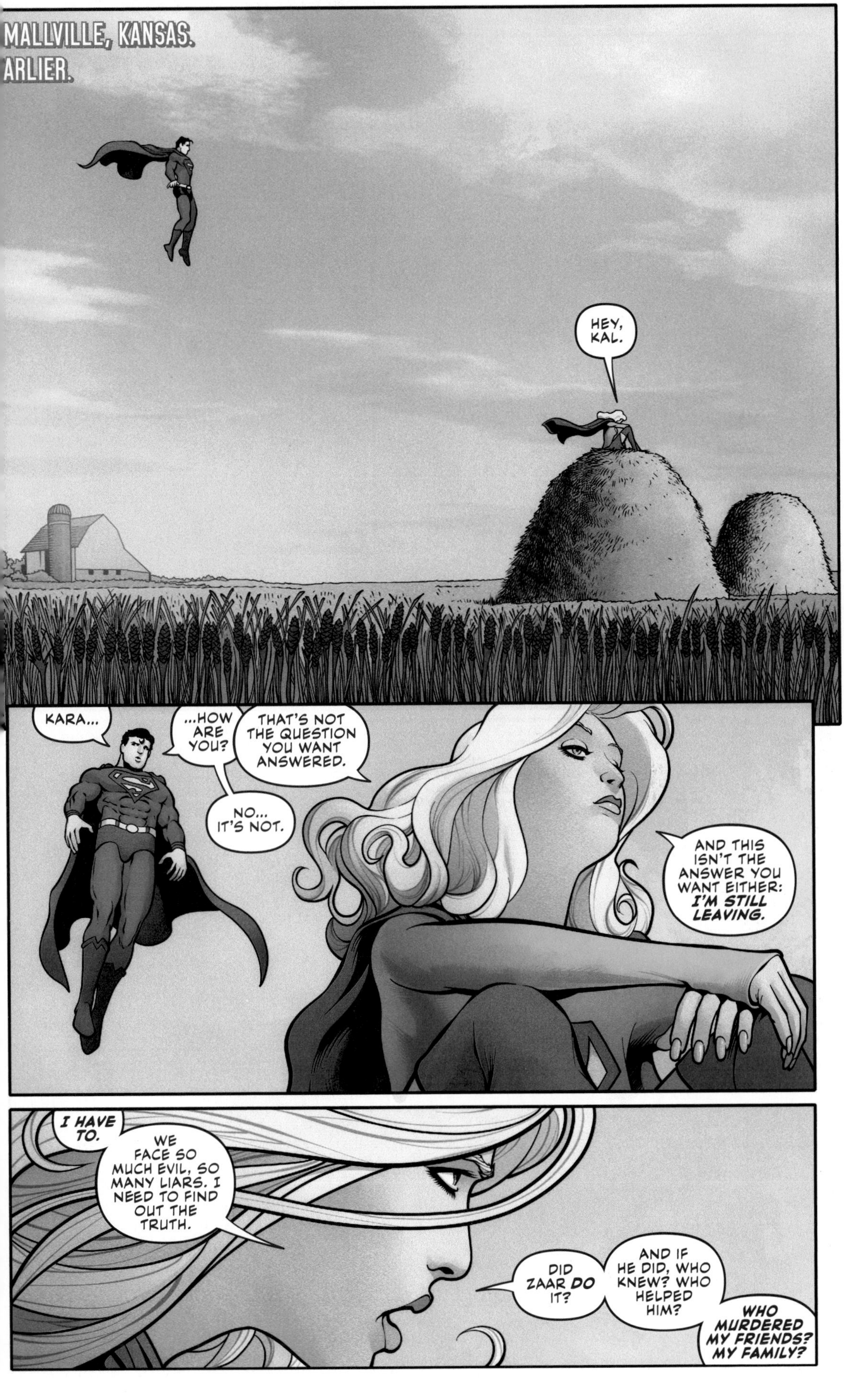
MALLVILLE, KANSAS.
ARLIER.
HEY, KAL.
KARA...
...HOW ARE YOU?
THAT'S NOT THE QUESTION YOU WANT ANSWERED.
NO... IT'S NOT.
AND THIS ISN'T THE ANSWER YOU WANT EITHER: *I'M STILL LEAVING.*
I HAVE TO.
WE FACE SO MUCH EVIL, SO MANY LIARS. I NEED TO FIND OUT THE TRUTH.
DID ZAAR *DO* IT?
AND IF HE DID, WHO KNEW? WHO HELPED HIM?
WHO MURDERED MY FRIENDS? MY FAMILY?

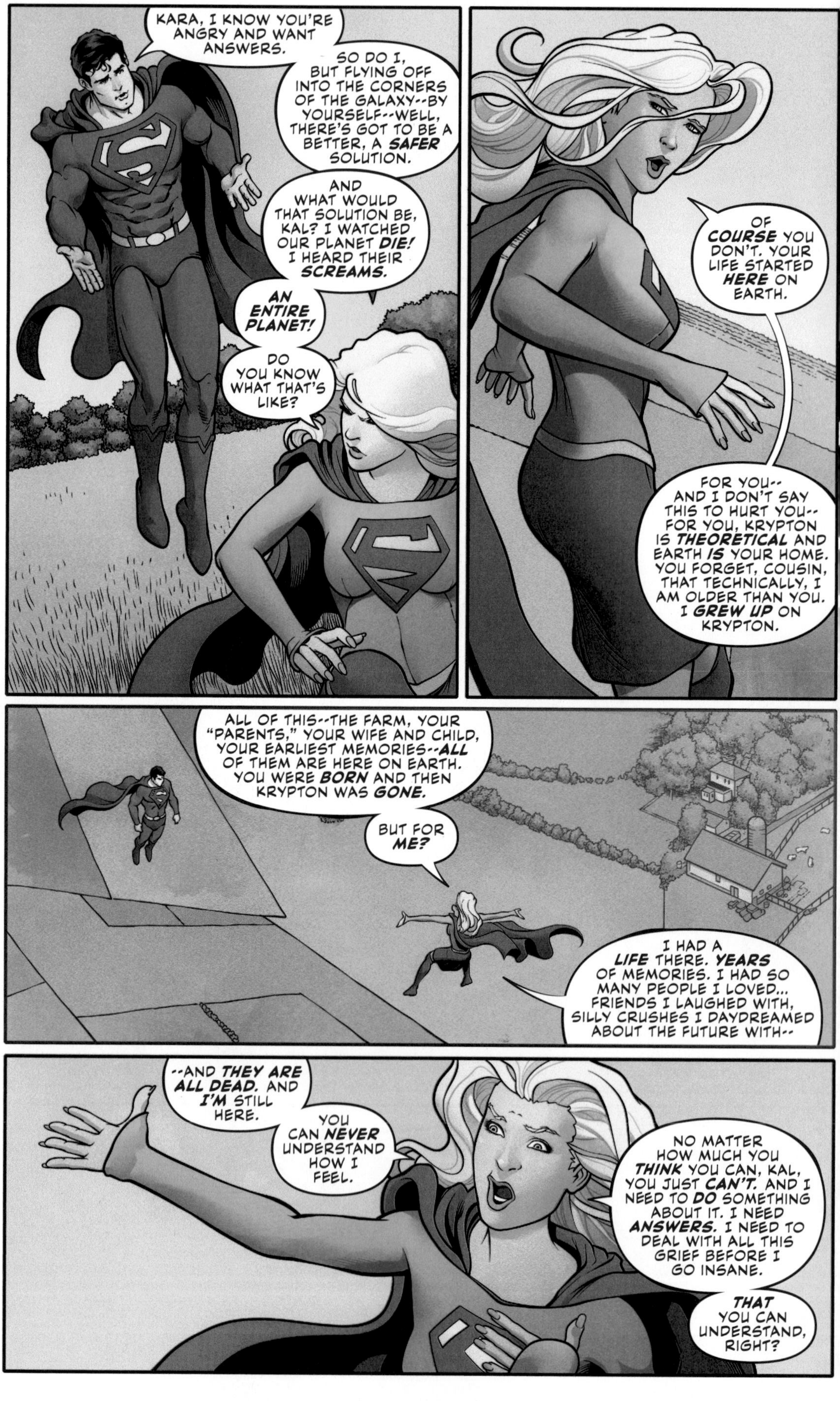
KARA, I KNOW YOU'RE ANGRY AND WANT ANSWERS.
SO DO I, BUT FLYING OFF INTO THE CORNERS OF THE GALAXY--BY YOURSELF--WELL, THERE'S GOT TO BE A BETTER, A SAFER SOLUTION.
AND WHAT WOULD THAT SOLUTION BE, KAL? I WATCHED OUR PLANET DIE! I HEARD THEIR SCREAMS.
AN ENTIRE PLANET!
DO YOU KNOW WHAT THAT'S LIKE?
OF COURSE YOU DON'T. YOUR LIFE STARTED HERE ON EARTH.
FOR YOU--AND I DON'T SAY THIS TO HURT YOU--FOR YOU, KRYPTON IS THEORETICAL AND EARTH IS YOUR HOME. YOU FORGET, COUSIN, THAT TECHNICALLY, I AM OLDER THAN YOU. I GREW UP ON KRYPTON.
ALL OF THIS--THE FARM, YOUR "PARENTS," YOUR WIFE AND CHILD, YOUR EARLIEST MEMORIES--ALL OF THEM ARE HERE ON EARTH. YOU WERE BORN AND THEN KRYPTON WAS GONE.
BUT FOR ME?
I HAD A LIFE THERE. YEARS OF MEMORIES. I HAD SO MANY PEOPLE I LOVED... FRIENDS I LAUGHED WITH, SILLY CRUSHES I DAYDREAMED ABOUT THE FUTURE WITH--
--AND THEY ARE ALL DEAD. AND I'M STILL HERE.
YOU CAN NEVER UNDERSTAND HOW I FEEL.
NO MATTER HOW MUCH YOU THINK YOU CAN, KAL, YOU JUST CAN'T. AND I NEED TO DO SOMETHING ABOUT IT. I NEED ANSWERS. I NEED TO DEAL WITH ALL THIS GRIEF BEFORE I GO INSANE.
THAT YOU CAN UNDERSTAND, RIGHT?

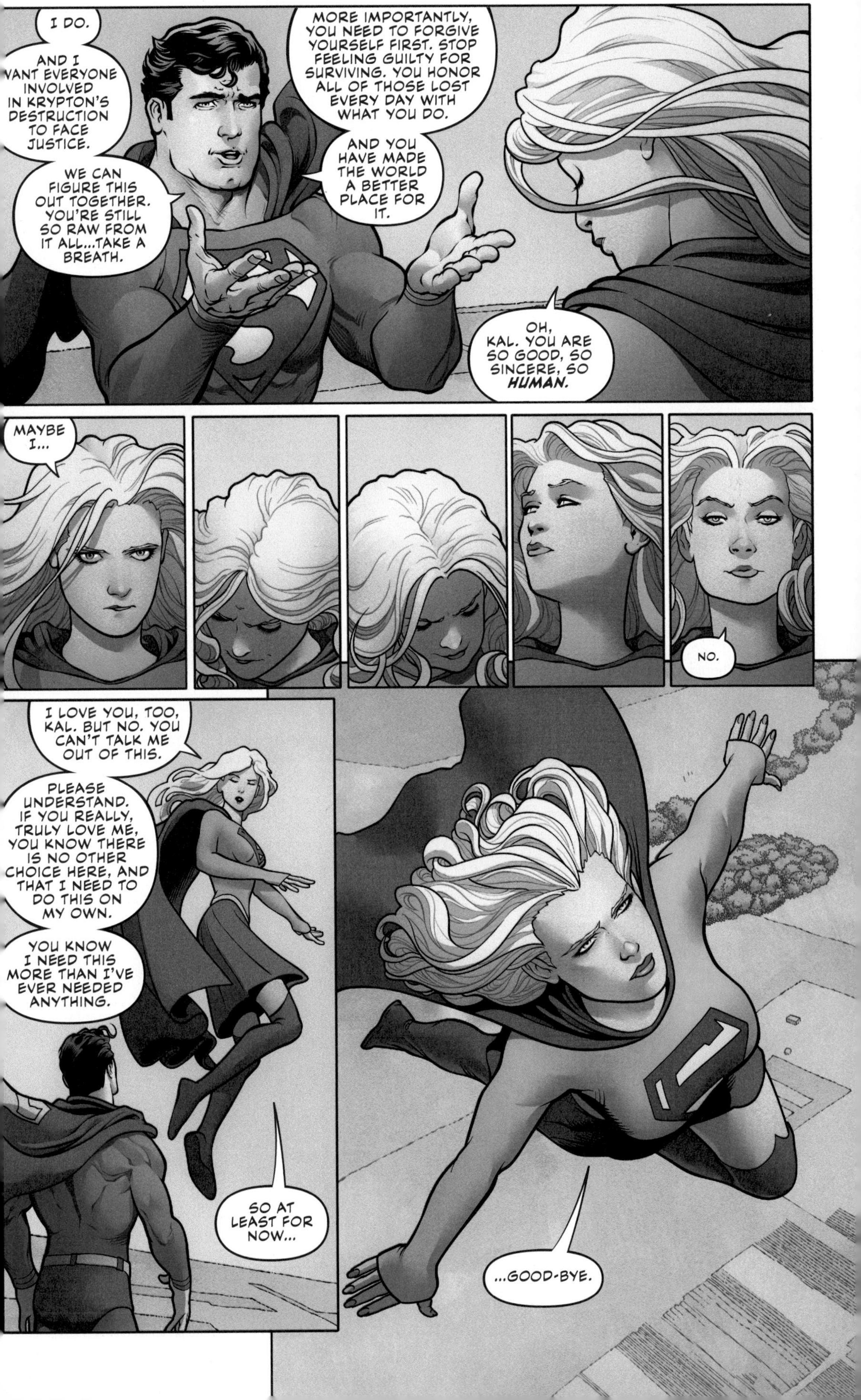
I DO.
AND I WANT EVERYONE INVOLVED IN KRYPTON'S DESTRUCTION TO FACE JUSTICE.
WE CAN FIGURE THIS OUT TOGETHER. YOU'RE STILL SO RAW FROM IT ALL...TAKE A BREATH.
MORE IMPORTANTLY, YOU NEED TO FORGIVE YOURSELF FIRST. STOP FEELING GUILTY FOR SURVIVING. YOU HONOR ALL OF THOSE LOST EVERY DAY WITH WHAT YOU DO.
AND YOU HAVE MADE THE WORLD A BETTER PLACE FOR IT.
OH, KAL. YOU ARE SO GOOD, SO SINCERE, SO ***HUMAN.***
MAYBE I...
NO.
I LOVE YOU, TOO, KAL. BUT NO. YOU CAN'T TALK ME OUT OF THIS.
PLEASE UNDERSTAND. IF YOU REALLY, TRULY LOVE ME, YOU KNOW THERE IS NO OTHER CHOICE HERE, AND THAT I NEED TO DO THIS ON MY OWN.
YOU KNOW I NEED THIS MORE THAN I'VE EVER NEEDED ANYTHING.
SO AT LEAST FOR NOW...
...GOOD-BYE.

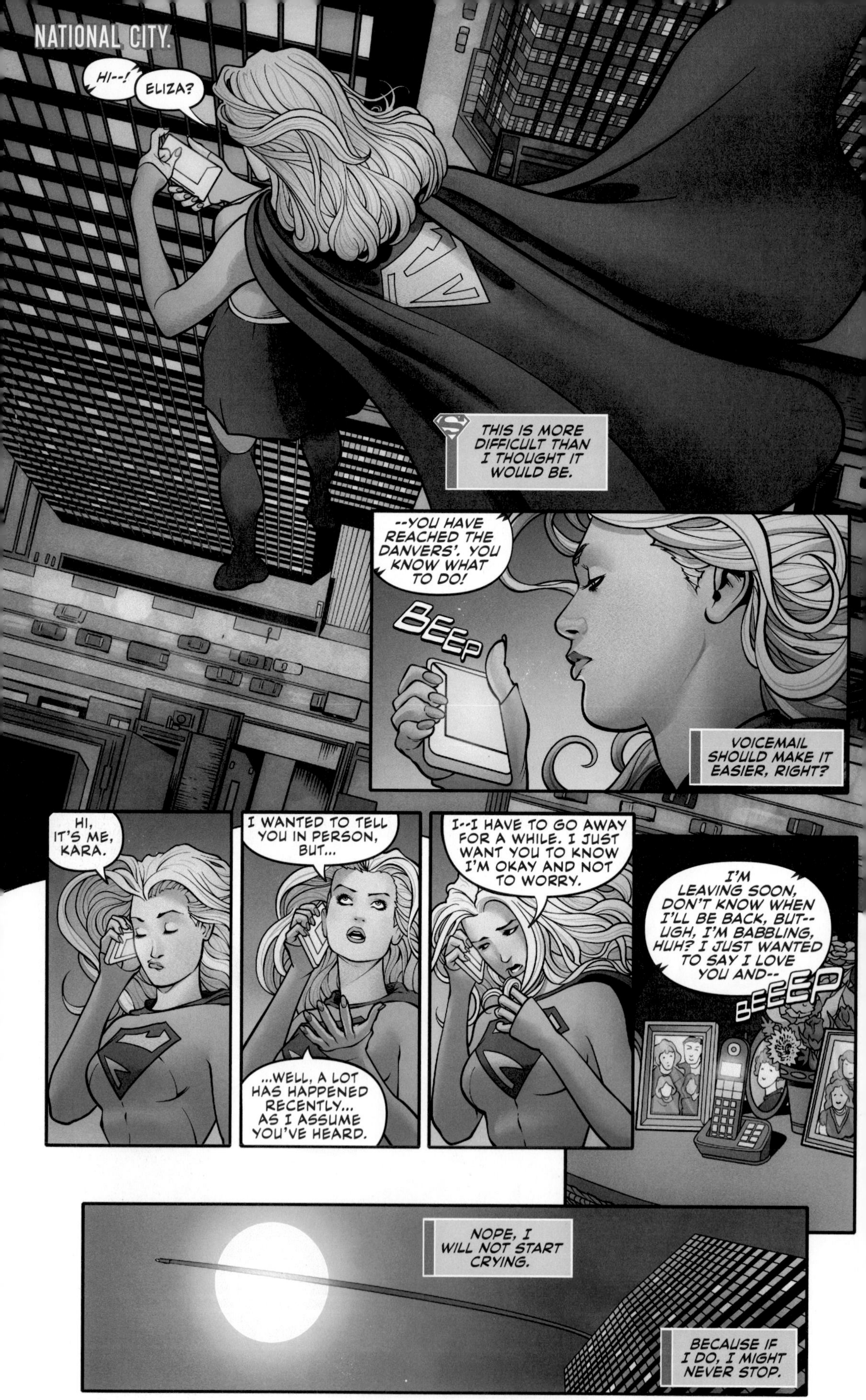
NATIONAL CITY.
HI--!
ELIZA?
THIS IS MORE DIFFICULT THAN I THOUGHT IT WOULD BE.
--YOU HAVE REACHED THE DANVERS'. YOU KNOW WHAT TO DO!
BEEP
VOICEMAIL SHOULD MAKE IT EASIER, RIGHT?
HI, IT'S ME, KARA.
I WANTED TO TELL YOU IN PERSON, BUT...
...WELL, A LOT HAS HAPPENED RECENTLY... AS I ASSUME YOU'VE HEARD.
I--I HAVE TO GO AWAY FOR A WHILE. I JUST WANT YOU TO KNOW I'M OKAY AND NOT TO WORRY.
I'M LEAVING SOON, DON'T KNOW WHEN I'LL BE BACK, BUT-- UGH, I'M BABBLING, HUH? I JUST WANTED TO SAY I LOVE YOU AND--
BEEEEP
NOPE, I WILL NOT START CRYING.
BECAUSE IF I DO, I MIGHT NEVER STOP.

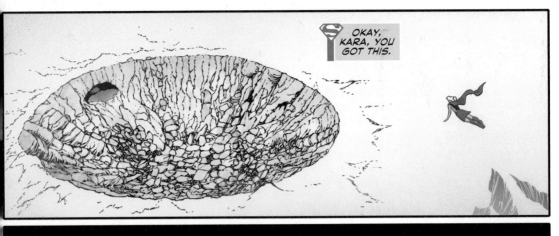

OKAY, KARA, YOU GOT THIS.

YOU'RE A STRONG, INDEPENDENT YOUNG WOMAN. HECK, YOU'RE A SUPERHERO. COUSIN OF *THE* SUPERHERO.

AND HE MUST'VE RUBBED OFF ON YOU. WHY ELSE DID I JUST USE THE WORD "HECK"?

BUT WHERE DO I START?

LIKE BATMAN ALWAYS SAYS (WHEN HE'S NOT SCARING SMALL CHILDREN)--

--"FOLLOW THE CLUES."

I'VE GOT YOUR VAUNTED WEAPON, ROGOL ZAAR, AND VERY SOON...

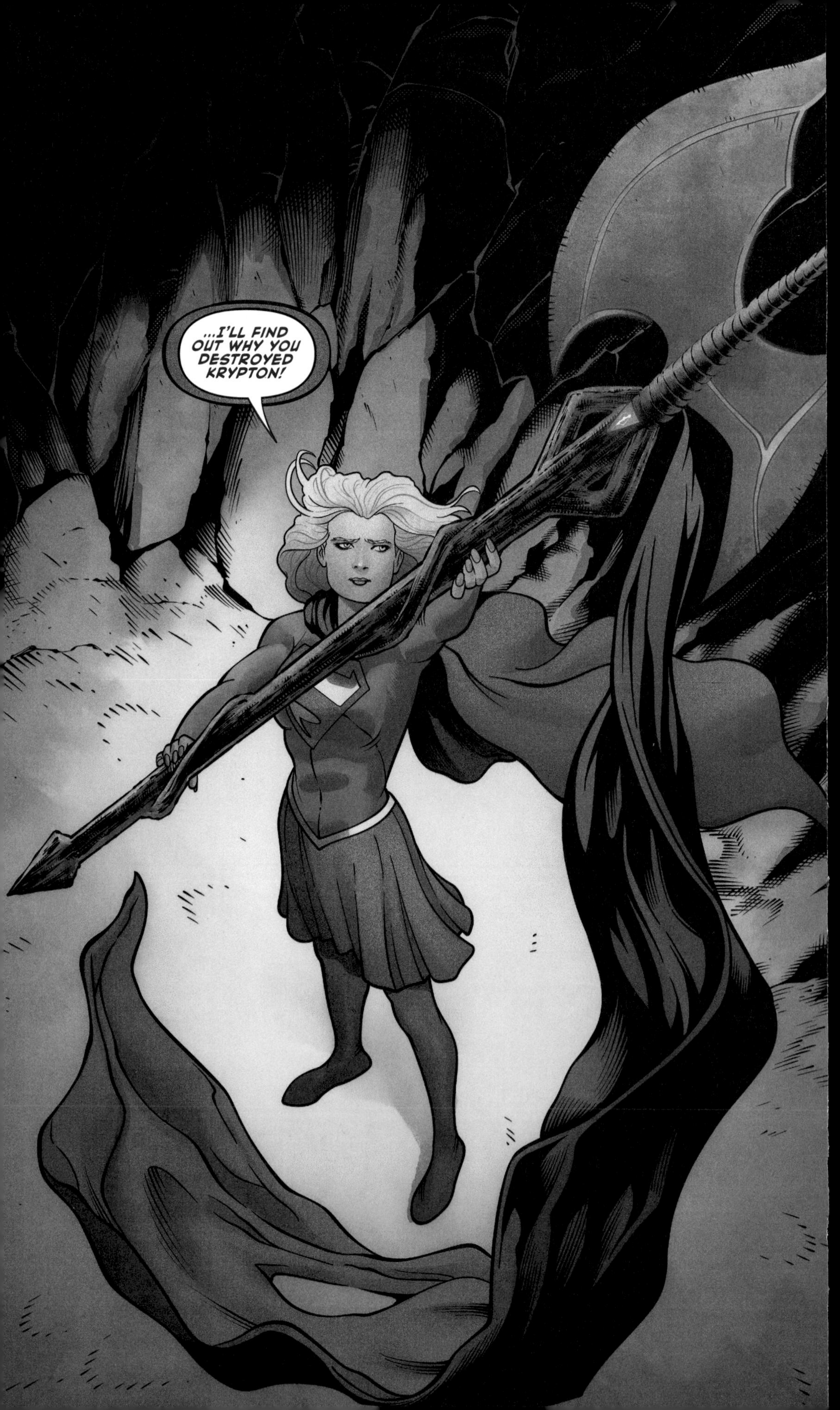
...I'LL FIND OUT WHY YOU DESTROYED KRYPTON!

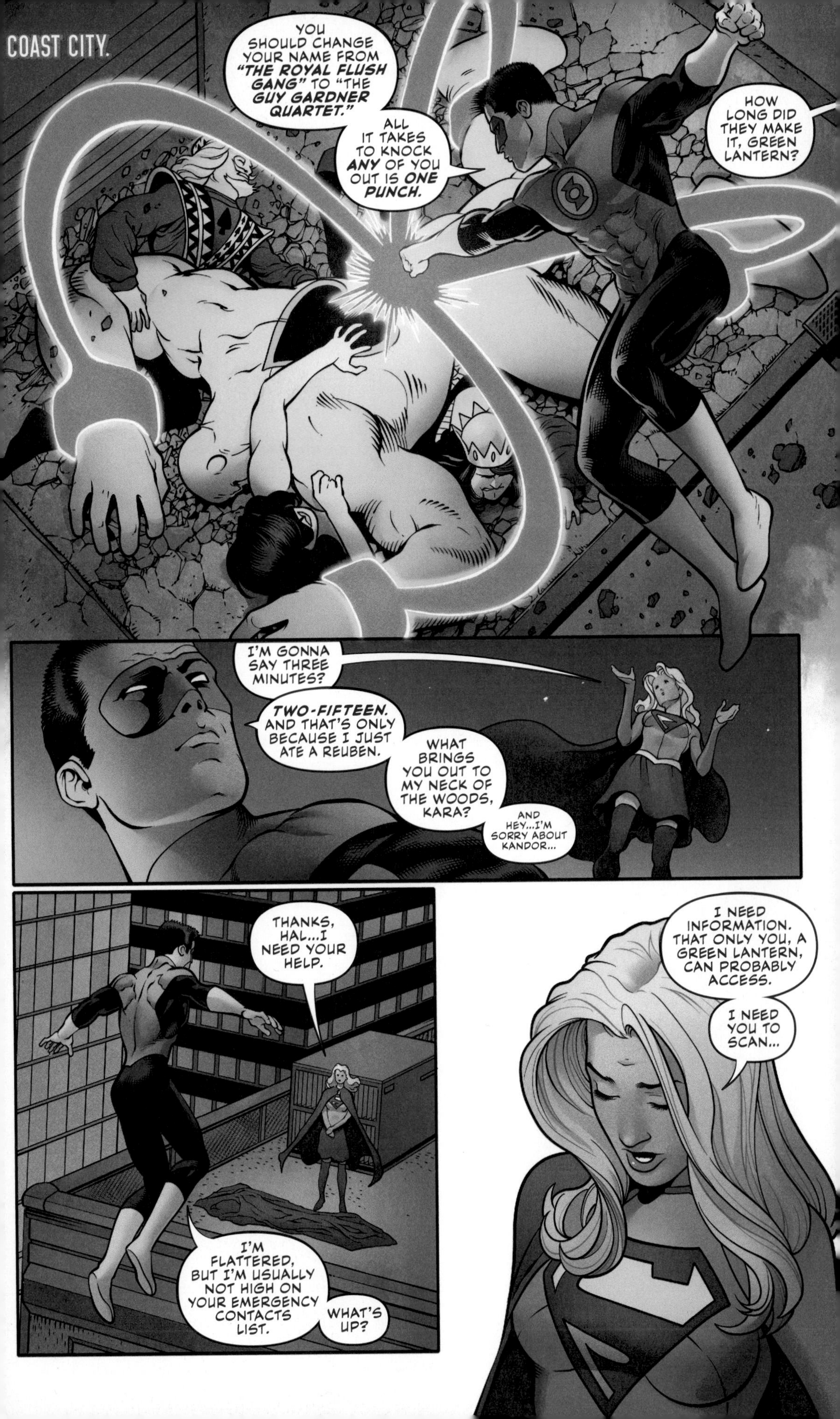
COAST CITY.
YOU SHOULD CHANGE YOUR NAME FROM *"THE ROYAL FLUSH GANG"* TO "THE *GUY GARDNER QUARTET."*
ALL IT TAKES TO KNOCK *ANY* OF YOU OUT IS *ONE PUNCH.*
HOW LONG DID THEY MAKE IT, GREEN LANTERN?
I'M GONNA SAY THREE MINUTES?
TWO-FIFTEEN. AND THAT'S ONLY BECAUSE I JUST ATE A REUBEN.
WHAT BRINGS YOU OUT TO MY NECK OF THE WOODS, KARA?
AND HEY...I'M SORRY ABOUT KANDOR...
THANKS, HAL...I NEED YOUR HELP.
I'M FLATTERED, BUT I'M USUALLY NOT HIGH ON YOUR EMERGENCY CONTACTS LIST.
WHAT'S UP?
I NEED INFORMATION. THAT ONLY YOU, A GREEN LANTERN, CAN PROBABLY ACCESS.
I NEED YOU TO SCAN...

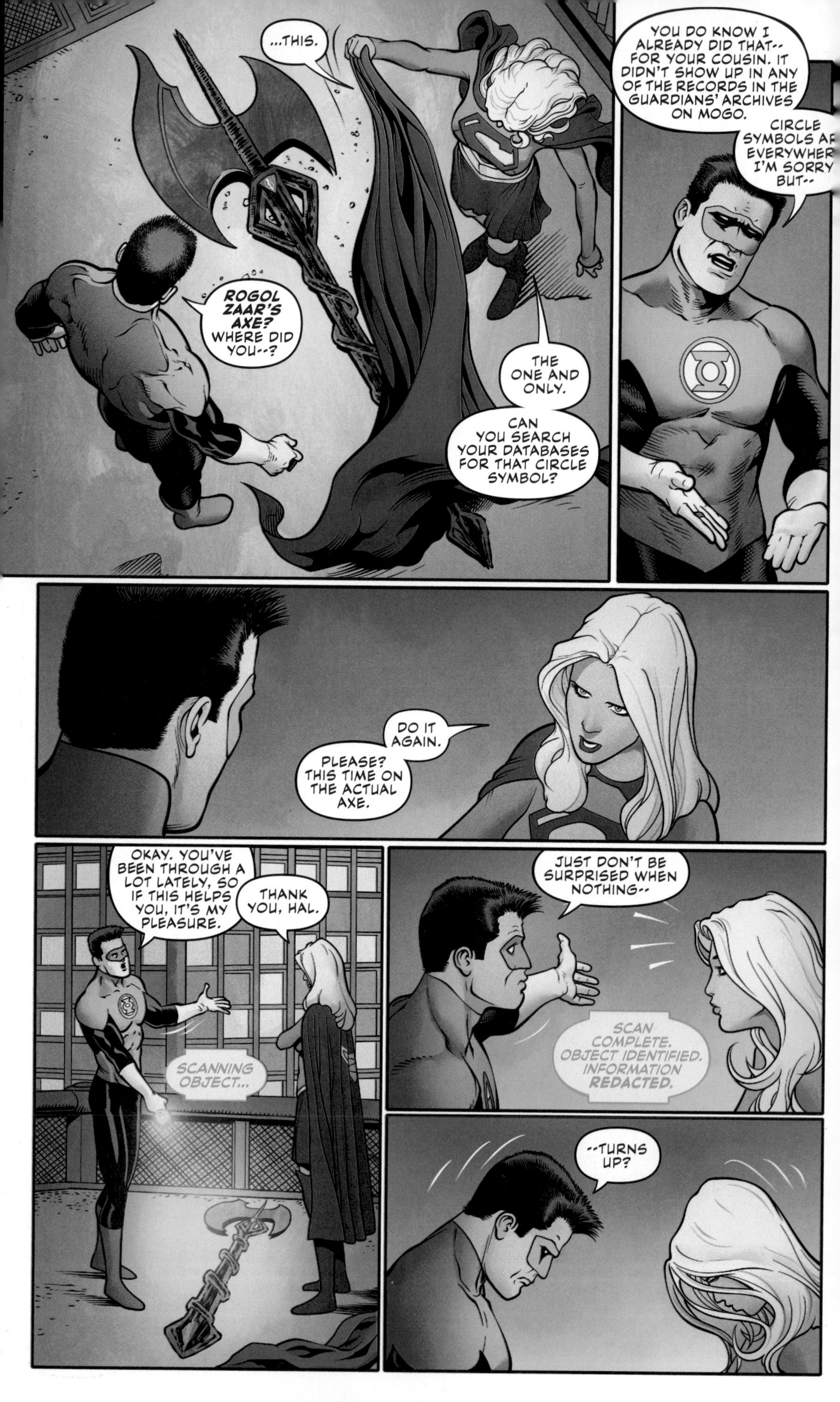

...THIS.
ROGOL ZAAR'S AXE? WHERE DID YOU--?
THE ONE AND ONLY.
CAN YOU SEARCH YOUR DATABASES FOR THAT CIRCLE SYMBOL?
YOU DO KNOW I ALREADY DID THAT-- FOR YOUR COUSIN. IT DIDN'T SHOW UP IN ANY OF THE RECORDS IN THE GUARDIANS' ARCHIVES ON MOGO.
DO IT AGAIN.
PLEASE? THIS TIME ON THE ACTUAL AXE.
OKAY. YOU'VE BEEN THROUGH A LOT LATELY, SO IF THIS HELPS YOU, IT'S MY PLEASURE.
THANK YOU, HAL.
SCANNING OBJECT...
JUST DON'T BE SURPRISED WHEN NOTHING--
SCAN COMPLETE. OBJECT IDENTIFIED. INFORMATION REDACTED.
--TURNS UP?

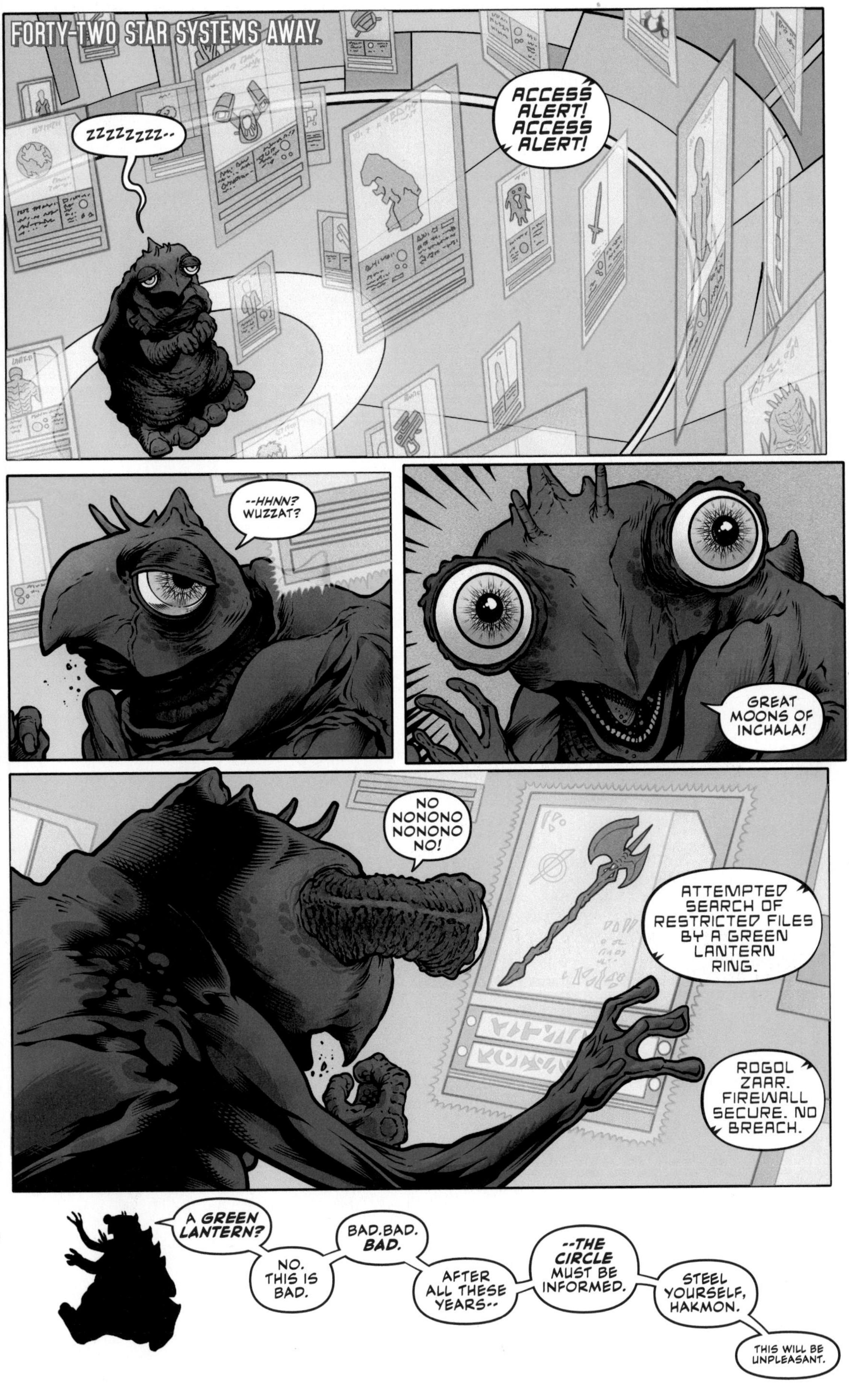

FORTY-TWO STAR SYSTEMS AWAY.
ZZZZZZZZ--
ACCESS ALERT! ACCESS ALERT!
--HHNN? WUZZAT?
GREAT MOONS OF INCHALA!
NO NONONO NONONO NO!
ATTEMPTED SEARCH OF RESTRICTED FILES BY A GREEN LANTERN RING.
ROGOL ZAAR. FIREWALL SECURE. NO BREACH.
A GREEN LANTERN?
NO. THIS IS BAD.
BAD.BAD. BAD.
AFTER ALL THESE YEARS--
--THE CIRCLE MUST BE INFORMED.
STEEL YOURSELF, HAKMON.
THIS WILL BE UNPLEASANT.

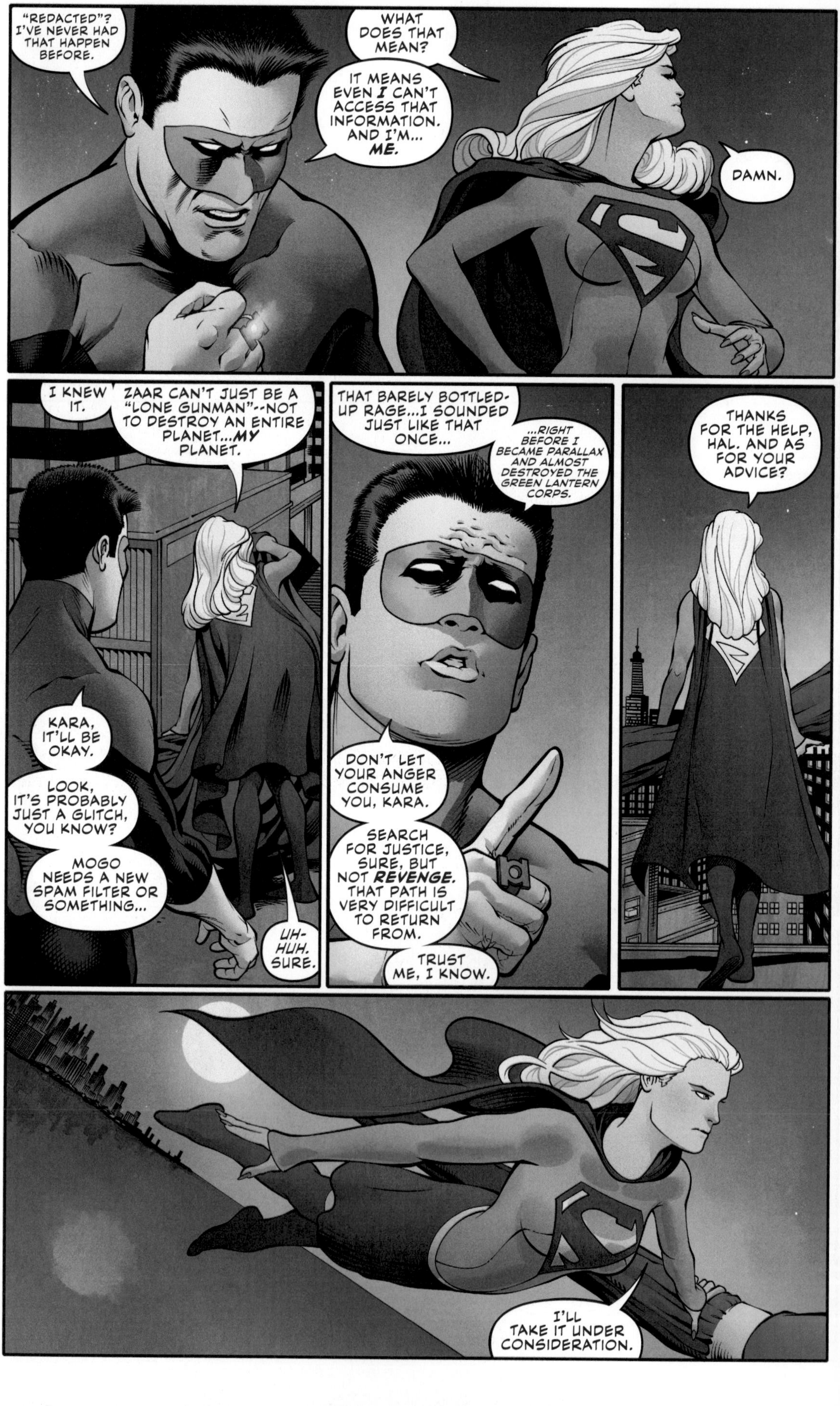
"REDACTED"? I'VE NEVER HAD THAT HAPPEN BEFORE.
WHAT DOES THAT MEAN?
IT MEANS EVEN I CAN'T ACCESS THAT INFORMATION. AND I'M... ME.
DAMN.
I KNEW IT.
ZAAR CAN'T JUST BE A "LONE GUNMAN"--NOT TO DESTROY AN ENTIRE PLANET...MY PLANET.
KARA, IT'LL BE OKAY.
LOOK, IT'S PROBABLY JUST A GLITCH, YOU KNOW?
MOGO NEEDS A NEW SPAM FILTER OR SOMETHING...
UH-HUH. SURE.
THAT BARELY BOTTLED-UP RAGE...I SOUNDED JUST LIKE THAT ONCE...
...RIGHT BEFORE I BECAME PARALLAX AND ALMOST DESTROYED THE GREEN LANTERN CORPS.
DON'T LET YOUR ANGER CONSUME YOU, KARA.
SEARCH FOR JUSTICE, SURE, BUT NOT REVENGE. THAT PATH IS VERY DIFFICULT TO RETURN FROM.
TRUST ME, I KNOW.
THANKS FOR THE HELP, HAL. AND AS FOR YOUR ADVICE?
I'LL TAKE IT UNDER CONSIDERATION.

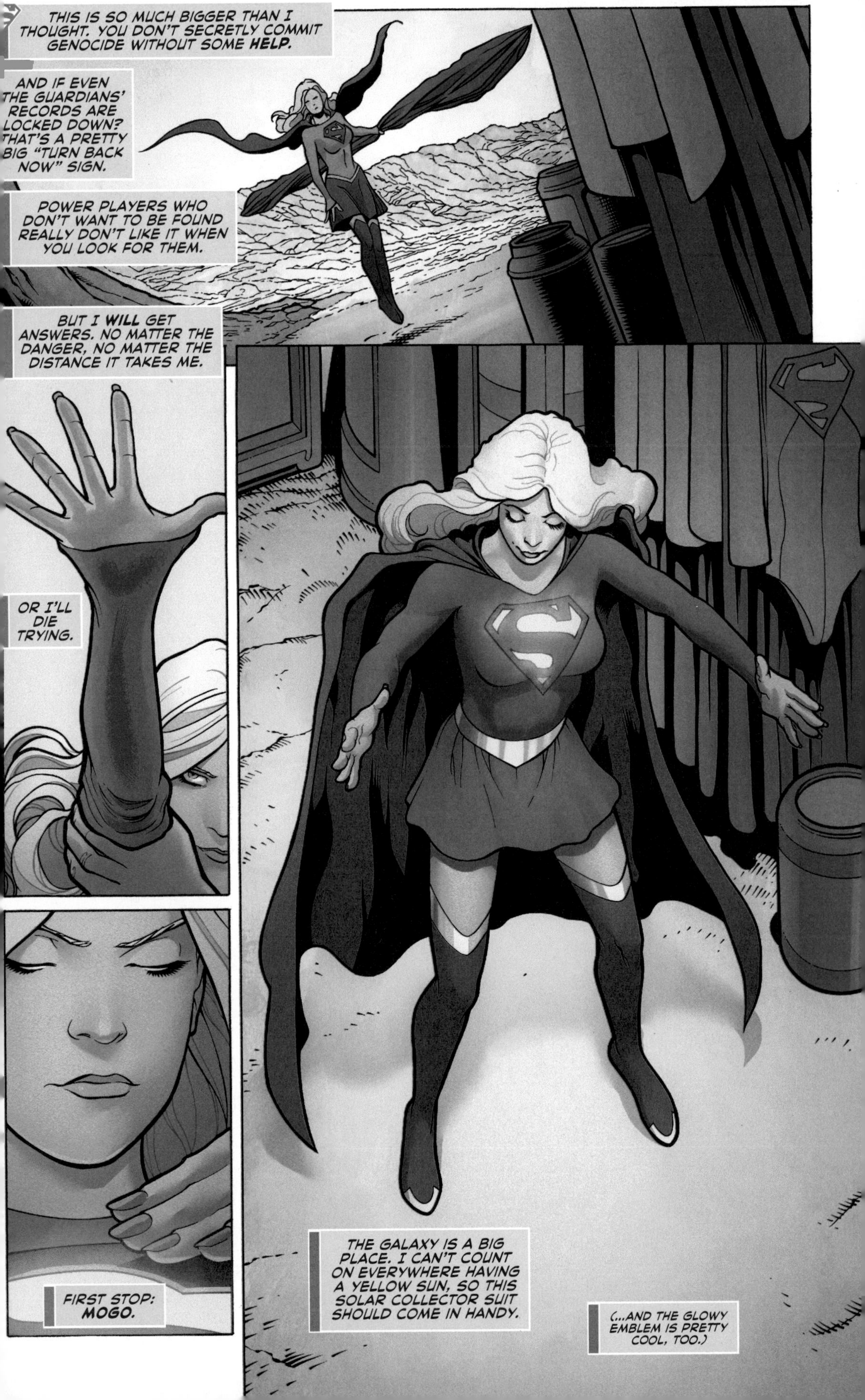
THIS IS SO MUCH BIGGER THAN I THOUGHT. YOU DON'T SECRETLY COMMIT GENOCIDE WITHOUT SOME HELP.
AND IF EVEN THE GUARDIANS' RECORDS ARE LOCKED DOWN? THAT'S A PRETTY BIG "TURN BACK NOW" SIGN.
POWER PLAYERS WHO DON'T WANT TO BE FOUND REALLY DON'T LIKE IT WHEN YOU LOOK FOR THEM.
BUT I WILL GET ANSWERS. NO MATTER THE DANGER, NO MATTER THE DISTANCE IT TAKES ME.
OR I'LL DIE TRYING.
FIRST STOP: MOGO.
THE GALAXY IS A BIG PLACE. I CAN'T COUNT ON EVERYWHERE HAVING A YELLOW SUN, SO THIS SOLAR COLLECTOR SUIT SHOULD COME IN HANDY.
(...AND THE GLOWY EMBLEM IS PRETTY COOL, TOO.)

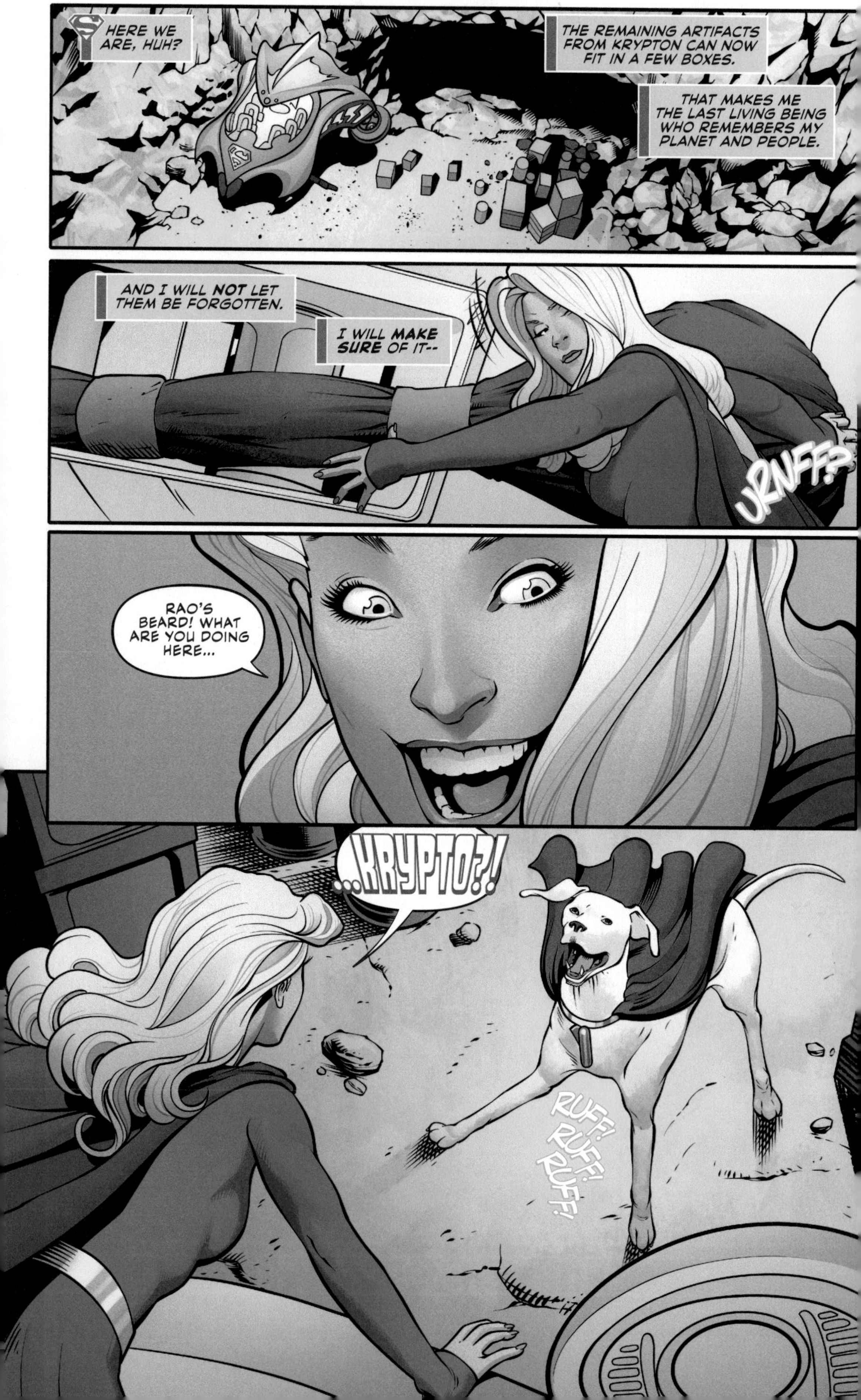
HERE WE ARE, HUH?
THE REMAINING ARTIFACTS FROM KRYPTON CAN NOW FIT IN A FEW BOXES.
THAT MAKES ME THE LAST LIVING BEING WHO REMEMBERS MY PLANET AND PEOPLE.
AND I WILL NOT LET THEM BE FORGOTTEN.
I WILL MAKE SURE OF IT--
URNFF?
RAO'S BEARD! WHAT ARE YOU DOING HERE...
...KRYPTO?!
RUFF! RUFF! RUFF!

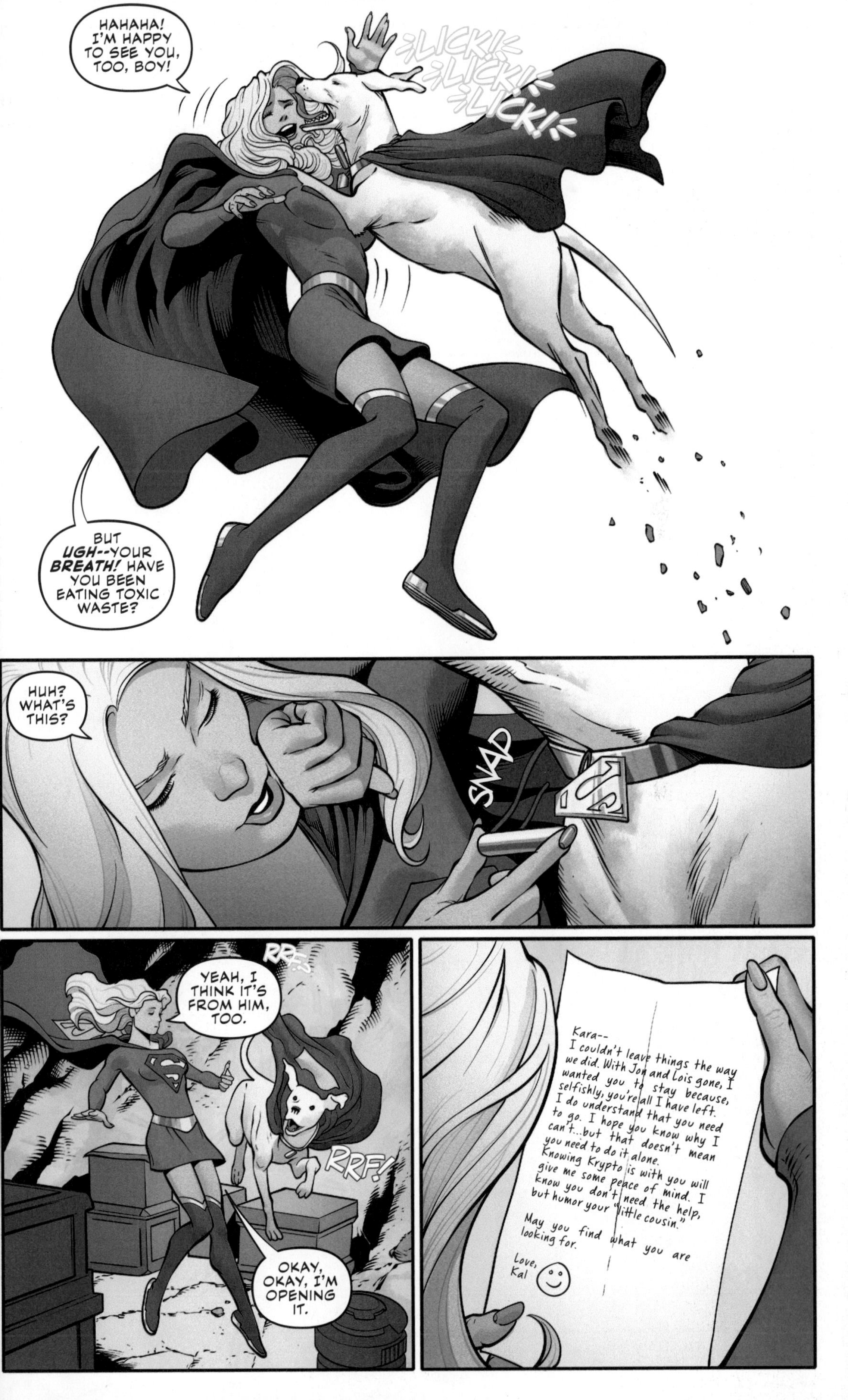
HAHAHA! I'M HAPPY TO SEE YOU, TOO, BOY!
LICK! LICK! LICK!
BUT UGH--YOUR BREATH! HAVE YOU BEEN EATING TOXIC WASTE?
HUH? WHAT'S THIS?
SNAP
RRF
YEAH, I THINK IT'S FROM HIM, TOO.
RRF!
OKAY, OKAY, I'M OPENING IT.
Kara--
I couldn't leave things the way we did. With Jon and Lois gone, I wanted you to stay because, selfishly, you're all I have left. I do understand that you need to go. I hope you know why I can't...but that doesn't mean you need to do it alone.
Knowing Krypto is with you will give me some peace of mind. I know you don't need the help, but humor your "little cousin."
May you find what you are looking for.
Love,
Kal

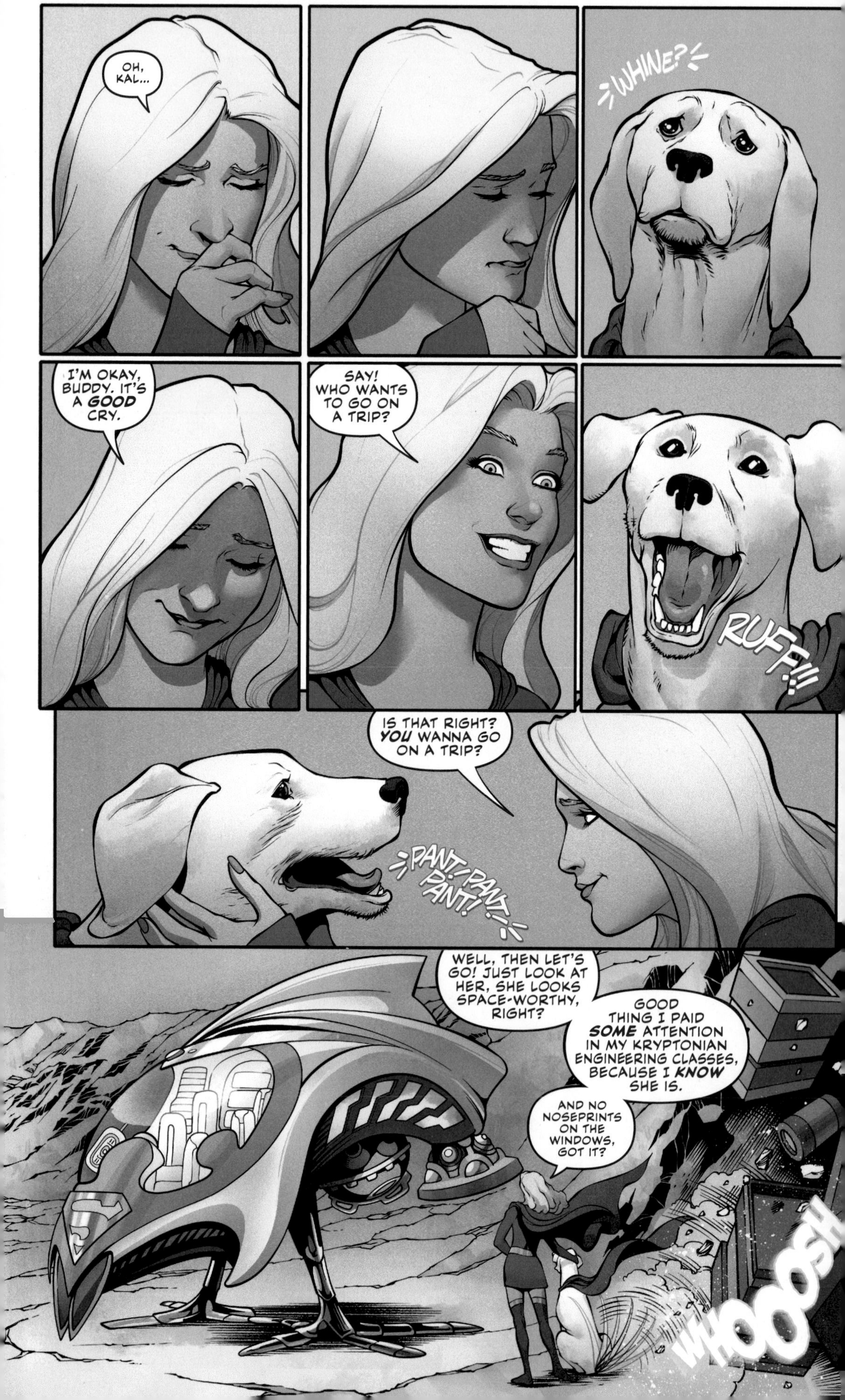
OH, KAL...
WHINE?
I'M OKAY, BUDDY. IT'S A GOOD CRY.
SAY! WHO WANTS TO GO ON A TRIP?
RUFF!!!
IS THAT RIGHT? YOU WANNA GO ON A TRIP?
PANT! PANT! PANT!
WELL, THEN LET'S GO! JUST LOOK AT HER, SHE LOOKS SPACE-WORTHY, RIGHT?
GOOD THING I PAID SOME ATTENTION IN MY KRYPTONIAN ENGINEERING CLASSES, BECAUSE I KNOW SHE IS.
AND NO NOSEPRINTS ON THE WINDOWS, GOT IT?
WHOOOSH

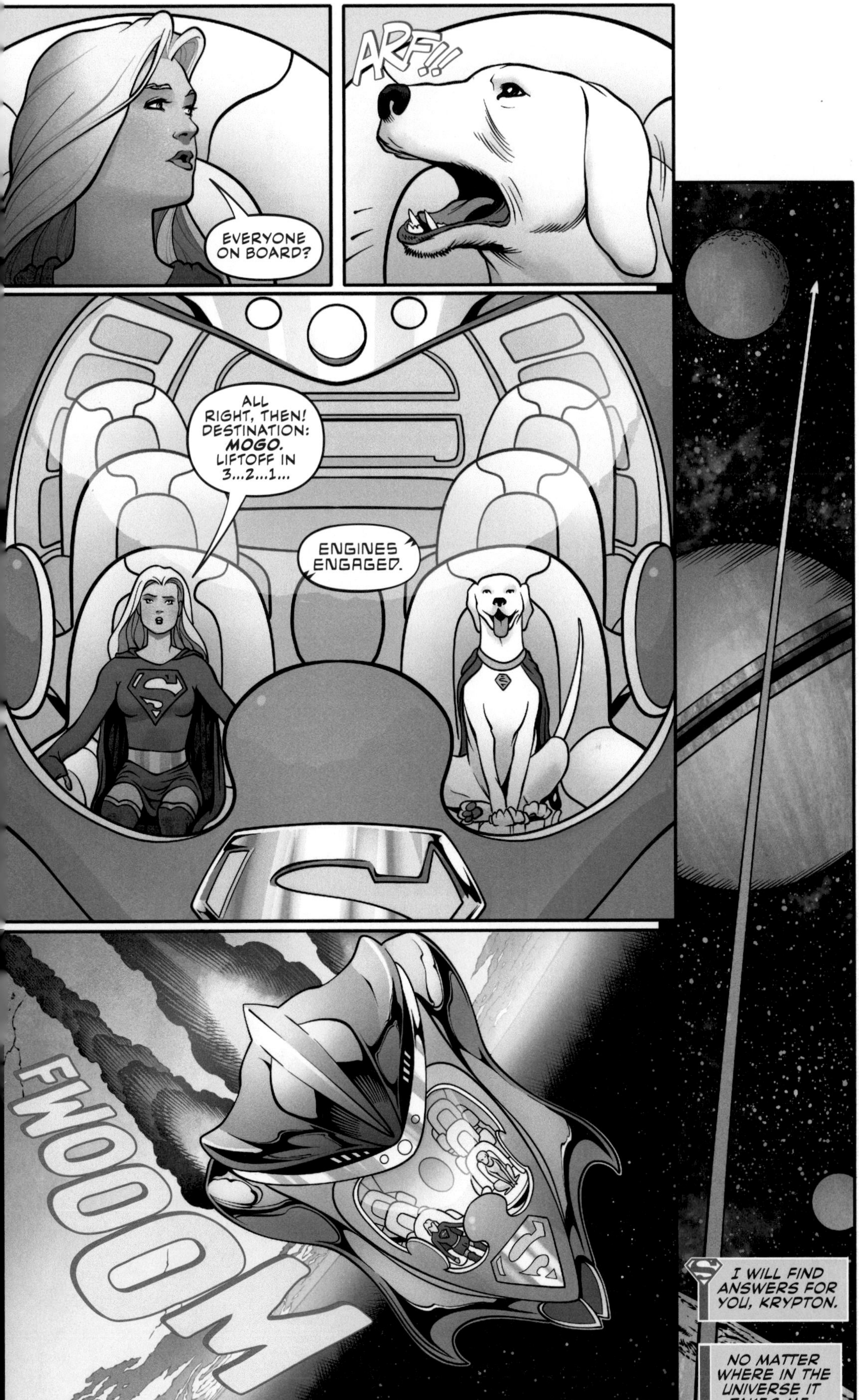
EVERYONE ON BOARD?
ARF!!!
ALL RIGHT, THEN! DESTINATION: MOGO. LIFTOFF IN 3...2...1...
ENGINES ENGAGED.
FWOOOM
I WILL FIND ANSWERS FOR YOU, KRYPTON.
NO MATTER WHERE IN THE UNIVERSE IT TAKES ME.

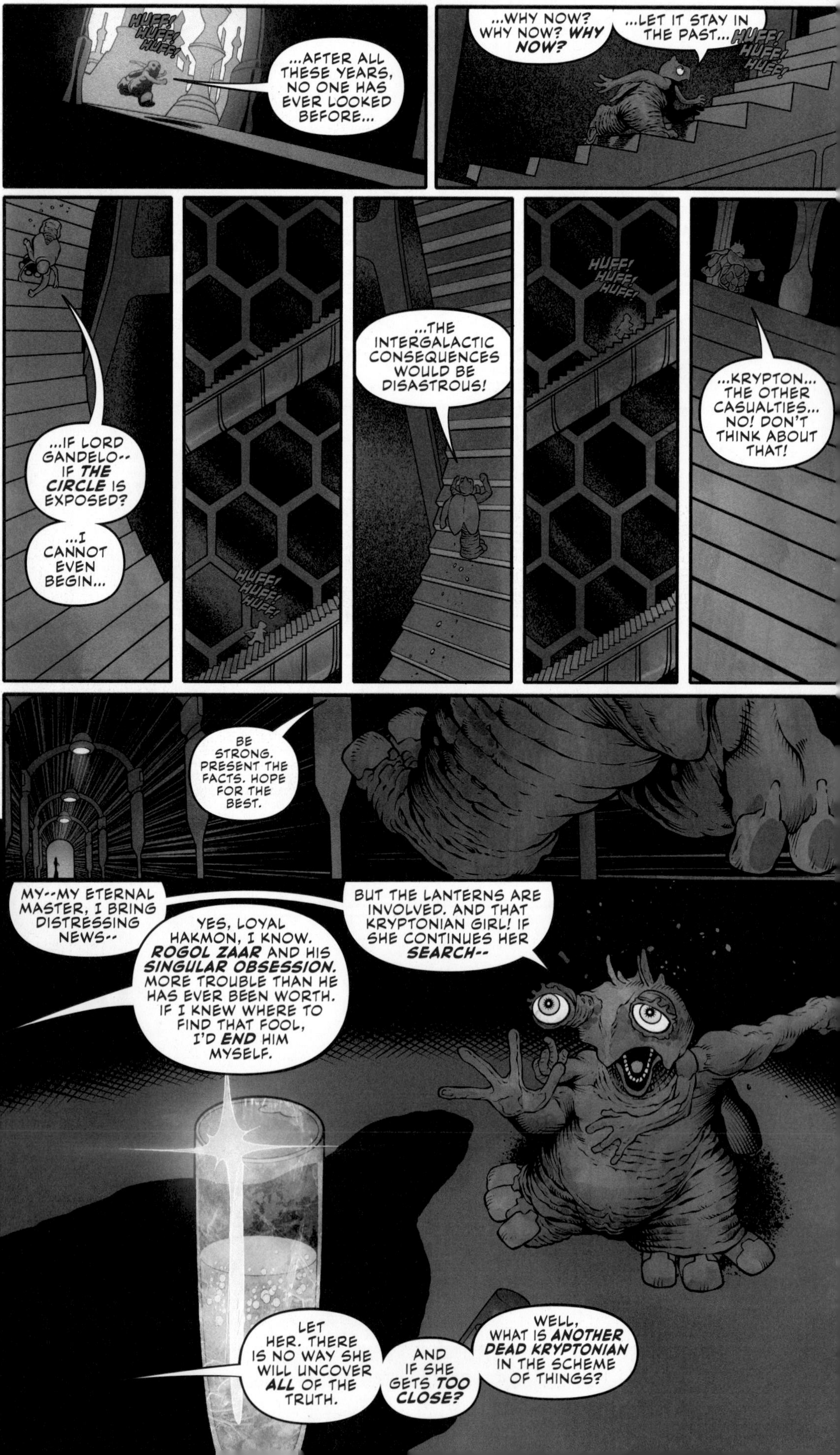
HUFF! HUFF! HUFF!
...AFTER ALL THESE YEARS, NO ONE HAS EVER LOOKED BEFORE...
...WHY NOW? WHY NOW? WHY NOW?
...LET IT STAY IN THE PAST... HUFF! HUFF! HUFF!
...IF LORD GANDELO-- IF THE CIRCLE IS EXPOSED?
...I CANNOT EVEN BEGIN...
HUFF! HUFF! HUFF!
...THE INTERGALACTIC CONSEQUENCES WOULD BE DISASTROUS!
HUFF! HUFF! HUFF!
...KRYPTON... THE OTHER CASUALTIES... NO! DON'T THINK ABOUT THAT!
BE STRONG. PRESENT THE FACTS. HOPE FOR THE BEST.
MY--MY ETERNAL MASTER, I BRING DISTRESSING NEWS--
YES, LOYAL HAKMON, I KNOW. ROGOL ZAAR AND HIS SINGULAR OBSESSION. MORE TROUBLE THAN HE HAS EVER BEEN WORTH. IF I KNEW WHERE TO FIND THAT FOOL, I'D END HIM MYSELF.
BUT THE LANTERNS ARE INVOLVED. AND THAT KRYPTONIAN GIRL! IF SHE CONTINUES HER SEARCH--
LET HER. THERE IS NO WAY SHE WILL UNCOVER ALL OF THE TRUTH.
AND IF SHE GETS TOO CLOSE?
WELL, WHAT IS ANOTHER DEAD KRYPTONIAN IN THE SCHEME OF THINGS?

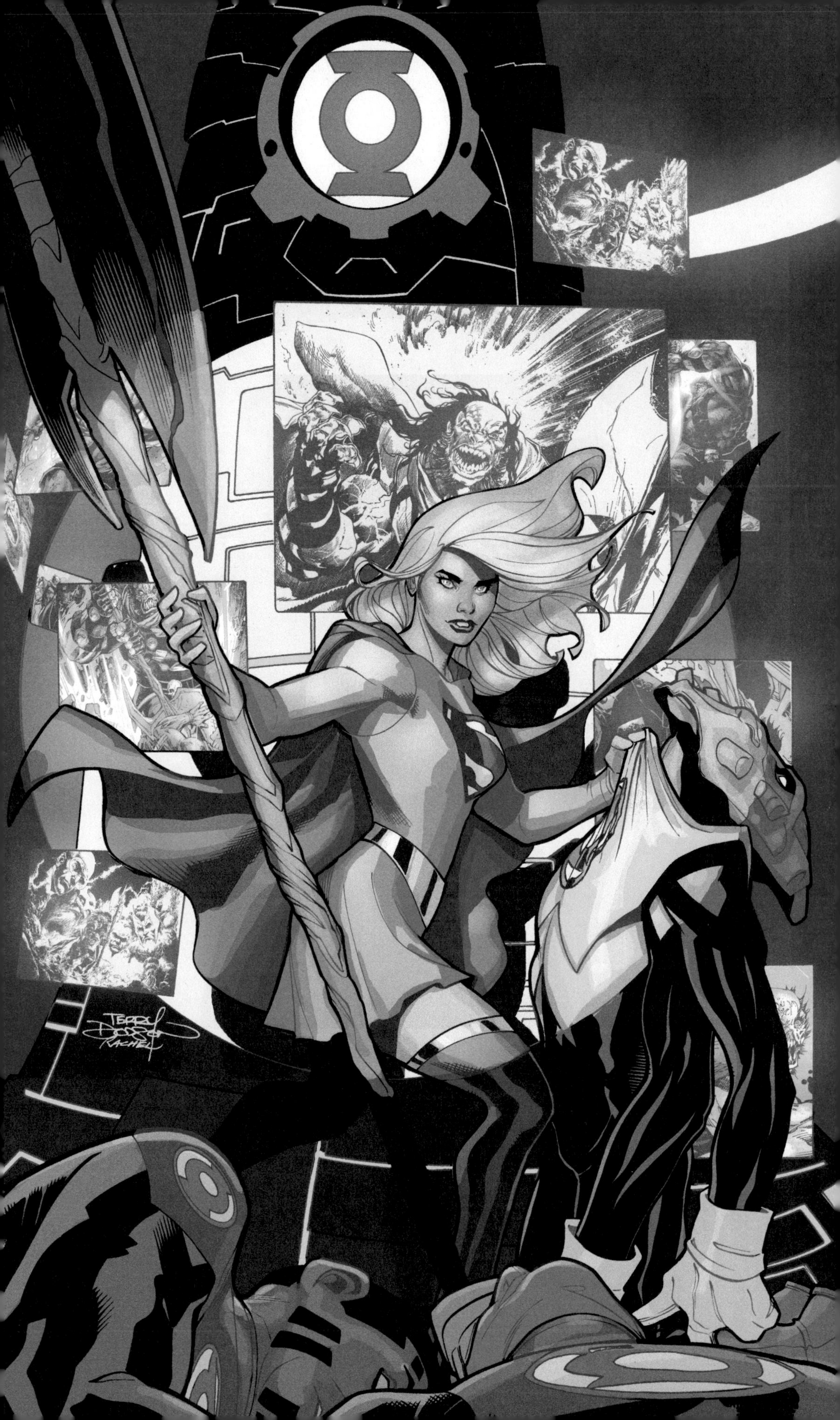

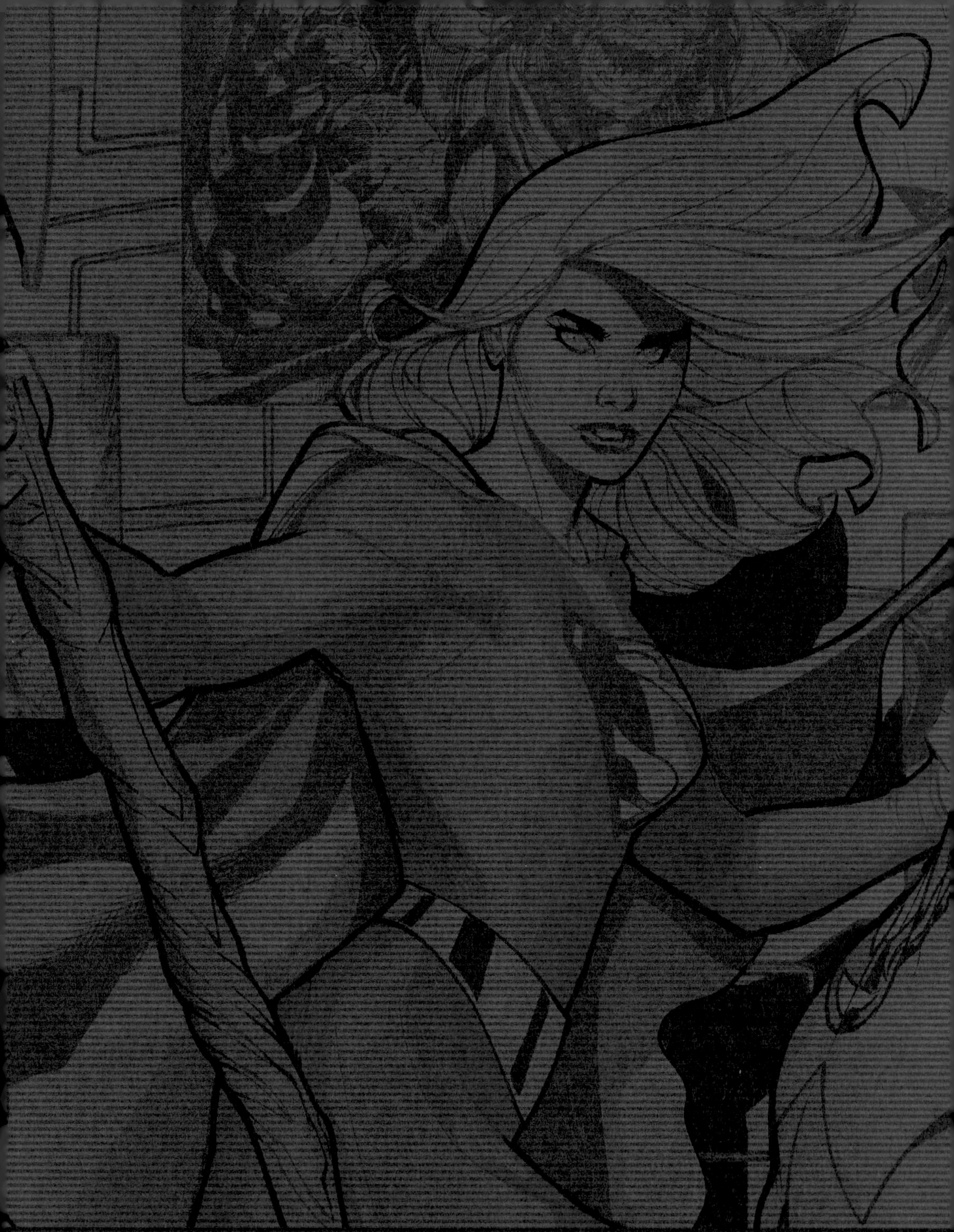

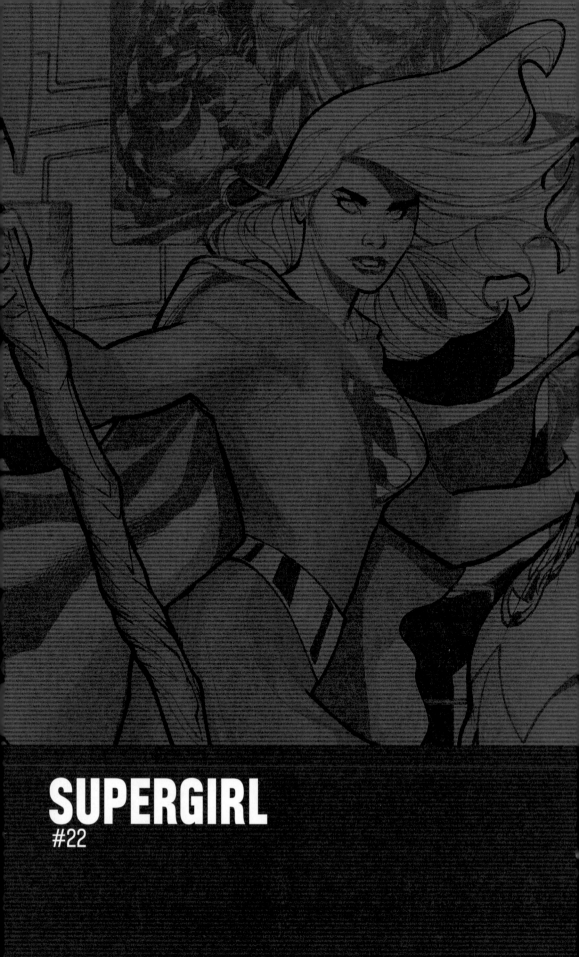

SUPERGIRL
#22

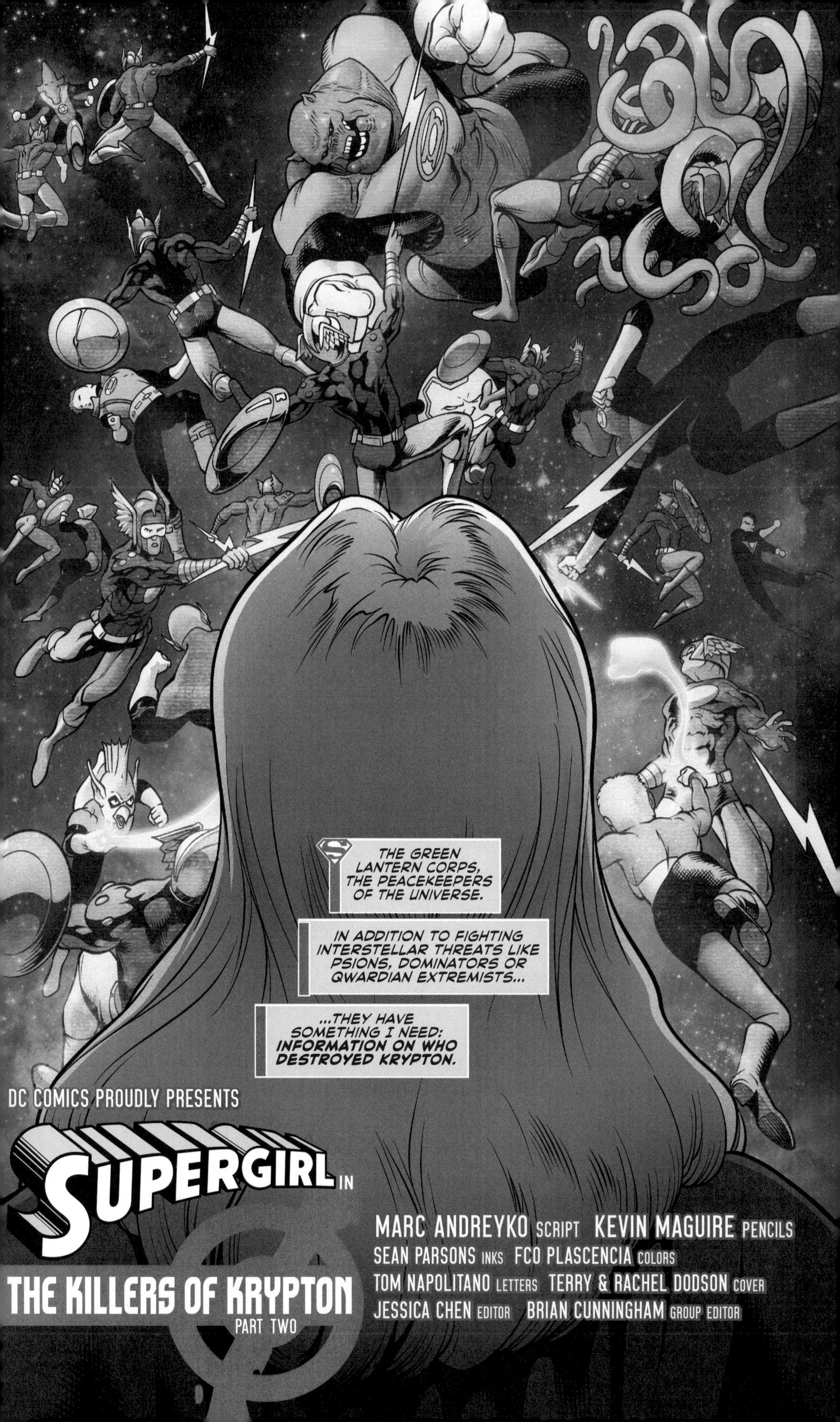
THE GREEN LANTERN CORPS, THE PEACEKEEPERS OF THE UNIVERSE.
IN ADDITION TO FIGHTING INTERSTELLAR THREATS LIKE PSIONS, DOMINATORS OR QWARDIAN EXTREMISTS...
...THEY HAVE SOMETHING I NEED: INFORMATION ON WHO DESTROYED KRYPTON.
DC COMICS PROUDLY PRESENTS
SUPERGIRL IN
THE KILLERS OF KRYPTON
PART TWO
MARC ANDREYKO SCRIPT KEVIN MAGUIRE PENCILS
SEAN PARSONS INKS FCO PLASCENCIA COLORS
TOM NAPOLITANO LETTERS TERRY & RACHEL DODSON COVER
JESSICA CHEN EDITOR BRIAN CUNNINGHAM GROUP EDITOR

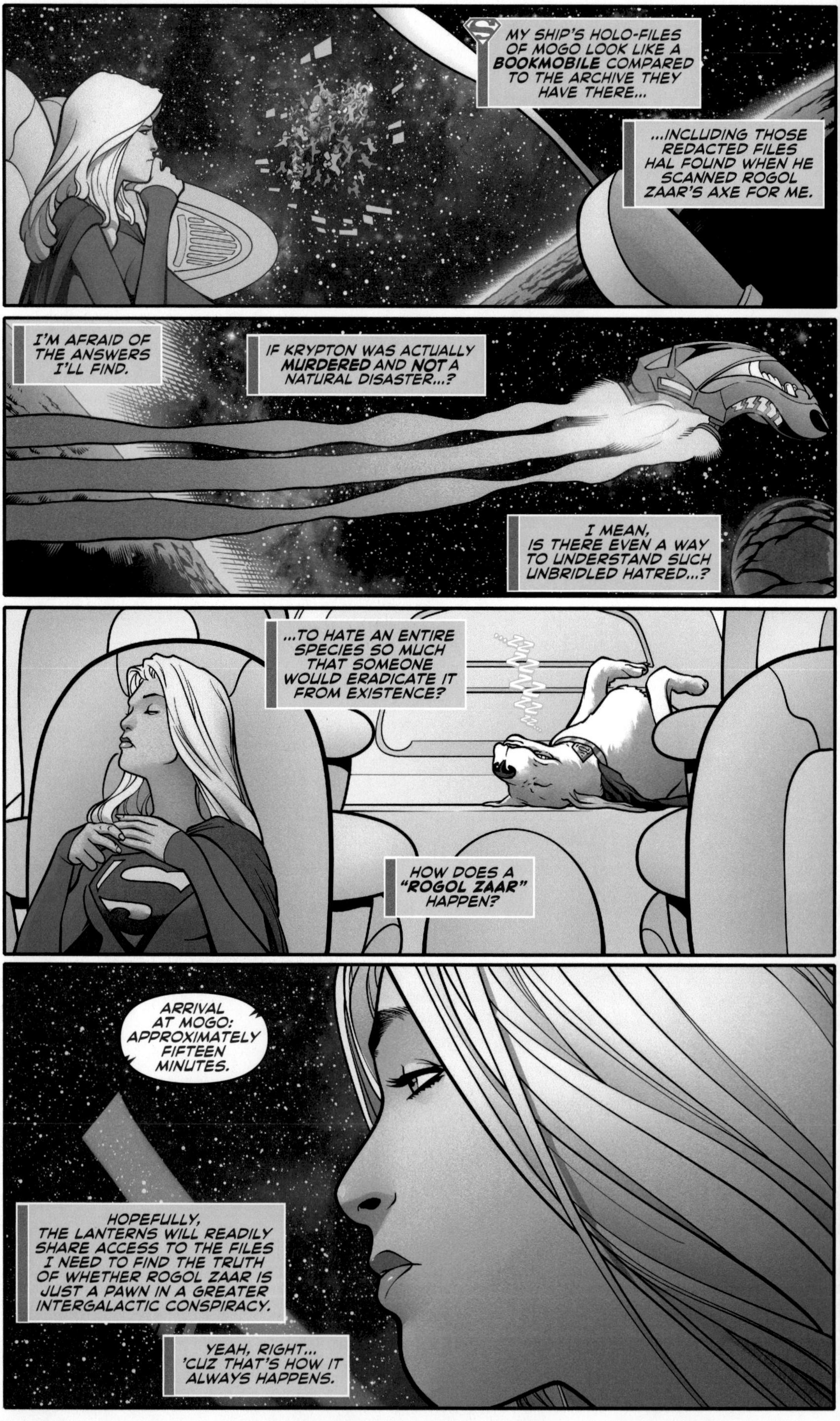

MY SHIP'S HOLO-FILES OF MOGO LOOK LIKE A **BOOKMOBILE** COMPARED TO THE ARCHIVE THEY HAVE THERE...
...INCLUDING THOSE REDACTED FILES HAL FOUND WHEN HE SCANNED ROGOL ZAAR'S AXE FOR ME.
I'M AFRAID OF THE ANSWERS I'LL FIND.
IF KRYPTON WAS ACTUALLY **MURDERED** AND **NOT** A NATURAL DISASTER...?
I MEAN, IS THERE EVEN A WAY TO UNDERSTAND SUCH UNBRIDLED HATRED...?
...TO HATE AN ENTIRE SPECIES SO MUCH THAT SOMEONE WOULD ERADICATE IT FROM EXISTENCE?
...ZZZZZZZ...
HOW DOES A **"ROGOL ZAAR"** HAPPEN?
ARRIVAL AT MOGO: APPROXIMATELY FIFTEEN MINUTES.
HOPEFULLY, THE LANTERNS WILL READILY SHARE ACCESS TO THE FILES I NEED TO FIND THE TRUTH OF WHETHER ROGOL ZAAR IS JUST A PAWN IN A GREATER INTERGALACTIC CONSPIRACY.
YEAH, RIGHT... 'CUZ THAT'S HOW IT ALWAYS HAPPENS.

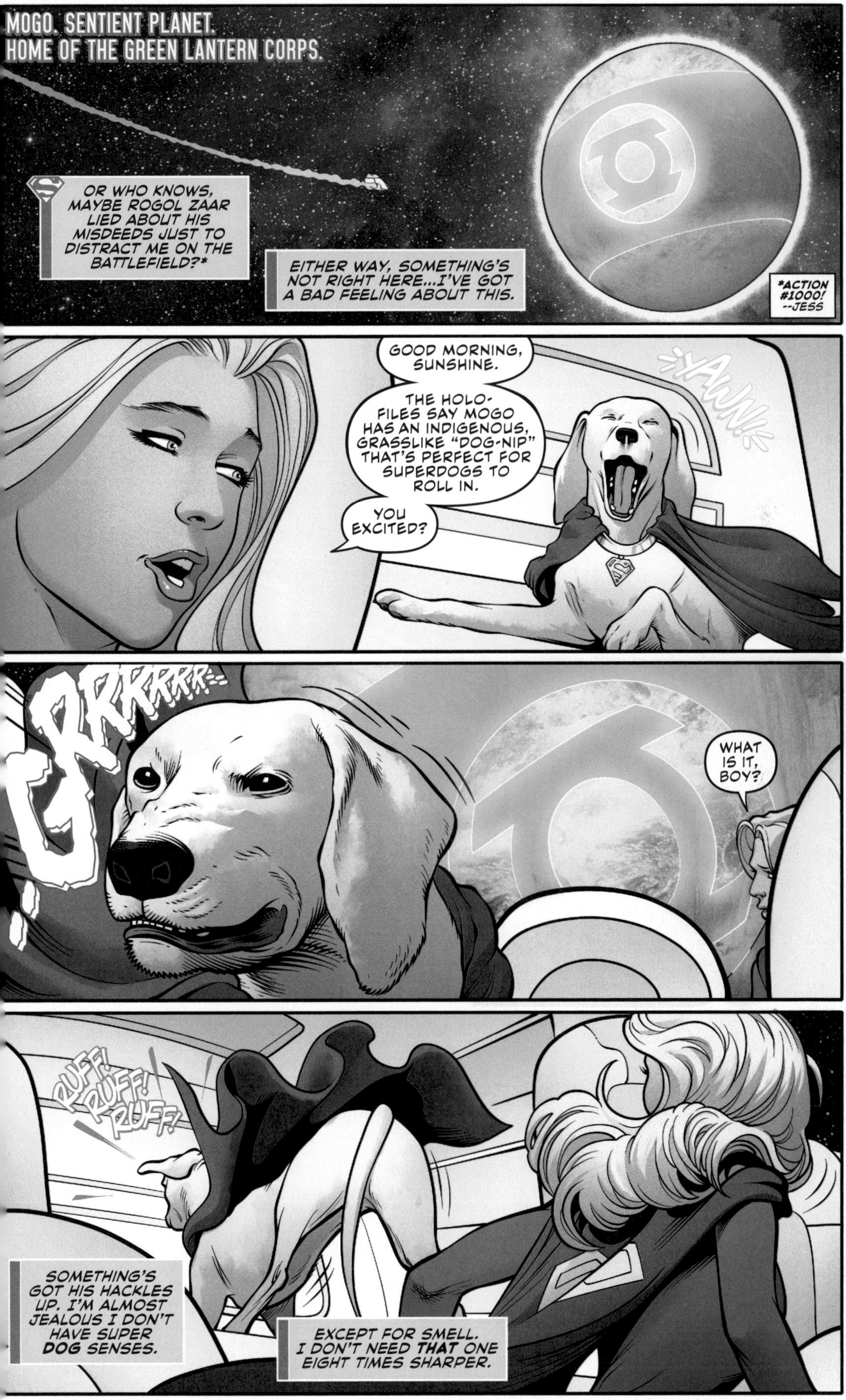
MOGO. SENTIENT PLANET.
HOME OF THE GREEN LANTERN CORPS.
OR WHO KNOWS, MAYBE ROGOL ZAAR LIED ABOUT HIS MISDEEDS JUST TO DISTRACT ME ON THE BATTLEFIELD?*
EITHER WAY, SOMETHING'S NOT RIGHT HERE...I'VE GOT A BAD FEELING ABOUT THIS.
*ACTION #1000! --JESS
GOOD MORNING, SUNSHINE.
YAWN!!
THE HOLO-FILES SAY MOGO HAS AN INDIGENOUS, GRASSLIKE "DOG-NIP" THAT'S PERFECT FOR SUPERDOGS TO ROLL IN.
YOU EXCITED?
GRRRRRR
WHAT IS IT, BOY?
RUFF! RUFF! RUFF!
SOMETHING'S GOT HIS HACKLES UP. I'M ALMOST JEALOUS I DON'T HAVE SUPER DOG SENSES.
EXCEPT FOR SMELL. I DON'T NEED THAT ONE EIGHT TIMES SHARPER.

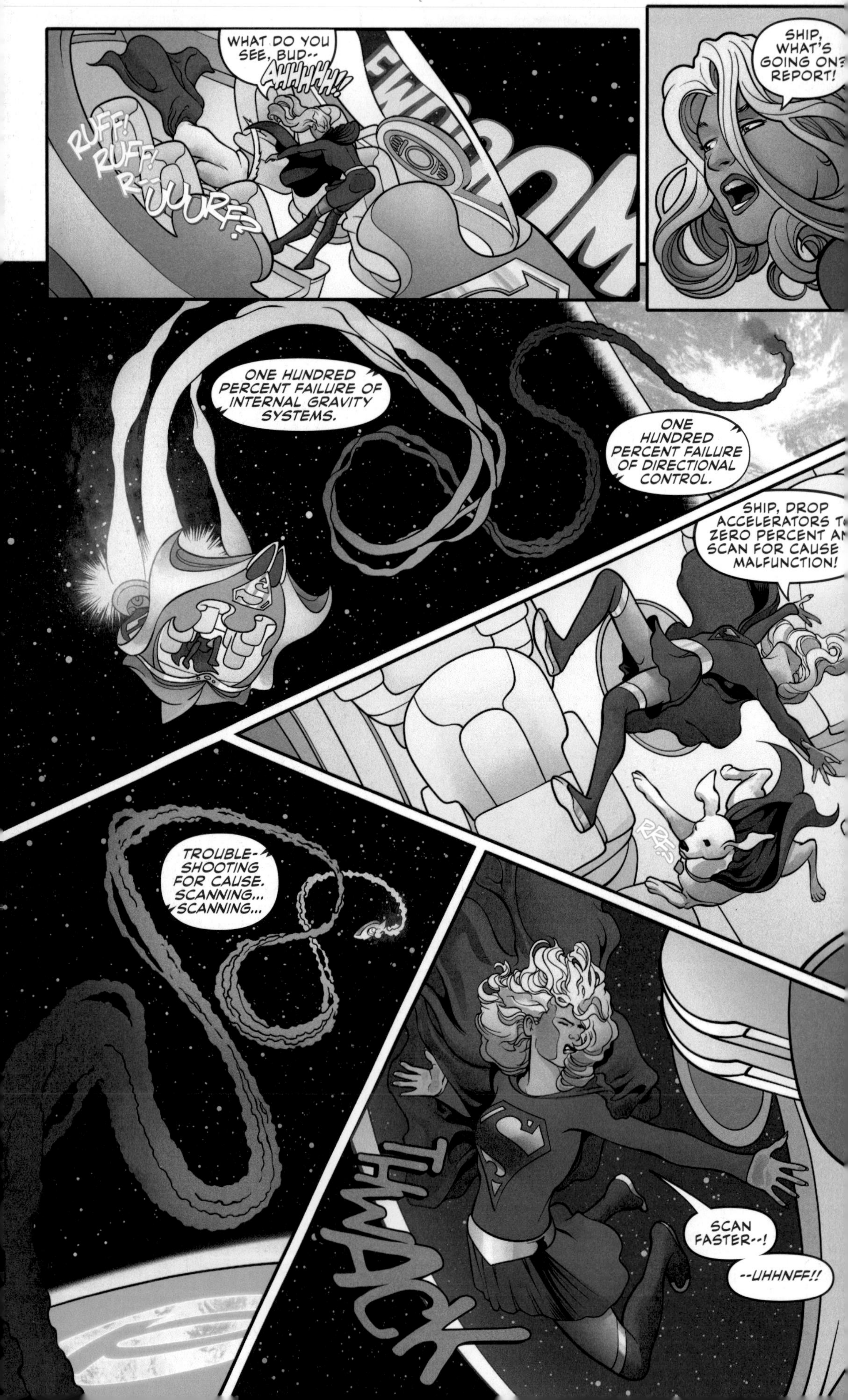
WHAT DO YOU SEE, BUD-- AHHHHH!!
RUFF! RUFF! R--UUURF?
SHIP, WHAT'S GOING ON? REPORT!
ONE HUNDRED PERCENT FAILURE OF INTERNAL GRAVITY SYSTEMS.
ONE HUNDRED PERCENT FAILURE OF DIRECTIONAL CONTROL.
SHIP, DROP ACCELERATORS T ZERO PERCENT AN SCAN FOR CAUSE MALFUNCTION!
TROUBLE-SHOOTING FOR CAUSE. SCANNING... SCANNING...
THWACK
SCAN FASTER--!
--UHHNFF!!

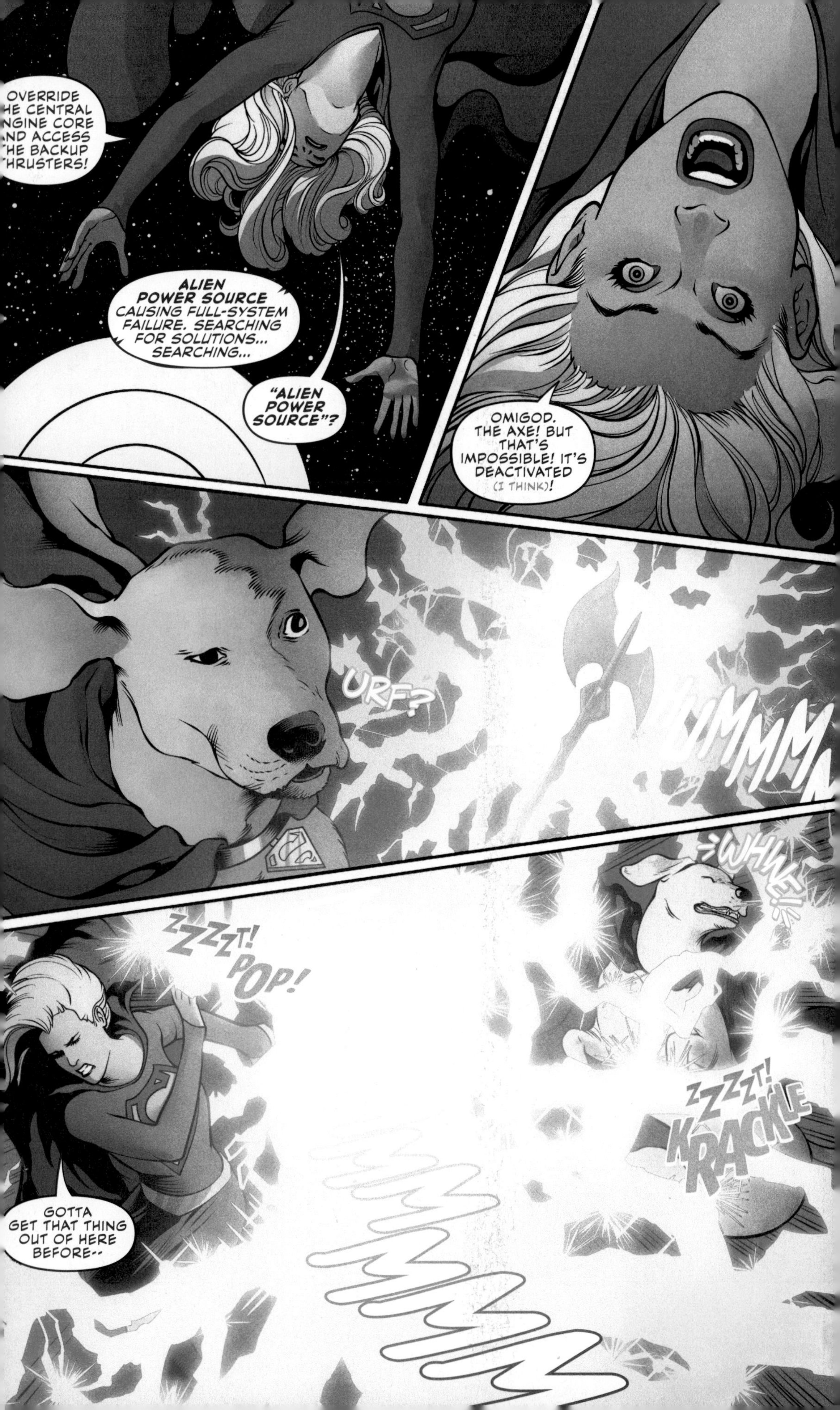
OVERRIDE HE CENTRAL NGINE CORE ND ACCESS THE BACKUP HRUSTERS!
ALIEN POWER SOURCE CAUSING FULL-SYSTEM FAILURE. SEARCHING FOR SOLUTIONS... SEARCHING...
"ALIEN POWER SOURCE"?
OMIGOD. THE AXE! BUT THAT'S IMPOSSIBLE! IT'S DEACTIVATED (I THINK)!
URF?
UMMM
WHINE!
ZZZZT! POP!
ZZZZT! KRACKLE
GOTTA GET THAT THING OUT OF HERE BEFORE--
MMMMMM

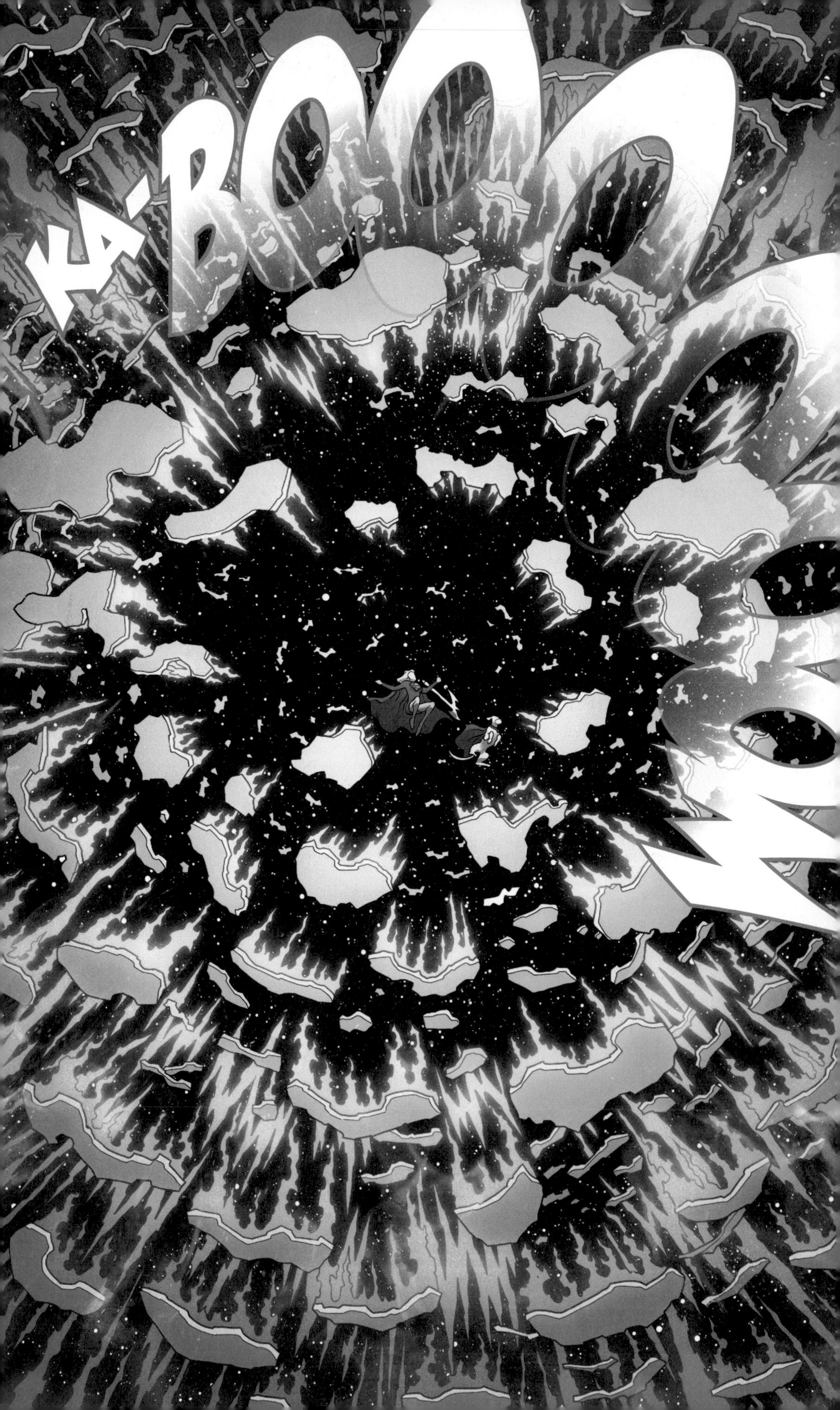
KA-BOOOOOOM

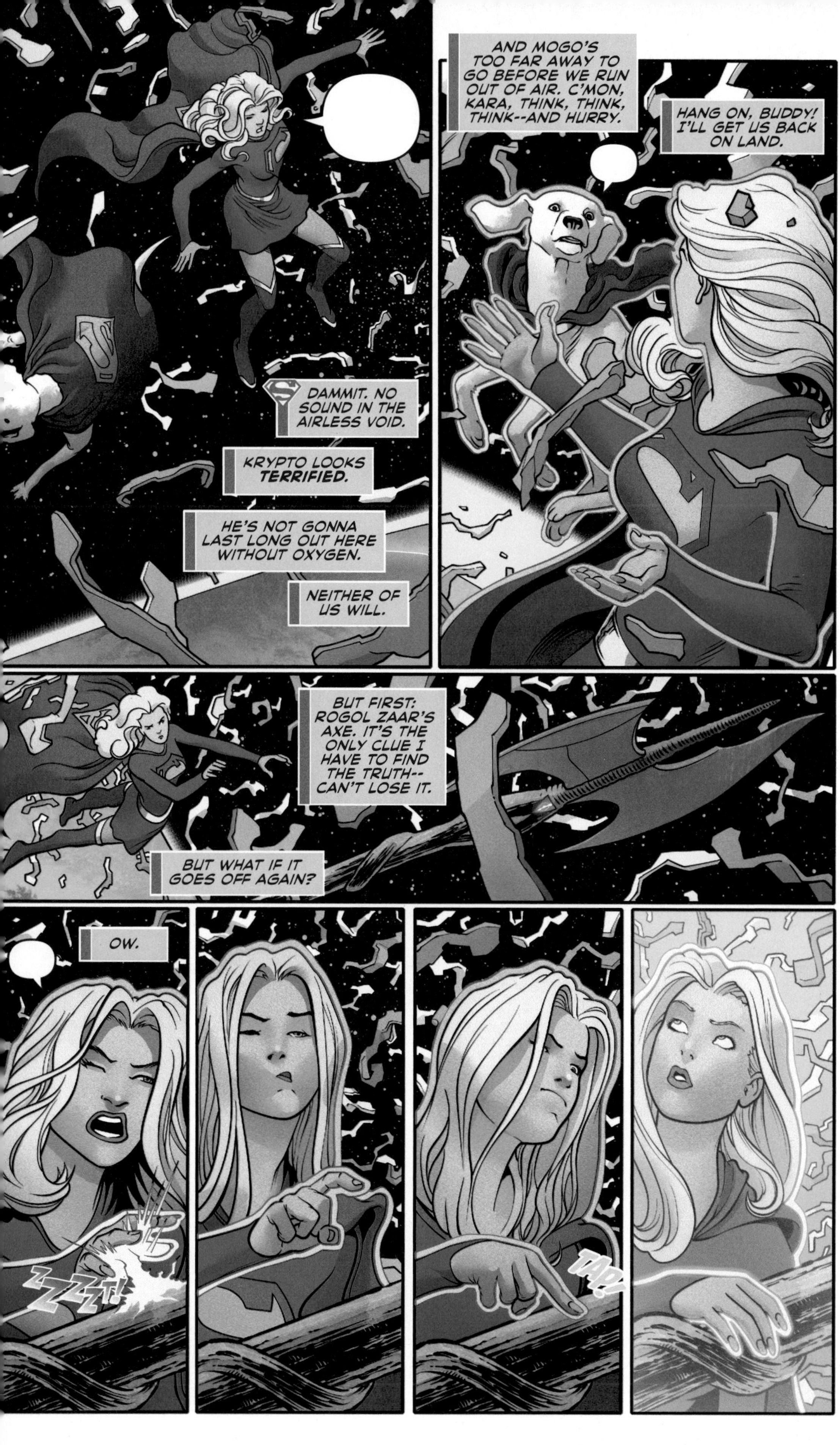
DAMMIT. NO SOUND IN THE AIRLESS VOID.
KRYPTO LOOKS TERRIFIED.
HE'S NOT GONNA LAST LONG OUT HERE WITHOUT OXYGEN.
NEITHER OF US WILL.
AND MOGO'S TOO FAR AWAY TO GO BEFORE WE RUN OUT OF AIR. C'MON, KARA, THINK, THINK, THINK--AND HURRY.
HANG ON, BUDDY! I'LL GET US BACK ON LAND.
BUT FIRST: ROGOL ZAAR'S AXE. IT'S THE ONLY CLUE I HAVE TO FIND THE TRUTH-- CAN'T LOSE IT.
BUT WHAT IF IT GOES OFF AGAIN?
OW.
ZZZZT!
TAP!

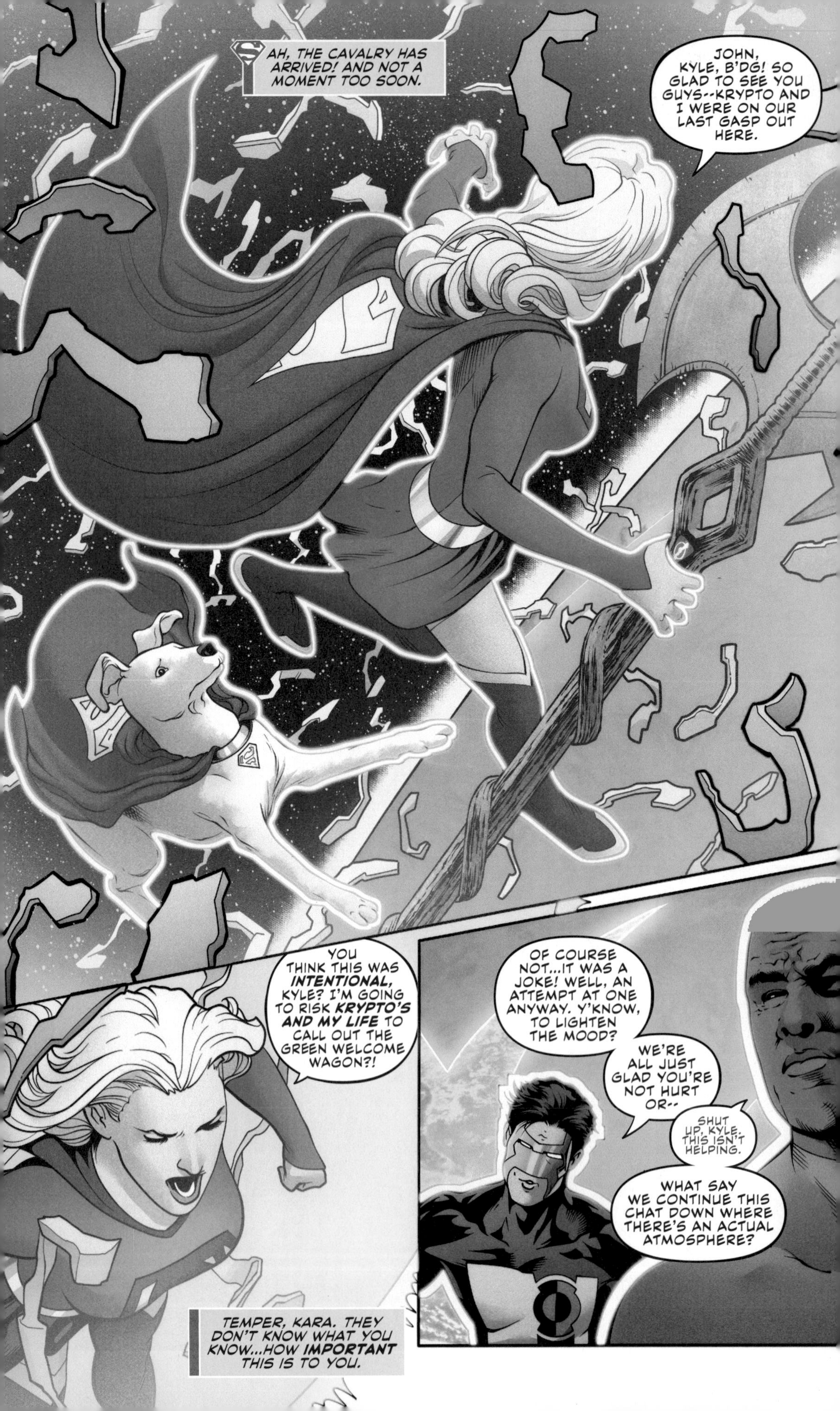
AH, THE CAVALRY HAS ARRIVED! AND NOT A MOMENT TOO SOON.
JOHN, KYLE, B'DG! SO GLAD TO SEE YOU GUYS--KRYPTO AND I WERE ON OUR LAST GASP OUT HERE.
YOU THINK THIS WAS *INTENTIONAL,* KYLE? I'M GOING TO RISK *KRYPTO'S AND MY LIFE* TO CALL OUT THE GREEN WELCOME WAGON?!
TEMPER, KARA. THEY DON'T KNOW WHAT YOU KNOW...HOW *IMPORTANT* THIS IS TO YOU.
OF COURSE NOT...IT WAS A JOKE! WELL, AN ATTEMPT AT ONE ANYWAY. Y'KNOW, TO LIGHTEN THE MOOD?
WE'RE ALL JUST GLAD YOU'RE NOT HURT OR--
SHUT UP, KYLE. THIS ISN'T HELPING.
WHAT SAY WE CONTINUE THIS CHAT DOWN WHERE THERE'S AN ACTUAL ATMOSPHERE?

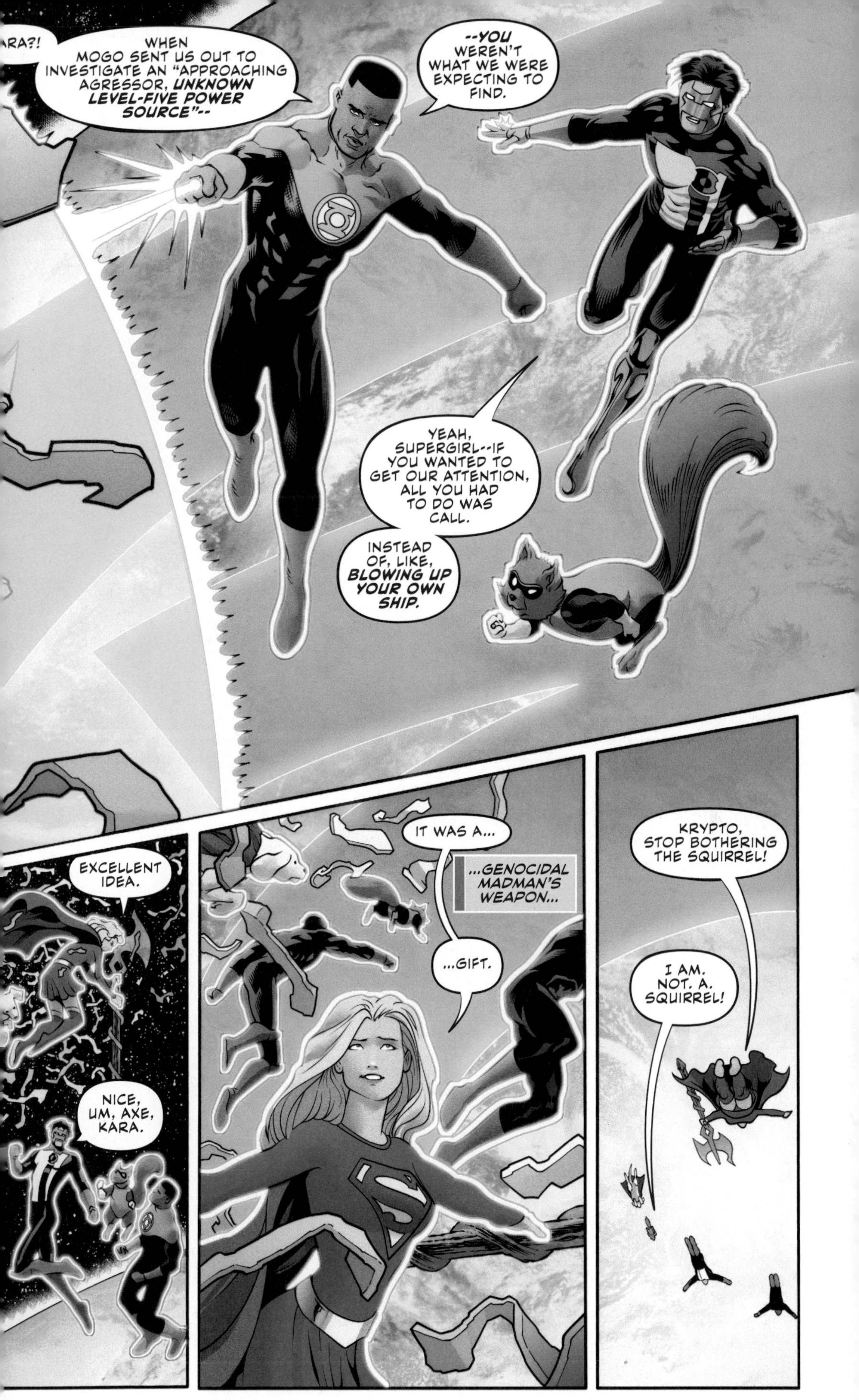

ARA?!
WHEN MOGO SENT US OUT TO INVESTIGATE AN "APPROACHING AGRESSOR, UNKNOWN LEVEL-FIVE POWER SOURCE"--
--YOU WEREN'T WHAT WE WERE EXPECTING TO FIND.
YEAH, SUPERGIRL--IF YOU WANTED TO GET OUR ATTENTION, ALL YOU HAD TO DO WAS CALL.
INSTEAD OF, LIKE, BLOWING UP YOUR OWN SHIP.
EXCELLENT IDEA.
NICE, UM, AXE, KARA.
IT WAS A...
...GENOCIDAL MADMAN'S WEAPON...
...GIFT.
KRYPTO, STOP BOTHERING THE SQUIRREL!
I AM. NOT. A. SQUIRREL!

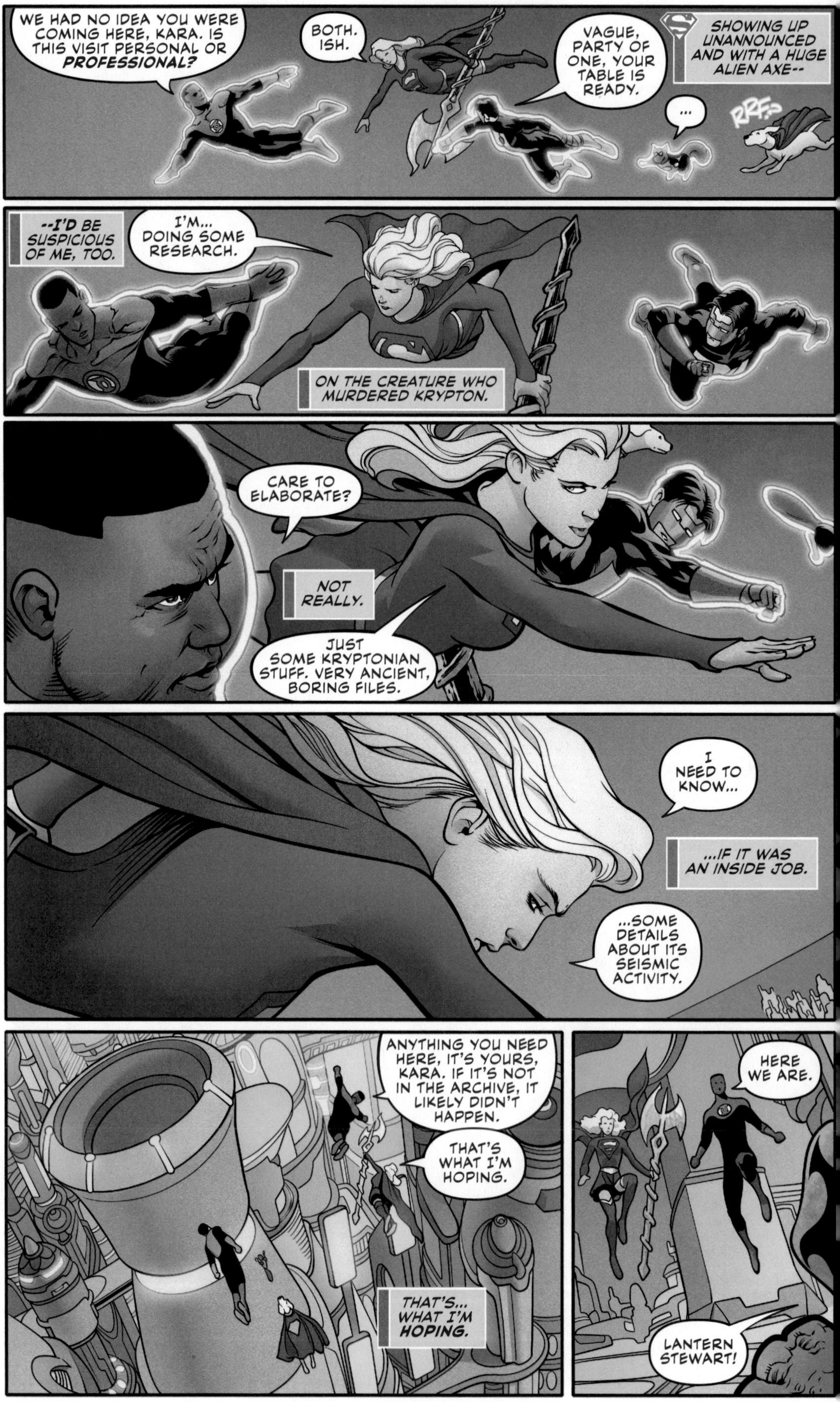
WE HAD NO IDEA YOU WERE COMING HERE, KARA. IS THIS VISIT PERSONAL OR PROFESSIONAL?
BOTH. ISH.
VAGUE, PARTY OF ONE, YOUR TABLE IS READY.
SHOWING UP UNANNOUNCED AND WITH A HUGE ALIEN AXE--
...
RRF?
--I'D BE SUSPICIOUS OF ME, TOO.
I'M... DOING SOME RESEARCH.
ON THE CREATURE WHO MURDERED KRYPTON.
CARE TO ELABORATE?
NOT REALLY.
JUST SOME KRYPTONIAN STUFF. VERY ANCIENT, BORING FILES.
I NEED TO KNOW...
...IF IT WAS AN INSIDE JOB.
...SOME DETAILS ABOUT ITS SEISMIC ACTIVITY.
ANYTHING YOU NEED HERE, IT'S YOURS, KARA. IF IT'S NOT IN THE ARCHIVE, IT LIKELY DIDN'T HAPPEN.
THAT'S WHAT I'M HOPING.
THAT'S... WHAT I'M HOPING.
HERE WE ARE.
LANTERN STEWART!

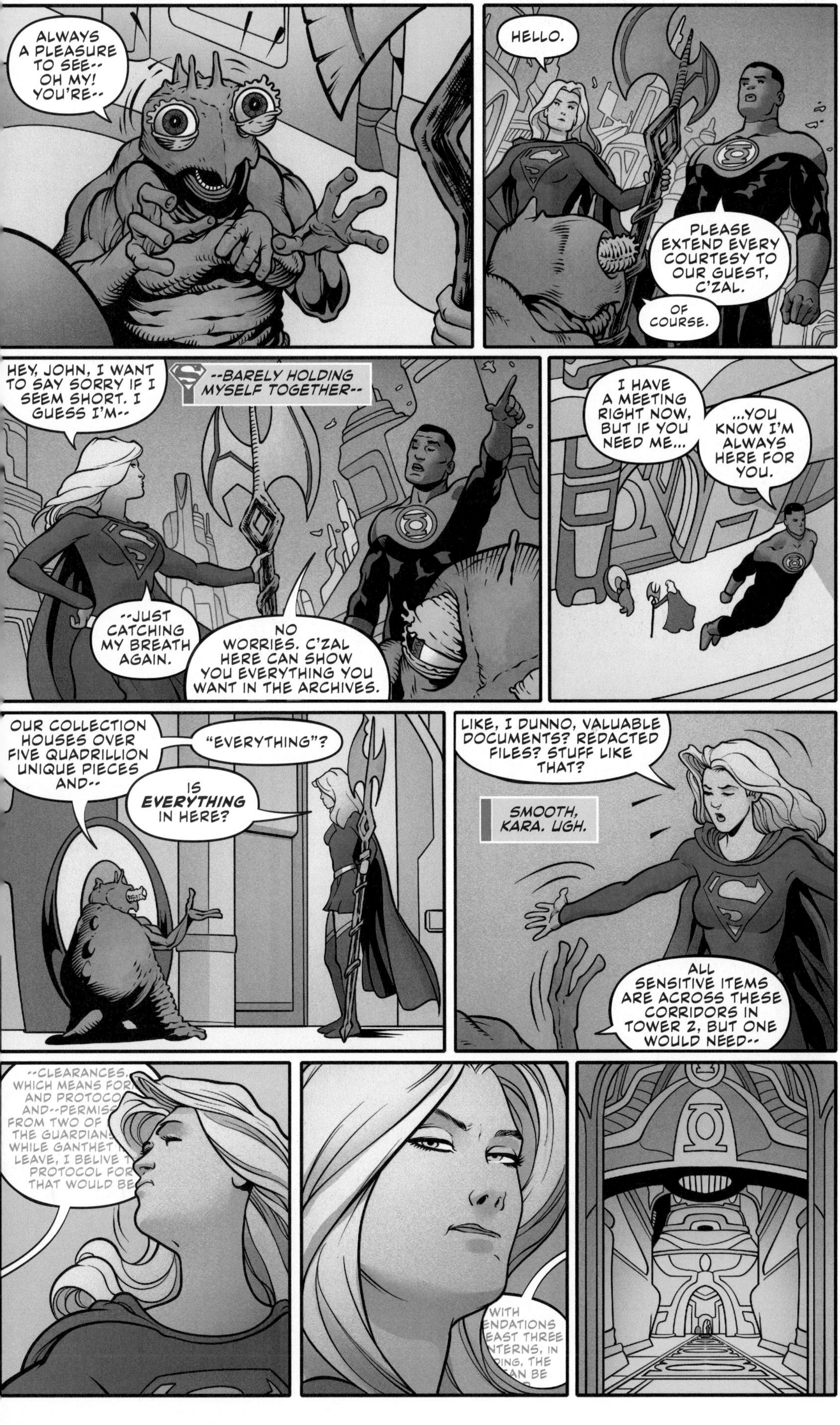
ALWAYS A PLEASURE TO SEE-- OH MY! YOU'RE--
HELLO.
PLEASE EXTEND EVERY COURTESY TO OUR GUEST, C'ZAL.
OF COURSE.
HEY, JOHN, I WANT TO SAY SORRY IF I SEEM SHORT. I GUESS I'M--
--BARELY HOLDING MYSELF TOGETHER--
--JUST CATCHING MY BREATH AGAIN.
NO WORRIES. C'ZAL HERE CAN SHOW YOU EVERYTHING YOU WANT IN THE ARCHIVES.
I HAVE A MEETING RIGHT NOW, BUT IF YOU NEED ME...
...YOU KNOW I'M ALWAYS HERE FOR YOU.
OUR COLLECTION HOUSES OVER FIVE QUADRILLION UNIQUE PIECES AND--
"EVERYTHING"?
IS EVERYTHING IN HERE?
LIKE, I DUNNO, VALUABLE DOCUMENTS? REDACTED FILES? STUFF LIKE THAT?
SMOOTH, KARA. UGH.
ALL SENSITIVE ITEMS ARE ACROSS THESE CORRIDORS IN TOWER 2, BUT ONE WOULD NEED--
--CLEARANCES, WHICH MEANS FOR AND PROTOCO AND--PERMIS FROM TWO OF THE GUARDIANS WHILE GANTHET LEAVE, I BELIVE T PROTOCOL FOR THAT WOULD BE
WITH ENDATIONS EAST THREE NTERNS, IN DING, THE AN BE

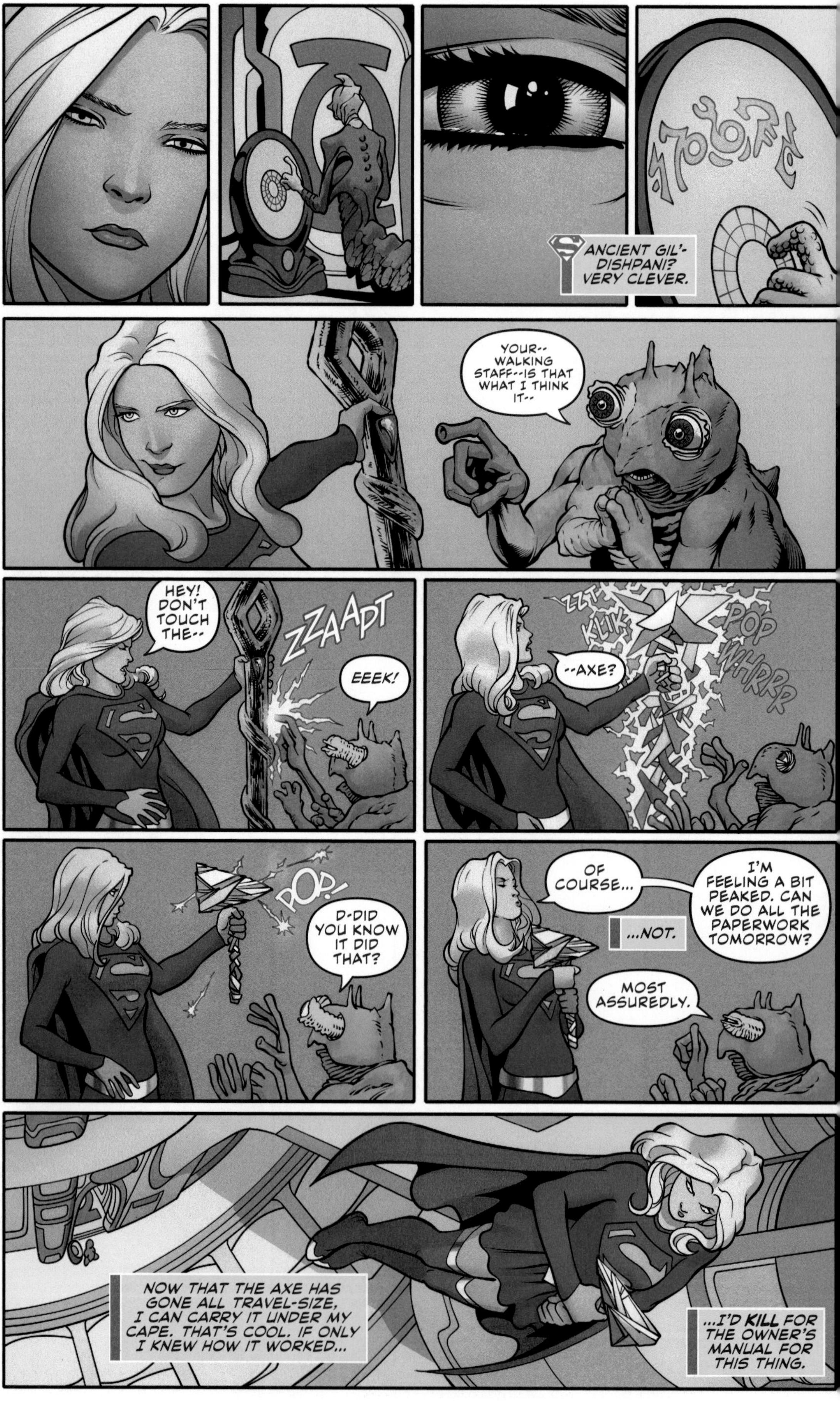
ANCIENT GIL'-DISHPANI? VERY CLEVER.
YOUR--WALKING STAFF--IS THAT WHAT I THINK IT--
HEY! DON'T TOUCH THE--
ZZAAPT
EEEK!
--AXE?
ZZZT
KLIK
POP
WHRRR
POP!
D-DID YOU KNOW IT DID THAT?
OF COURSE...
...NOT.
I'M FEELING A BIT PEAKED. CAN WE DO ALL THE PAPERWORK TOMORROW?
MOST ASSUREDLY.
NOW THAT THE AXE HAS GONE ALL TRAVEL-SIZE, I CAN CARRY IT UNDER MY CAPE. THAT'S COOL. IF ONLY I KNEW HOW IT WORKED...
...I'D KILL FOR THE OWNER'S MANUAL FOR THIS THING.

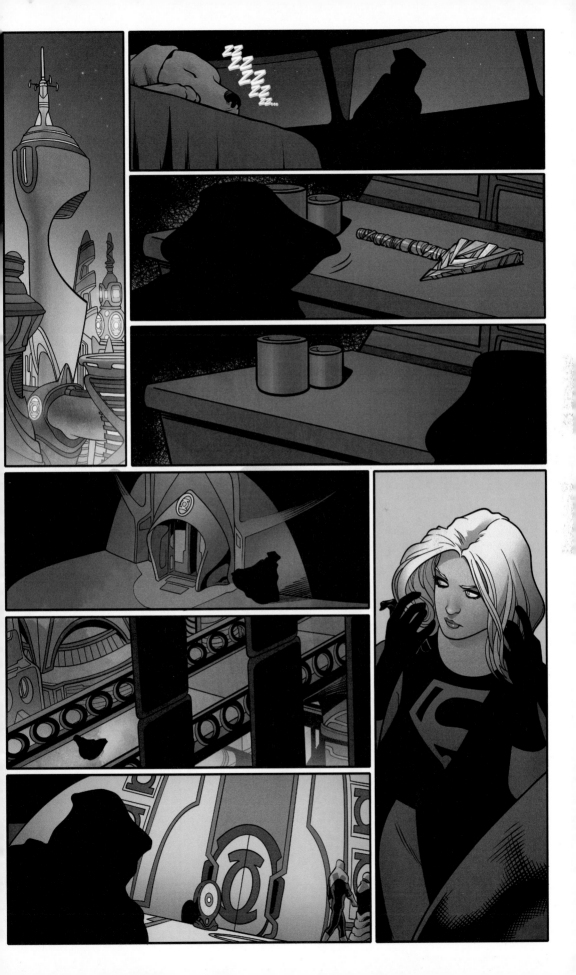

ZZZZ ZZZZ ZZ...

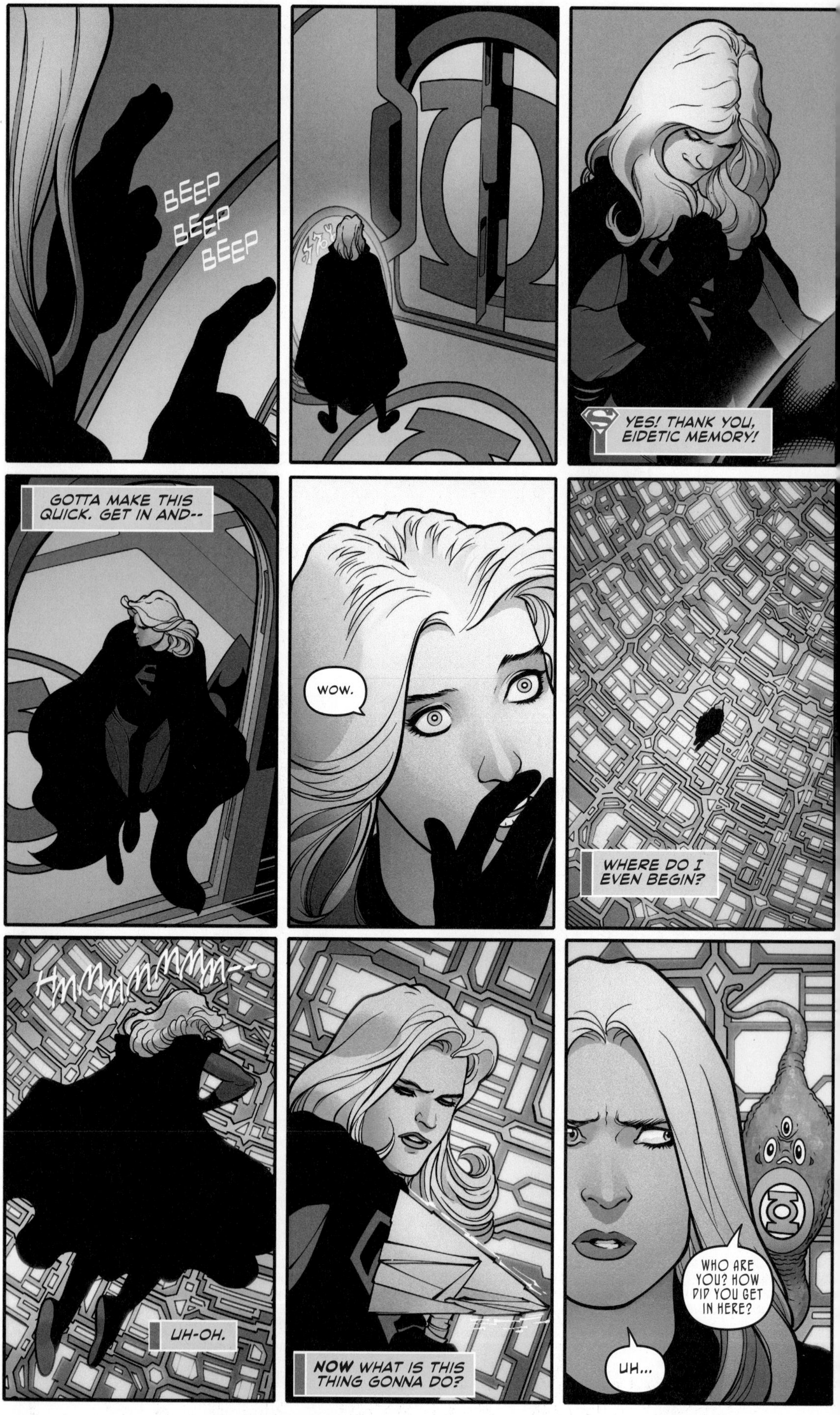
BEEP
BEEP
BEEP
YES! THANK YOU, EIDETIC MEMORY!
GOTTA MAKE THIS QUICK. GET IN AND--
WOW.
WHERE DO I EVEN BEGIN?
HMMMMMMM--
UH-OH.
NOW WHAT IS THIS THING GONNA DO?
WHO ARE YOU? HOW DID YOU GET IN HERE?
UH...

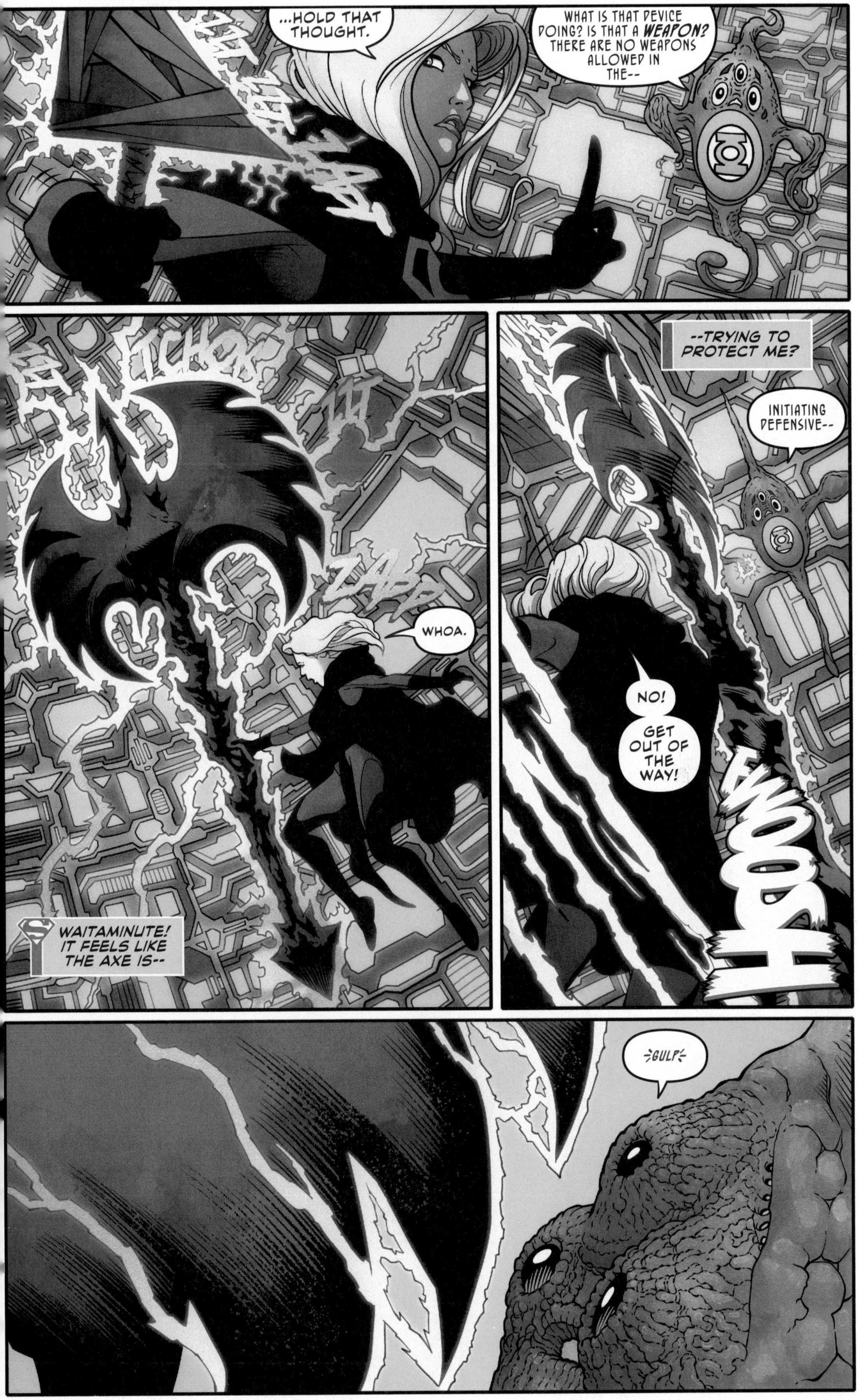
...HOLD THAT THOUGHT.
WHAT IS THAT DEVICE DOING? IS THAT A WEAPON? THERE ARE NO WEAPONS ALLOWED IN THE--
WHOA.
WAITAMINUTE! IT FEELS LIKE THE AXE IS--
--TRYING TO PROTECT ME?
INITIATING DEFENSIVE--
NO!
GET OUT OF THE WAY!
WHOOSH
GULP

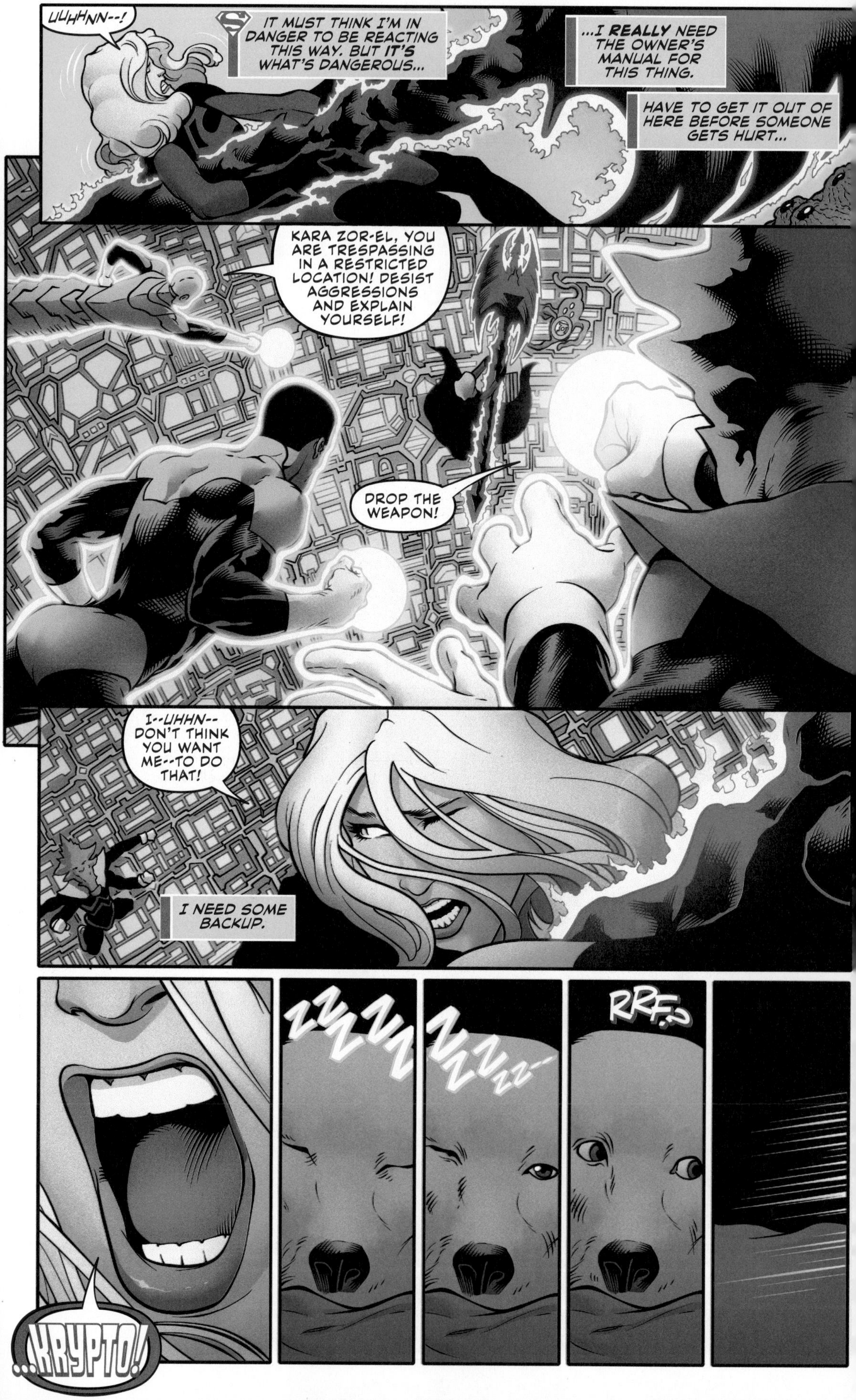
UUHHNN--!
IT MUST THINK I'M IN DANGER TO BE REACTING THIS WAY. BUT IT'S WHAT'S DANGEROUS...
...I REALLY NEED THE OWNER'S MANUAL FOR THIS THING.
HAVE TO GET IT OUT OF HERE BEFORE SOMEONE GETS HURT...
KARA ZOR-EL, YOU ARE TRESPASSING IN A RESTRICTED LOCATION! DESIST AGGRESSIONS AND EXPLAIN YOURSELF!
DROP THE WEAPON!
I--UHHN--DON'T THINK YOU WANT ME--TO DO THAT!
I NEED SOME BACKUP.
...KRYPTO!
ZZZZZ
ZZZZZZ--
RRF?

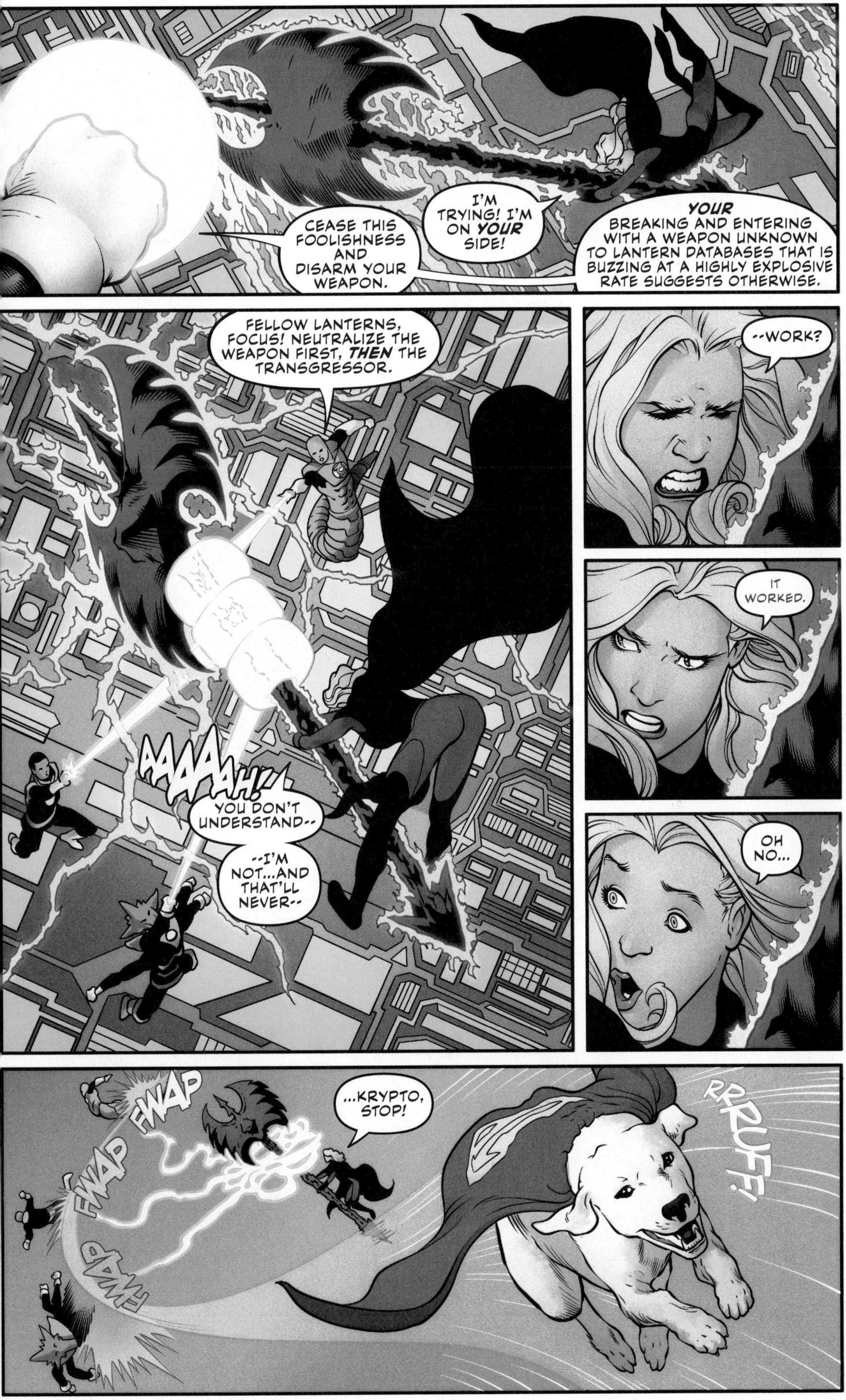
CEASE THIS FOOLISHNESS AND DISARM YOUR WEAPON.
I'M TRYING! I'M ON YOUR SIDE!
YOUR BREAKING AND ENTERING WITH A WEAPON UNKNOWN TO LANTERN DATABASES THAT IS BUZZING AT A HIGHLY EXPLOSIVE RATE SUGGESTS OTHERWISE.
FELLOW LANTERNS, FOCUS! NEUTRALIZE THE WEAPON FIRST, THEN THE TRANSGRESSOR.
AAAAAH!
YOU DON'T UNDERSTAND--
--I'M NOT...AND THAT'LL NEVER--
--WORK?
IT WORKED.
OH NO...
FWAP
FWAP
FWAP
FWAP
...KRYPTO, STOP!
RRRUFF!

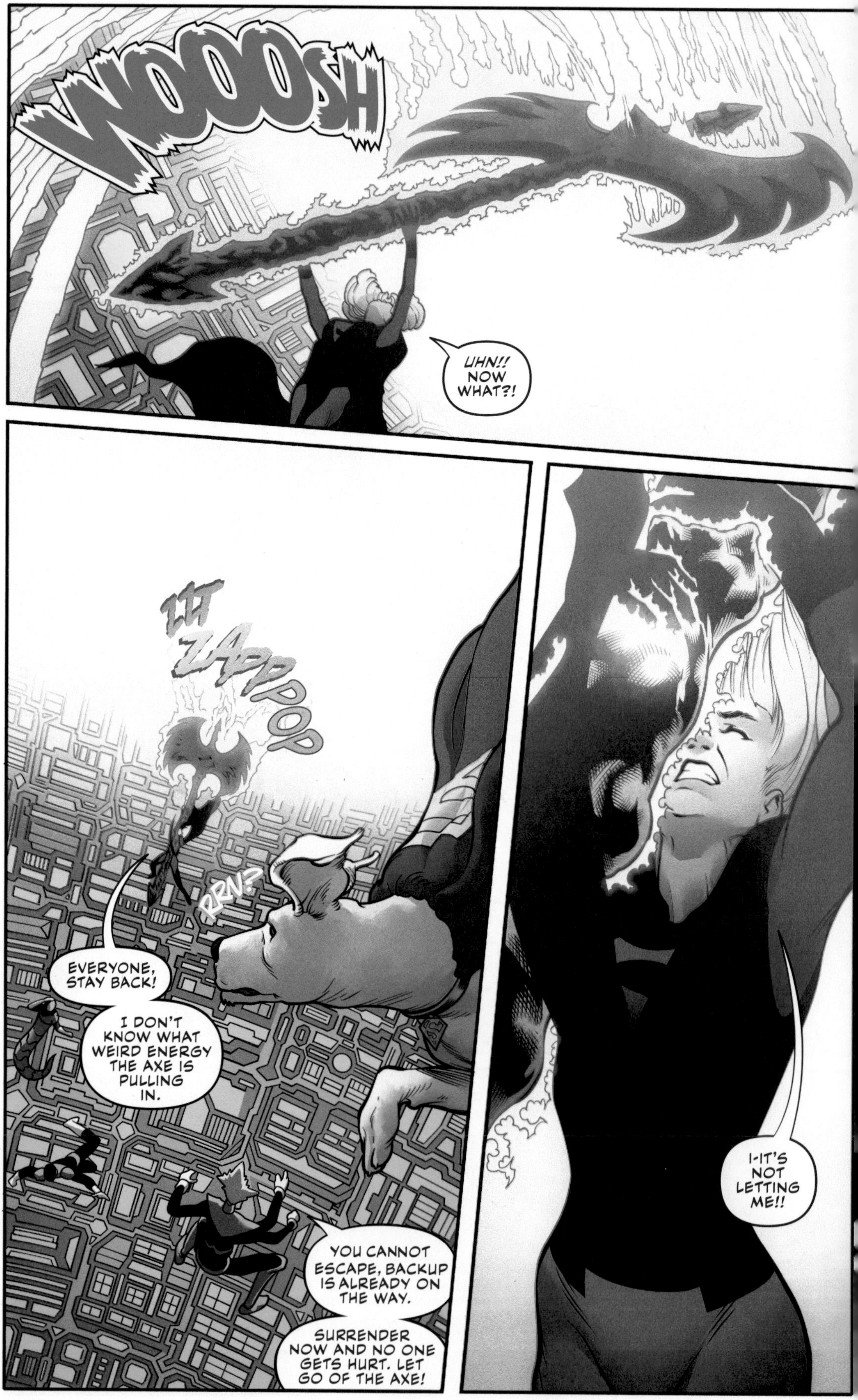
WOOOSH
UHN!! NOW WHAT?!
ZZT ZAPPPOP
RRN?
EVERYONE, STAY BACK!
I DON'T KNOW WHAT WEIRD ENERGY THE AXE IS PULLING IN.
YOU CANNOT ESCAPE, BACKUP IS ALREADY ON THE WAY.
SURRENDER NOW AND NO ONE GETS HURT. LET GO OF THE AXE!
I-IT'S NOT LETTING ME!!

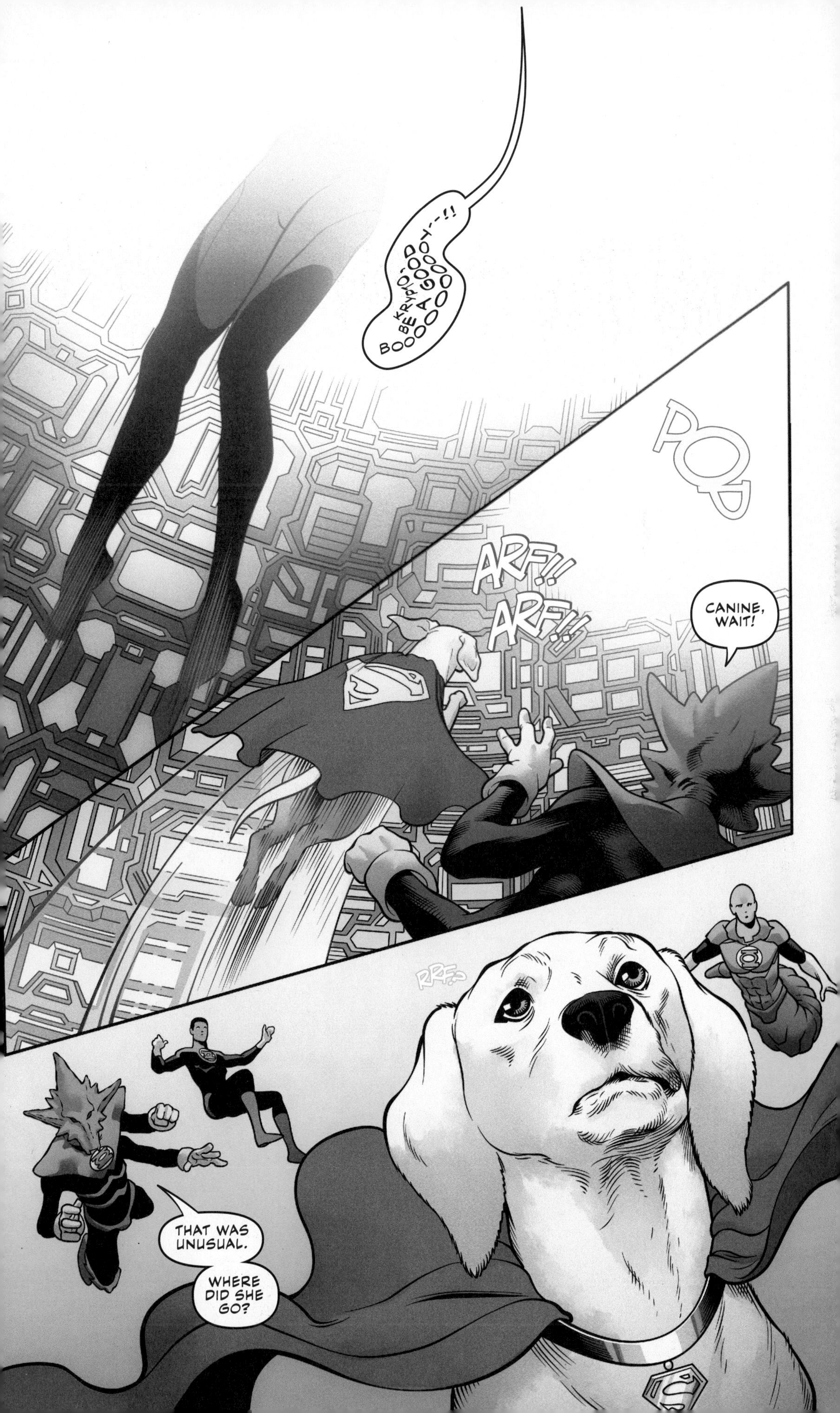
KRYPTO, BE A GOOOD BOOOOOOOOOY--!!
POP
ARF!! ARF!!
CANINE, WAIT!
RRF?
THAT WAS UNUSUAL.
WHERE DID SHE GO?

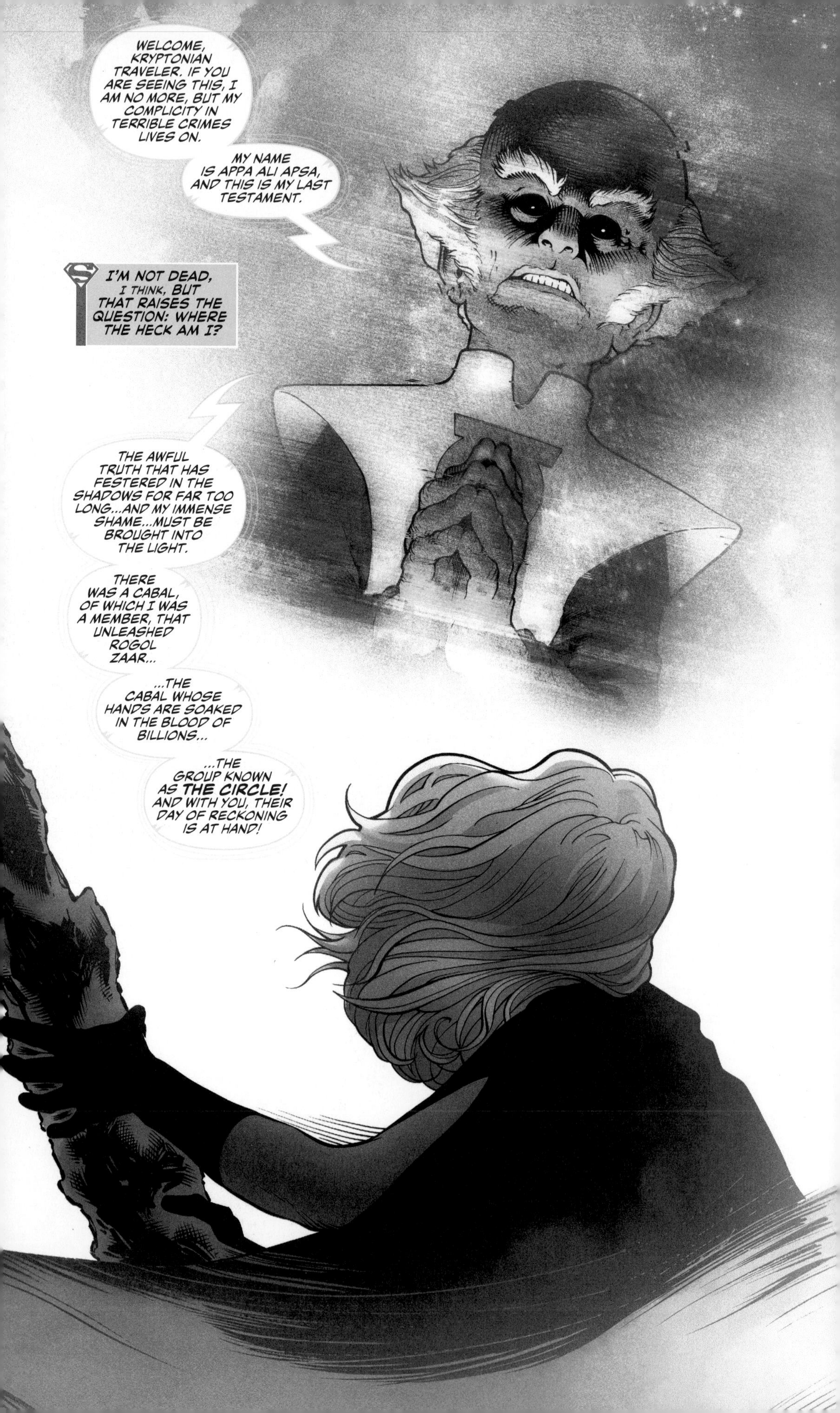
WELCOME, KRYPTONIAN TRAVELER. IF YOU ARE SEEING THIS, I AM NO MORE, BUT MY COMPLICITY IN TERRIBLE CRIMES LIVES ON.
MY NAME IS APPA ALI APSA, AND THIS IS MY LAST TESTAMENT.
I'M NOT DEAD, I THINK, BUT THAT RAISES THE QUESTION: WHERE THE HECK AM I?
THE AWFUL TRUTH THAT HAS FESTERED IN THE SHADOWS FOR FAR TOO LONG...AND MY IMMENSE SHAME...MUST BE BROUGHT INTO THE LIGHT.
THERE WAS A CABAL, OF WHICH I WAS A MEMBER, THAT UNLEASHED ROGOL ZAAR...
...THE CABAL WHOSE HANDS ARE SOAKED IN THE BLOOD OF BILLIONS...
...THE GROUP KNOWN AS **THE CIRCLE!** AND WITH YOU, THEIR DAY OF RECKONING IS AT HAND!

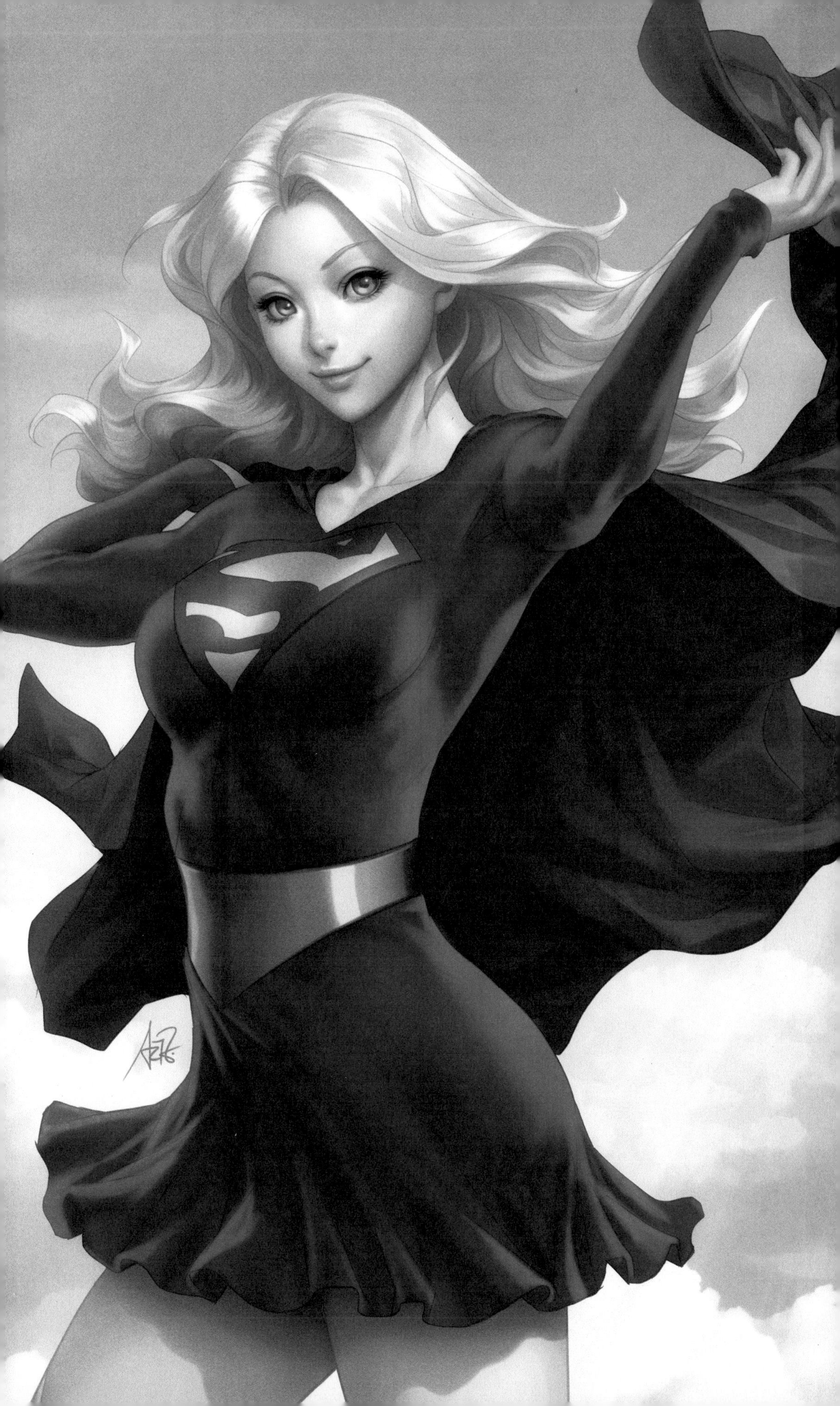

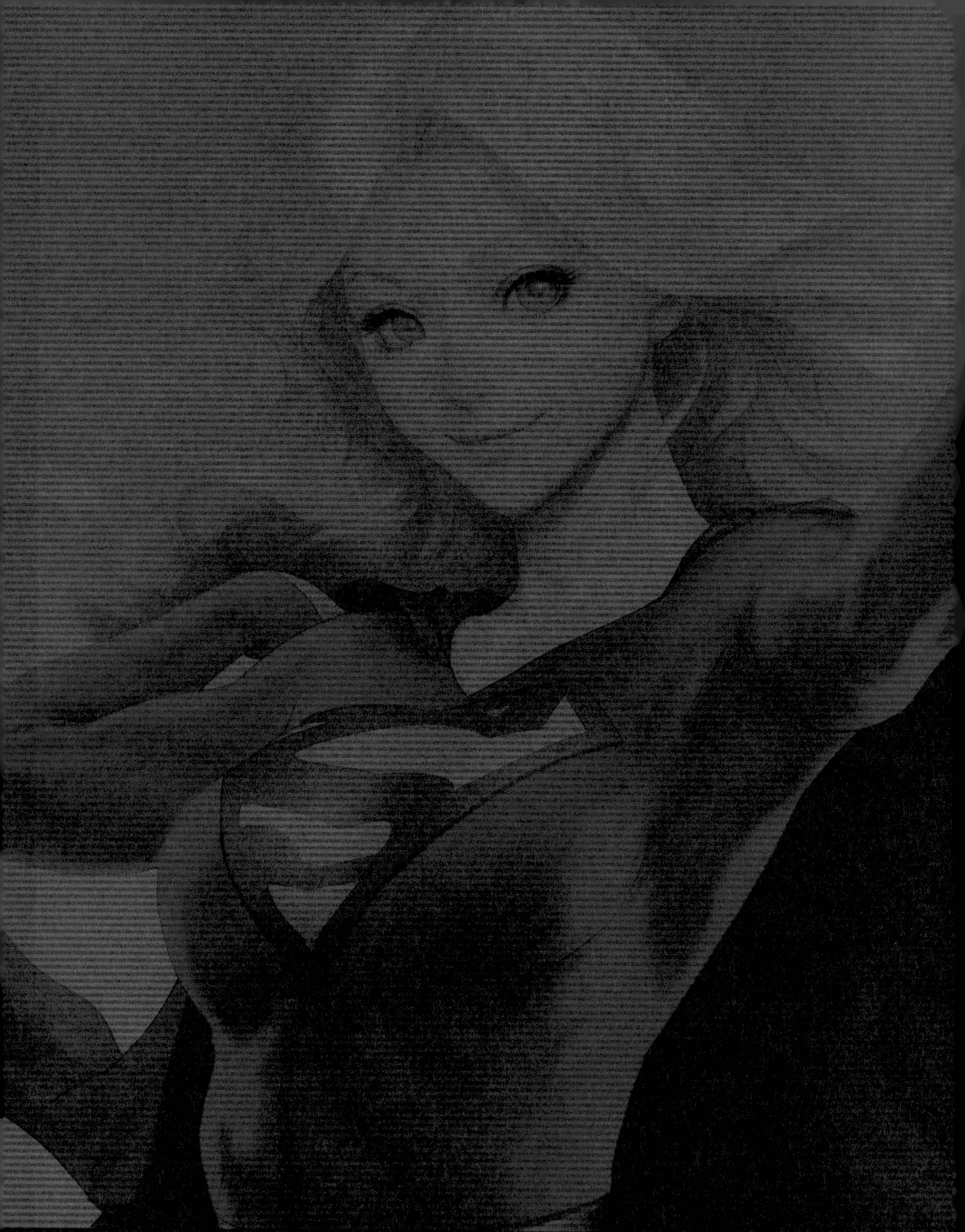

SUPERGIRL
#23

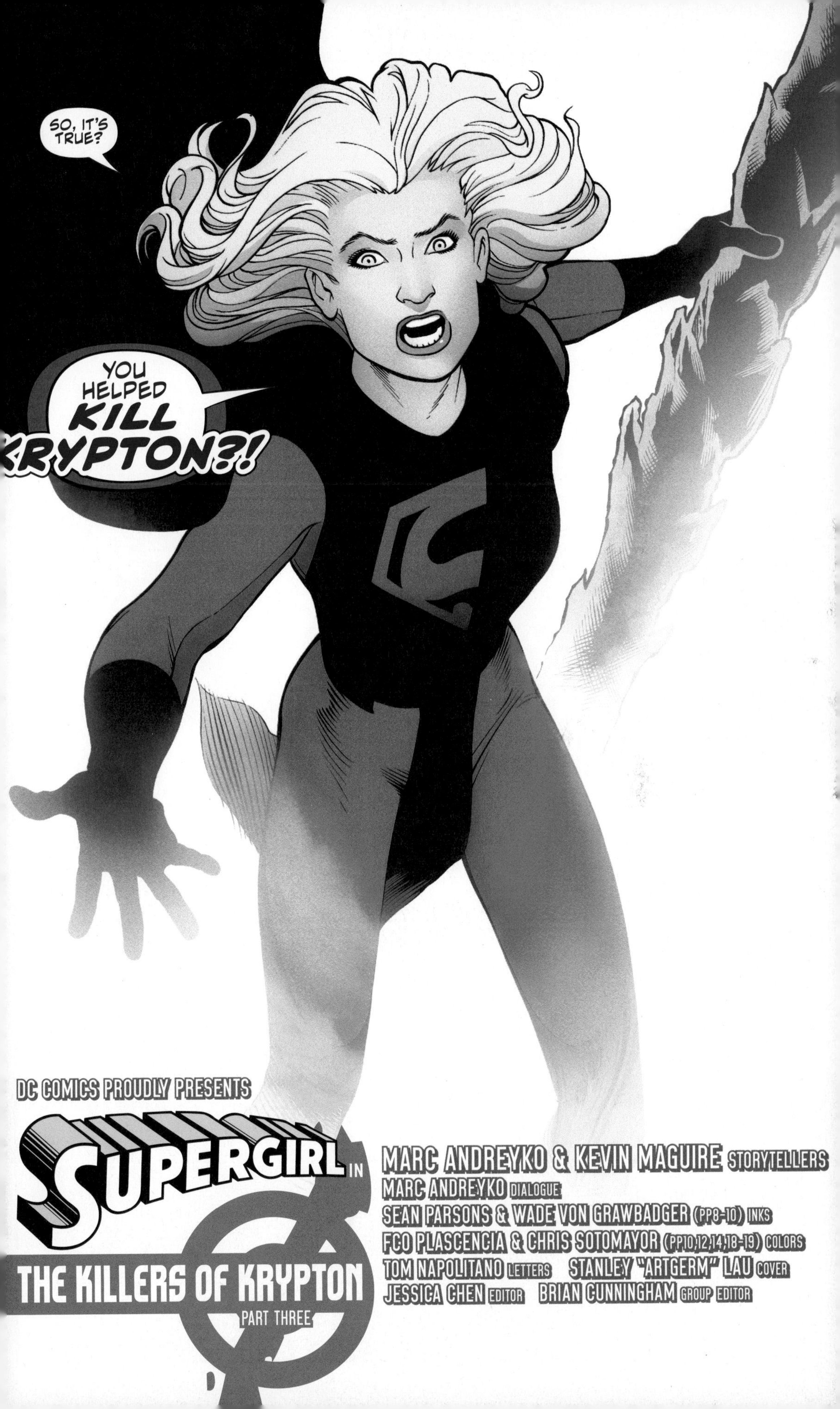

SO, IT'S TRUE?
YOU HELPED KILL KRYPTON?!
DC COMICS PROUDLY PRESENTS
SUPERGIRL IN
THE KILLERS OF KRYPTON
PART THREE
MARC ANDREYKO & KEVIN MAGUIRE STORYTELLERS
MARC ANDREYKO DIALOGUE
SEAN PARSONS & WADE VON GRAWBADGER (PP8-10) INKS
FCO PLASCENCIA & CHRIS SOTOMAYOR (PP10,12,14,18-19) COLORS
TOM NAPOLITANO LETTERS
STANLEY "ARTGERM" LAU COVER
JESSICA CHEN EDITOR
BRIAN CUNNINGHAM GROUP EDITOR

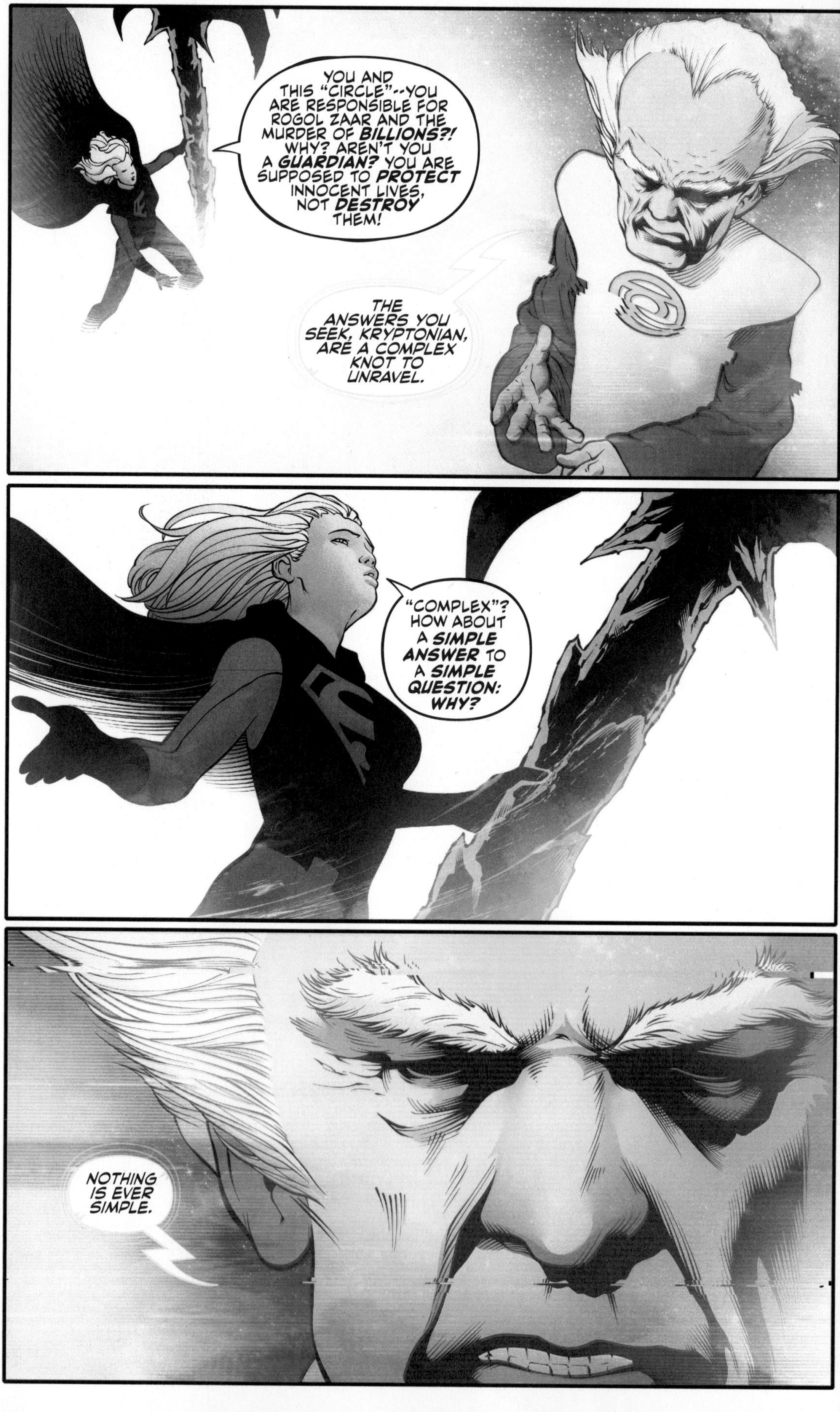
YOU AND THIS "CIRCLE"--YOU ARE RESPONSIBLE FOR ROGOL ZAAR AND THE MURDER OF **BILLIONS?!** WHY? AREN'T YOU A **GUARDIAN?** YOU ARE SUPPOSED TO **PROTECT** INNOCENT LIVES, NOT **DESTROY** THEM!
THE ANSWERS YOU SEEK, KRYPTONIAN, ARE A COMPLEX KNOT TO UNRAVEL.
"COMPLEX"? HOW ABOUT A **SIMPLE ANSWER** TO A **SIMPLE QUESTION: WHY?**
NOTHING IS EVER SIMPLE.

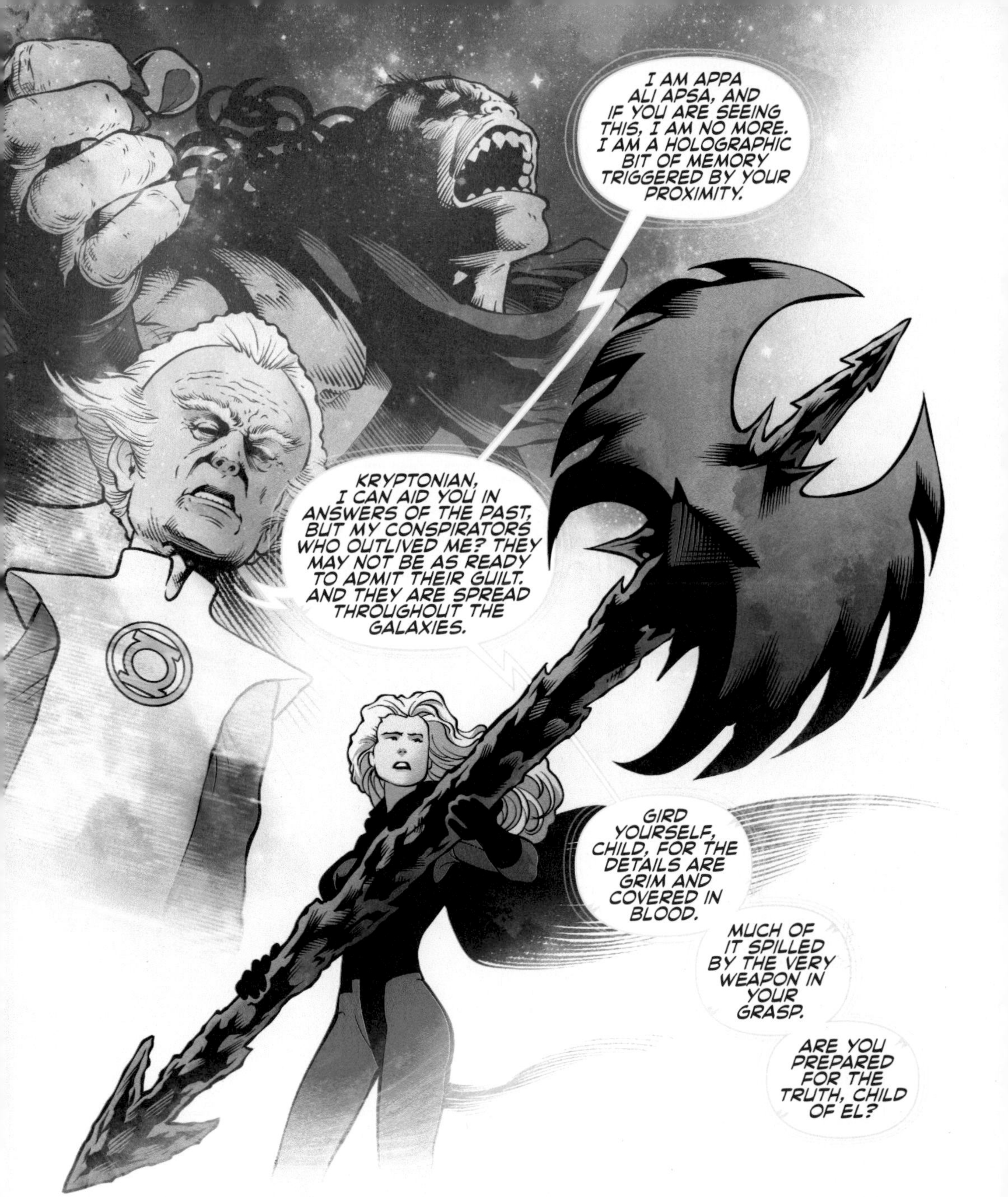
I AM APPA ALI APSA, AND IF YOU ARE SEEING THIS, I AM NO MORE. I AM A HOLOGRAPHIC BIT OF MEMORY TRIGGERED BY YOUR PROXIMITY.
KRYPTONIAN, I CAN AID YOU IN ANSWERS OF THE PAST, BUT MY CONSPIRATORS WHO OUTLIVED ME? THEY MAY NOT BE AS READY TO ADMIT THEIR GUILT. AND THEY ARE SPREAD THROUGHOUT THE GALAXIES.
GIRD YOURSELF, CHILD, FOR THE DETAILS ARE GRIM AND COVERED IN BLOOD.
MUCH OF IT SPILLED BY THE VERY WEAPON IN YOUR GRASP.
ARE YOU PREPARED FOR THE TRUTH, CHILD OF EL?

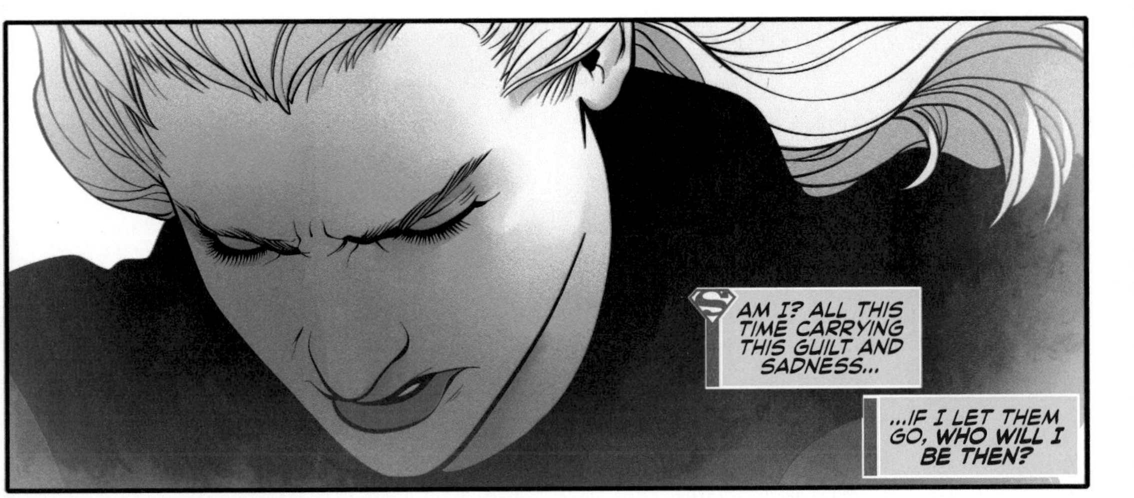
AM I? ALL THIS TIME CARRYING THIS GUILT AND SADNESS...
...IF I LET THEM GO, WHO WILL I BE THEN?

YES.

ZZZAP

TELL ME EVERYTHING.

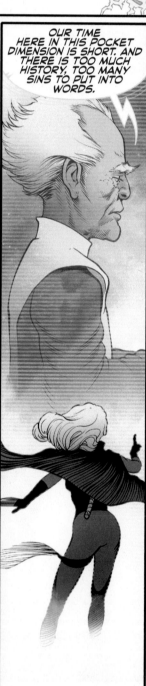

OUR TIME HERE IN THIS POCKET DIMENSION IS SHORT. AND THERE IS TOO MUCH HISTORY, TOO MANY SINS TO PUT INTO WORDS.

TAKE THIS AND SOME OF YOUR QUESTIONS WILL SOON BE ANSWERED.

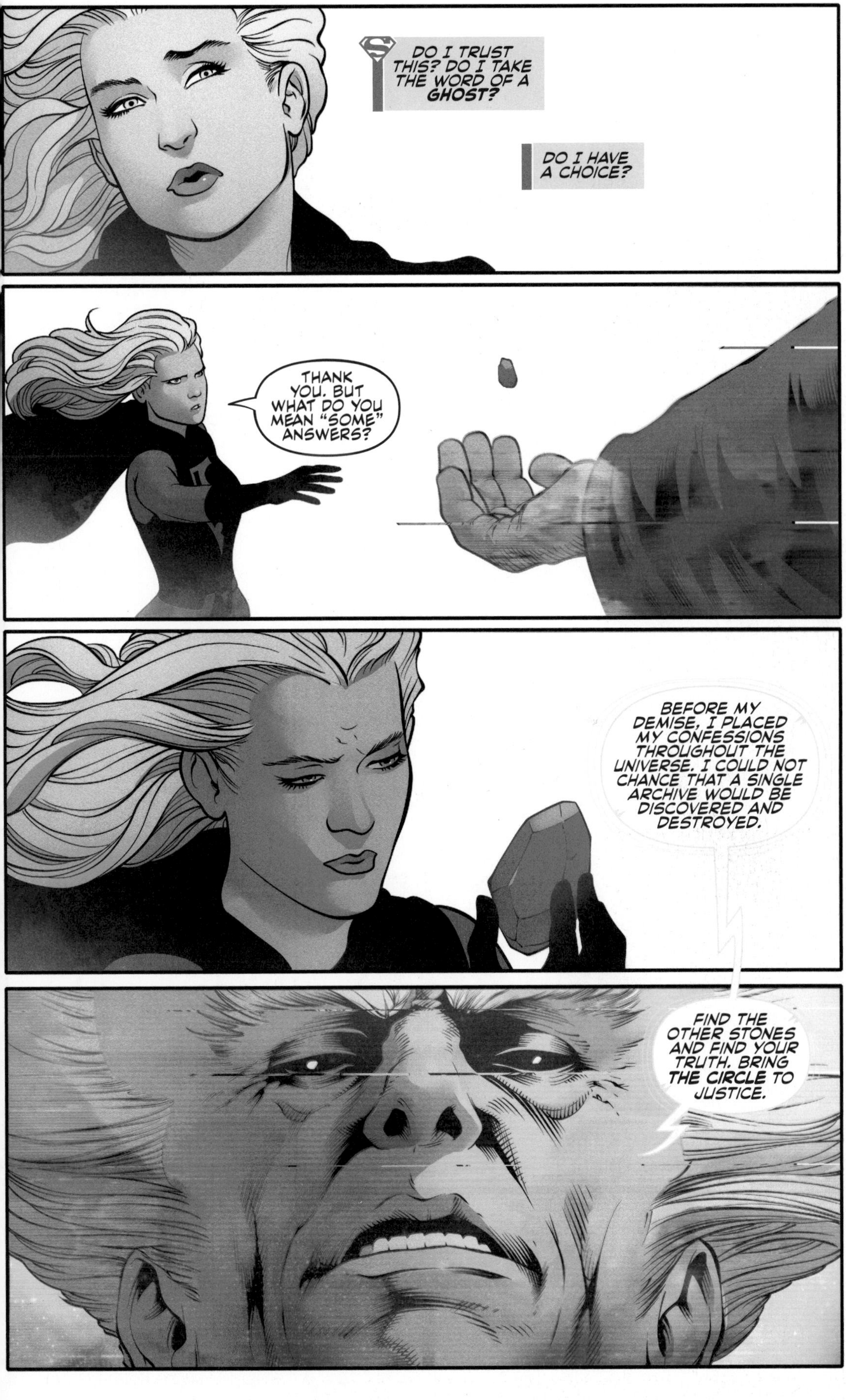
DO I TRUST THIS? DO I TAKE THE WORD OF A GHOST?
DO I HAVE A CHOICE?
THANK YOU. BUT WHAT DO YOU MEAN "SOME" ANSWERS?
BEFORE MY DEMISE, I PLACED MY CONFESSIONS THROUGHOUT THE UNIVERSE. I COULD NOT CHANCE THAT A SINGLE ARCHIVE WOULD BE DISCOVERED AND DESTROYED.
FIND THE OTHER STONES AND FIND YOUR TRUTH. BRING THE CIRCLE TO JUSTICE.

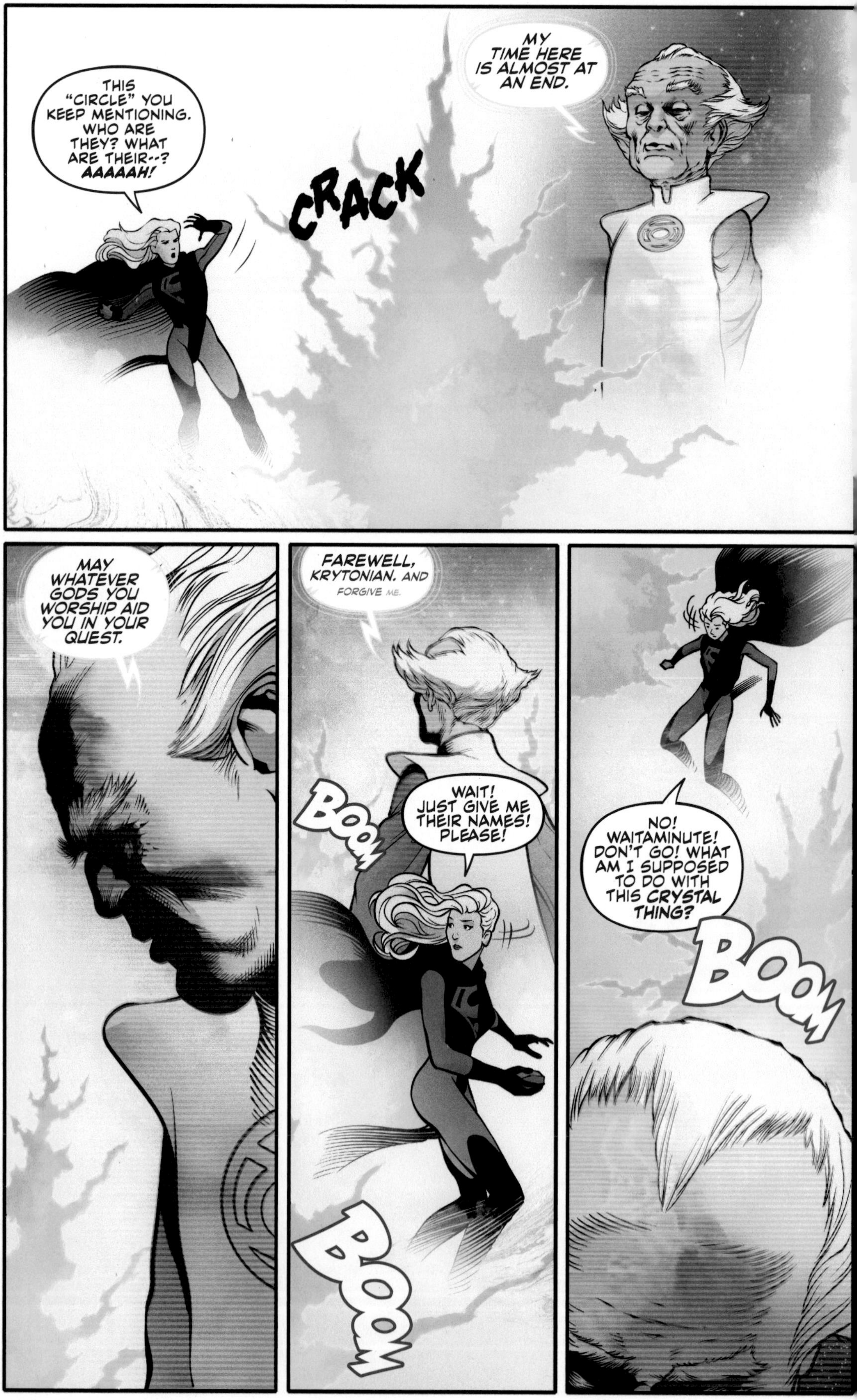
THIS "CIRCLE" YOU KEEP MENTIONING. WHO ARE THEY? WHAT ARE THEIR--? AAAAAH!
CRACK
MY TIME HERE IS ALMOST AT AN END.
MAY WHATEVER GODS YOU WORSHIP AID YOU IN YOUR QUEST.
FAREWELL, KRYTONIAN. AND FORGIVE ME.
BOOM
WAIT! JUST GIVE ME THEIR NAMES! PLEASE!
BOOM
NO! WAITAMINUTE! DON'T GO! WHAT AM I SUPPOSED TO DO WITH THIS CRYSTAL THING?
BOOM

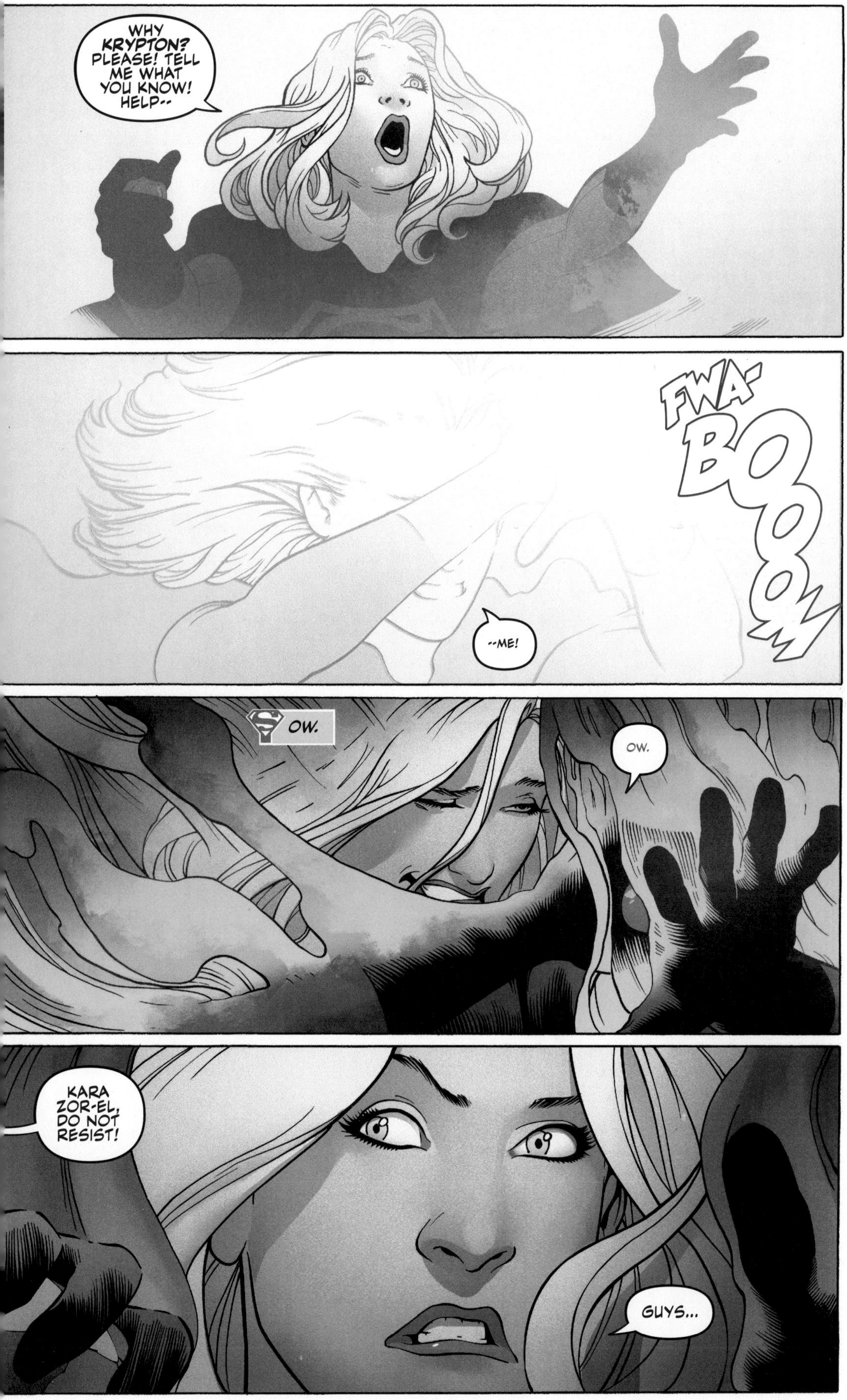
WHY KRYPTON? PLEASE! TELL ME WHAT YOU KNOW! HELP--
FWA-BOOOOM
--ME!
OW.
OW.
KARA ZOR-EL, DO NOT RESIST!
GUYS...

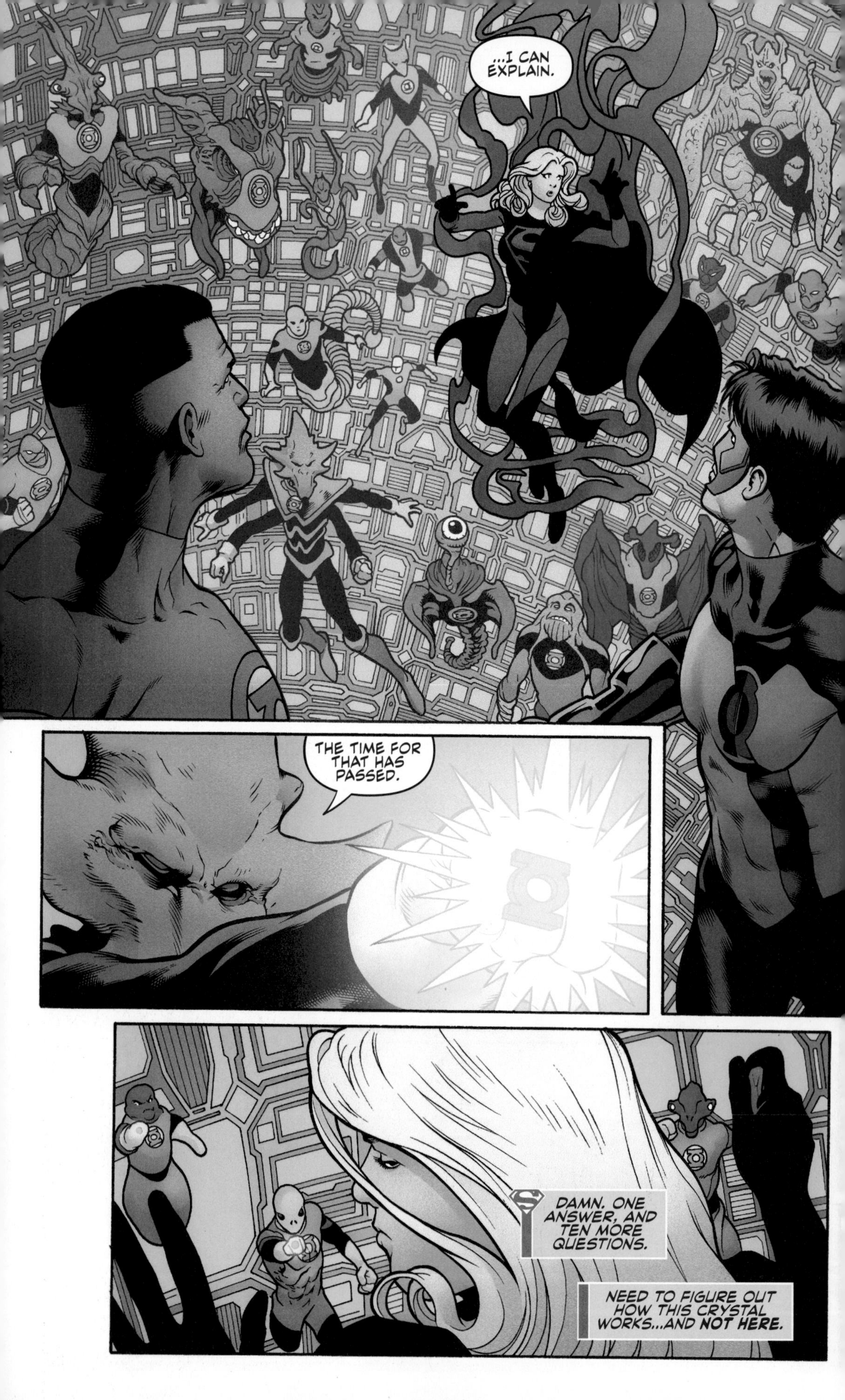
...I CAN EXPLAIN.
THE TIME FOR THAT HAS PASSED.
DAMN. ONE ANSWER, AND TEN MORE QUESTIONS.
NEED TO FIGURE OUT HOW THIS CRYSTAL WORKS...AND NOT HERE.

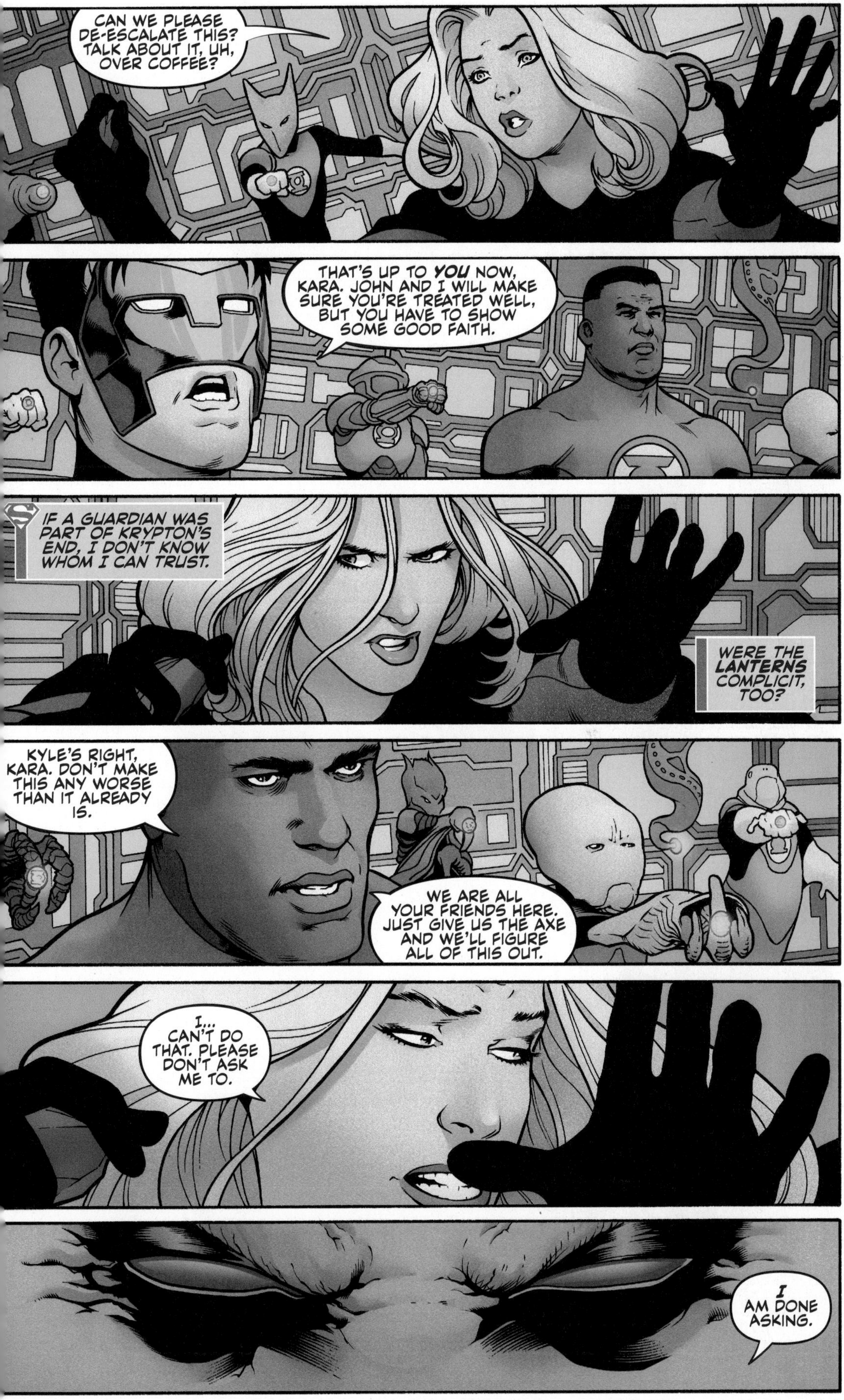

CAN WE PLEASE DE-ESCALATE THIS? TALK ABOUT IT, UH, OVER COFFEE?
THAT'S UP TO *YOU* NOW, KARA. JOHN AND I WILL MAKE SURE YOU'RE TREATED WELL, BUT YOU HAVE TO SHOW SOME GOOD FAITH.
IF A GUARDIAN WAS PART OF KRYPTON'S END, I DON'T KNOW WHOM I CAN TRUST.
WERE THE *LANTERNS* COMPLICIT, TOO?
KYLE'S RIGHT, KARA. DON'T MAKE THIS ANY WORSE THAN IT ALREADY IS.
WE ARE ALL YOUR FRIENDS HERE. JUST GIVE US THE AXE AND WE'LL FIGURE ALL OF THIS OUT.
I... CAN'T DO THAT. PLEASE DON'T ASK ME TO.
I AM DONE ASKING.

I'M SORRY, JOHN, KYLE...

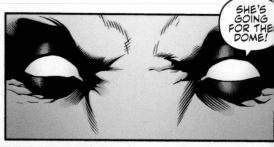

SHE'S GOING FOR THE DOME!

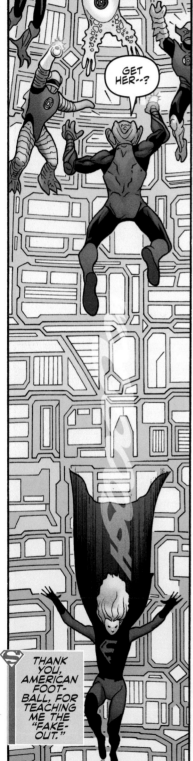

GET HER--?

THANK YOU, AMERICAN FOOTBALL, FOR TEACHING ME THE "FAKE-OUT."

I KNEW THIS WAS GONNA HAPPEN.

LANTERNS, STAND DOWN! RAYNER AND I HAVE THIS!

YOU DO?

YOU MADE ME DO THIS, KARA! I TRIED TO ASK NICELY.

CHOMP

"AUDREY II"? FOR REAL, KYLE?! YOUR MUSICAL-THEATER FETISH IS SHOWING--!

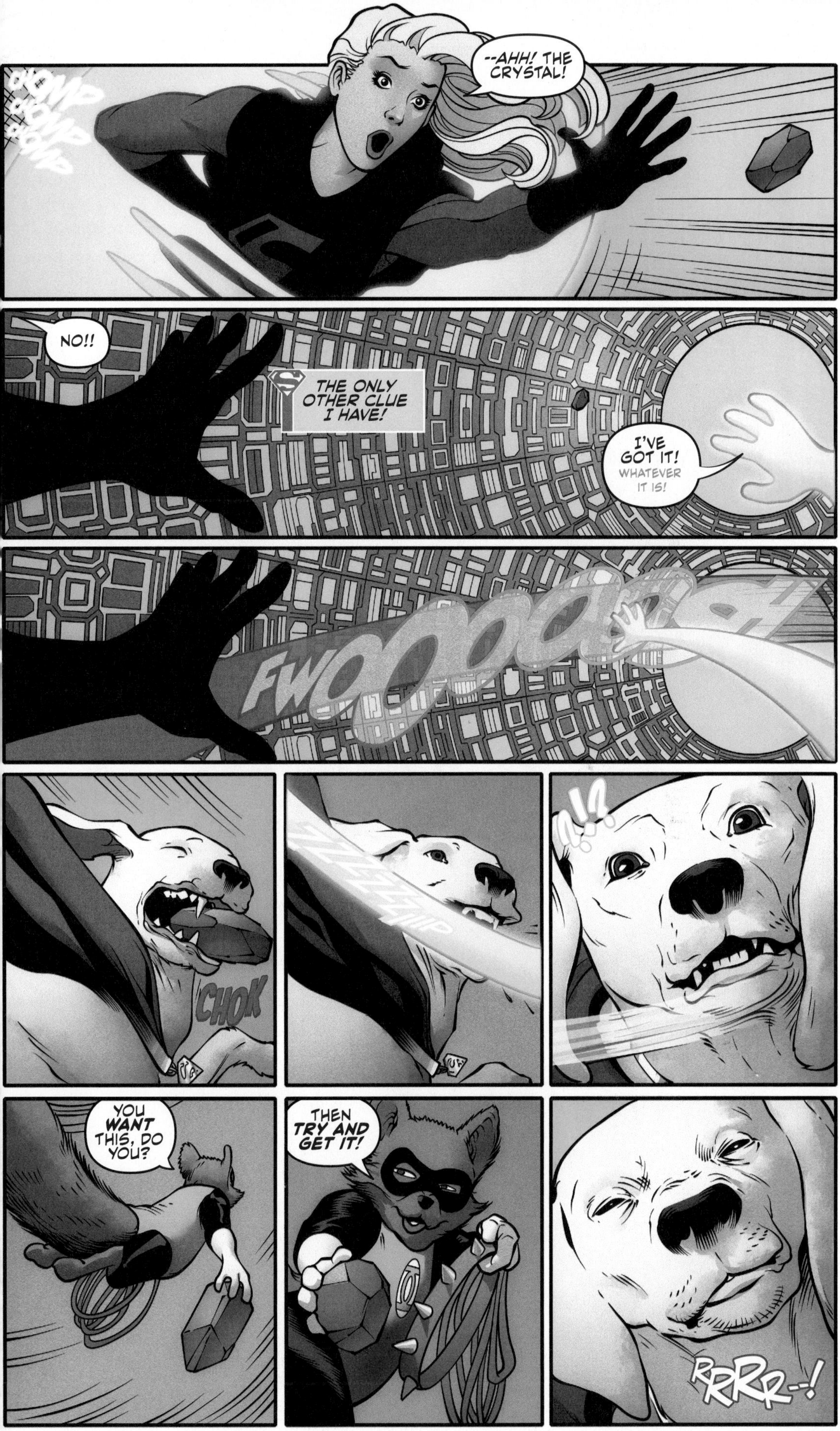

CHOMP CHOMP CHOMP
--AHH! THE CRYSTAL!
NO!!
THE ONLY OTHER CLUE I HAVE!
I'VE GOT IT! WHATEVER IT IS!
FWOOOOOSH
CHOK
!!?
YOU WANT THIS, DO YOU?
THEN TRY AND GET IT!
RRRR--!

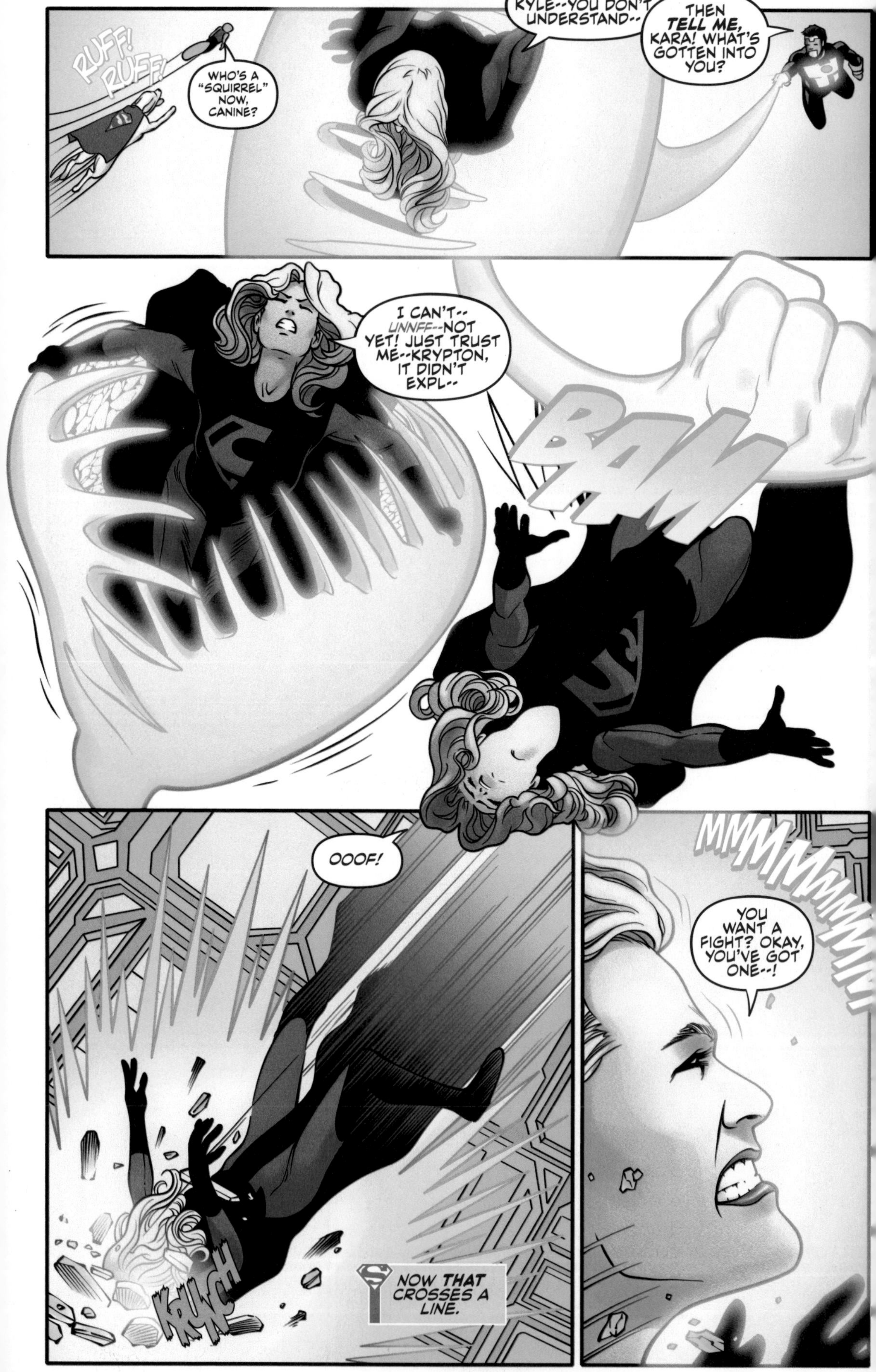
RUFF! RUFF!
WHO'S A "SQUIRREL" NOW, CANINE?
UUHN-- KYLE--YOU DON'T UNDERSTAND--
THEN TELL ME, KARA! WHAT'S GOTTEN INTO YOU?
I CAN'T-- UNNFF--NOT YET! JUST TRUST ME--KRYPTON, IT DIDN'T EXPL--
BAM
OOOF!
KRUNCH
NOW THAT CROSSES A LINE.
MMMMMMMMM
YOU WANT A FIGHT? OKAY, YOU'VE GOT ONE--!

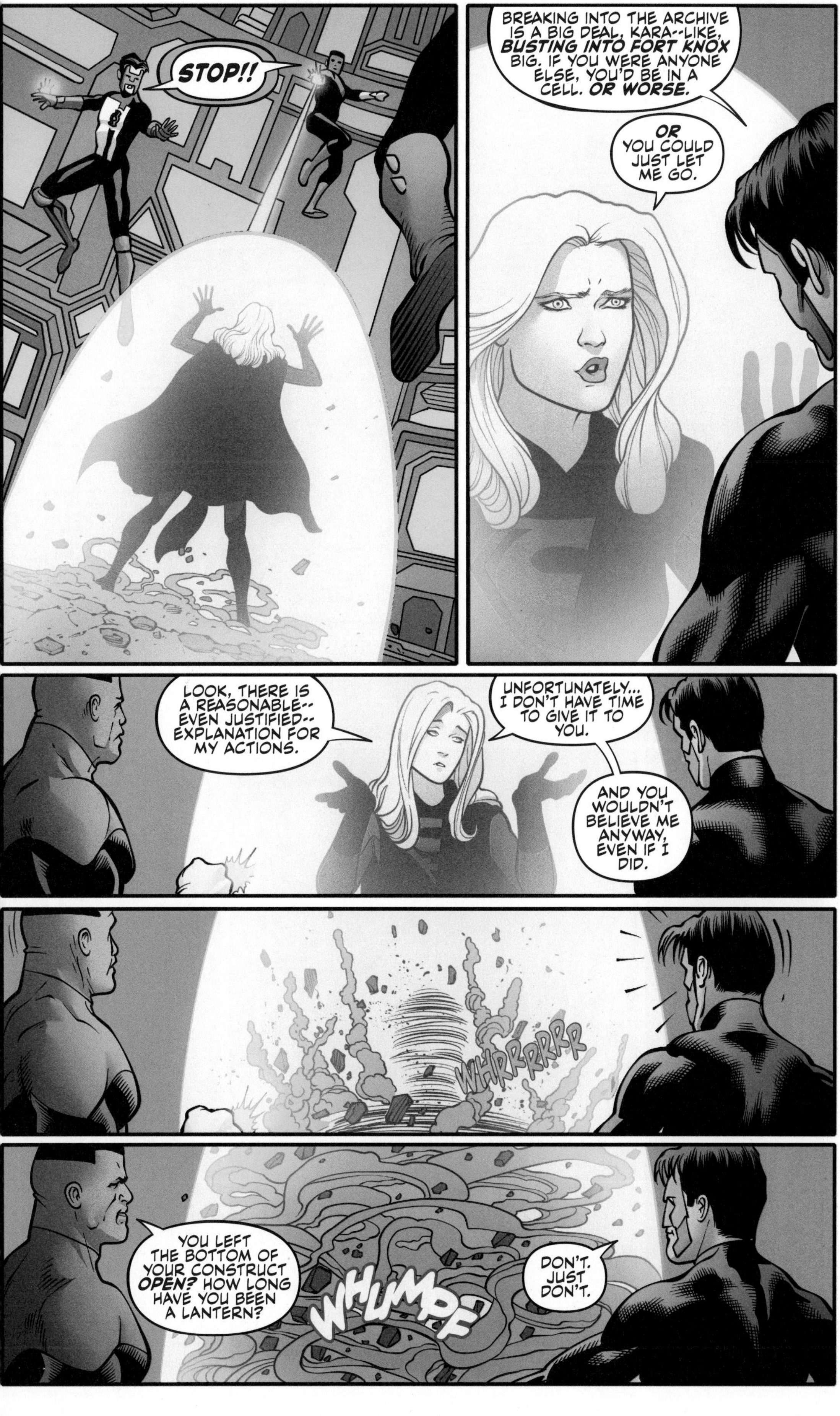
STOP!!
BREAKING INTO THE ARCHIVE IS A BIG DEAL, KARA--LIKE, BUSTING INTO FORT KNOX BIG. IF YOU WERE ANYONE ELSE, YOU'D BE IN A CELL. OR WORSE.
OR YOU COULD JUST LET ME GO.
LOOK, THERE IS A REASONABLE-- EVEN JUSTIFIED-- EXPLANATION FOR MY ACTIONS.
UNFORTUNATELY... I DON'T HAVE TIME TO GIVE IT TO YOU.
AND YOU WOULDN'T BELIEVE ME ANYWAY, EVEN IF I DID.
WHRRRRRR
YOU LEFT THE BOTTOM OF YOUR CONSTRUCT OPEN? HOW LONG HAVE YOU BEEN A LANTERN?
WHUMPF
DON'T. JUST DON'T.

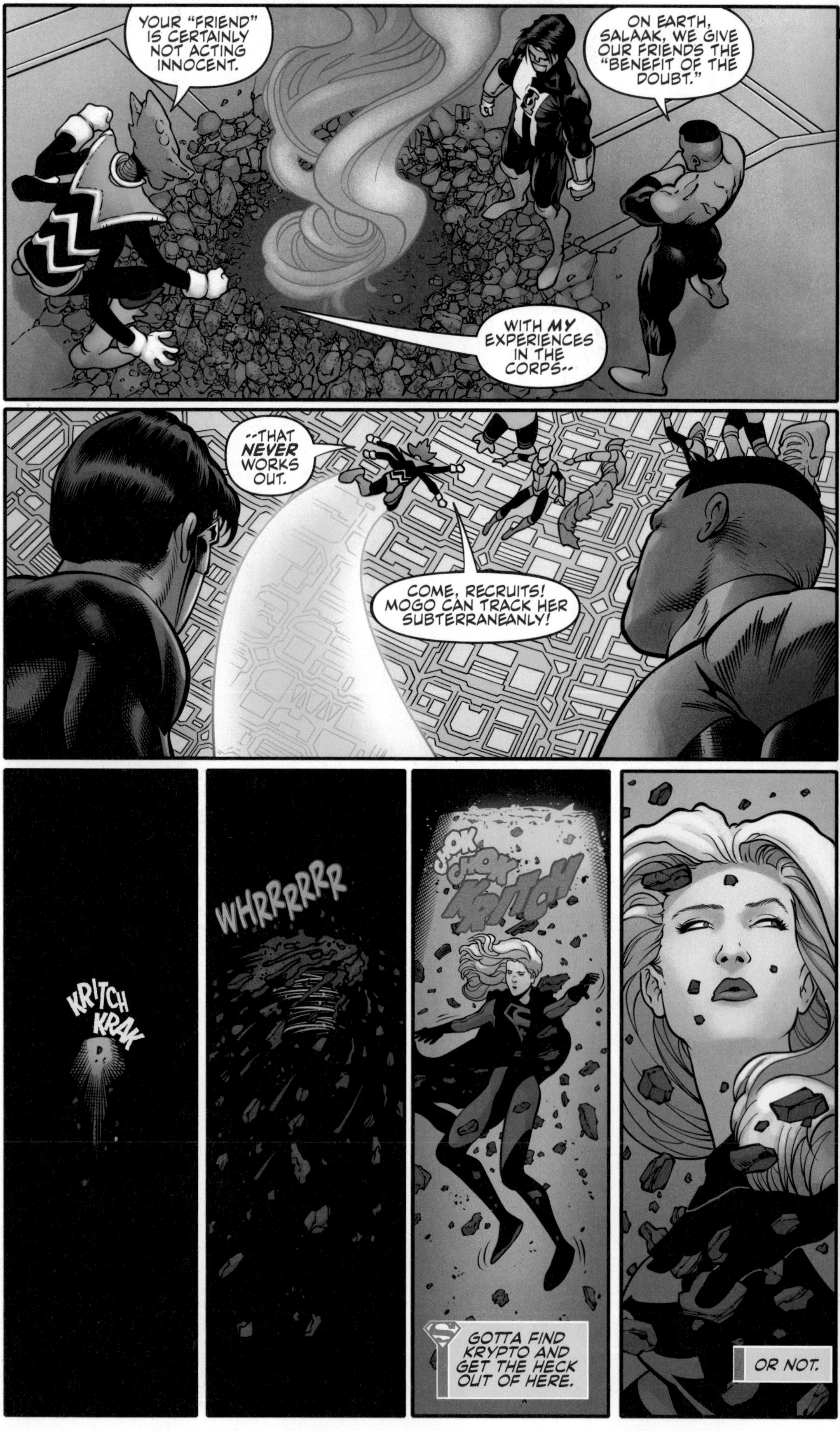

YOUR "FRIEND" IS CERTAINLY NOT ACTING INNOCENT.
ON EARTH, SALAAK, WE GIVE OUR FRIENDS THE "BENEFIT OF THE DOUBT."
WITH MY EXPERIENCES IN THE CORPS--
--THAT NEVER WORKS OUT.
COME, RECRUITS! MOGO CAN TRACK HER SUBTERRANEANLY!
KRITCH KRAK
WHRRRRRR
CHOK CHOK KRITCH
GOTTA FIND KRYPTO AND GET THE HECK OUT OF HERE.
OR NOT.

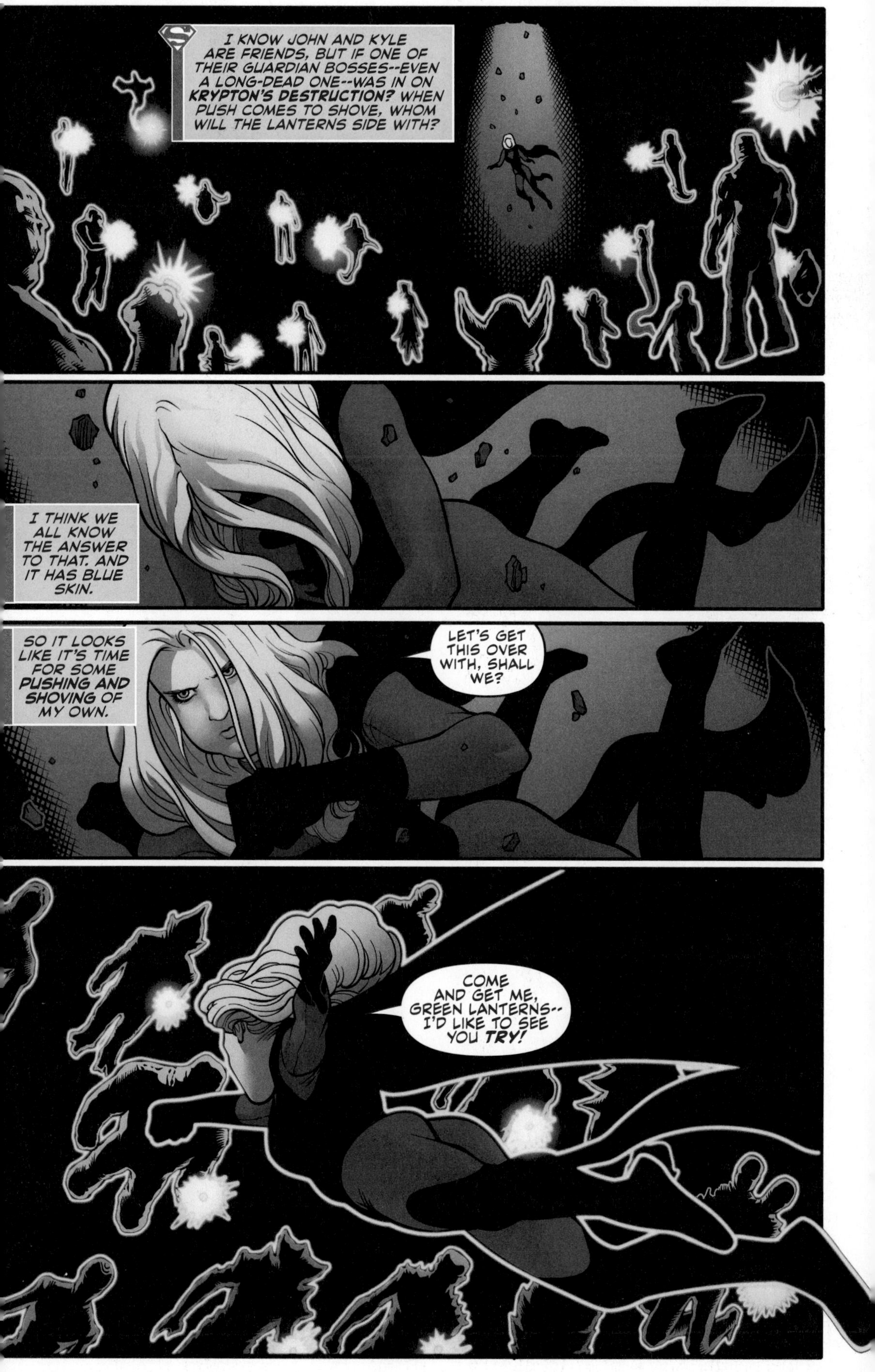
I KNOW JOHN AND KYLE ARE FRIENDS, BUT IF ONE OF THEIR GUARDIAN BOSSES--EVEN A LONG-DEAD ONE--WAS IN ON KRYPTON'S DESTRUCTION? WHEN PUSH COMES TO SHOVE, WHOM WILL THE LANTERNS SIDE WITH?
I THINK WE ALL KNOW THE ANSWER TO THAT. AND IT HAS BLUE SKIN.
SO IT LOOKS LIKE IT'S TIME FOR SOME PUSHING AND SHOVING OF MY OWN.
LET'S GET THIS OVER WITH, SHALL WE?
COME AND GET ME, GREEN LANTERNS--I'D LIKE TO SEE YOU TRY!

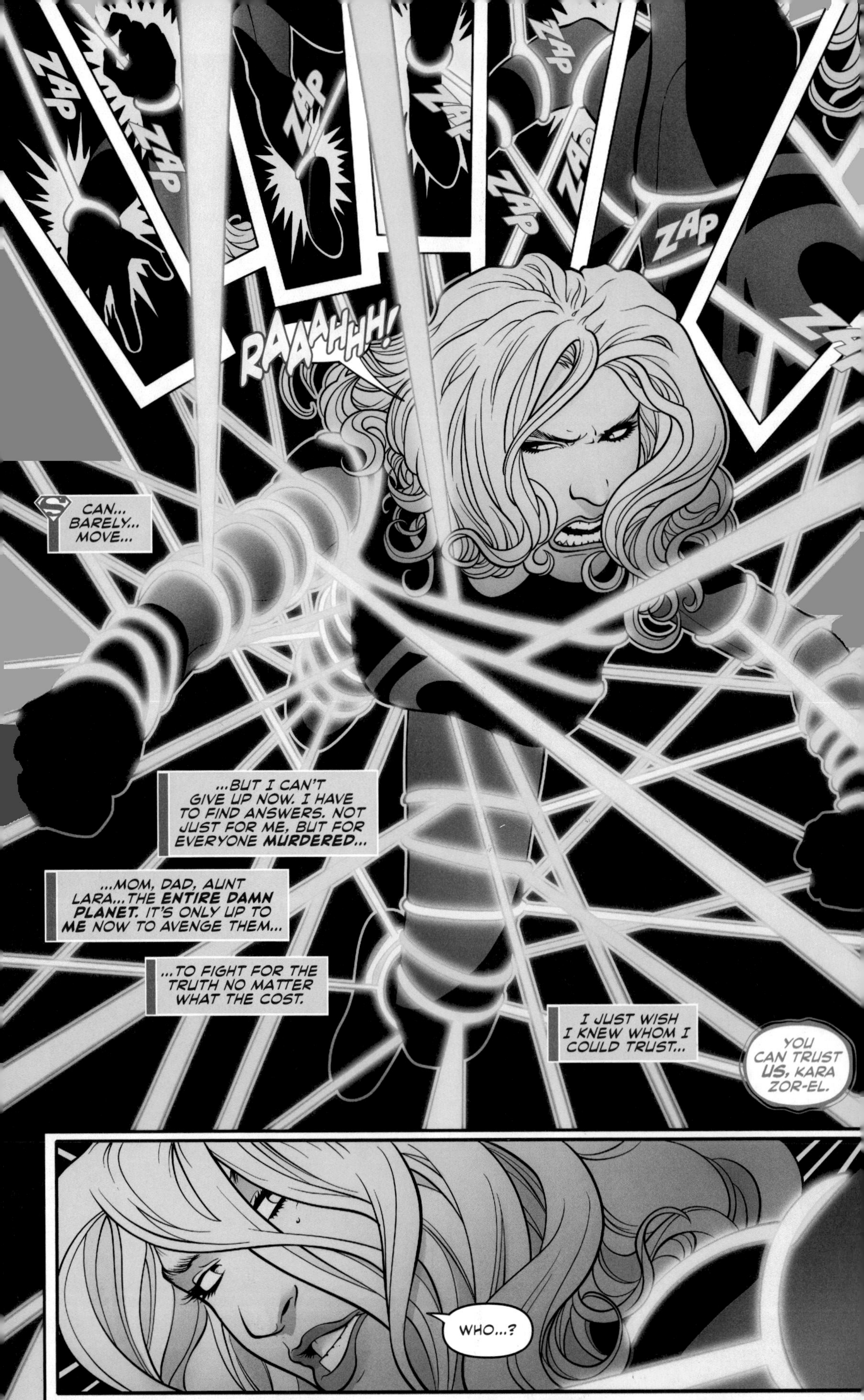
ZAP
ZAP
ZAP
ZAP
ZAP
ZAP
ZAP
ZAP
ZAP
RAAAHHH!
CAN... BARELY... MOVE...
...BUT I CAN'T GIVE UP NOW. I HAVE TO FIND ANSWERS. NOT JUST FOR ME, BUT FOR EVERYONE MURDERED...
...MOM, DAD, AUNT LARA...THE ENTIRE DAMN PLANET. IT'S ONLY UP TO ME NOW TO AVENGE THEM...
...TO FIGHT FOR THE TRUTH NO MATTER WHAT THE COST.
I JUST WISH I KNEW WHOM I COULD TRUST...
YOU CAN TRUST US, KARA ZOR-EL.
WHO...?

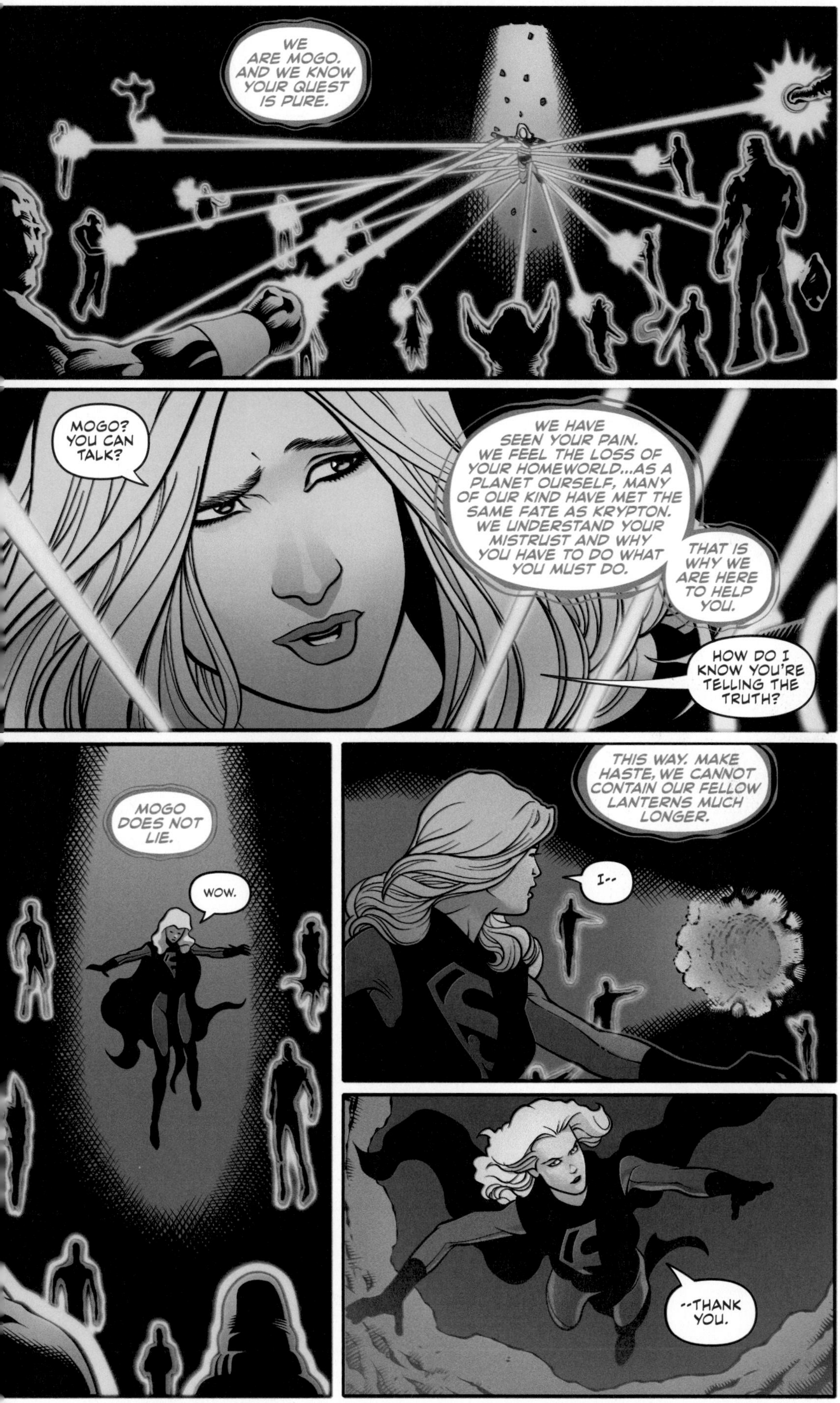
WE ARE MOGO. AND WE KNOW YOUR QUEST IS PURE.
MOGO? YOU CAN TALK?
WE HAVE SEEN YOUR PAIN. WE FEEL THE LOSS OF YOUR HOMEWORLD...AS A PLANET OURSELF, MANY OF OUR KIND HAVE MET THE SAME FATE AS KRYPTON. WE UNDERSTAND YOUR MISTRUST AND WHY YOU HAVE TO DO WHAT YOU MUST DO.
THAT IS WHY WE ARE HERE TO HELP YOU.
HOW DO I KNOW YOU'RE TELLING THE TRUTH?
MOGO DOES NOT LIE.
WOW.
THIS WAY. MAKE HASTE, WE CANNOT CONTAIN OUR FELLOW LANTERNS MUCH LONGER.
I--
--THANK YOU.

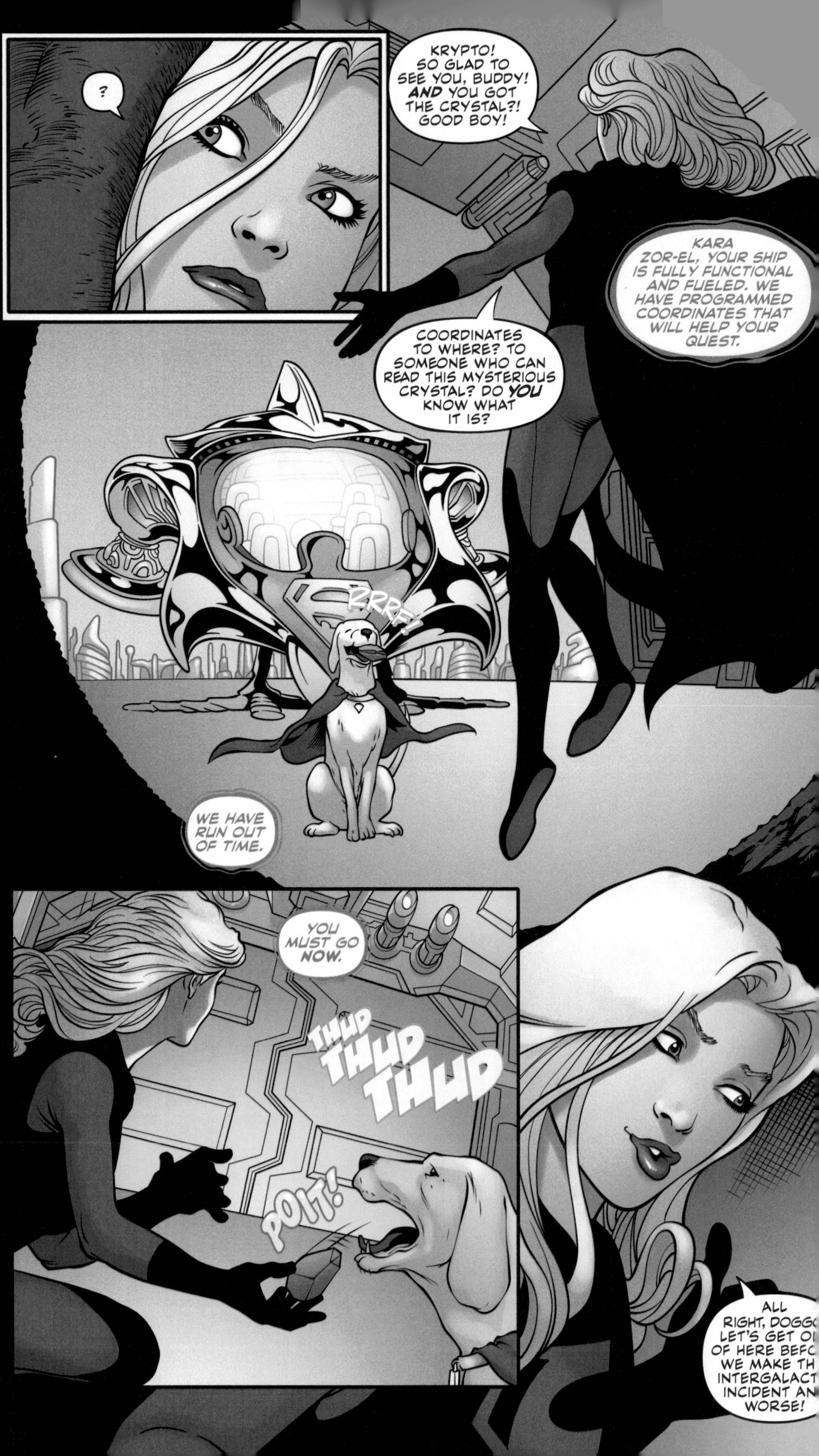
?
KRYPTO! SO GLAD TO SEE YOU, BUDDY! AND YOU GOT THE CRYSTAL?! GOOD BOY!
KARA ZOR-EL, YOUR SHIP IS FULLY FUNCTIONAL AND FUELED. WE HAVE PROGRAMMED COORDINATES THAT WILL HELP YOUR QUEST.
COORDINATES TO WHERE? TO SOMEONE WHO CAN READ THIS MYSTERIOUS CRYSTAL? DO YOU KNOW WHAT IT IS?
RRRF!
WE HAVE RUN OUT OF TIME.
YOU MUST GO NOW.
THUD THUD THUD
POIT!
ALL RIGHT, DOGG LET'S GET O OF HERE BEFO WE MAKE TH INTERGALACT INCIDENT AN WORSE!

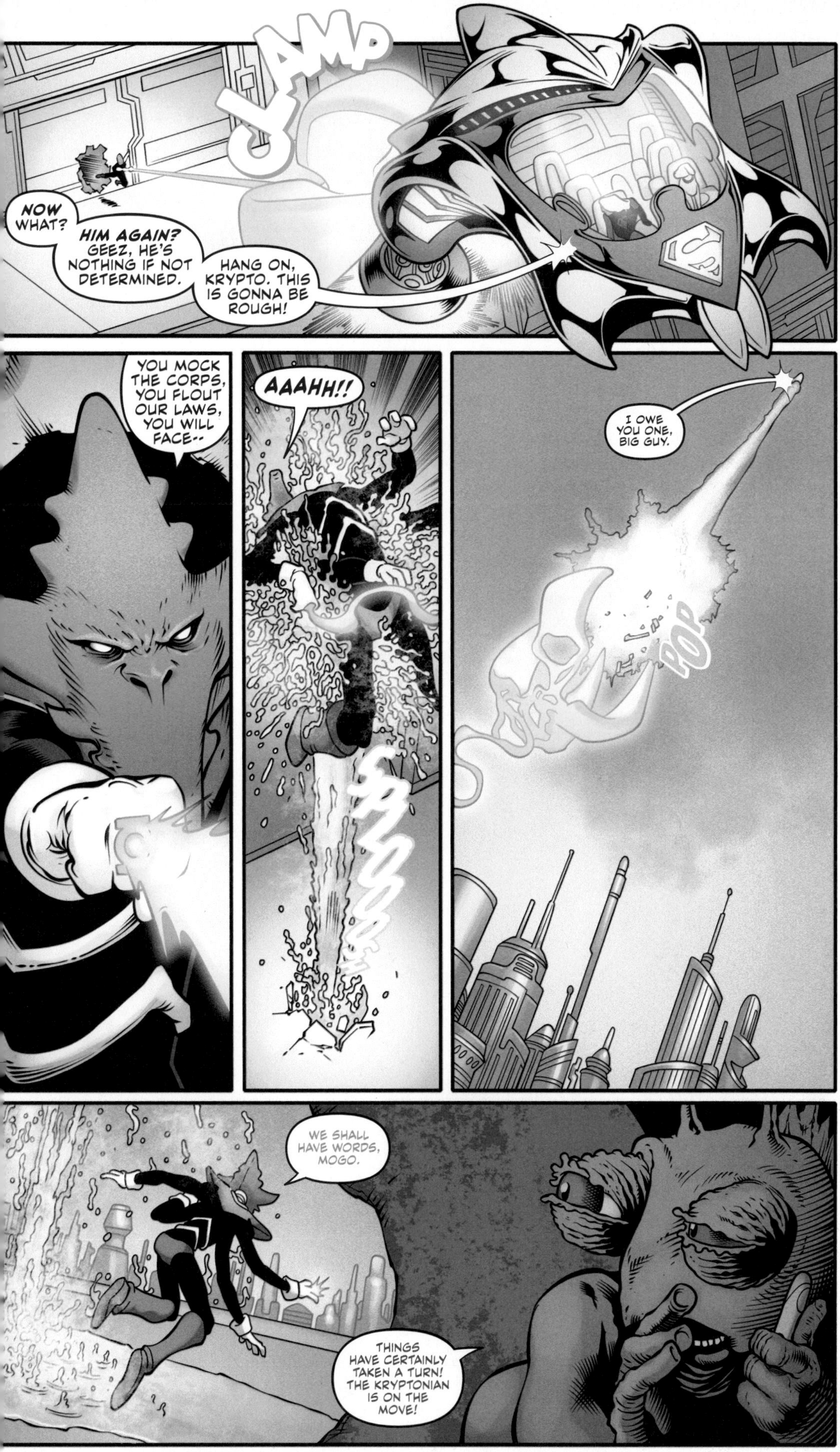
CLAMP
NOW WHAT?
HIM AGAIN? GEEZ, HE'S NOTHING IF NOT DETERMINED.
HANG ON, KRYPTO. THIS IS GONNA BE ROUGH!
YOU MOCK THE CORPS, YOU FLOUT OUR LAWS, YOU WILL FACE--
AAAHH!!
I OWE YOU ONE, BIG GUY.
POP
WE SHALL HAVE WORDS, MOGO.
THINGS HAVE CERTAINLY TAKEN A TURN! THE KRYPTONIAN IS ON THE MOVE!

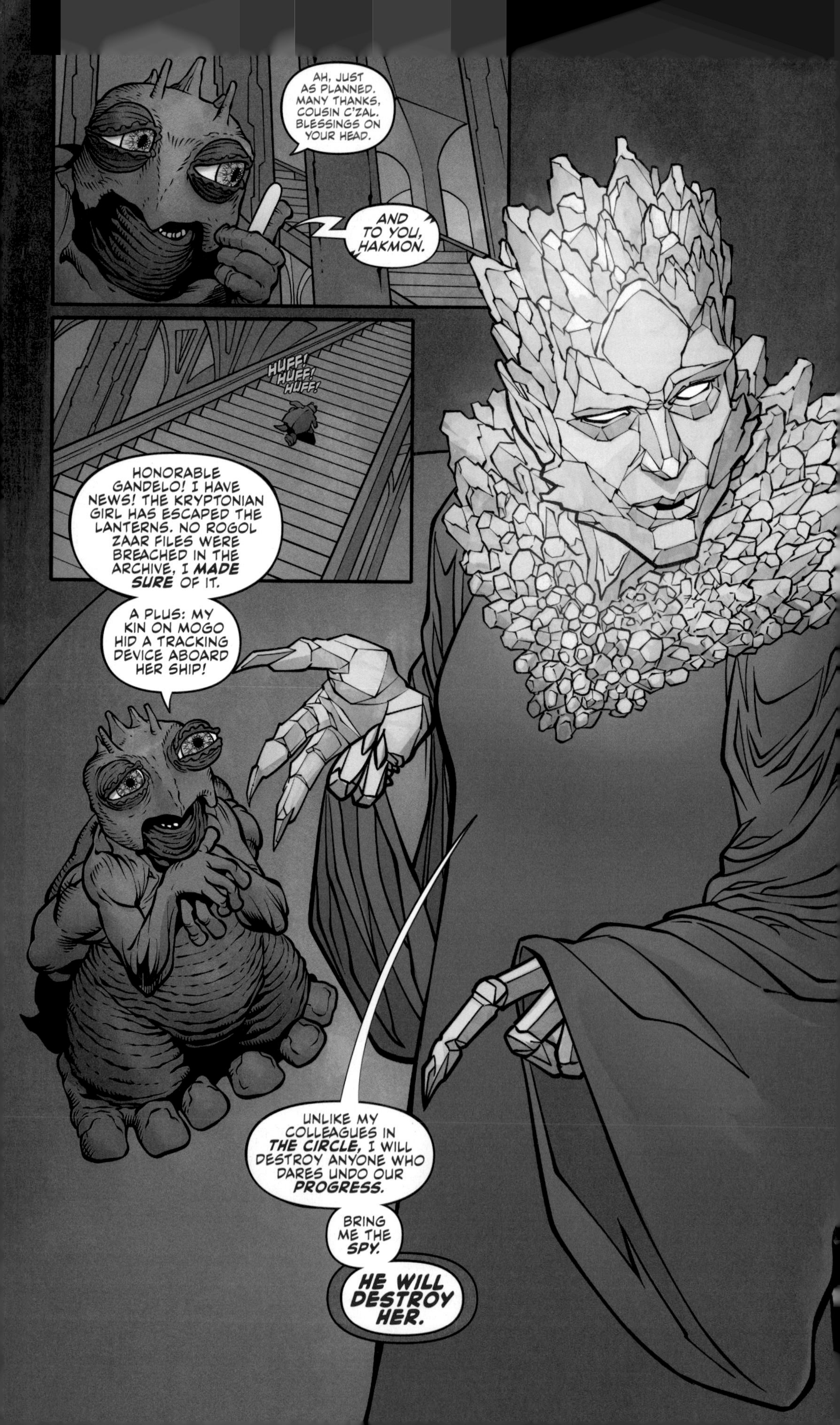
AH, JUST AS PLANNED. MANY THANKS, COUSIN C'ZAL. BLESSINGS ON YOUR HEAD.
AND TO YOU, HAKMON.
HUFF! HUFF! HUFF!
HONORABLE GANDELO! I HAVE NEWS! THE KRYPTONIAN GIRL HAS ESCAPED THE LANTERNS. NO ROGOL ZAAR FILES WERE BREACHED IN THE ARCHIVE, I MADE SURE OF IT.
A PLUS: MY KIN ON MOGO HID A TRACKING DEVICE ABOARD HER SHIP!
UNLIKE MY COLLEAGUES IN THE CIRCLE, I WILL DESTROY ANYONE WHO DARES UNDO OUR PROGRESS.
BRING ME THE SPY.
HE WILL DESTROY HER.

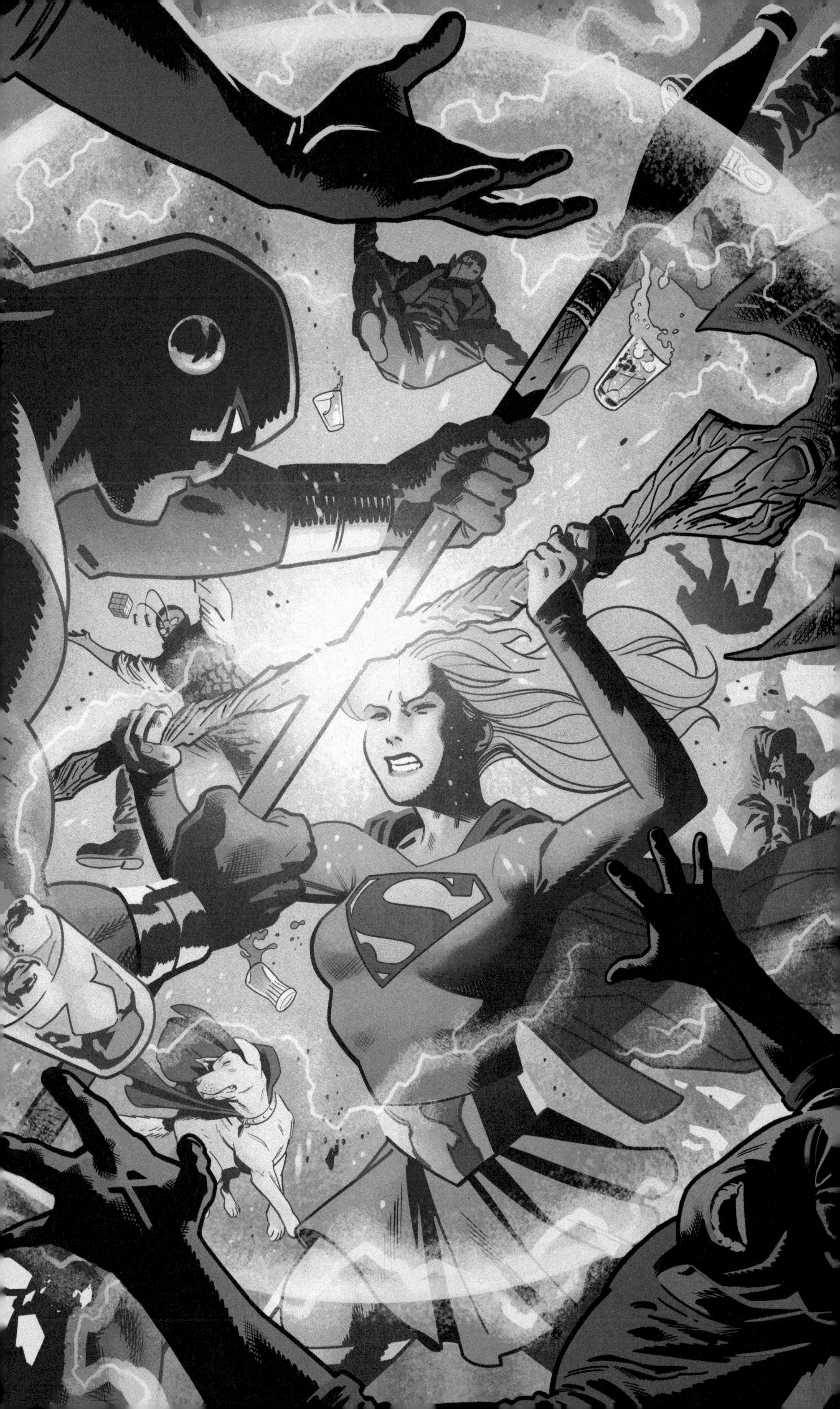

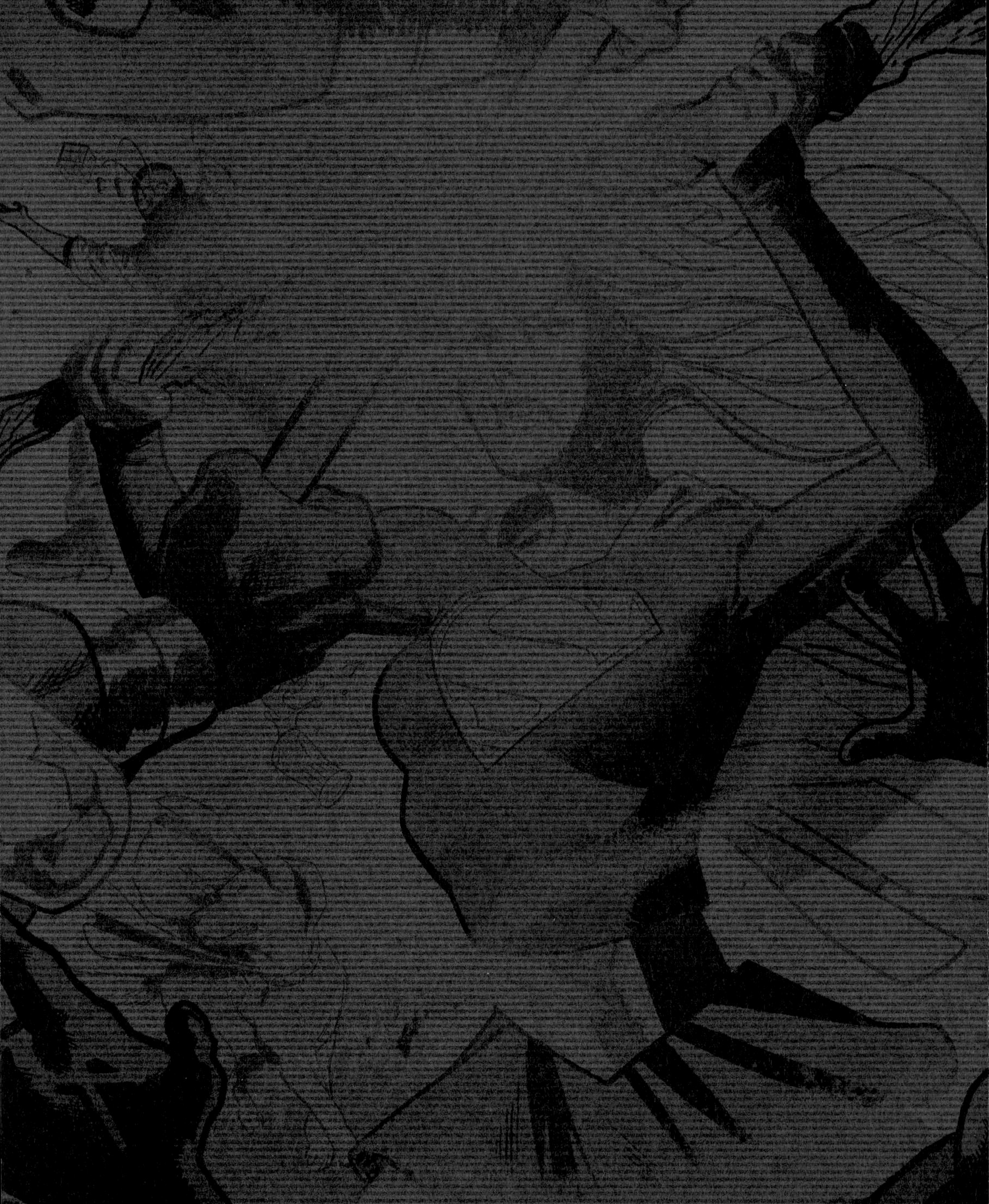

SUPERGIRL

#24

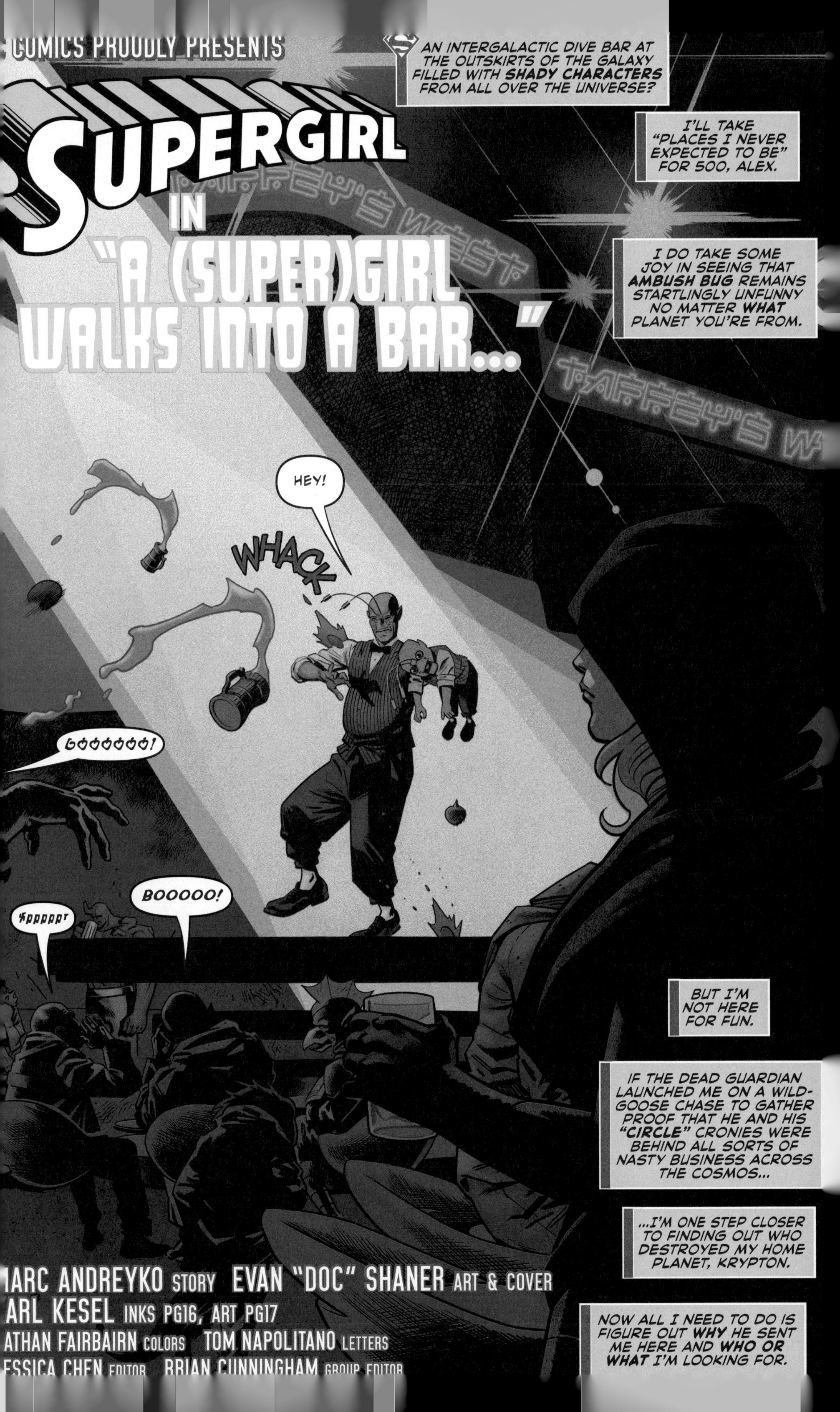
COMICS PROUDLY PRESENTS
SUPERGIRL
IN
"A (SUPER)GIRL WALKS INTO A BAR..."
AN INTERGALACTIC DIVE BAR AT THE OUTSKIRTS OF THE GALAXY FILLED WITH SHADY CHARACTERS FROM ALL OVER THE UNIVERSE?
I'LL TAKE "PLACES I NEVER EXPECTED TO BE" FOR 500, ALEX.
I DO TAKE SOME JOY IN SEEING THAT AMBUSH BUG REMAINS STARTLINGLY UNFUNNY NO MATTER WHAT PLANET YOU'RE FROM.
HEY!
WHACK
BOOOOO!
BUT I'M NOT HERE FOR FUN.
IF THE DEAD GUARDIAN LAUNCHED ME ON A WILD-GOOSE CHASE TO GATHER PROOF THAT HE AND HIS "CIRCLE" CRONIES WERE BEHIND ALL SORTS OF NASTY BUSINESS ACROSS THE COSMOS...
...I'M ONE STEP CLOSER TO FINDING OUT WHO DESTROYED MY HOME PLANET, KRYPTON.
NOW ALL I NEED TO DO IS FIGURE OUT WHY HE SENT ME HERE AND WHO OR WHAT I'M LOOKING FOR.
IARC ANDREYKO STORY EVAN "DOC" SHANER ART & COVER
ARL KESEL INKS PG16, ART PG17
ATHAN FAIRBAIRN COLORS TOM NAPOLITANO LETTERS
ESSICA CHEN EDITOR BRIAN CUNNINGHAM GROUP EDITOR

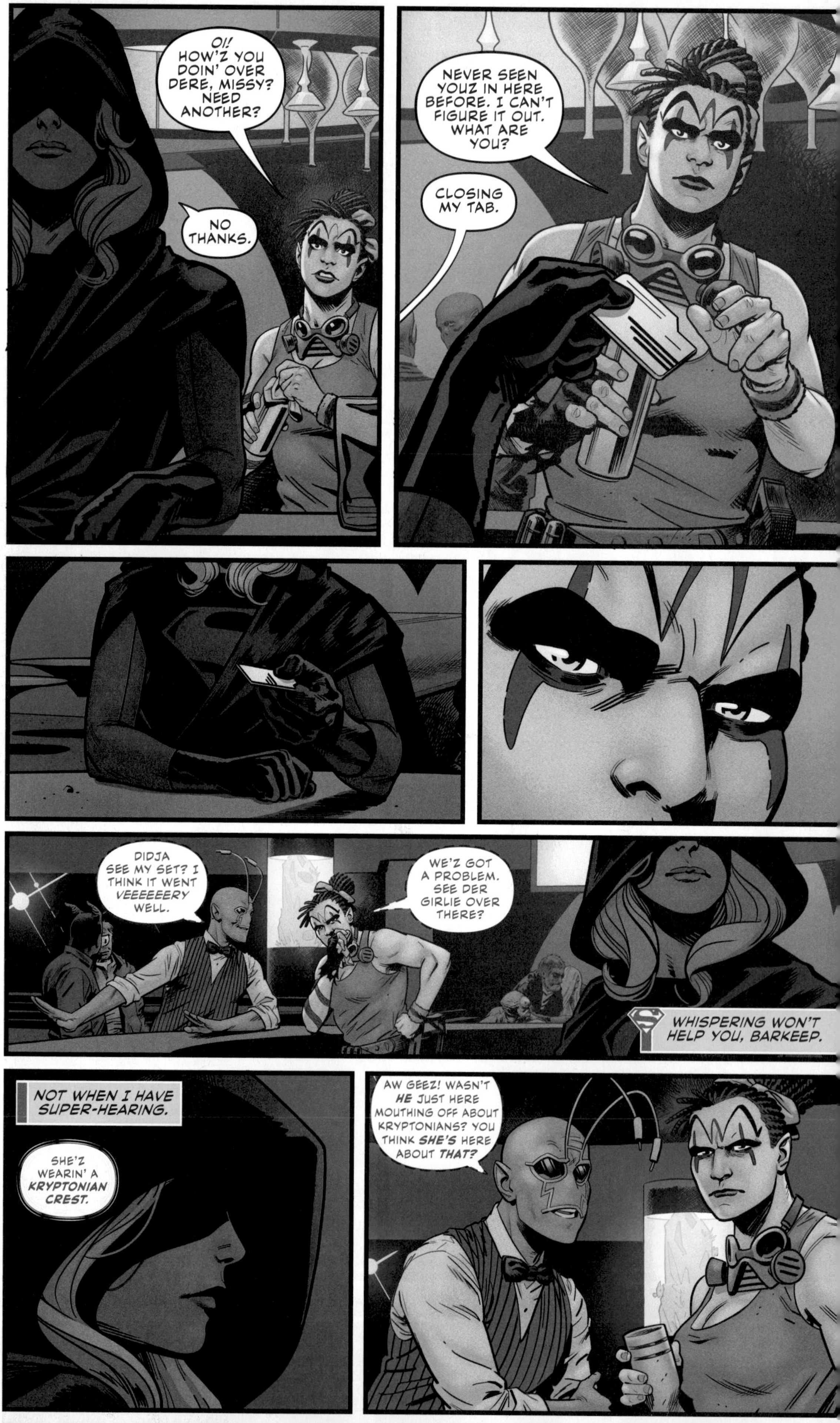

OI! HOW'Z YOU DOIN' OVER DERE, MISSY? NEED ANOTHER?
NO THANKS.
NEVER SEEN YOUZ IN HERE BEFORE. I CAN'T FIGURE IT OUT. WHAT ARE YOU?
CLOSING MY TAB.
DIDJA SEE MY SET? I THINK IT WENT VEEEEEERY WELL.
WE'Z GOT A PROBLEM. SEE DER GIRLIE OVER THERE?
WHISPERING WON'T HELP YOU, BARKEEP.
NOT WHEN I HAVE SUPER-HEARING.
SHE'Z WEARIN' A KRYPTONIAN CREST.
AW GEEZ! WASN'T HE JUST HERE MOUTHING OFF ABOUT KRYPTONIANS? YOU THINK SHE'S HERE ABOUT THAT?

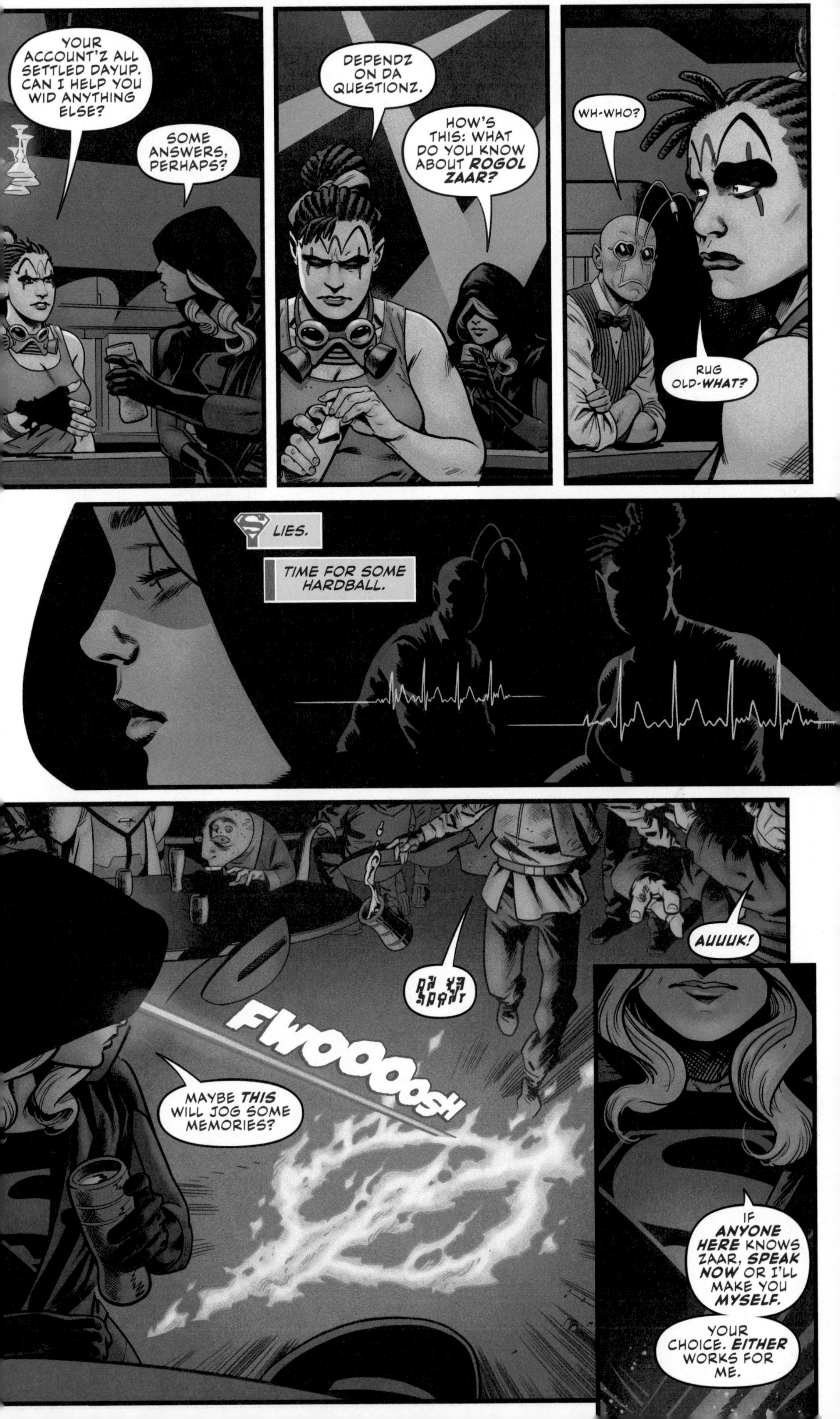
YOUR ACCOUNT'Z ALL SETTLED DAYUP. CAN I HELP YOU WID ANYTHING ELSE?
SOME ANSWERS, PERHAPS?
DEPENDZ ON DA QUESTIONZ.
HOW'S THIS: WHAT DO YOU KNOW ABOUT ROGOL ZAAR?
WH-WHO?
RUG OLD-WHAT?
LIES.
TIME FOR SOME HARDBALL.
AUUUK!
FWOOOOSH
MAYBE THIS WILL JOG SOME MEMORIES?
IF ANYONE HERE KNOWS ZAAR, SPEAK NOW OR I'LL MAKE YOU MYSELF.
YOUR CHOICE. EITHER WORKS FOR ME.

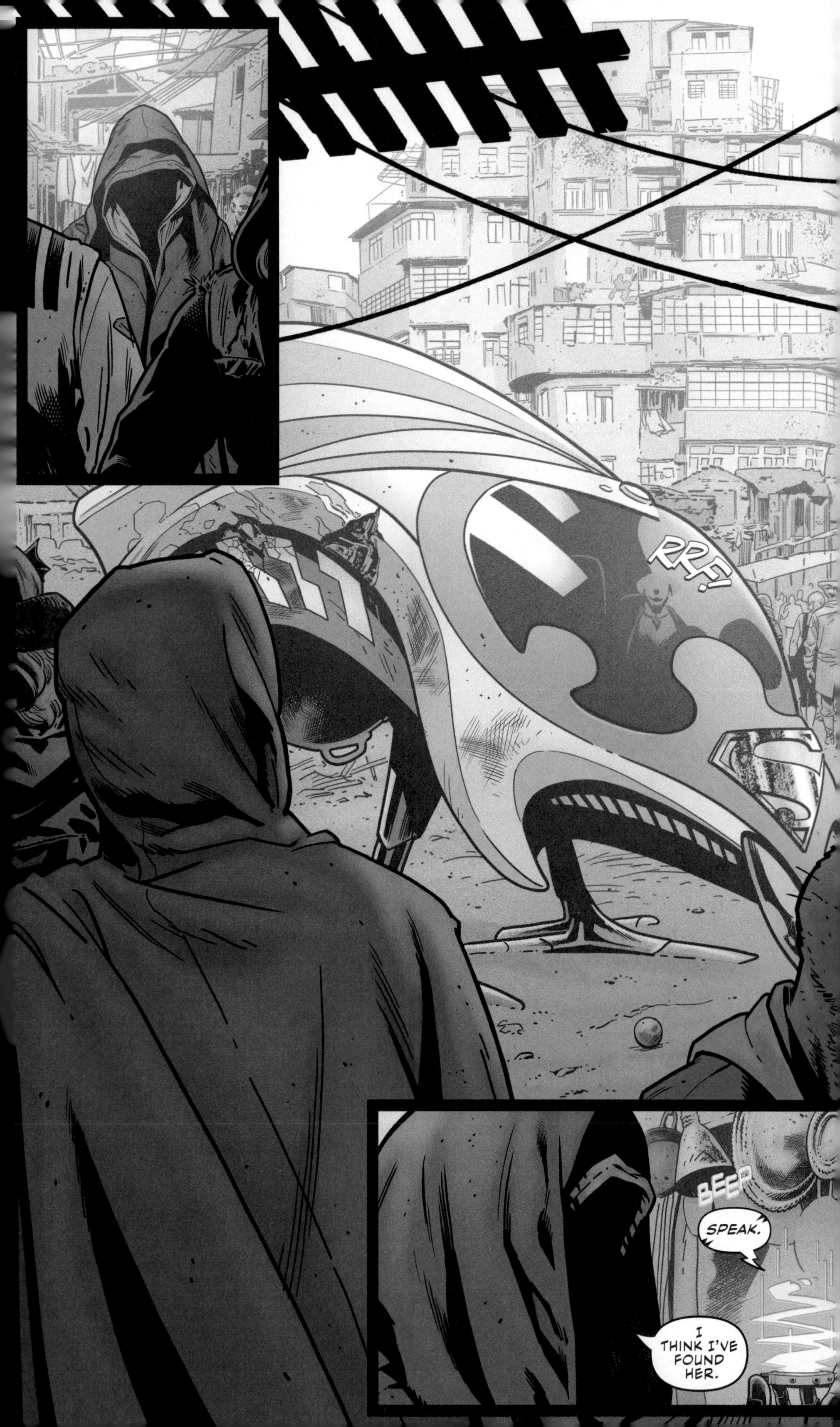
RRF!
BEEP
SPEAK.
I THINK I'VE FOUND HER.

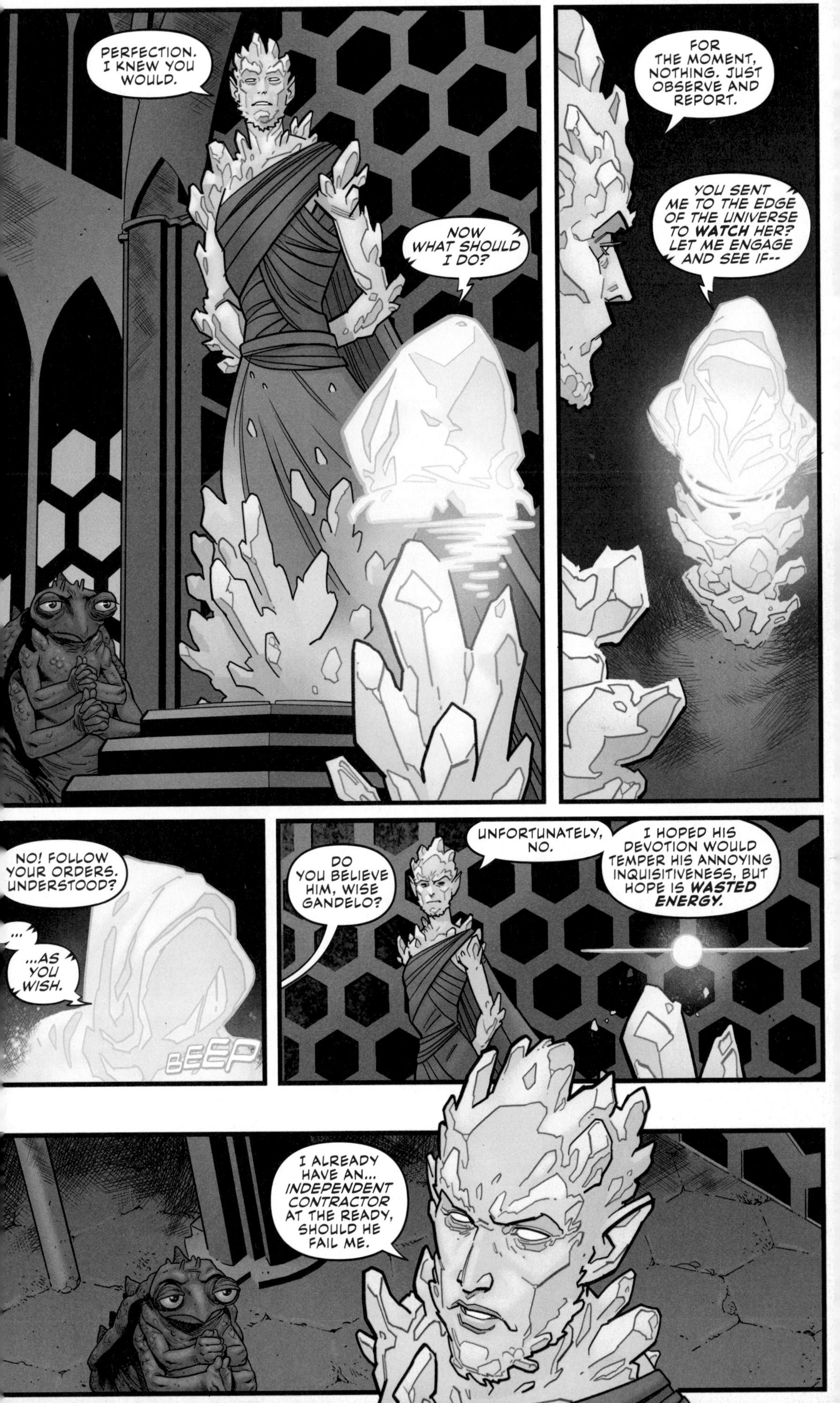
PERFECTION. I KNEW YOU WOULD.
NOW WHAT SHOULD I DO?
FOR THE MOMENT, NOTHING. JUST OBSERVE AND REPORT.
YOU SENT ME TO THE EDGE OF THE UNIVERSE TO WATCH HER? LET ME ENGAGE AND SEE IF--
NO! FOLLOW YOUR ORDERS. UNDERSTOOD?
...
...AS YOU WISH.
BEEP
DO YOU BELIEVE HIM, WISE GANDELO?
UNFORTUNATELY, NO.
I HOPED HIS DEVOTION WOULD TEMPER HIS ANNOYING INQUISITIVENESS, BUT HOPE IS WASTED ENERGY.
I ALREADY HAVE AN... INDEPENDENT CONTRACTOR AT THE READY, SHOULD HE FAIL ME.

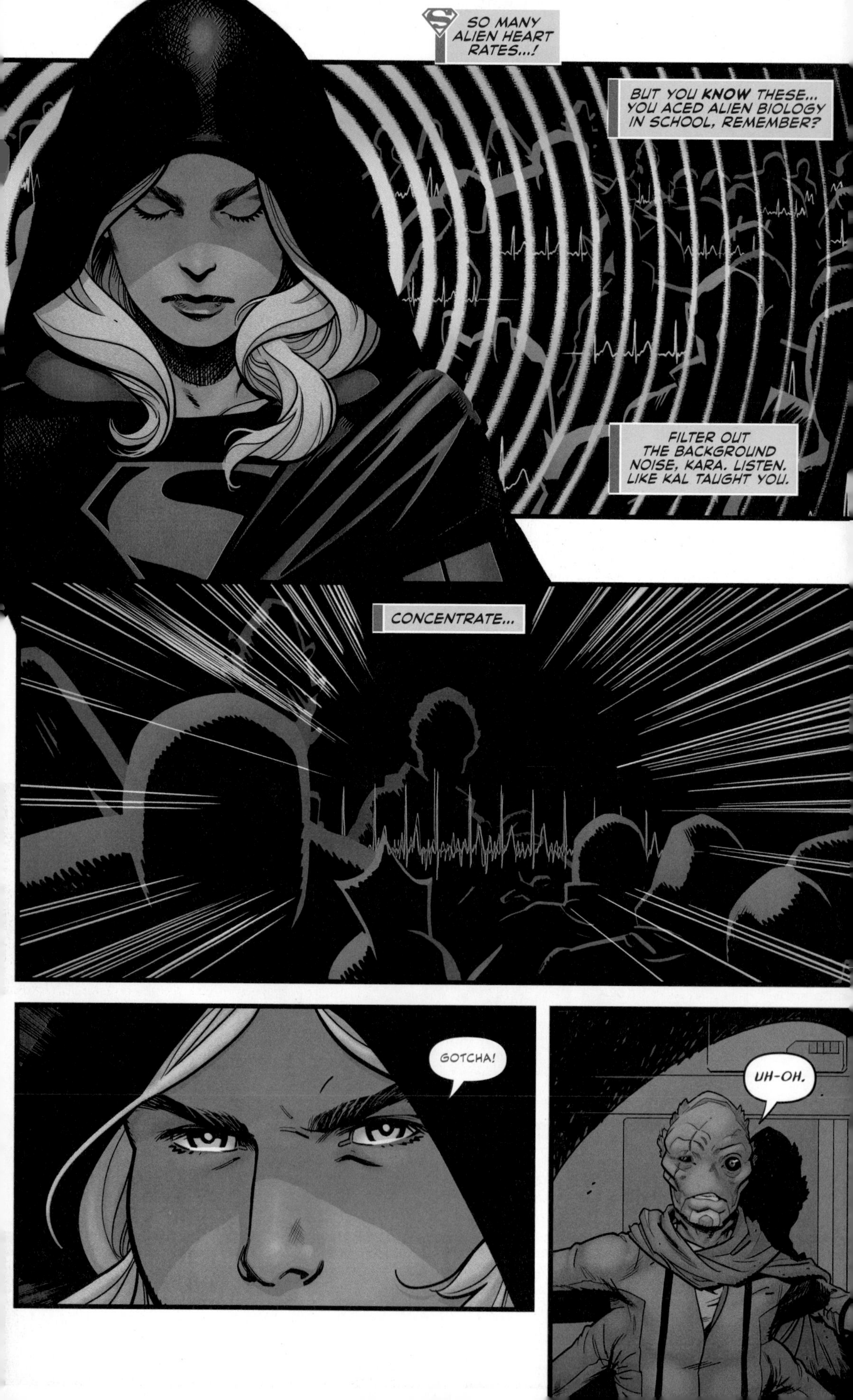
SO MANY ALIEN HEART RATES...!
BUT YOU KNOW THESE... YOU ACED ALIEN BIOLOGY IN SCHOOL, REMEMBER?
FILTER OUT THE BACKGROUND NOISE, KARA. LISTEN. LIKE KAL TAUGHT YOU.
CONCENTRATE...
GOTCHA!
UH-OH.

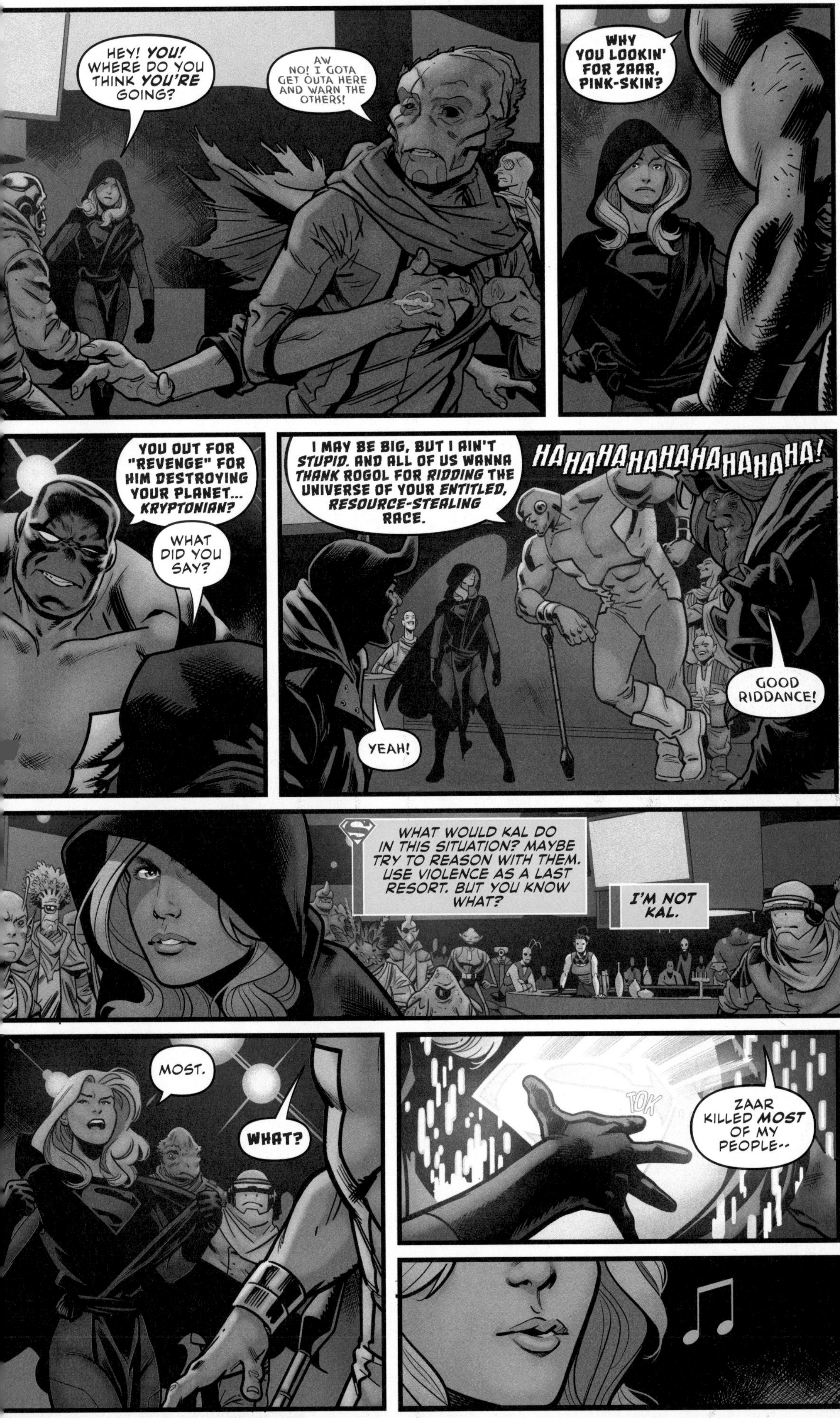
HEY! YOU! WHERE DO YOU THINK YOU'RE GOING?
AW NO! I GOTA GET OUTA HERE AND WARN THE OTHERS!
WHY YOU LOOKIN' FOR ZAAR, PINK-SKIN?
YOU OUT FOR "REVENGE" FOR HIM DESTROYING YOUR PLANET... KRYPTONIAN?
WHAT DID YOU SAY?
I MAY BE BIG, BUT I AIN'T STUPID. AND ALL OF US WANNA THANK ROGOL FOR RIDDING THE UNIVERSE OF YOUR ENTITLED, RESOURCE-STEALING RACE.
HAHAHAHAHAHAHAHAHAHA!
YEAH!
GOOD RIDDANCE!
WHAT WOULD KAL DO IN THIS SITUATION? MAYBE TRY TO REASON WITH THEM. USE VIOLENCE AS A LAST RESORT. BUT YOU KNOW WHAT?
I'M NOT KAL.
MOST.
WHAT?
TOK
ZAAR KILLED MOST OF MY PEOPLE--

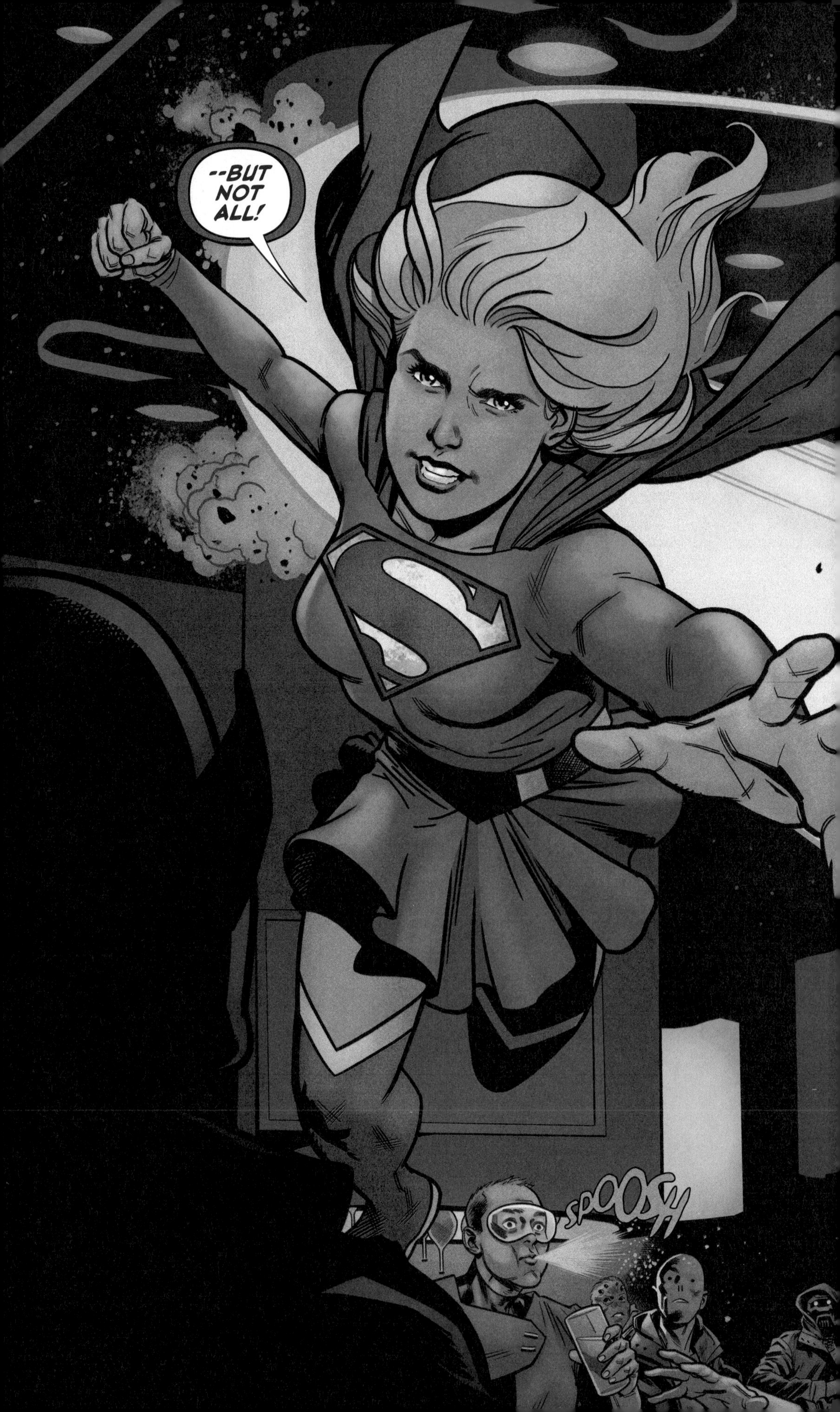
--BUT NOT ALL!
SPOOSH

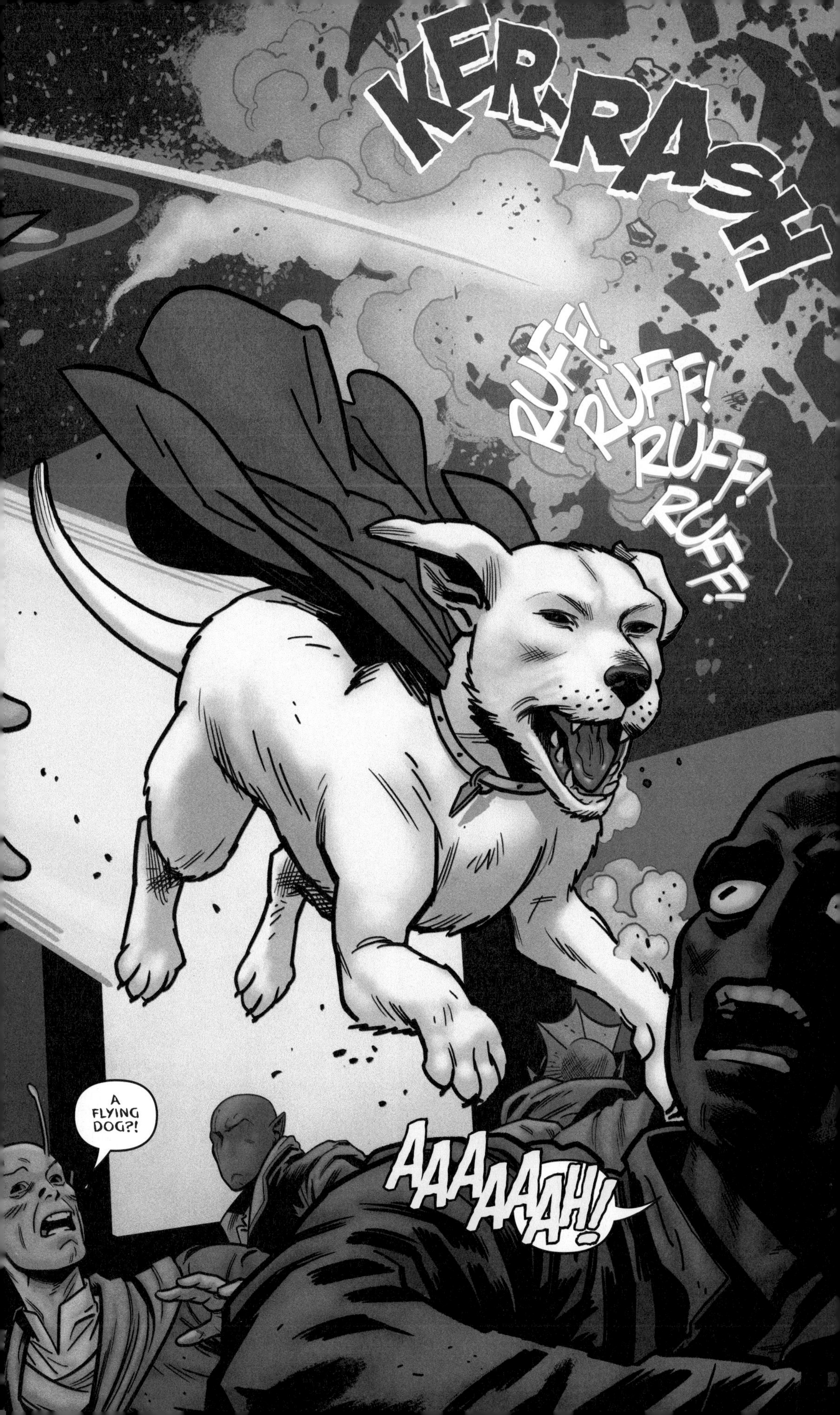
KER-RASH
RUFF! RUFF! RUFF! RUFF!
A FLYING DOG?!
AAAAAAH!!

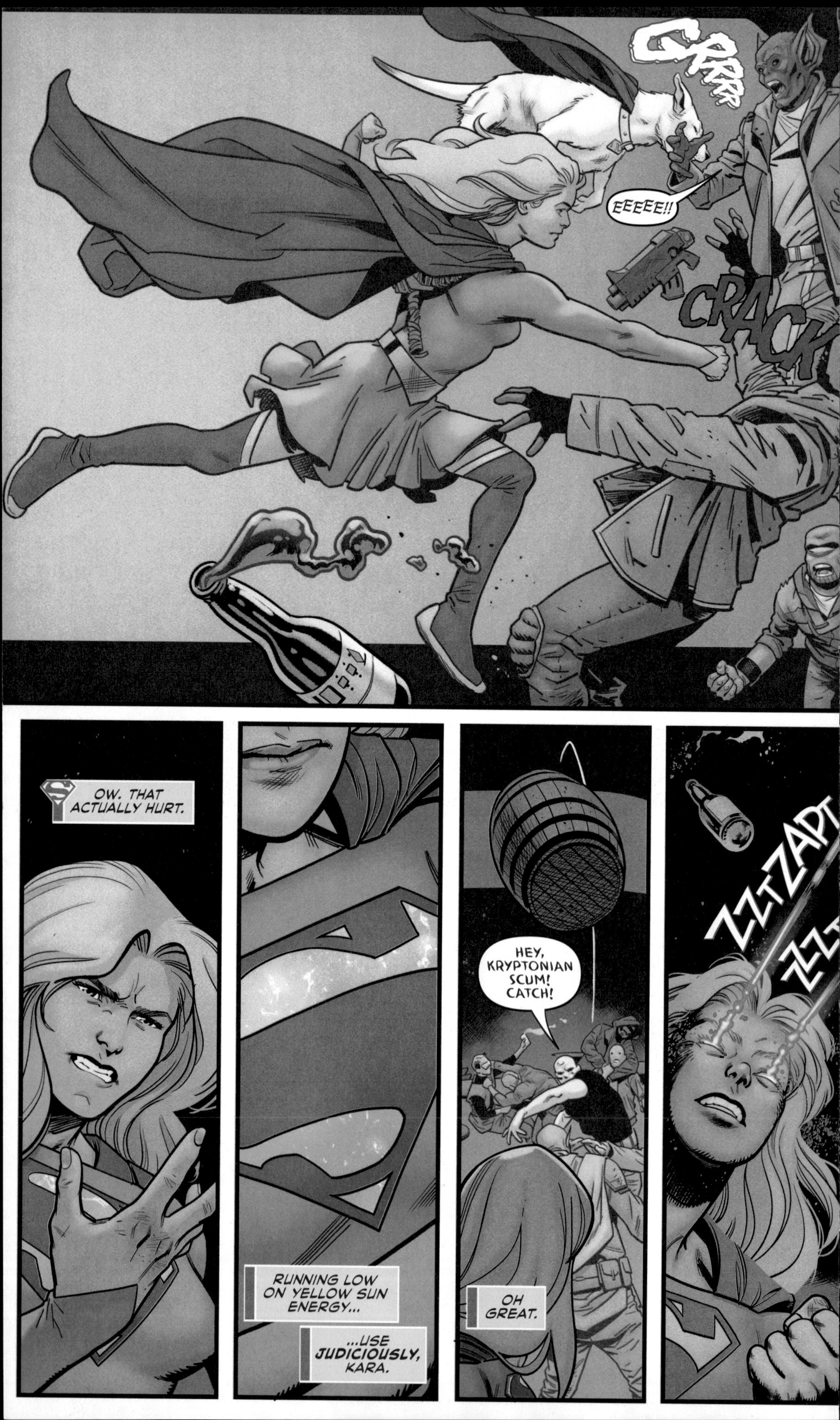
GRRRR
EEEEE!!
CRACK
OW. THAT ACTUALLY HURT.
RUNNING LOW ON YELLOW SUN ENERGY...
...USE JUDICIOUSLY, KARA.
HEY, KRYPTONIAN SCUM! CATCH!
OH GREAT.
ZZZTZAPT

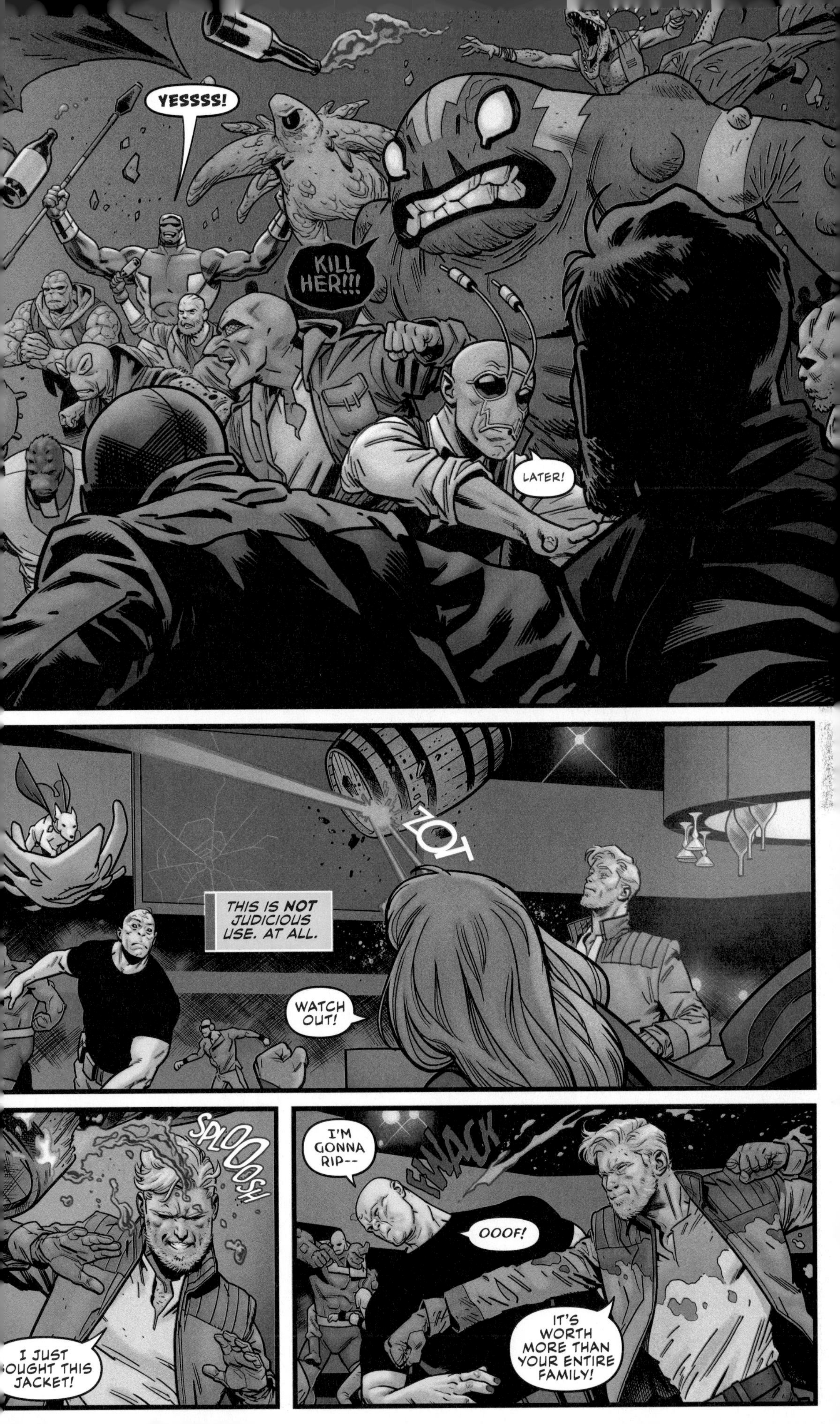
YESSSS!
KILL HER!!!
LATER!
THIS IS NOT JUDICIOUS USE. AT ALL.
ZOT
WATCH OUT!
SPLOOOSH
I JUST OUGHT THIS JACKET!
I'M GONNA RIP--
OOOF!
IT'S WORTH MORE THAN YOUR ENTIRE FAMILY!

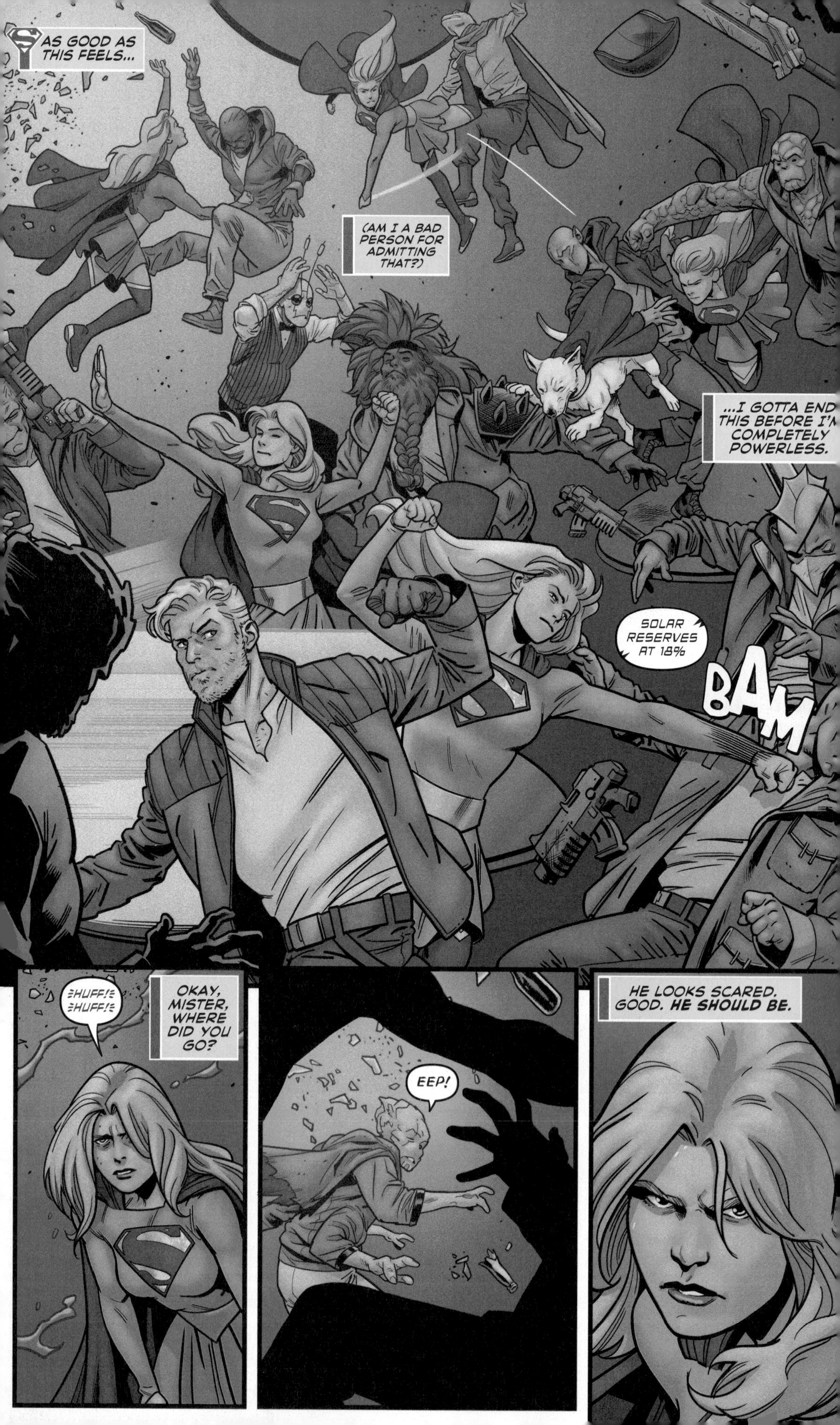
AS GOOD AS THIS FEELS...
(AM I A BAD PERSON FOR ADMITTING THAT?)
...I GOTTA END THIS BEFORE I'M COMPLETELY POWERLESS.
SOLAR RESERVES AT 18%
BAM
HUFF! HUFF!
OKAY, MISTER, WHERE DID YOU GO?
EEP!
HE LOOKS SCARED. GOOD. **HE SHOULD BE.**

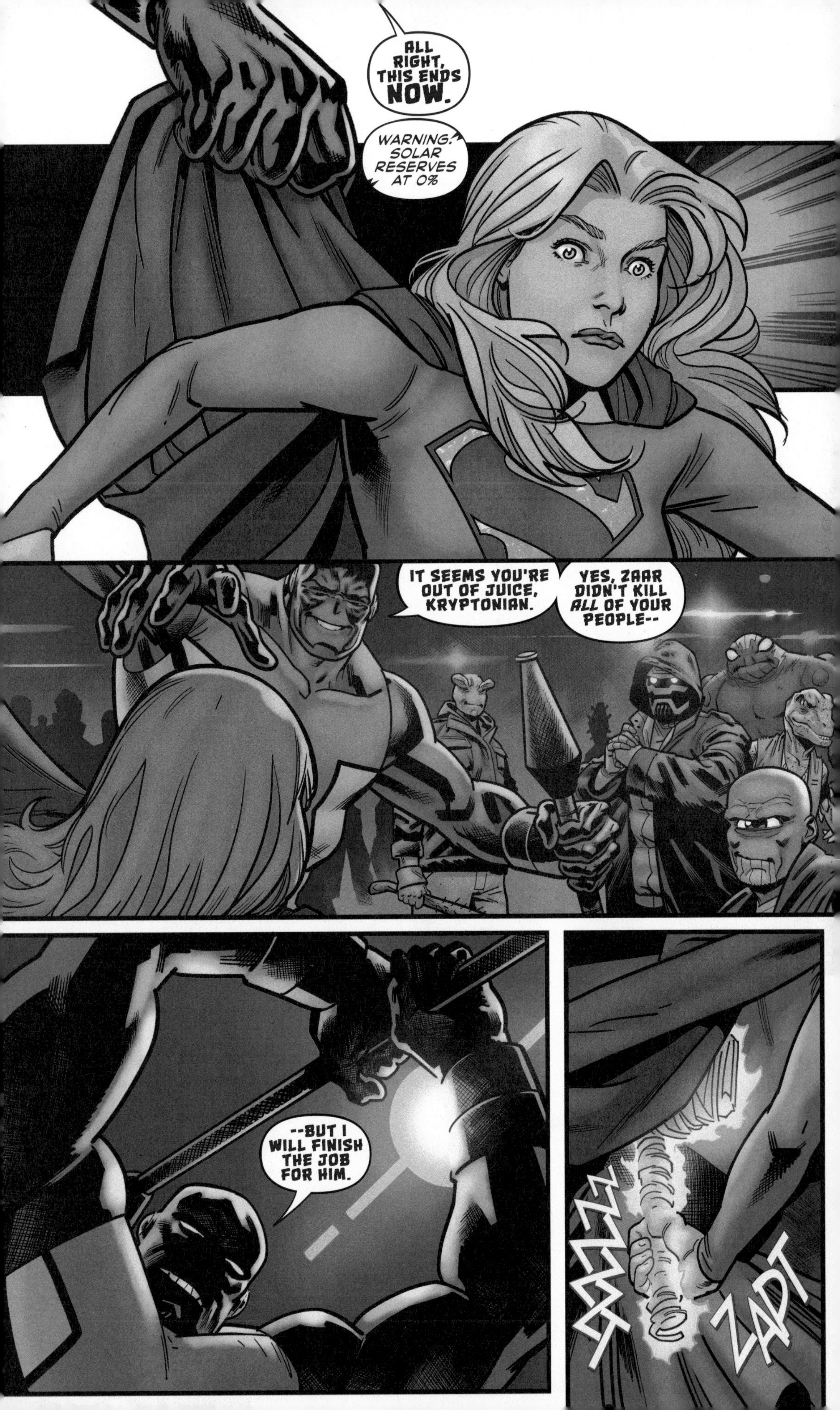
ALL RIGHT, THIS ENDS NOW.
WARNING: SOLAR RESERVES AT 0%
IT SEEMS YOU'RE OUT OF JUICE, KRYPTONIAN.
YES, ZAAR DIDN'T KILL ALL OF YOUR PEOPLE--
--BUT I WILL FINISH THE JOB FOR HIM.
ZZZZZT
ZAPT

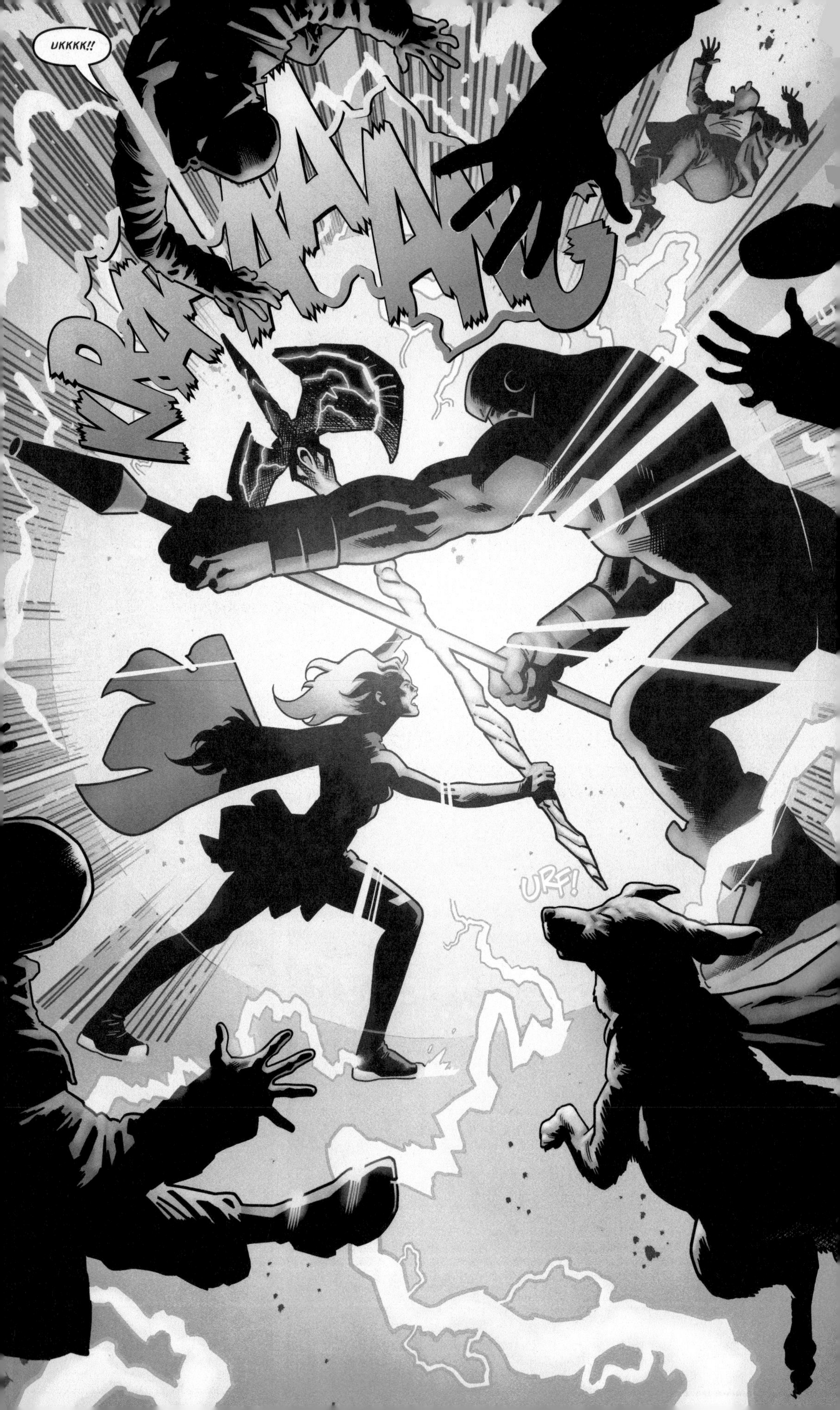
UKKKK!!
KRAAANG
URF!

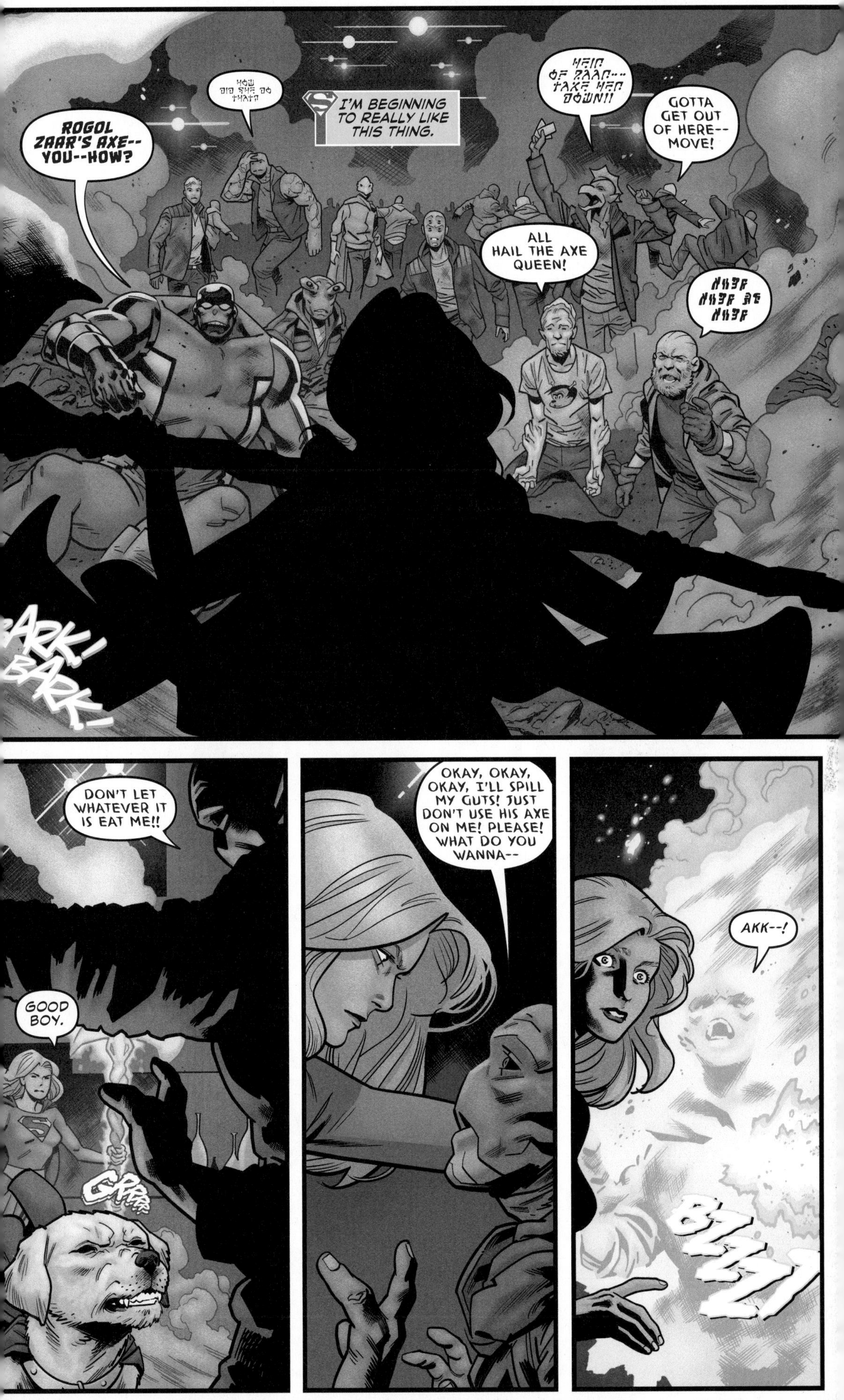
ROGOL ZAAR'S AXE--YOU--HOW?
I'M BEGINNING TO REALLY LIKE THIS THING.
GOTTA GET OUT OF HERE--MOVE!
ALL HAIL THE AXE QUEEN!
ARK! BARK!
DON'T LET WHATEVER IT IS EAT ME!!
GOOD BOY.
GRRR
OKAY, OKAY, OKAY, I'LL SPILL MY GUTS! JUST DON'T USE HIS AXE ON ME! PLEASE! WHAT DO YOU WANNA--
AKK--!
BZZZ

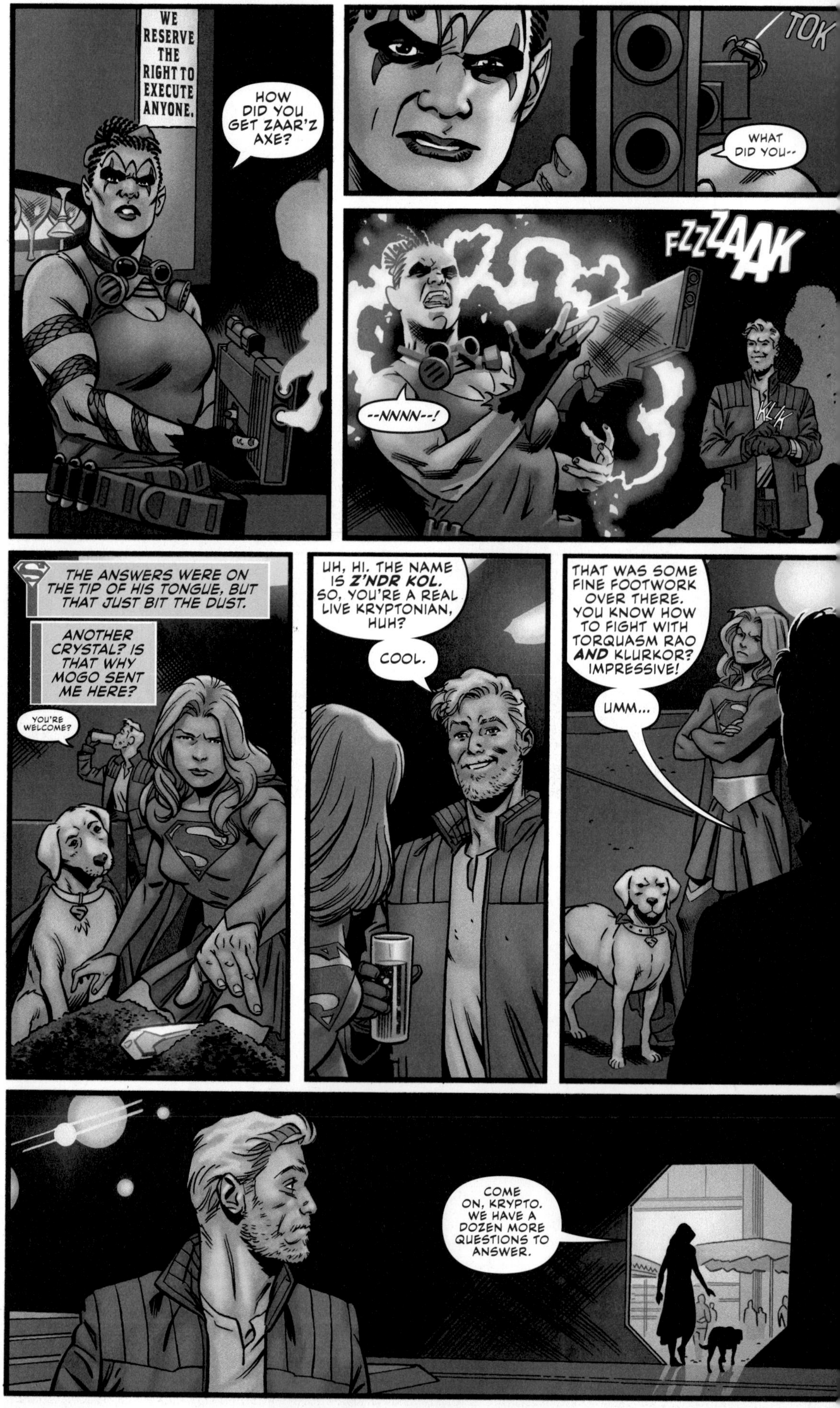
WE RESERVE THE RIGHT TO EXECUTE ANYONE.
HOW DID YOU GET ZAAR'Z AXE?
TOK
WHAT DID YOU--
FZZZAAAK
--NNNN--!
KLIK
THE ANSWERS WERE ON THE TIP OF HIS TONGUE, BUT THAT JUST BIT THE DUST.
ANOTHER CRYSTAL? IS THAT WHY MOGO SENT ME HERE?
YOU'RE WELCOME?
UH, HI. THE NAME IS Z'NDR KOL. SO, YOU'RE A REAL LIVE KRYPTONIAN, HUH?
COOL.
THAT WAS SOME FINE FOOTWORK OVER THERE. YOU KNOW HOW TO FIGHT WITH TORQUASM RAO AND KLURKOR? IMPRESSIVE!
UMM...
COME ON, KRYPTO. WE HAVE A DOZEN MORE QUESTIONS TO ANSWER.

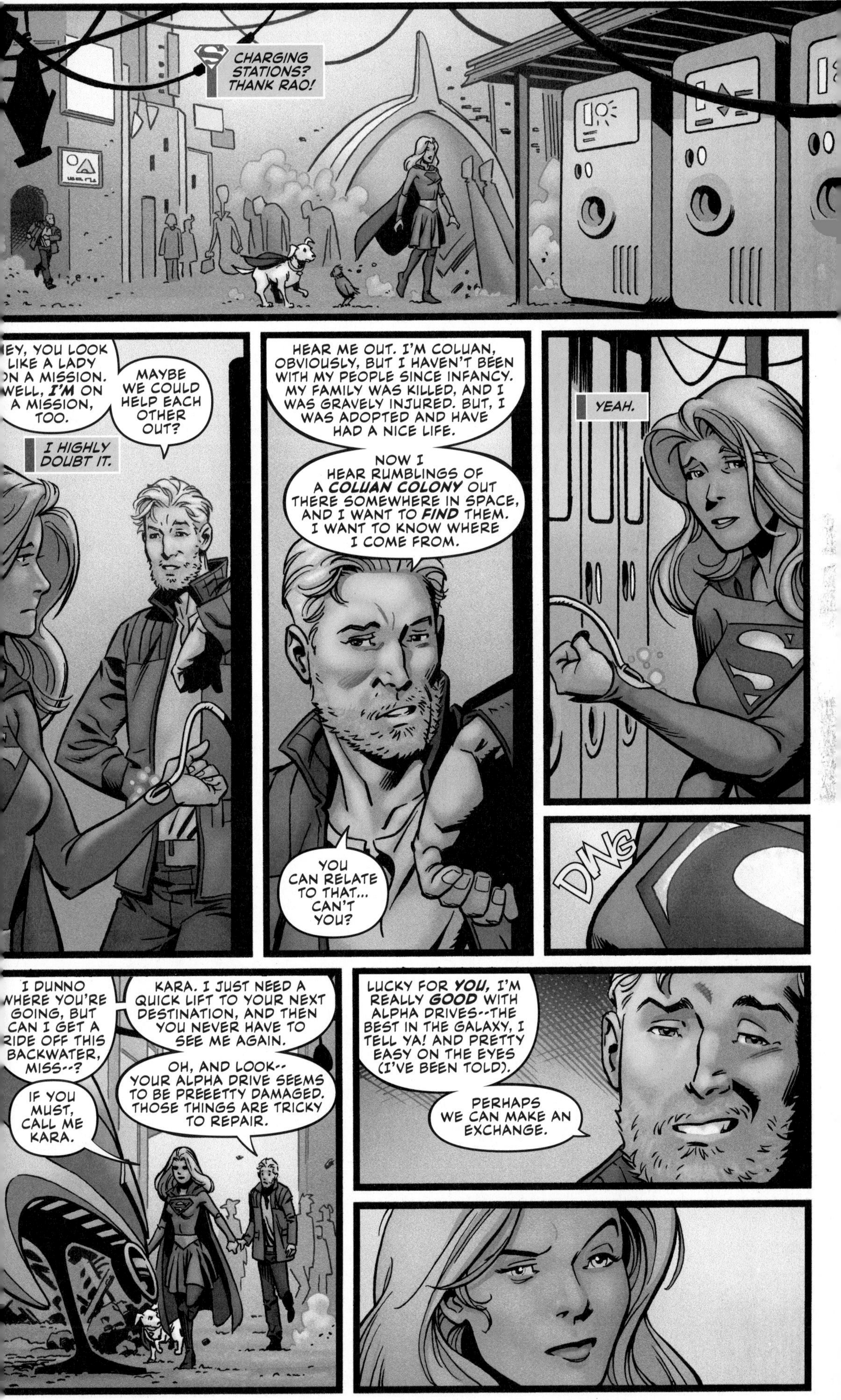
CHARGING STATIONS? THANK RAO!
EY, YOU LOOK LIKE A LADY ON A MISSION. WELL, I'M ON A MISSION, TOO.
MAYBE WE COULD HELP EACH OTHER OUT?
I HIGHLY DOUBT IT.
HEAR ME OUT. I'M COLUAN, OBVIOUSLY, BUT I HAVEN'T BEEN WITH MY PEOPLE SINCE INFANCY. MY FAMILY WAS KILLED, AND I WAS GRAVELY INJURED. BUT, I WAS ADOPTED AND HAVE HAD A NICE LIFE.
NOW I HEAR RUMBLINGS OF A COLUAN COLONY OUT THERE SOMEWHERE IN SPACE, AND I WANT TO FIND THEM. I WANT TO KNOW WHERE I COME FROM.
YOU CAN RELATE TO THAT... CAN'T YOU?
YEAH.
DNG
I DUNNO WHERE YOU'RE GOING, BUT CAN I GET A RIDE OFF THIS BACKWATER, MISS--?
IF YOU MUST, CALL ME KARA.
KARA. I JUST NEED A QUICK LIFT TO YOUR NEXT DESTINATION, AND THEN YOU NEVER HAVE TO SEE ME AGAIN.
OH, AND LOOK-- YOUR ALPHA DRIVE SEEMS TO BE PREEETTY DAMAGED. THOSE THINGS ARE TRICKY TO REPAIR.
LUCKY FOR YOU, I'M REALLY GOOD WITH ALPHA DRIVES--THE BEST IN THE GALAXY, I TELL YA! AND PRETTY EASY ON THE EYES (I'VE BEEN TOLD).
PERHAPS WE CAN MAKE AN EXCHANGE.

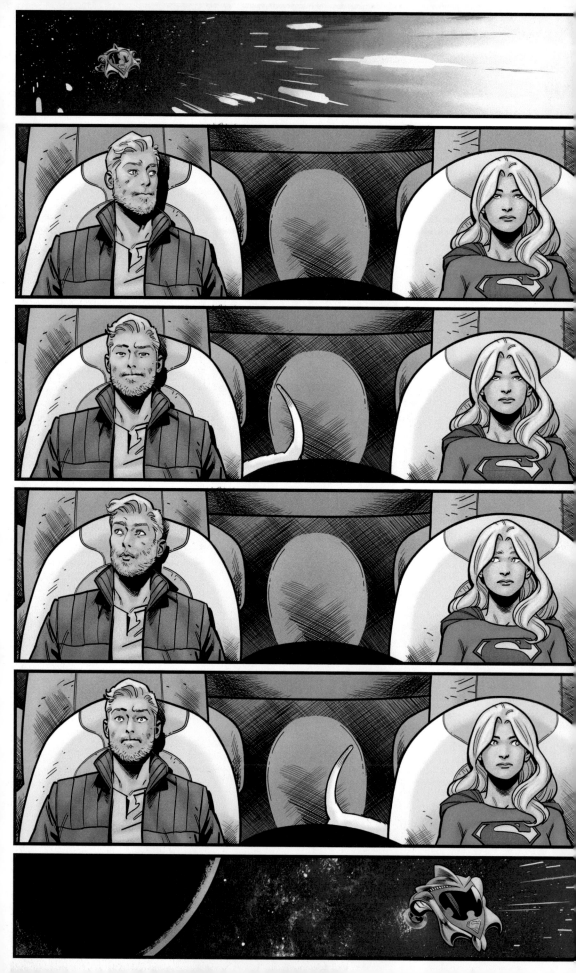

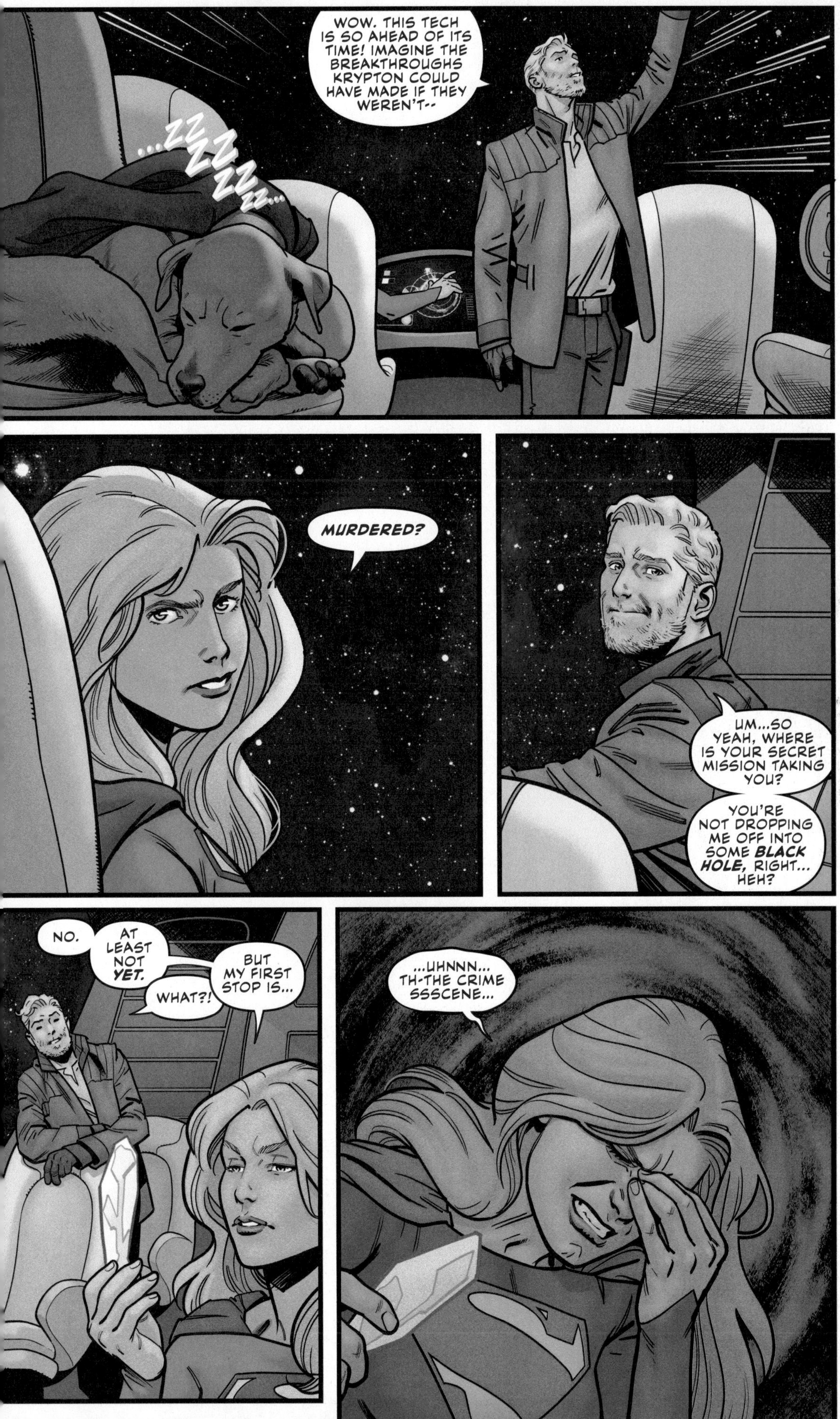
...ZZZZZZZZZ...
WOW. THIS TECH IS SO AHEAD OF ITS TIME! IMAGINE THE BREAKTHROUGHS KRYPTON COULD HAVE MADE IF THEY WEREN'T--
MURDERED?
UM...SO YEAH, WHERE IS YOUR SECRET MISSION TAKING YOU?
YOU'RE NOT DROPPING ME OFF INTO SOME BLACK HOLE, RIGHT... HEH?
NO.
AT LEAST NOT YET.
WHAT?!
BUT MY FIRST STOP IS...
...UHNNN... TH-THE CRIME SSSCENE...

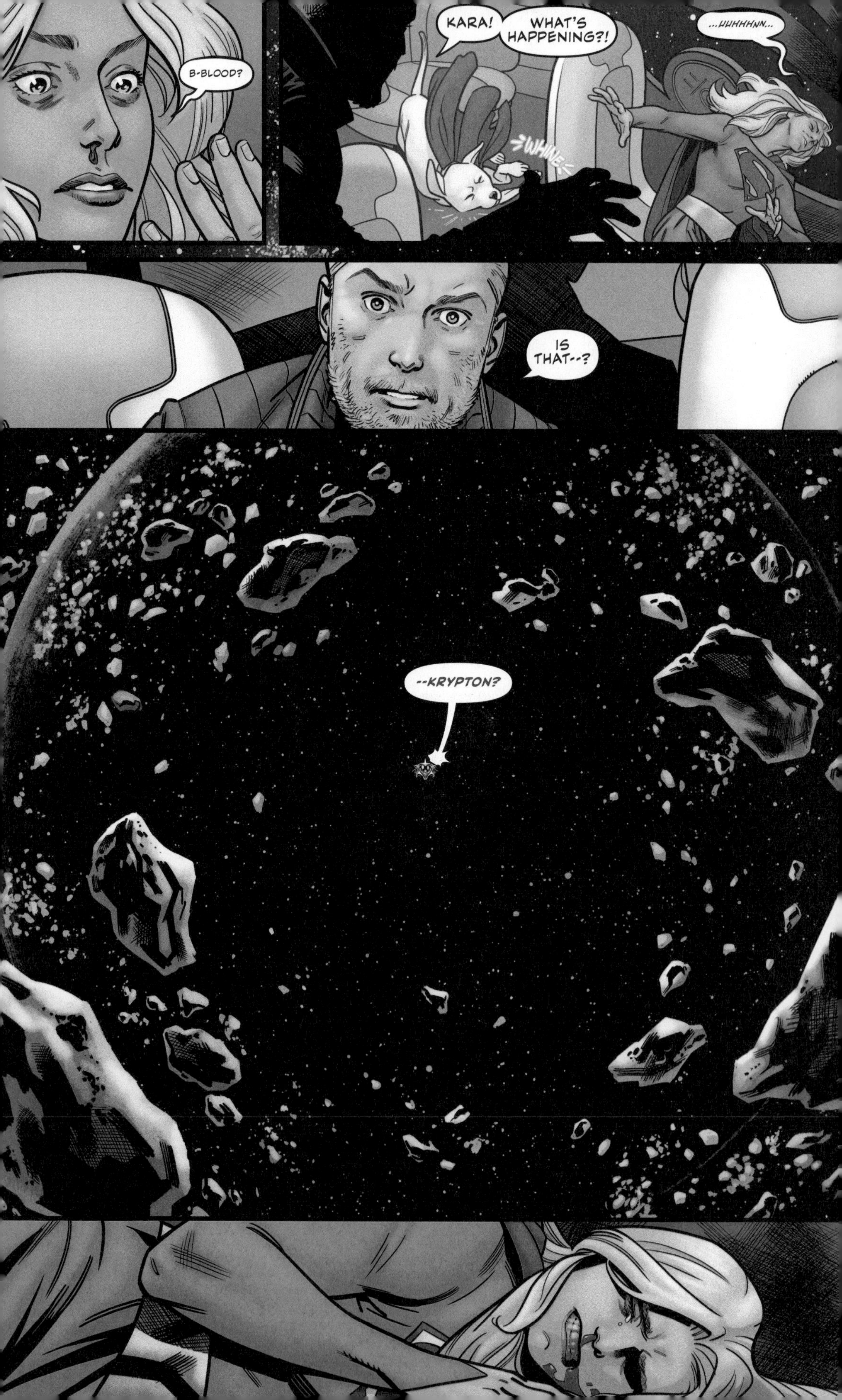
B-BLOOD?
KARA!
WHAT'S HAPPENING?!
...UHHHHNN...
WHINE
IS THAT--?
--KRYPTON?

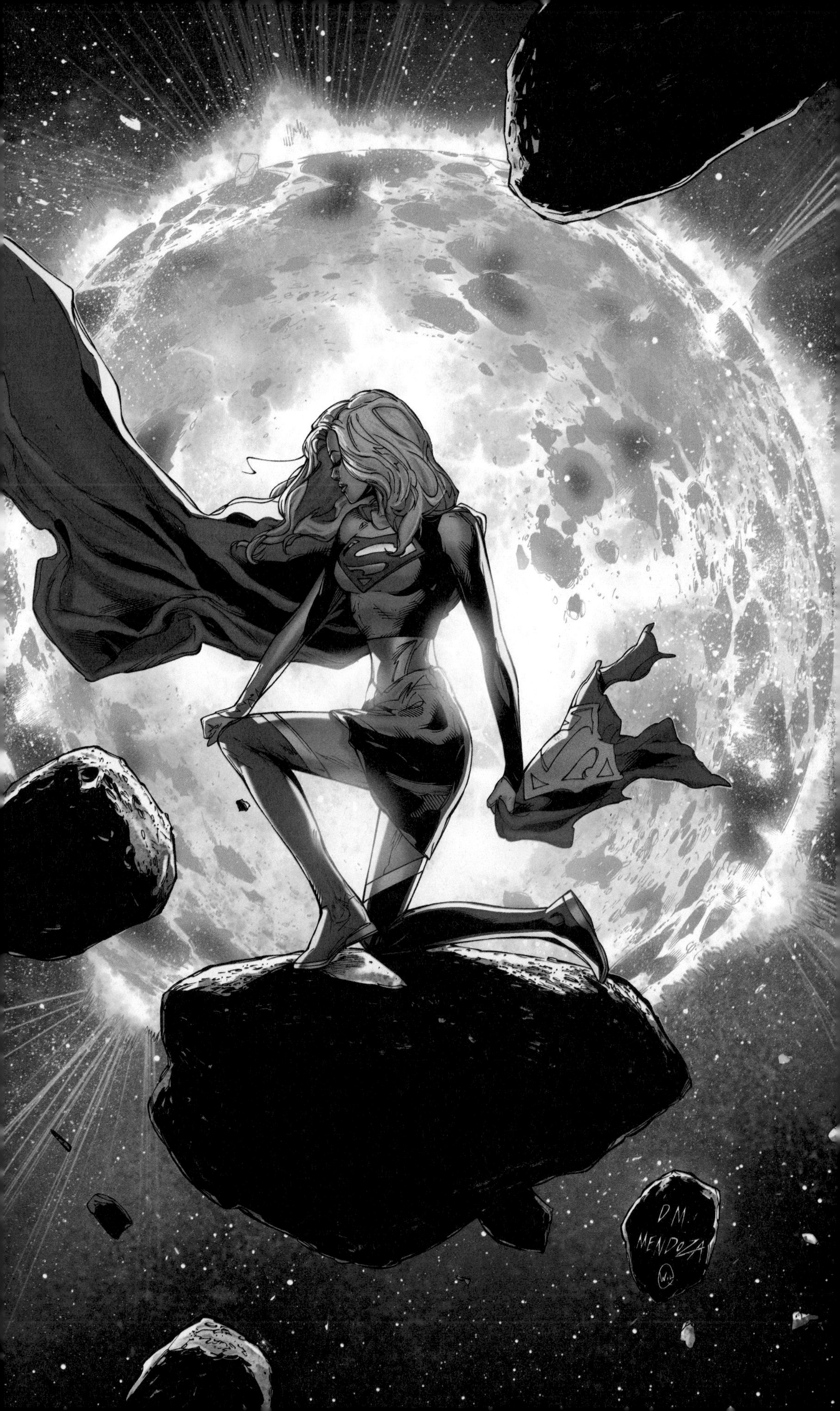
D.M.
MENDOZA

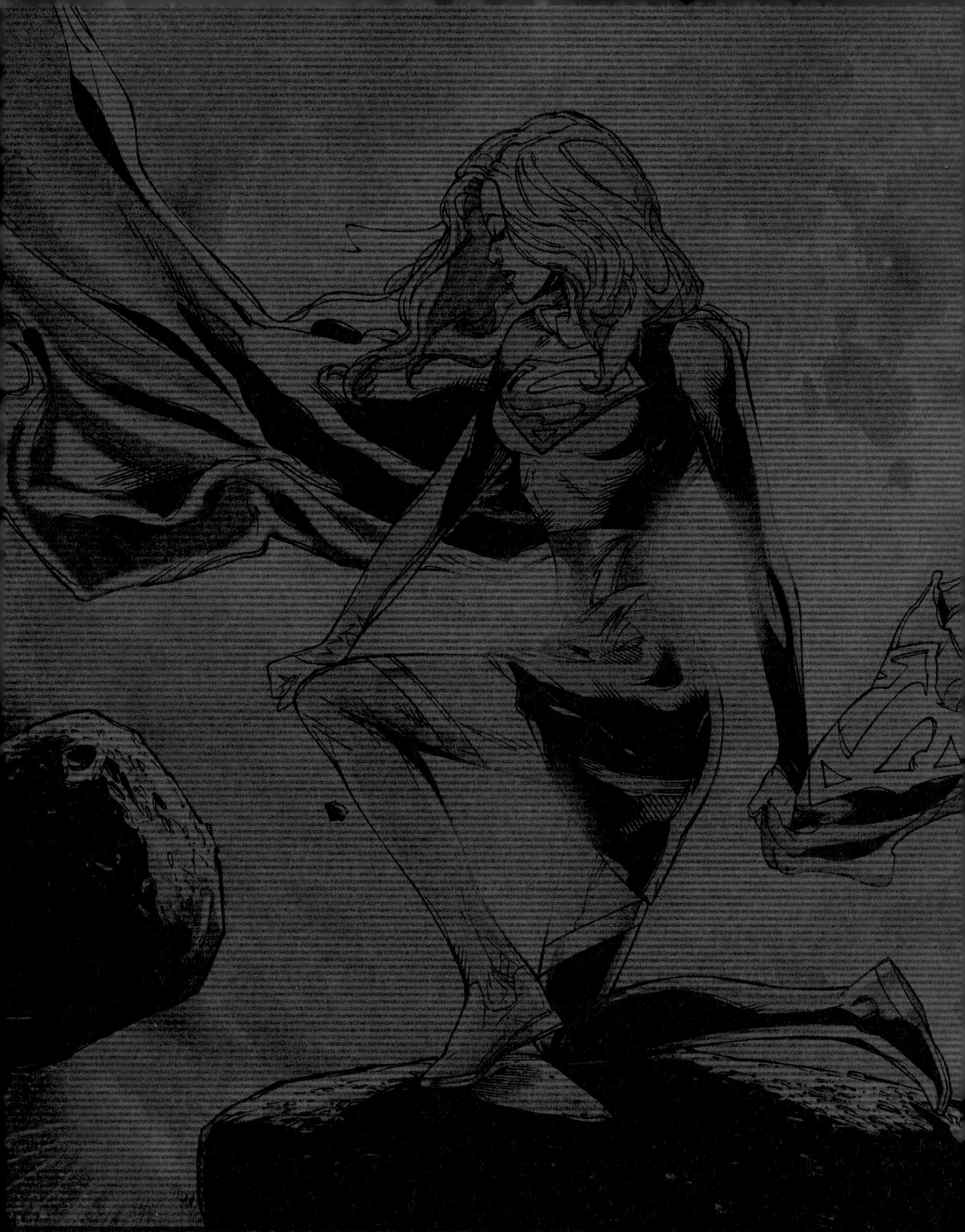

SUPERGIRL
#25

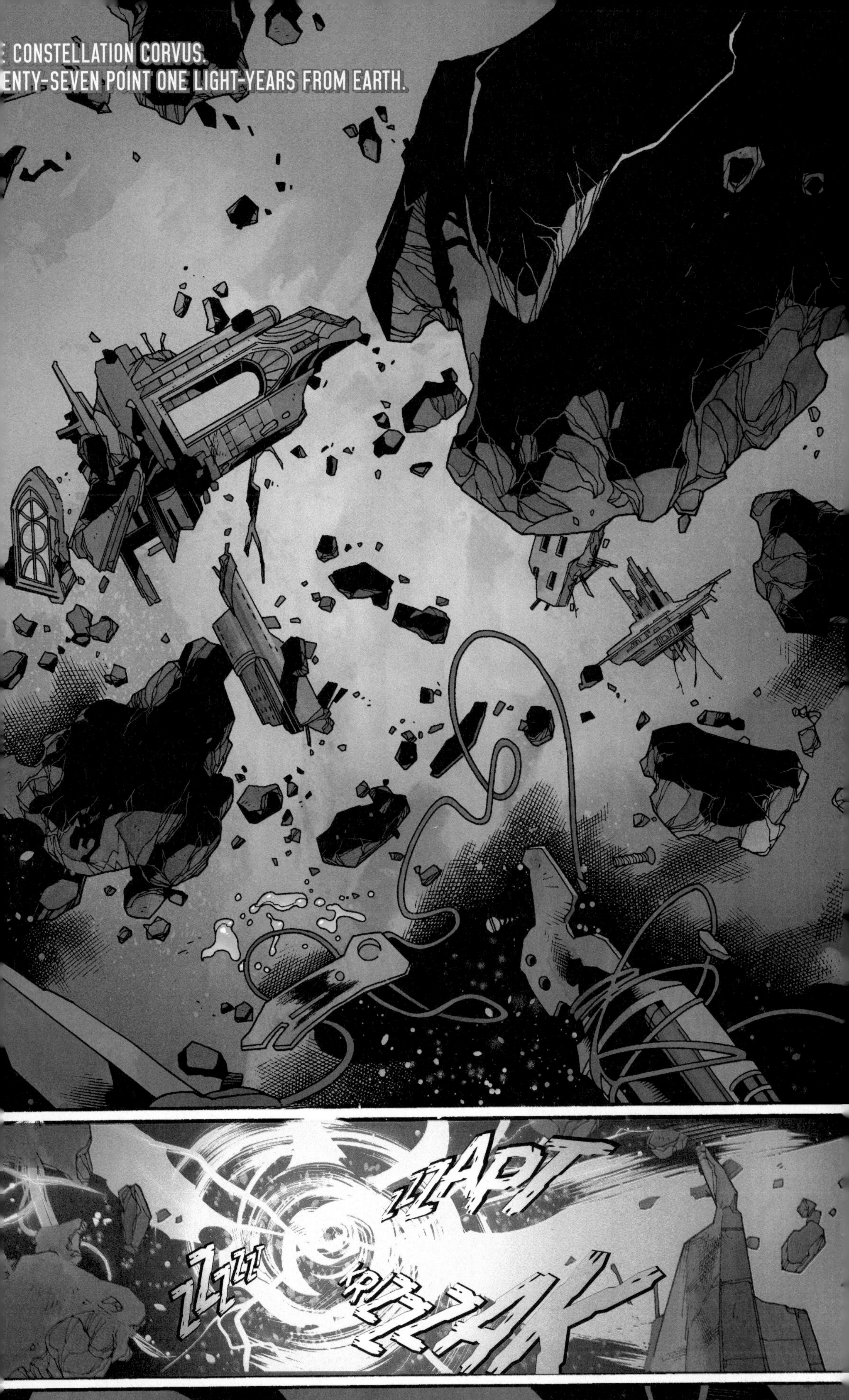
E CONSTELLATION CORVUS.
ENTY-SEVEN POINT ONE LIGHT-YEARS FROM EARTH.
ZZZAPT
ZZZZZT
KRIZZZAK

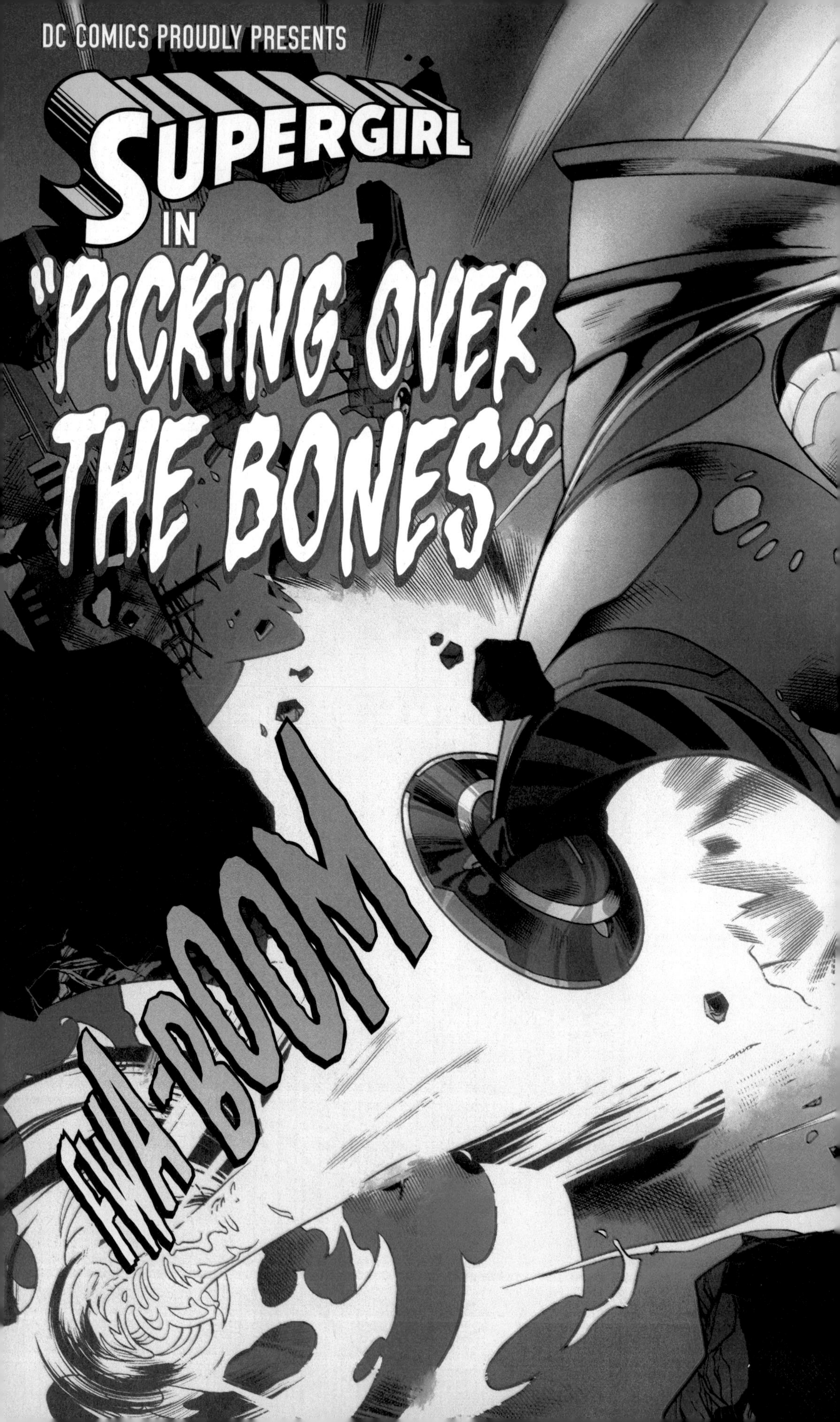
DC COMICS PROUDLY PRESENTS
SUPERGIRL
IN
"PICKING OVER THE BONES"
WHA-BOOM

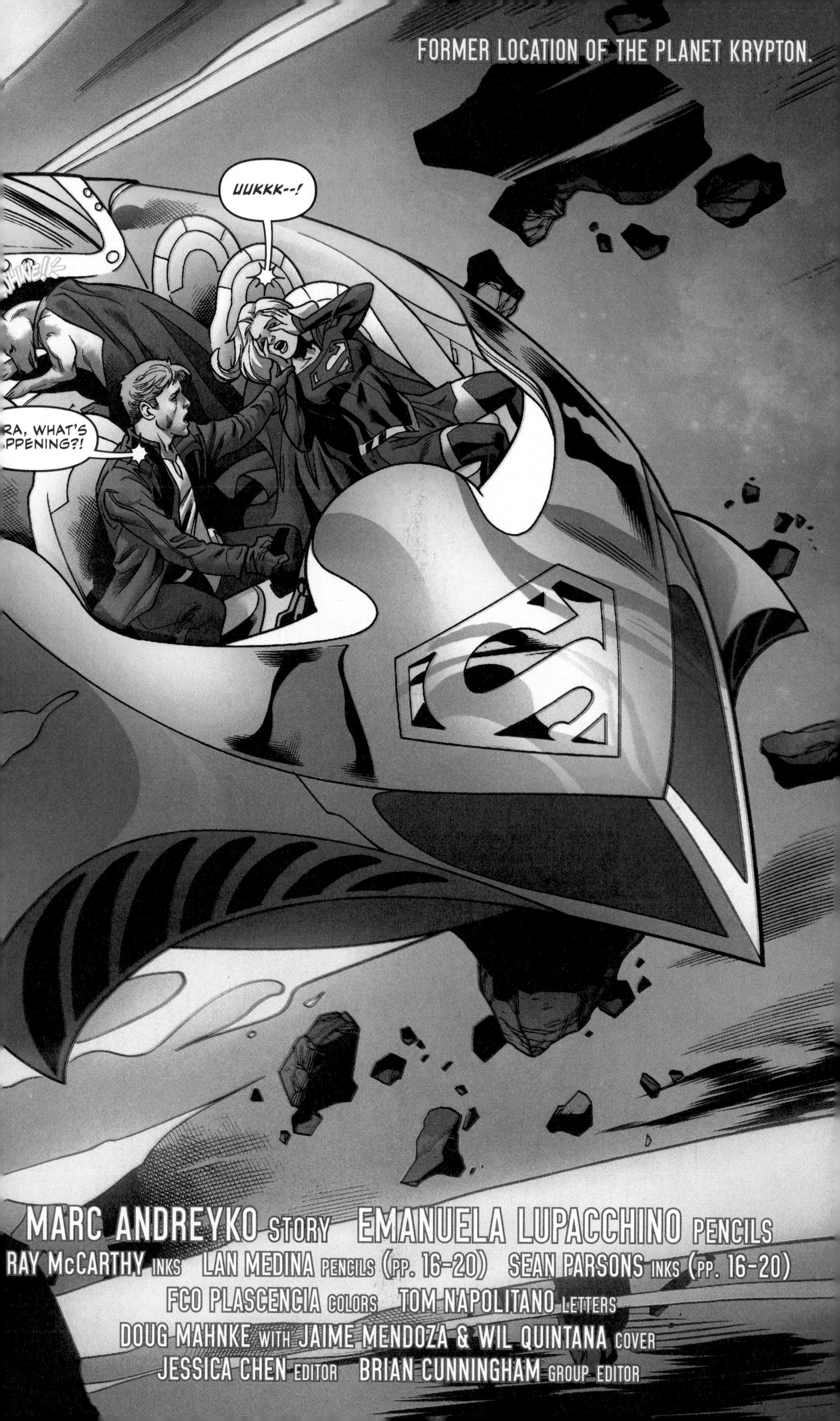
FORMER LOCATION OF THE PLANET KRYPTON.
UUKKK--!
RA, WHAT'S PPENING?!
MARC ANDREYKO STORY EMANUELA LUPACCHINO PENCILS
RAY McCARTHY INKS LAN MEDINA PENCILS (PP. 16-20) SEAN PARSONS INKS (PP. 16-20)
FCO PLASCENCIA COLORS TOM NAPOLITANO LETTERS
DOUG MAHNKE WITH JAIME MENDOZA & WIL QUINTANA COVER
JESSICA CHEN EDITOR BRIAN CUNNINGHAM GROUP EDITOR

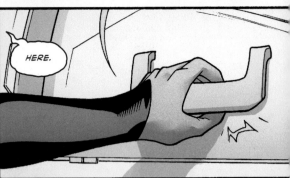

C'MON KARA, DON'T DIE ON ME--I'M A DOCTOR, BUT NOT *THAT* KIND OF ONE!

...SPACESUITS...

GOT IT! SPACESUITS!

UH, AND THEY ARE...?

HERE.

H-HELP ME GET IT ON... ...WILL FIL-FILTER OUT...

OKAY, OKAY. I GOT IT.

THERE! BETTER?

Y-YEAH. MUCH.

WOW, THAT WAS *UTTERLY TERRIFYING*. WHAT HAPPENED?

I UNDERESTIMATED THE POTENCY OF ALL THE KRYPTONITE RADIATION HERE. THE SUIT WILL FILTER OUT MOST OF IT.

MOST OF IT?

I'LL EXPLAIN LATER. JUST GET THIS ON KRYPTO!

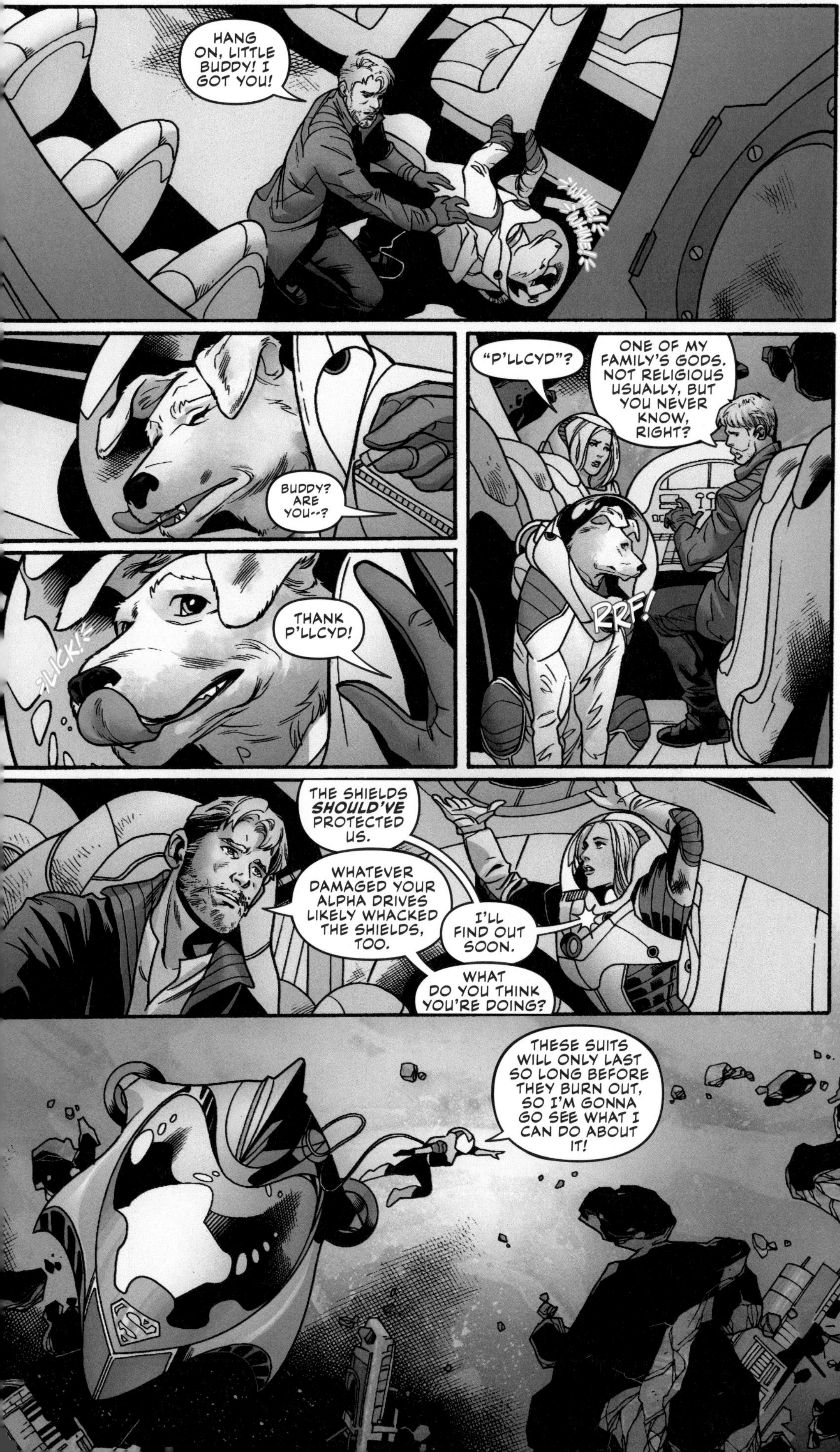
HANG ON, LITTLE BUDDY! I GOT YOU!
WHINE! WHINE!
BUDDY? ARE YOU--?
THANK P'LLCYD!
LICK!
"P'LLCYD"?
ONE OF MY FAMILY'S GODS. NOT RELIGIOUS USUALLY, BUT YOU NEVER KNOW, RIGHT?
RRF!
THE SHIELDS *SHOULD'VE* PROTECTED US.
WHATEVER DAMAGED YOUR ALPHA DRIVES LIKELY WHACKED THE SHIELDS, TOO.
I'LL FIND OUT SOON.
WHAT DO YOU THINK YOU'RE DOING?
THESE SUITS WILL ONLY LAST SO LONG BEFORE THEY BURN OUT, SO I'M GONNA GO SEE WHAT I CAN DO ABOUT IT!

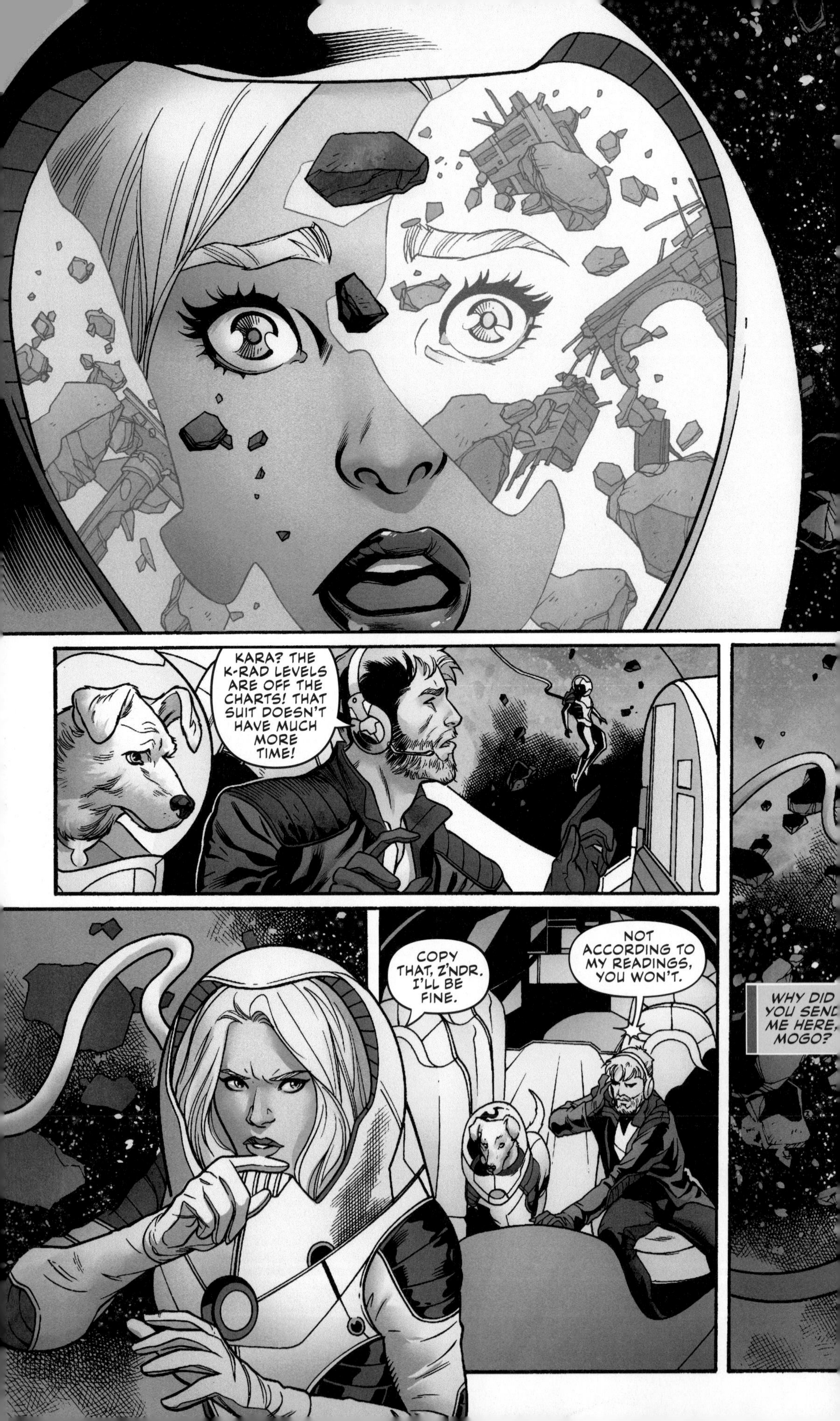
KARA? THE K-RAD LEVELS ARE OFF THE CHARTS! THAT SUIT DOESN'T HAVE MUCH MORE TIME!
COPY THAT, Z'NDR. I'LL BE FINE.
NOT ACCORDING TO MY READINGS, YOU WON'T.
WHY DID YOU SEND ME HERE, MOGO?

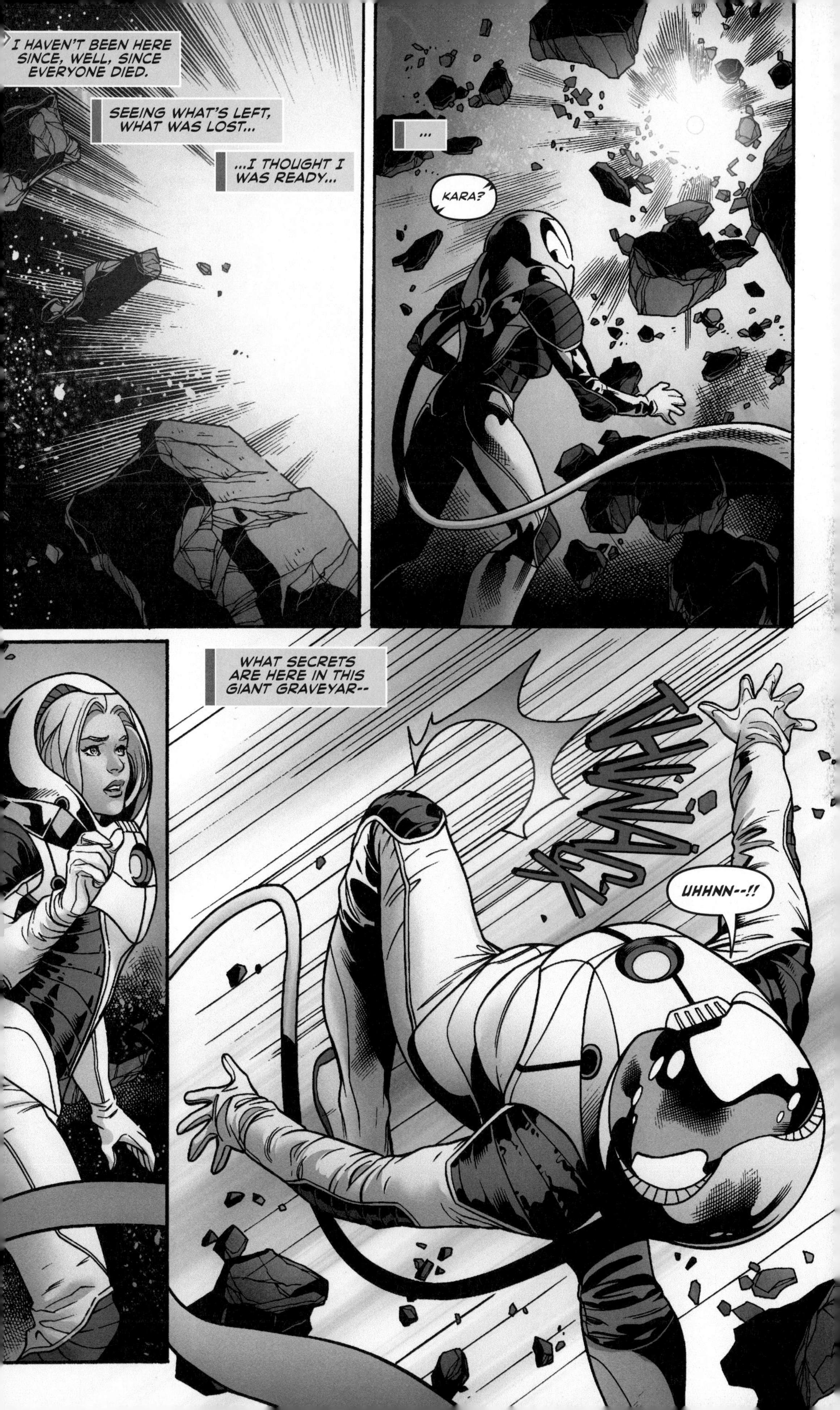

I HAVEN'T BEEN HERE SINCE, WELL, SINCE EVERYONE DIED.
SEEING WHAT'S LEFT, WHAT WAS LOST...
...I THOUGHT I WAS READY...
...
KARA?
WHAT SECRETS ARE HERE IN THIS GIANT GRAVEYAR--
THWAKK
UHHNN--!!

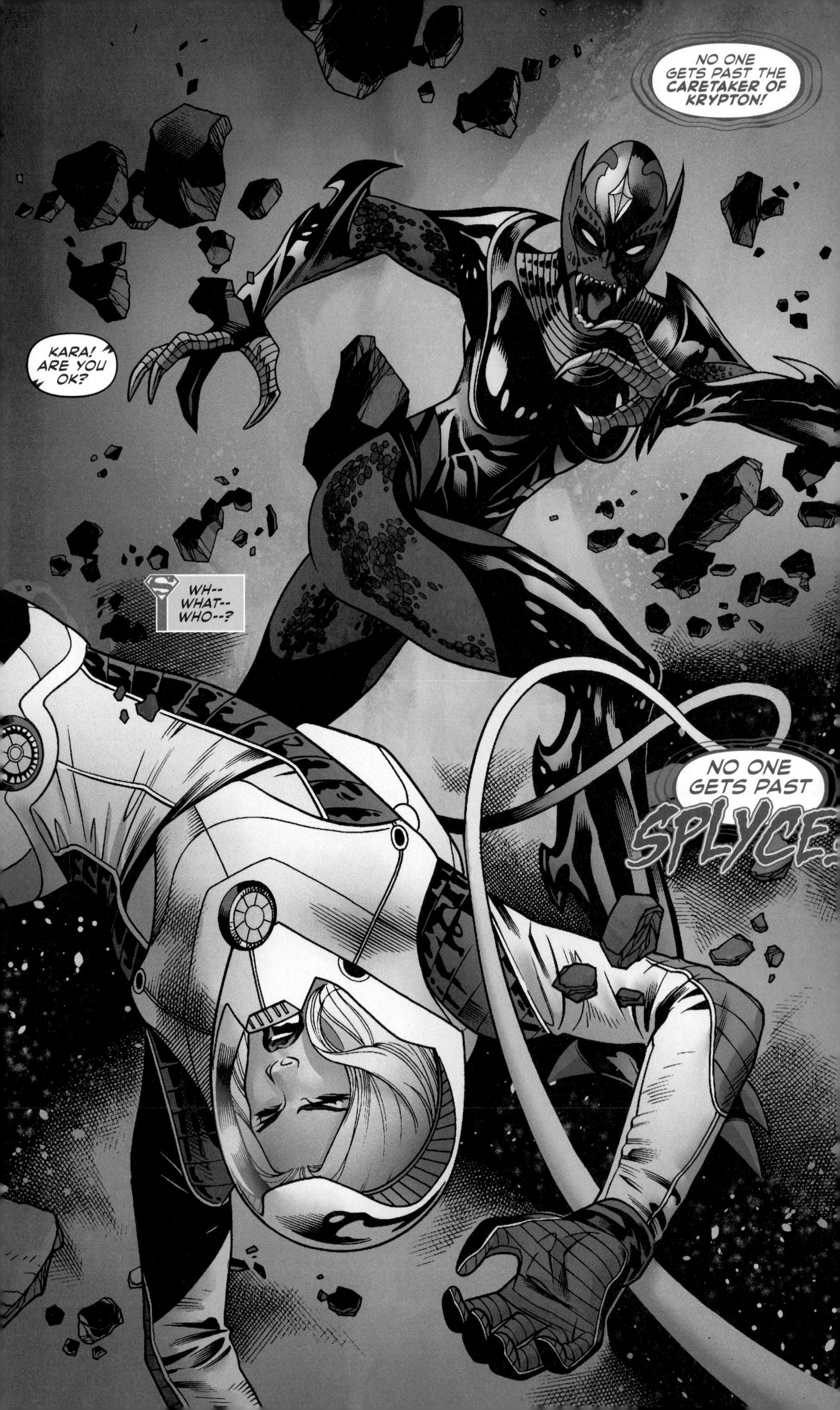

NO ONE GETS PAST THE CARETAKER OF KRYPTON!
KARA! ARE YOU OK?
WH-- WHAT-- WHO--?
NO ONE GETS PAST SPLYCE!

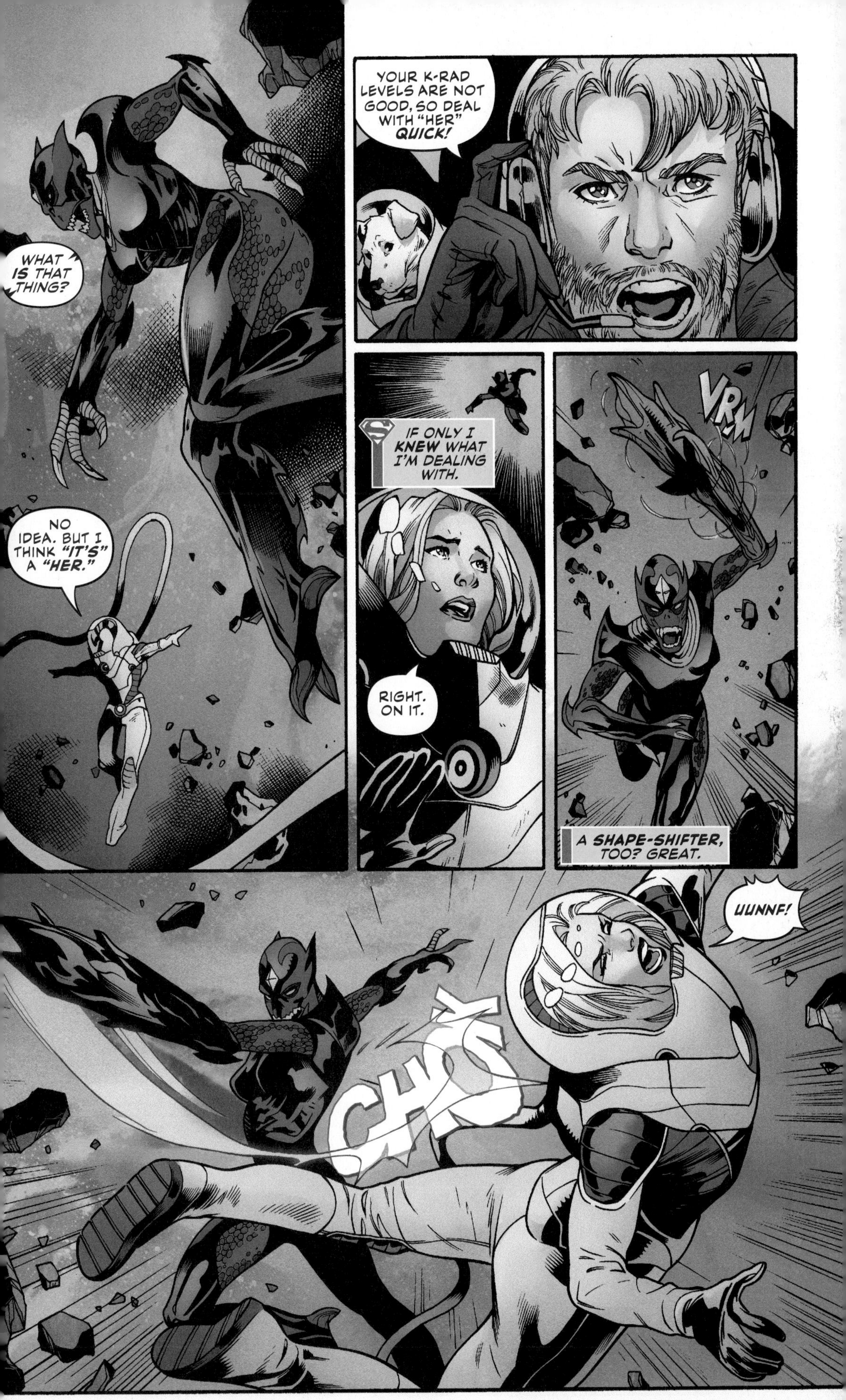
YOUR K-RAD LEVELS ARE NOT GOOD, SO DEAL WITH "HER" QUICK!
WHAT IS THAT THING?
NO IDEA. BUT I THINK "IT'S" A "HER."
IF ONLY I KNEW WHAT I'M DEALING WITH.
RIGHT. ON IT.
VRM
A SHAPE-SHIFTER, TOO? GREAT.
UUNNF!
CHK

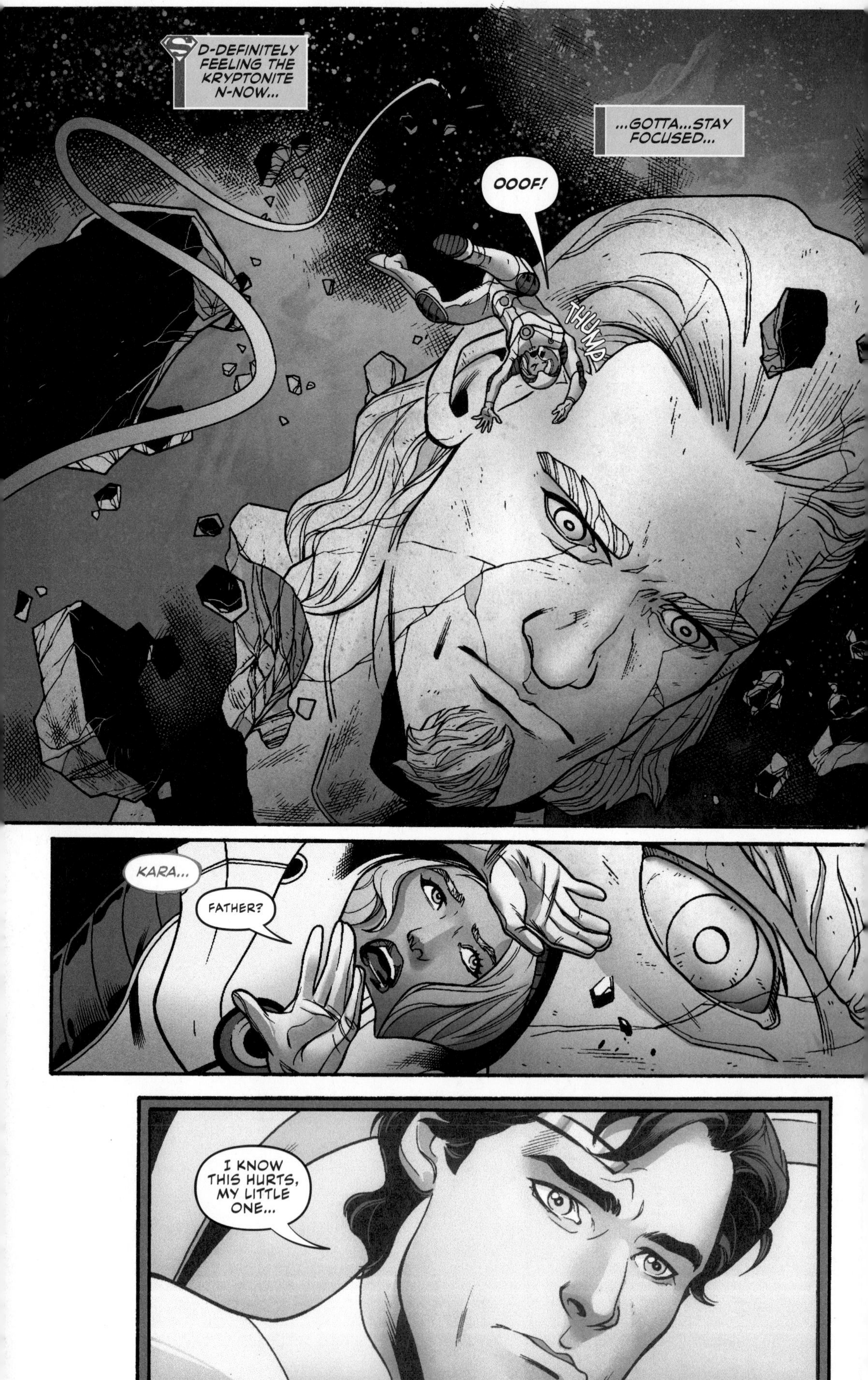
D-DEFINITELY FEELING THE KRYPTONITE N-NOW...
...GOTTA...STAY FOCUSED...
OOOF!
THUMP
KARA...
FATHER?
I KNOW THIS HURTS, MY LITTLE ONE...

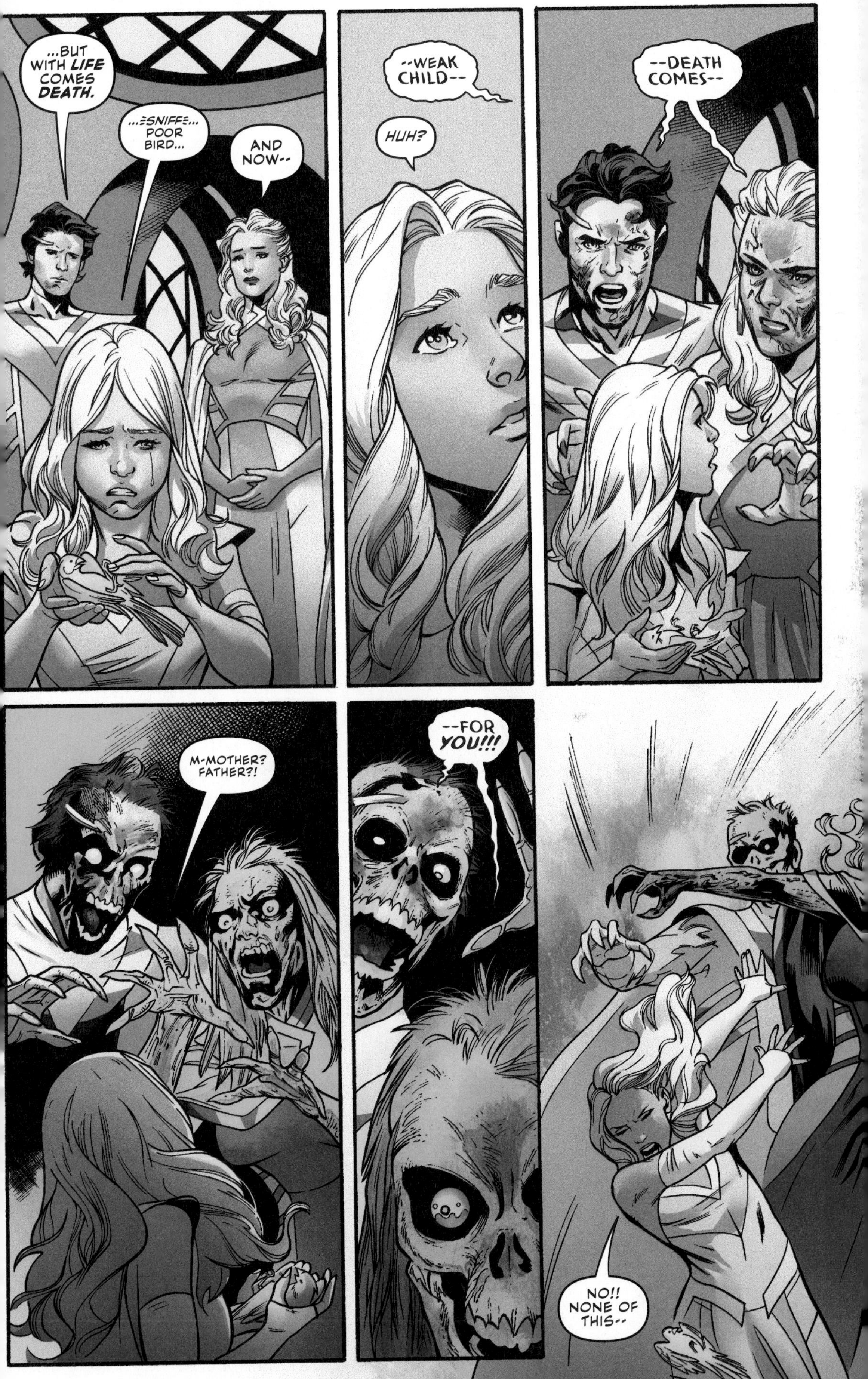
...BUT WITH LIFE COMES DEATH.
...SNIFF... POOR BIRD...
AND NOW--
--WEAK CHILD--
HUH?
--DEATH COMES--
M-MOTHER? FATHER?!
--FOR YOU!!!
NO!! NONE OF THIS--

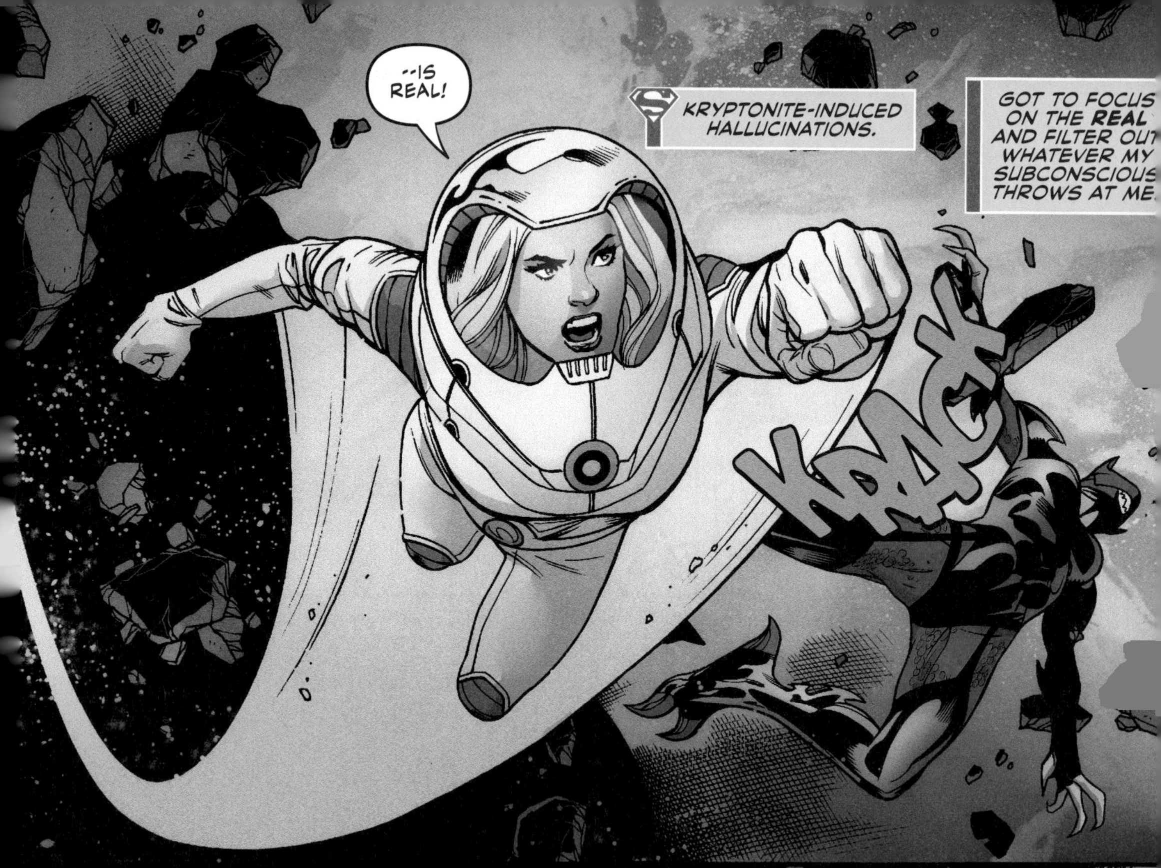
--IS REAL!
KRYPTONITE-INDUCED HALLUCINATIONS.
GOT TO FOCUS ON THE **REAL** AND FILTER OUT WHATEVER MY SUBCONSCIOUS THROWS AT ME.
KRACK

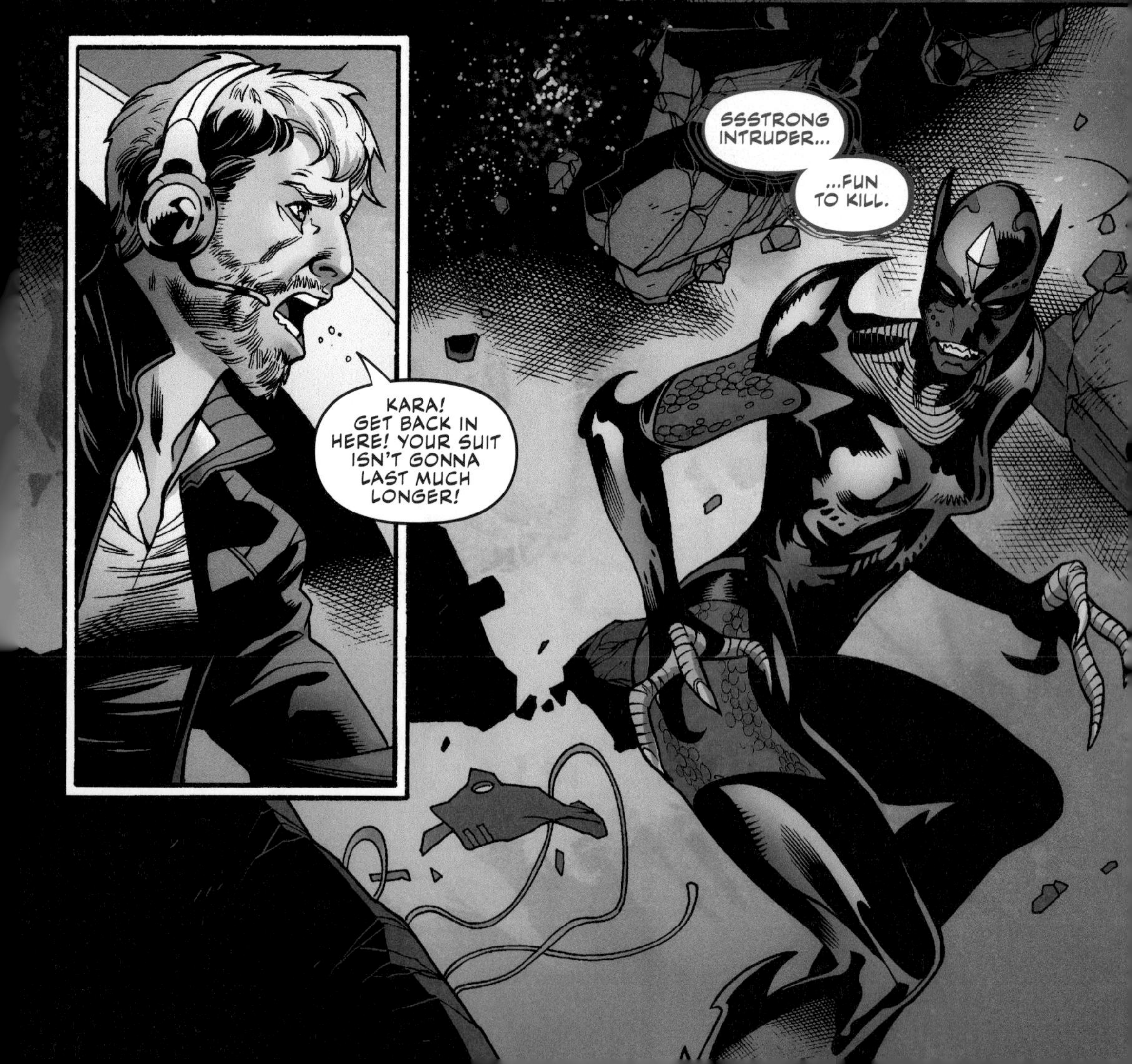
SSSTRONG INTRUDER...
...FUN TO KILL.
KARA! GET BACK IN HERE! YOUR SUIT ISN'T GONNA LAST MUCH LONGER!

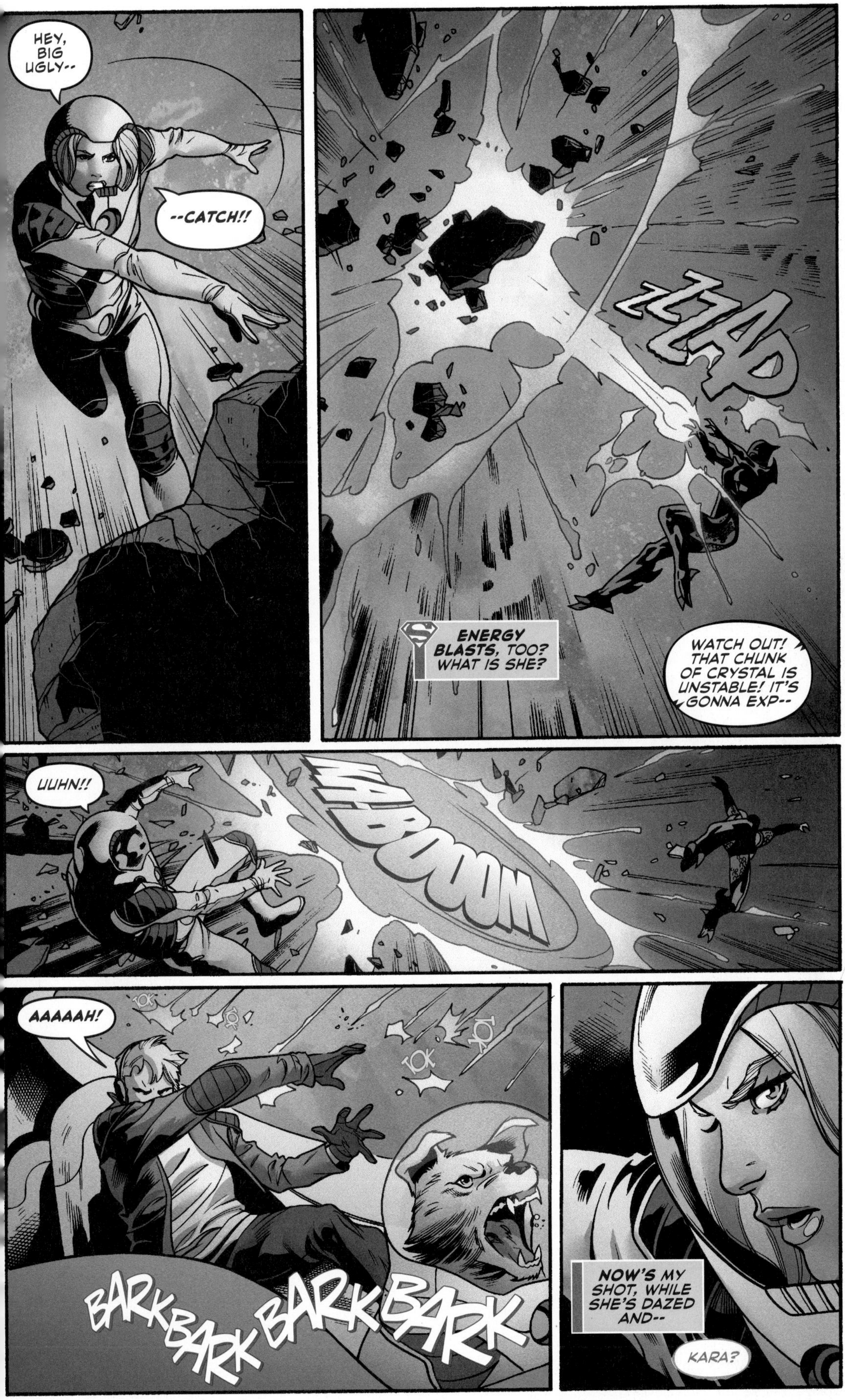
HEY, BIG UGLY--
--CATCH!!
ZZZAP
ENERGY BLASTS, TOO? WHAT IS SHE?
WATCH OUT! THAT CHUNK OF CRYSTAL IS UNSTABLE! IT'S GONNA EXP--
UUHN!!
KA-BOOOM
AAAAAH!
TOK
TOK
TOK
BARK BARK BARK BARK
NOW'S MY SHOT, WHILE SHE'S DAZED AND--
KARA?

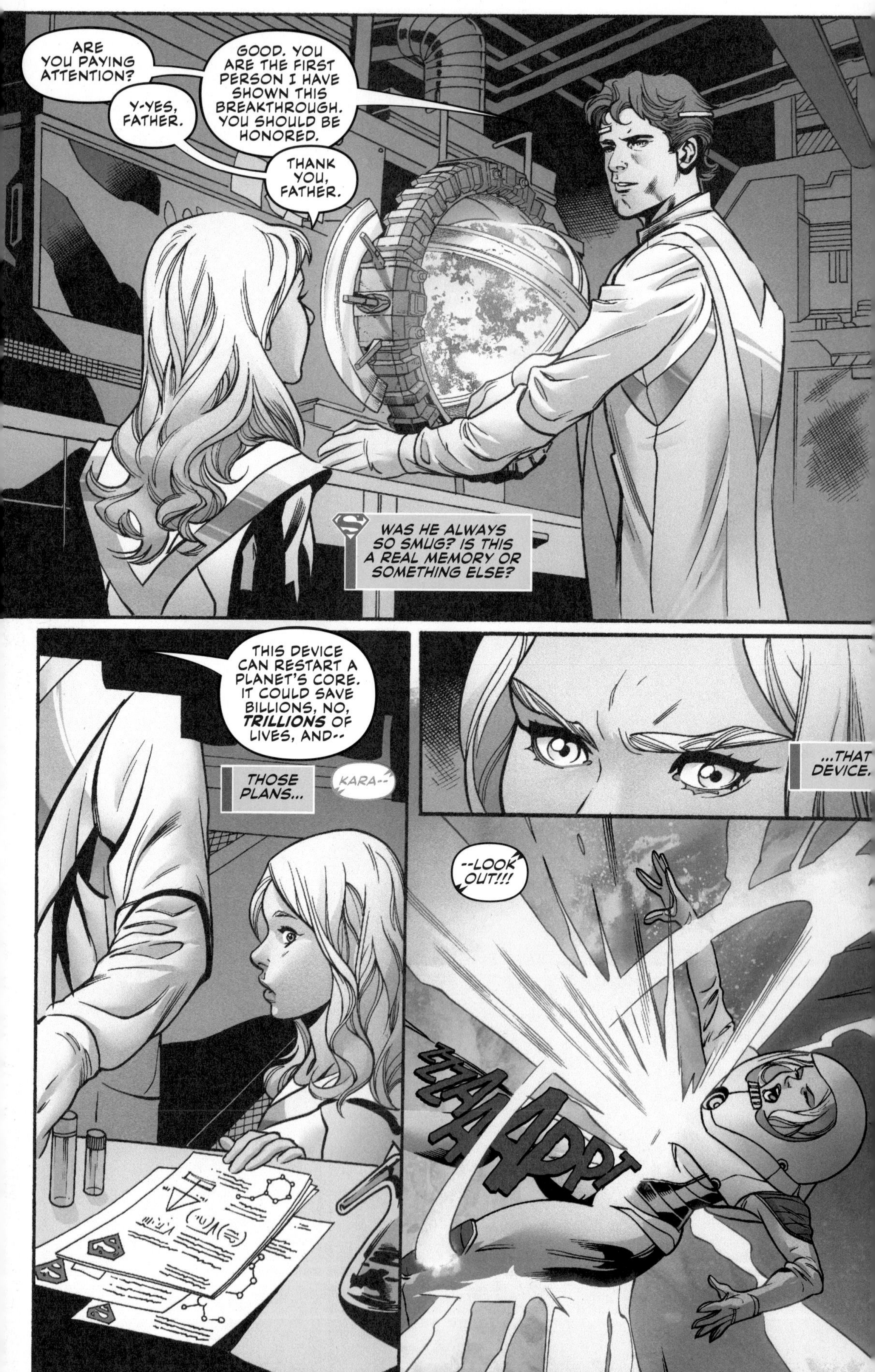
ARE YOU PAYING ATTENTION?
Y-YES, FATHER.
GOOD. YOU ARE THE FIRST PERSON I HAVE SHOWN THIS BREAKTHROUGH. YOU SHOULD BE HONORED.
THANK YOU, FATHER.
WAS HE ALWAYS SO SMUG? IS THIS A REAL MEMORY OR SOMETHING ELSE?
THIS DEVICE CAN RESTART A PLANET'S CORE. IT COULD SAVE BILLIONS, NO, TRILLIONS OF LIVES, AND--
THOSE PLANS...
KARA--
...THAT DEVICE.
--LOOK OUT!!!
ZZZAAAPPT

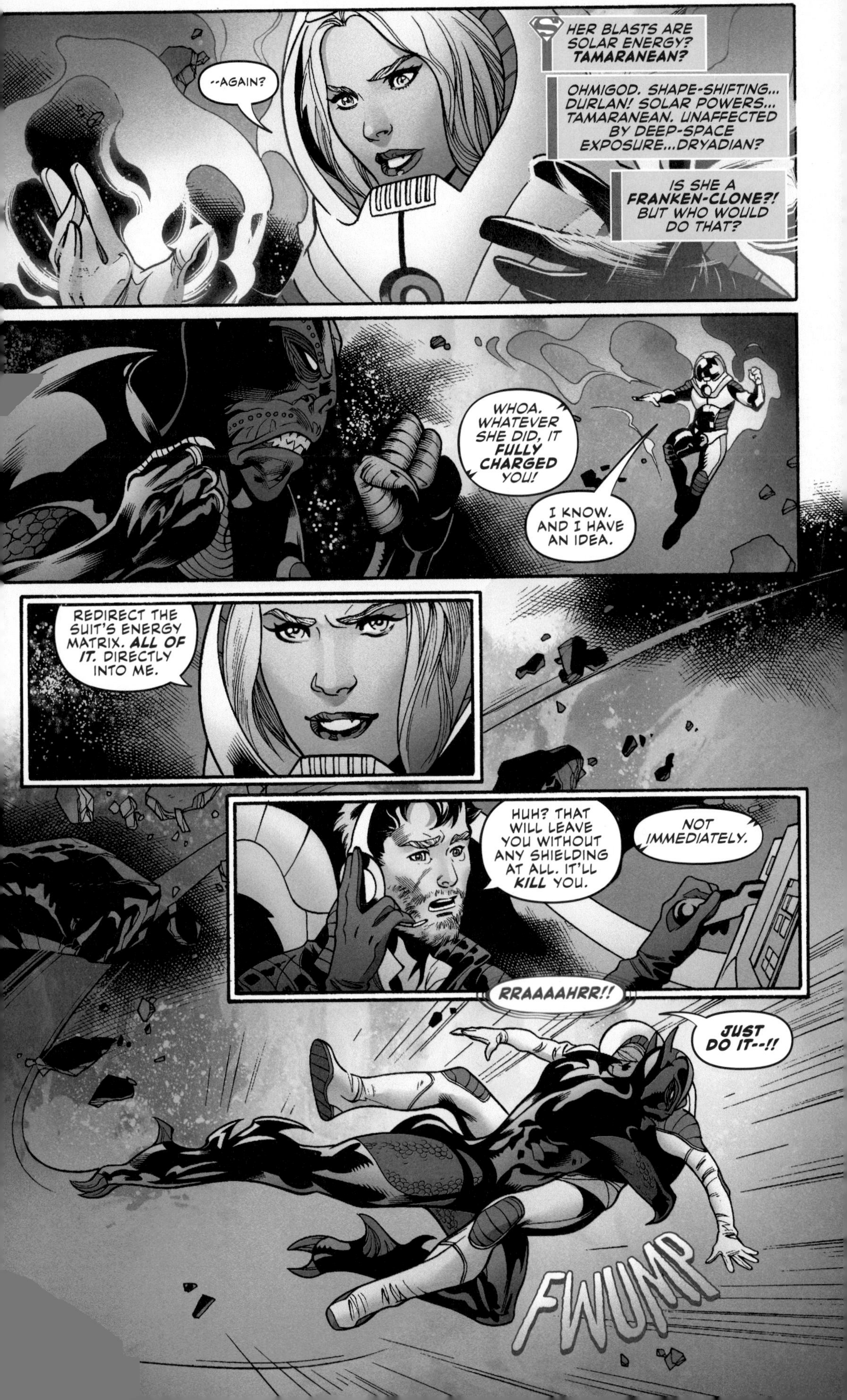

--AGAIN?
HER BLASTS ARE SOLAR ENERGY? TAMARANEAN?
OHMIGOD. SHAPE-SHIFTING... DURLAN! SOLAR POWERS... TAMARANEAN. UNAFFECTED BY DEEP-SPACE EXPOSURE...DRYADIAN?
IS SHE A FRANKEN-CLONE?! BUT WHO WOULD DO THAT?
WHOA. WHATEVER SHE DID, IT FULLY CHARGED YOU!
I KNOW. AND I HAVE AN IDEA.
REDIRECT THE SUIT'S ENERGY MATRIX. ALL OF IT. DIRECTLY INTO ME.
HUH? THAT WILL LEAVE YOU WITHOUT ANY SHIELDING AT ALL. IT'LL KILL YOU.
NOT IMMEDIATELY.
RRAAAAHRR!!
JUST DO IT--!!
FWUMP

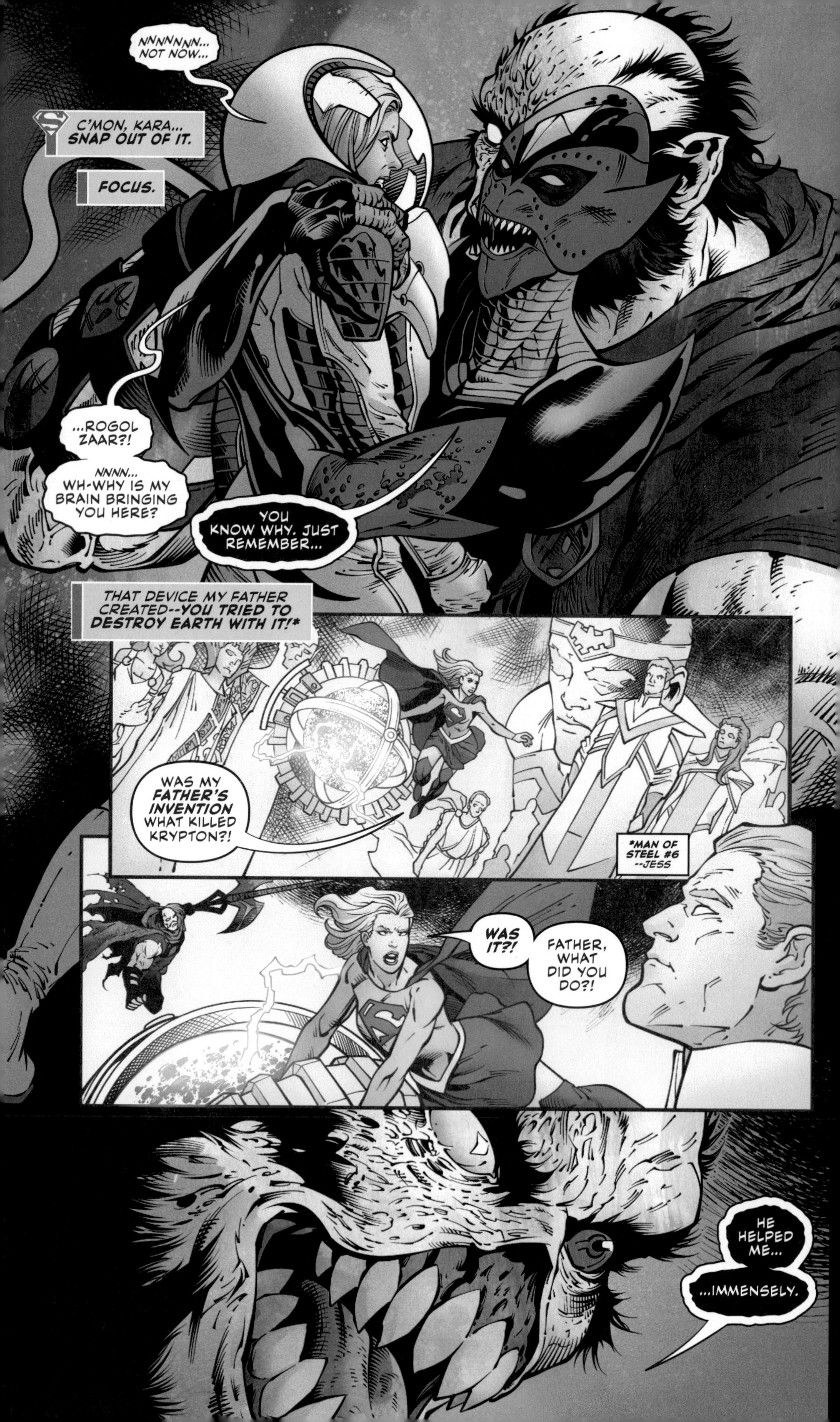
NNNNNNN... NOT NOW...
C'MON, KARA... SNAP OUT OF IT.
FOCUS.
...ROGOL ZAAR?!
NNNN... WH-WHY IS MY BRAIN BRINGING YOU HERE?
YOU KNOW WHY. JUST REMEMBER...
THAT DEVICE MY FATHER CREATED--YOU TRIED TO DESTROY EARTH WITH IT!*
WAS MY FATHER'S INVENTION WHAT KILLED KRYPTON?!
*MAN OF STEEL #6 --JESS
WAS IT?!
FATHER, WHAT DID YOU DO?!
HE HELPED ME...
...IMMENSELY.

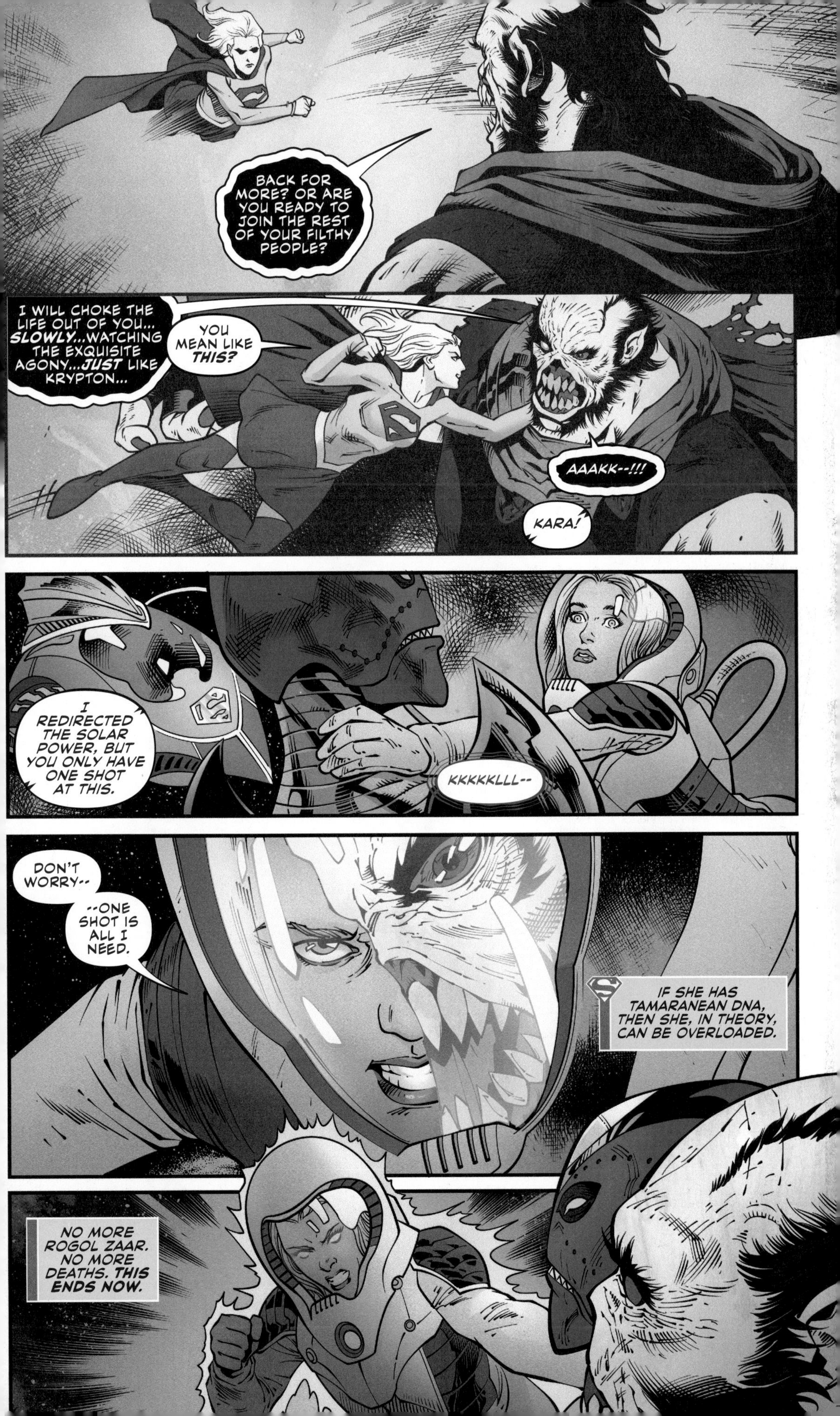
BACK FOR MORE? OR ARE YOU READY TO JOIN THE REST OF YOUR FILTHY PEOPLE?
I WILL CHOKE THE LIFE OUT OF YOU... SLOWLY...WATCHING THE EXQUISITE AGONY...JUST LIKE KRYPTON...
YOU MEAN LIKE THIS?
AAAKK--!!!
KARA!
I REDIRECTED THE SOLAR POWER, BUT YOU ONLY HAVE ONE SHOT AT THIS.
KKKKKLLL--
DON'T WORRY--
--ONE SHOT IS ALL I NEED.
IF SHE HAS TAMARANEAN DNA, THEN SHE, IN THEORY, CAN BE OVERLOADED.
NO MORE ROGOL ZAAR. NO MORE DEATHS. THIS ENDS NOW.

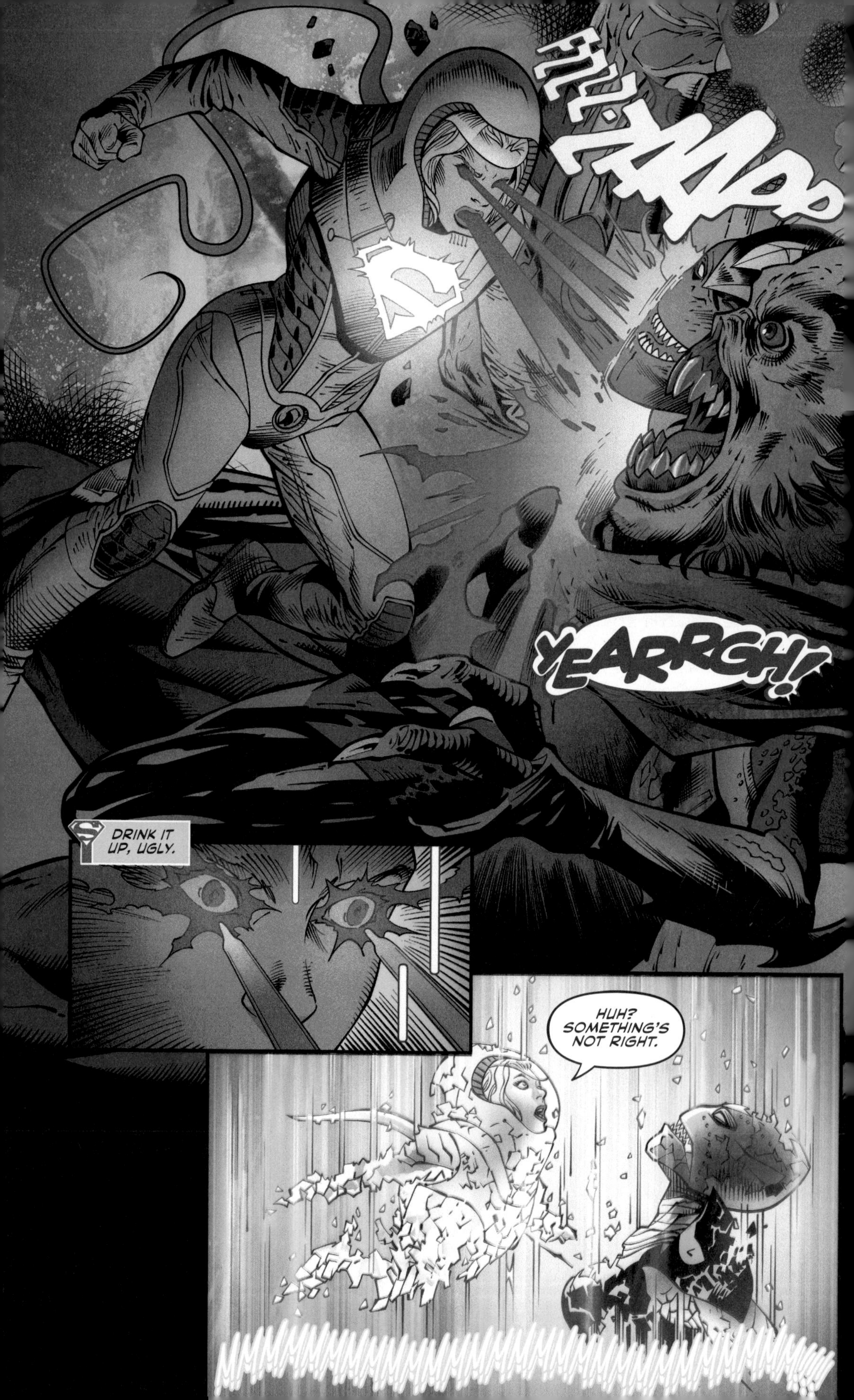
FZZZ-ZAAAP
YEARRGH!
DRINK IT UP, UGLY.
HUH? SOMETHING'S NOT RIGHT.
MMMMMMMMMMMMMMMMMMMMMMMMMMMMMMMMMM

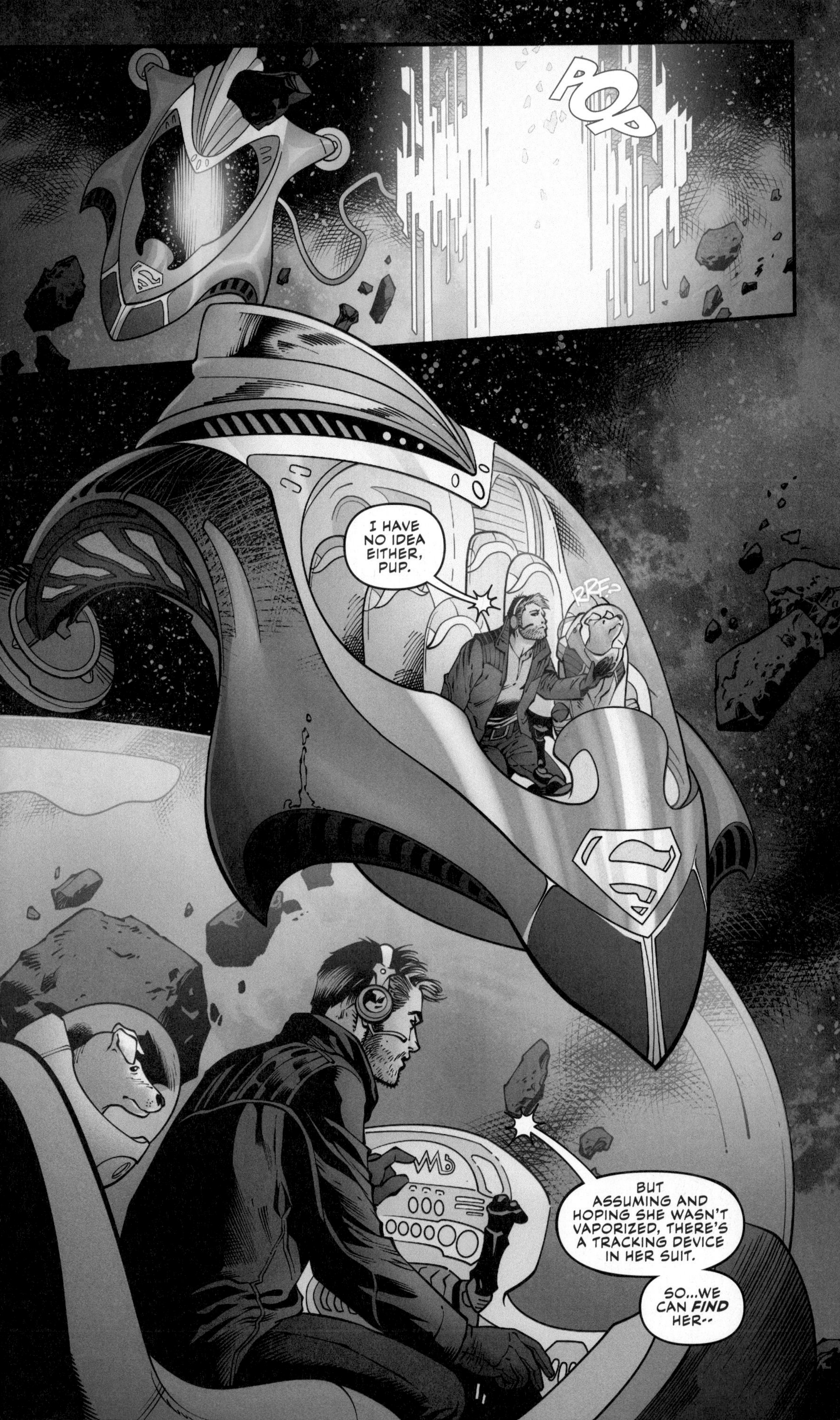
POP
I HAVE NO IDEA EITHER, PUP.
RRF?
BUT ASSUMING AND HOPING SHE WASN'T VAPORIZED, THERE'S A TRACKING DEVICE IN HER SUIT.
SO...WE CAN *FIND* HER--

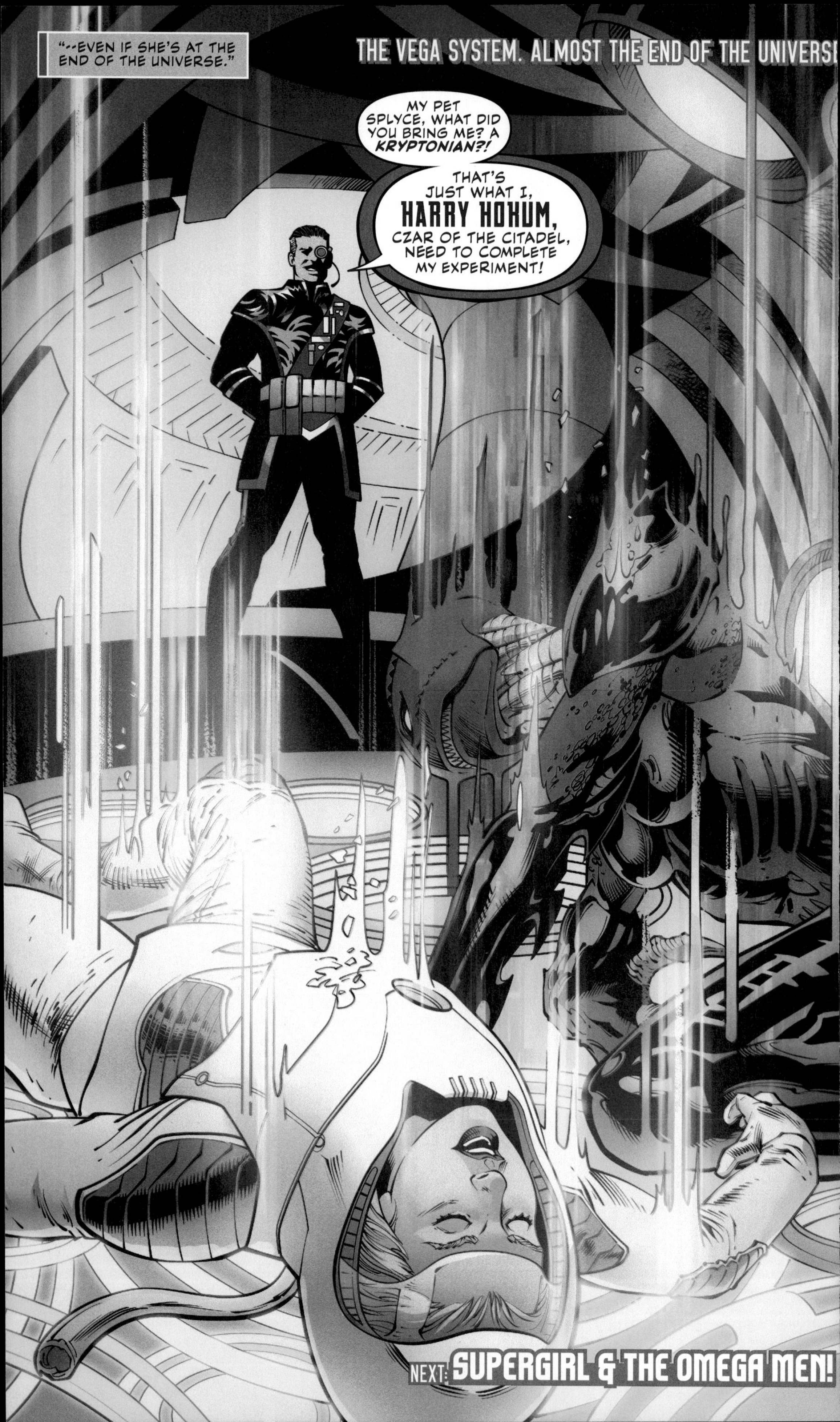
"--EVEN IF SHE'S AT THE END OF THE UNIVERSE."
THE VEGA SYSTEM. ALMOST THE END OF THE UNIVERSE
MY PET SPLYCE, WHAT DID YOU BRING ME? A KRYPTONIAN?!
THAT'S JUST WHAT I, HARRY HOKUM, CZAR OF THE CITADEL, NEED TO COMPLETE MY EXPERIMENT!
NEXT: SUPERGIRL & THE OMEGA MEN!

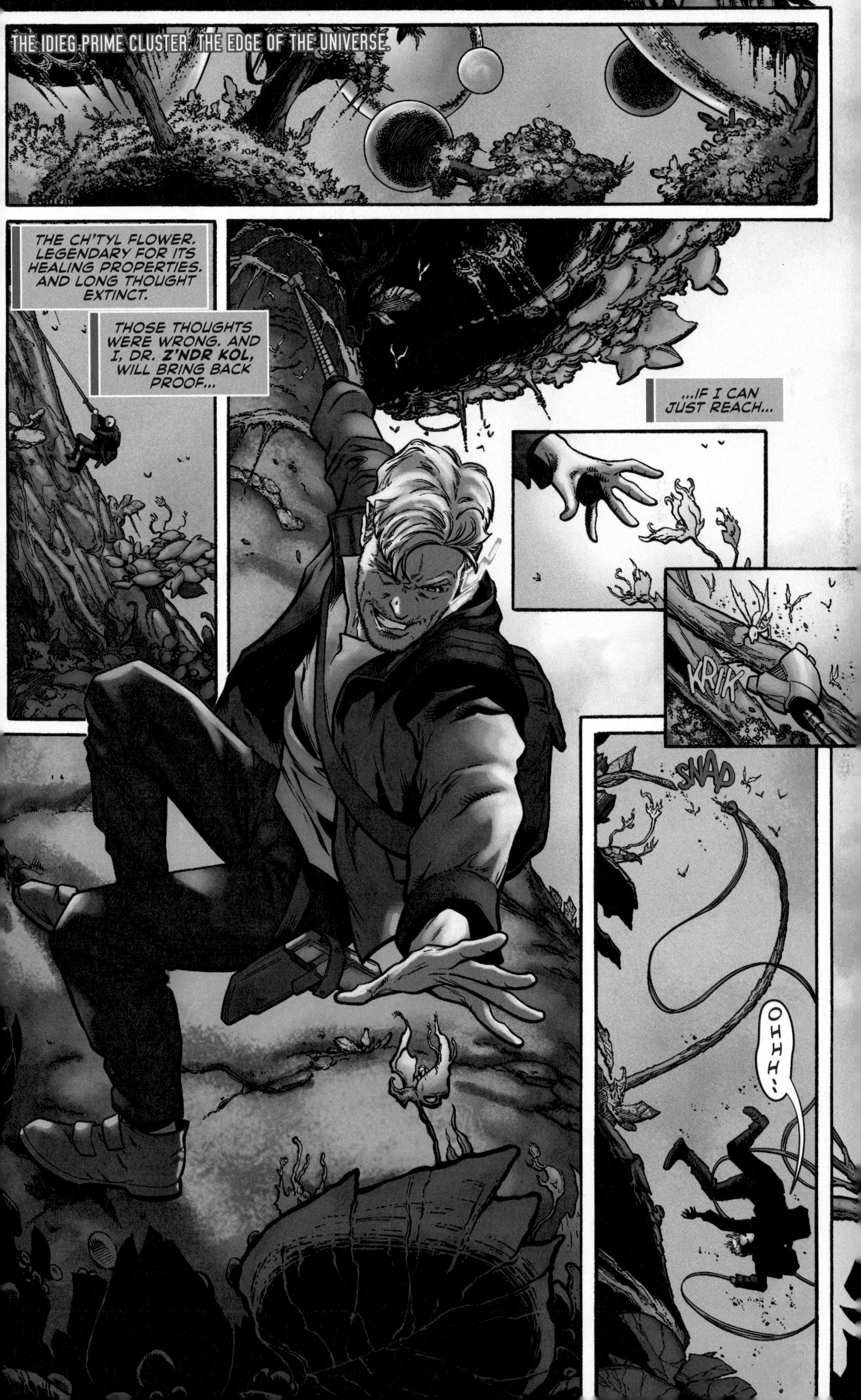
THE IDIEG PRIME CLUSTER. THE EDGE OF THE UNIVERSE.
THE CH'TYL FLOWER. LEGENDARY FOR ITS HEALING PROPERTIES. AND LONG THOUGHT EXTINCT.
THOSE THOUGHTS WERE WRONG. AND I, DR. **Z'NDR KOL,** WILL BRING BACK PROOF...
...IF I CAN JUST REACH...
KRIK
SNAP
OHHH!

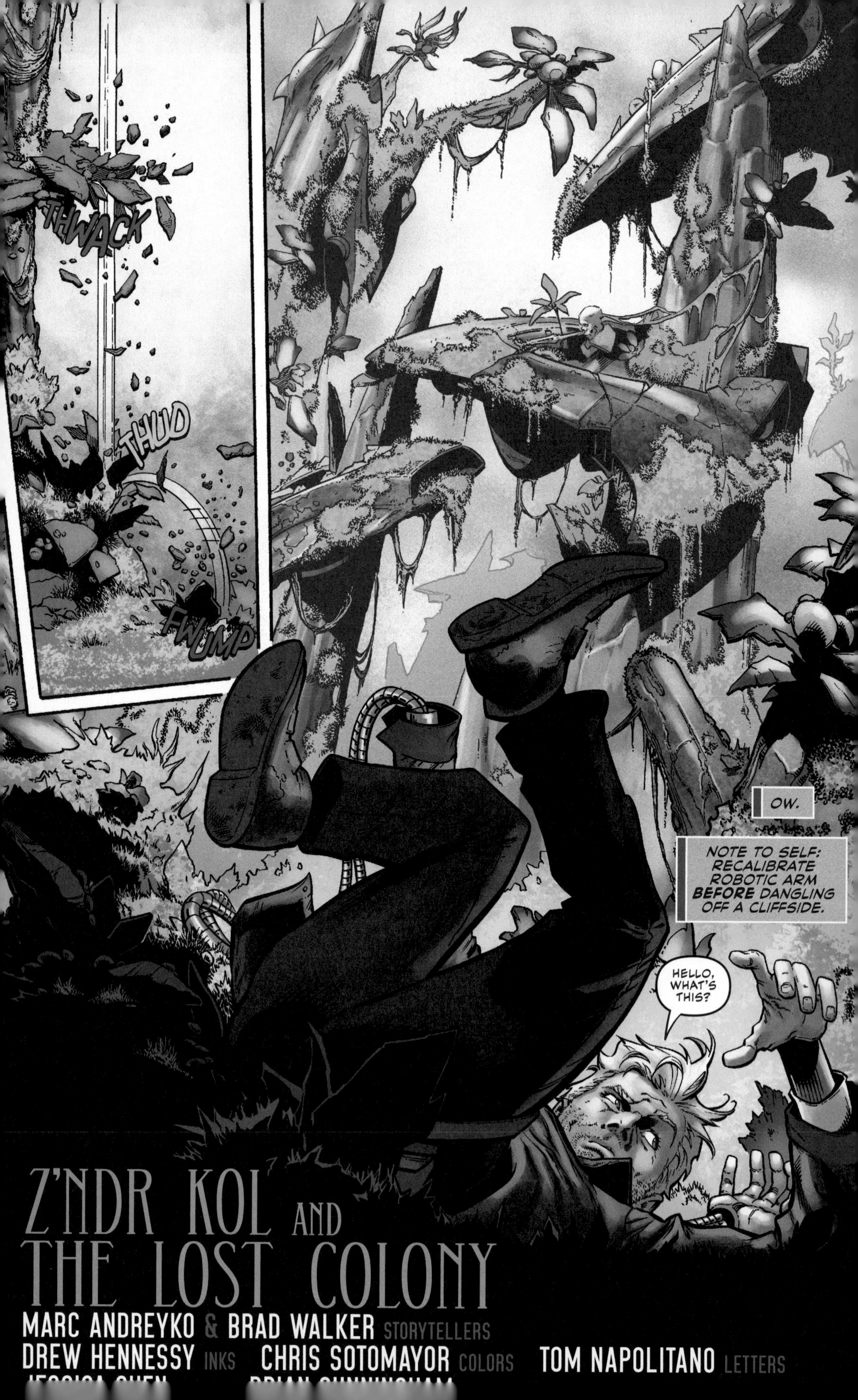
THWACK
THUD
FWUMP
OW.
NOTE TO SELF: RECALIBRATE ROBOTIC ARM BEFORE DANGLING OFF A CLIFFSIDE.
HELLO, WHAT'S THIS?

Z'NDR KOL AND THE LOST COLONY

MARC ANDREYKO & BRAD WALKER STORYTELLERS
DREW HENNESSY INKS CHRIS SOTOMAYOR COLORS TOM NAPOLITANO LETTERS

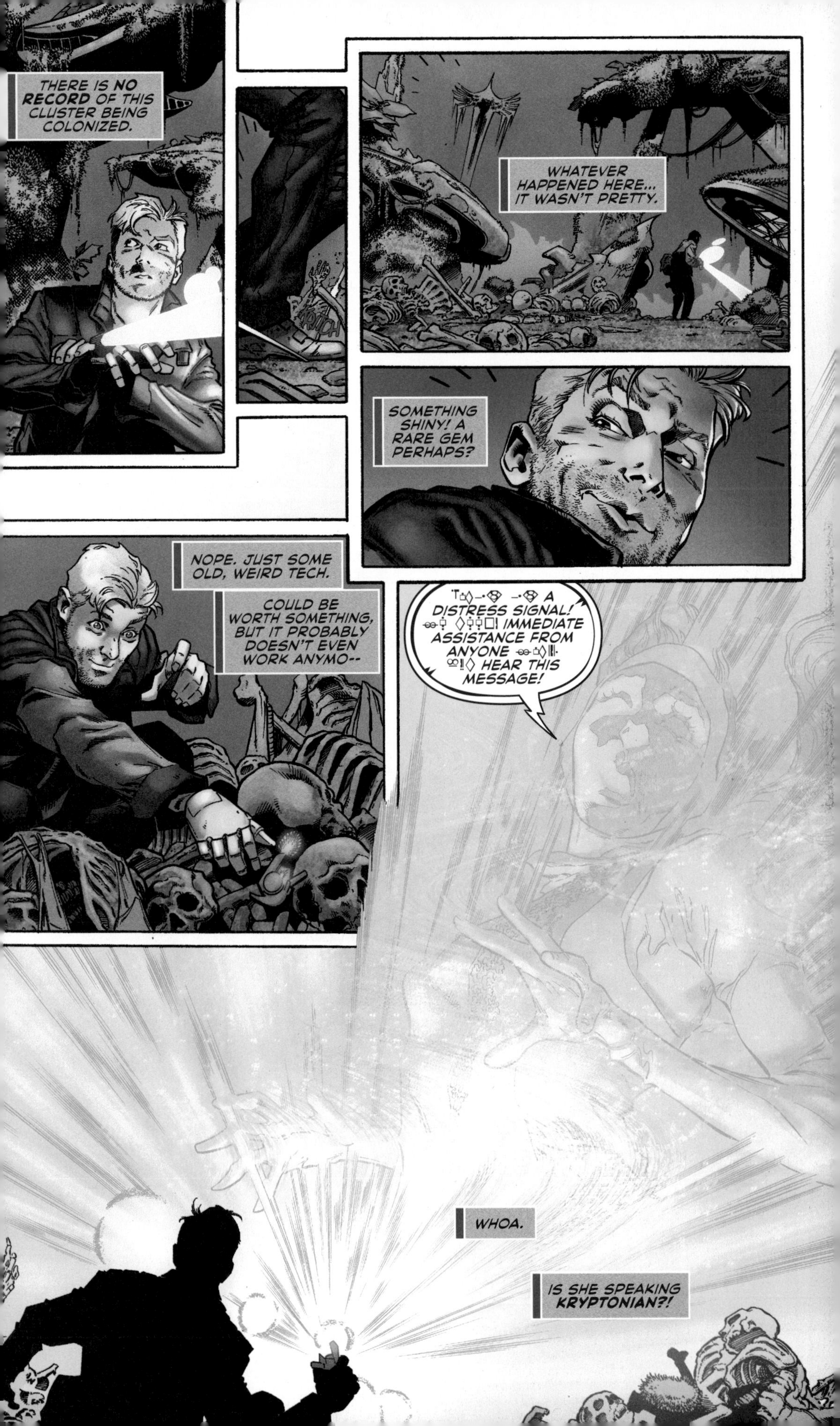

THERE IS NO RECORD OF THIS CLUSTER BEING COLONIZED.
WHATEVER HAPPENED HERE... IT WASN'T PRETTY.
SOMETHING SHINY! A RARE GEM PERHAPS?
NOPE. JUST SOME OLD, WEIRD TECH.
COULD BE WORTH SOMETHING, BUT IT PROBABLY DOESN'T EVEN WORK ANYMO--
A DISTRESS SIGNAL! IMMEDIATE ASSISTANCE FROM ANYONE HEAR THIS MESSAGE!
WHOA.
IS SHE SPEAKING KRYPTONIAN?!

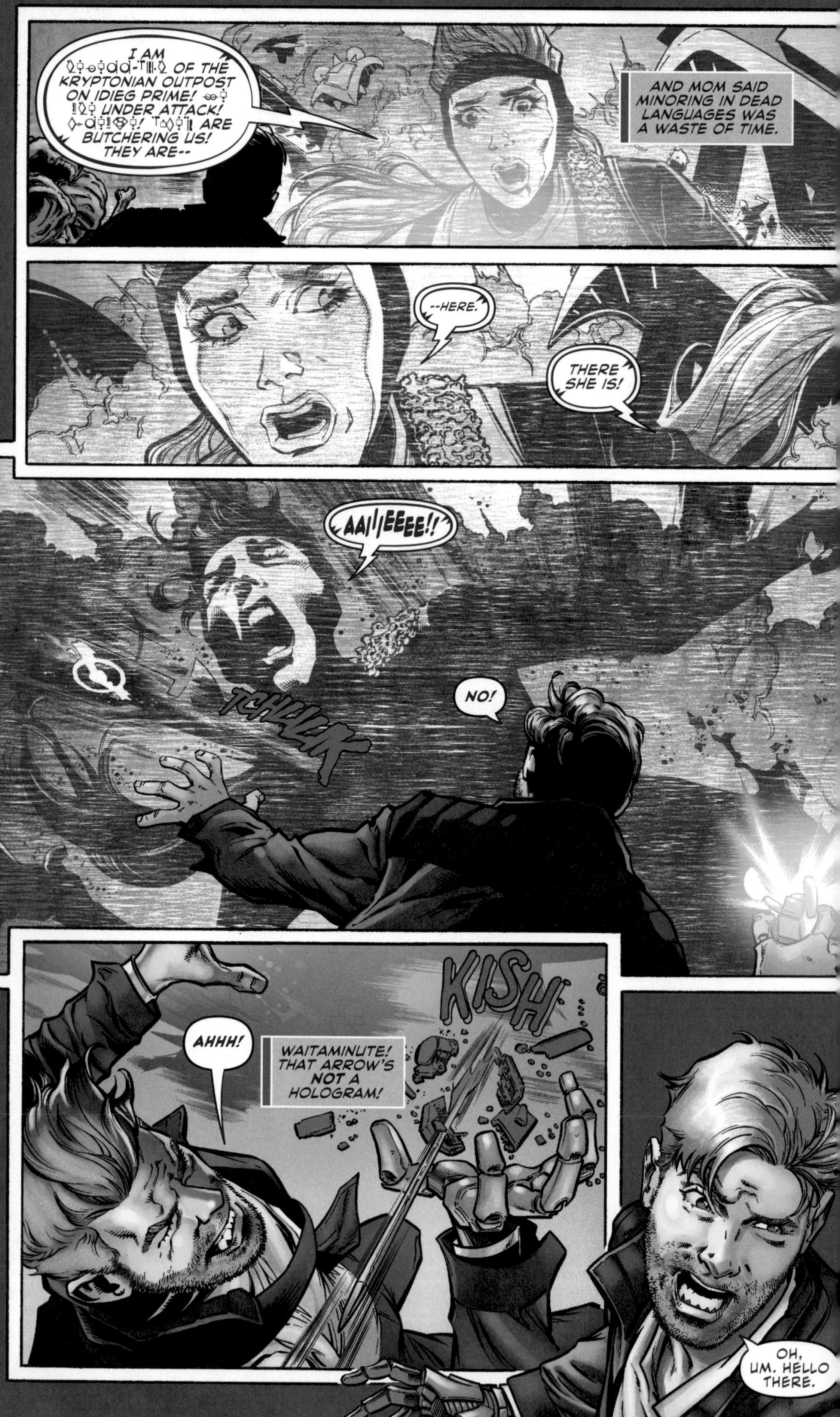
I AM ... OF THE KRYPTONIAN OUTPOST ON IDIEG PRIME! ... UNDER ATTACK! ... ARE BUTCHERING US! THEY ARE--
AND MOM SAID MINORING IN DEAD LANGUAGES WAS A WASTE OF TIME.
--HERE.
THERE SHE IS!
AAIIIEEEE!!
TCHULK
NO!
KISH
AHHH!
WAITAMINUTE! THAT ARROW'S NOT A HOLOGRAM!
OH, UM. HELLO THERE.

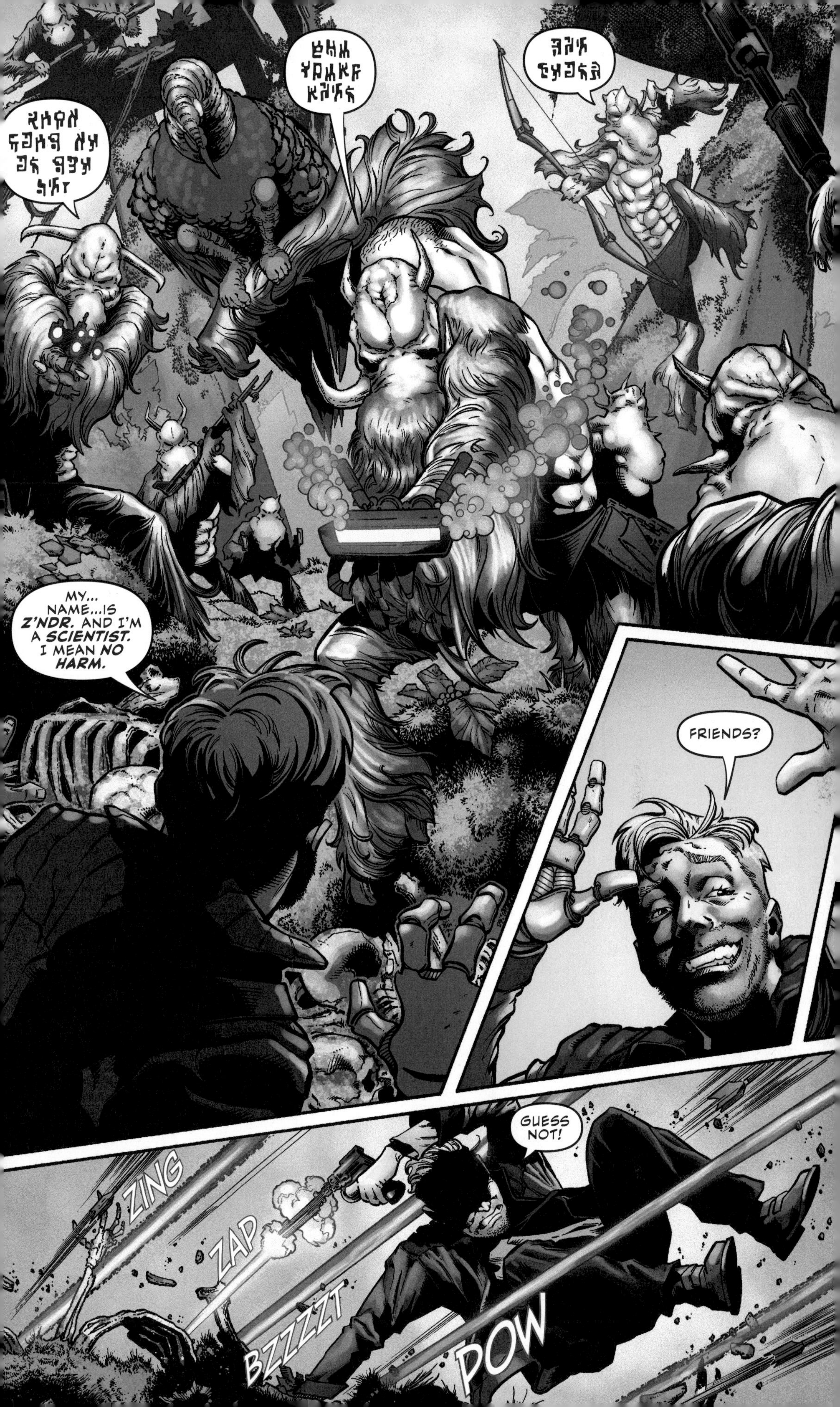
MY... NAME...IS Z'NDR. AND I'M A SCIENTIST. I MEAN NO HARM.
FRIENDS?
GUESS NOT!
ZING
ZAP
BZZZZT
POW

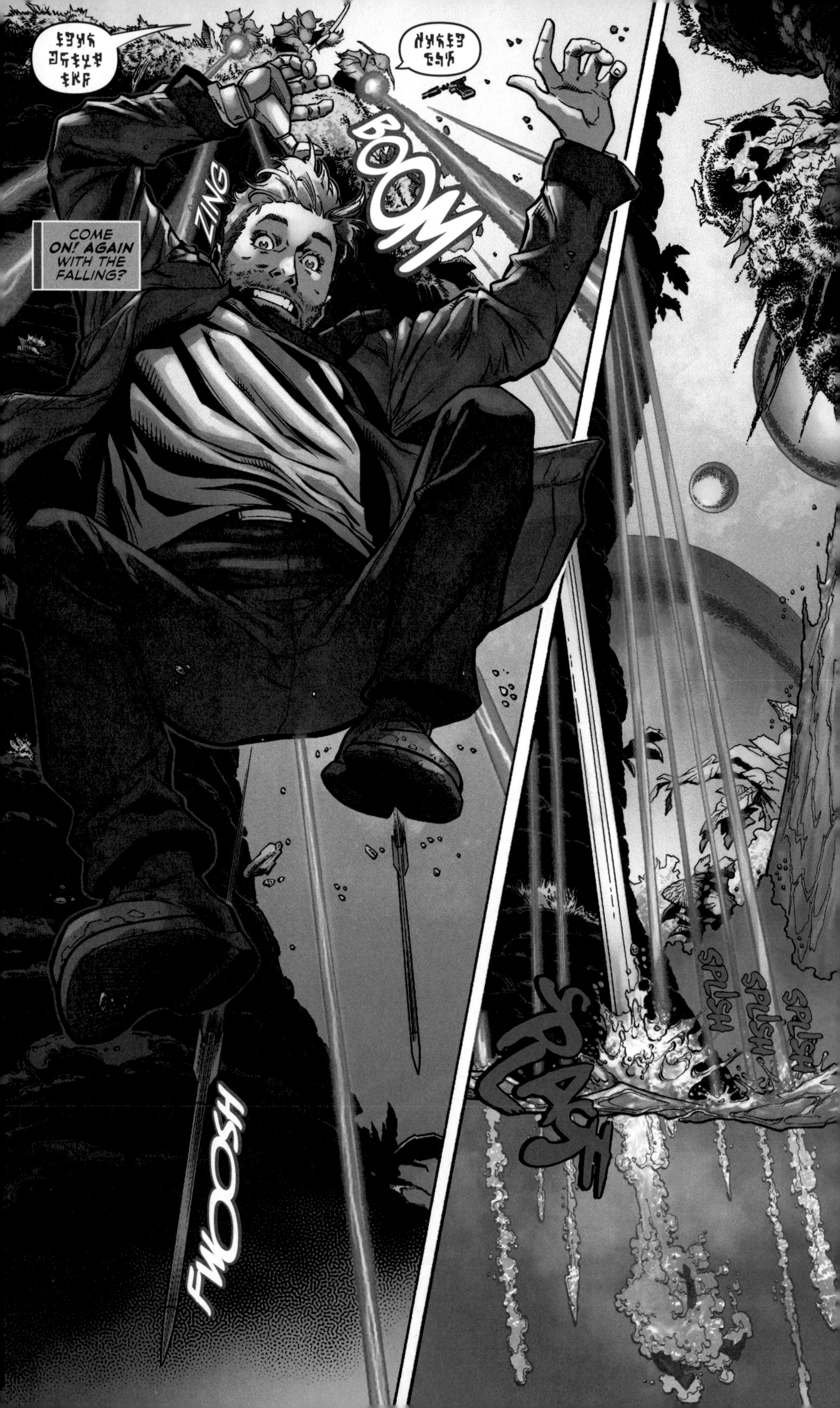
COME ON! AGAIN WITH THE FALLING?
ZING
BOOM
FWOOSH
SPLASH
SPLSH
SPLSH
SPLSH

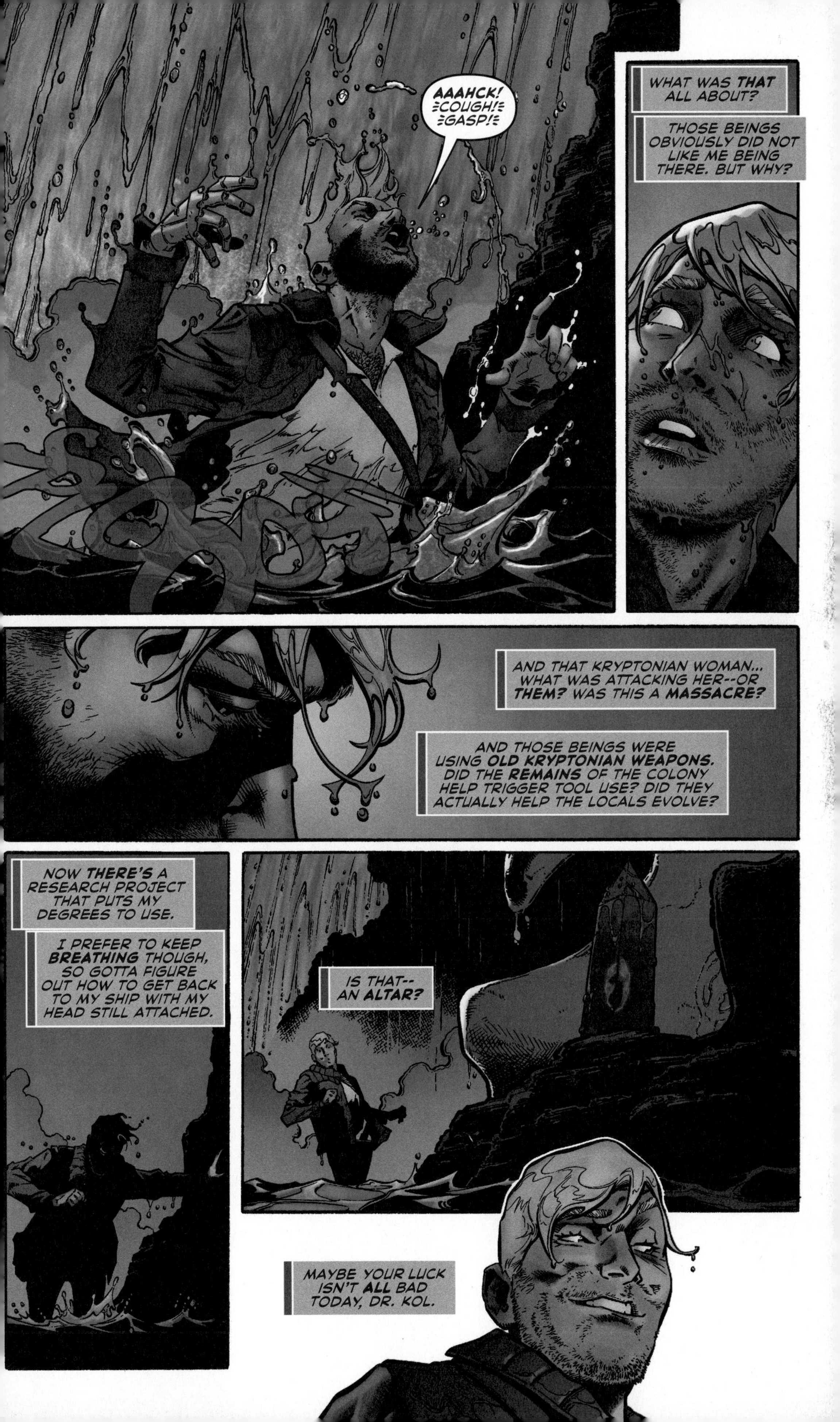
AAAHCK! COUGH! GASP!
WHAT WAS THAT ALL ABOUT?
THOSE BEINGS OBVIOUSLY DID NOT LIKE ME BEING THERE. BUT WHY?
AND THAT KRYPTONIAN WOMAN... WHAT WAS ATTACKING HER--OR THEM? WAS THIS A MASSACRE?
AND THOSE BEINGS WERE USING OLD KRYPTONIAN WEAPONS. DID THE REMAINS OF THE COLONY HELP TRIGGER TOOL USE? DID THEY ACTUALLY HELP THE LOCALS EVOLVE?
NOW THERE'S A RESEARCH PROJECT THAT PUTS MY DEGREES TO USE.
I PREFER TO KEEP BREATHING THOUGH, SO GOTTA FIGURE OUT HOW TO GET BACK TO MY SHIP WITH MY HEAD STILL ATTACHED.
IS THAT-- AN ALTAR?
MAYBE YOUR LUCK ISN'T ALL BAD TODAY, DR. KOL.

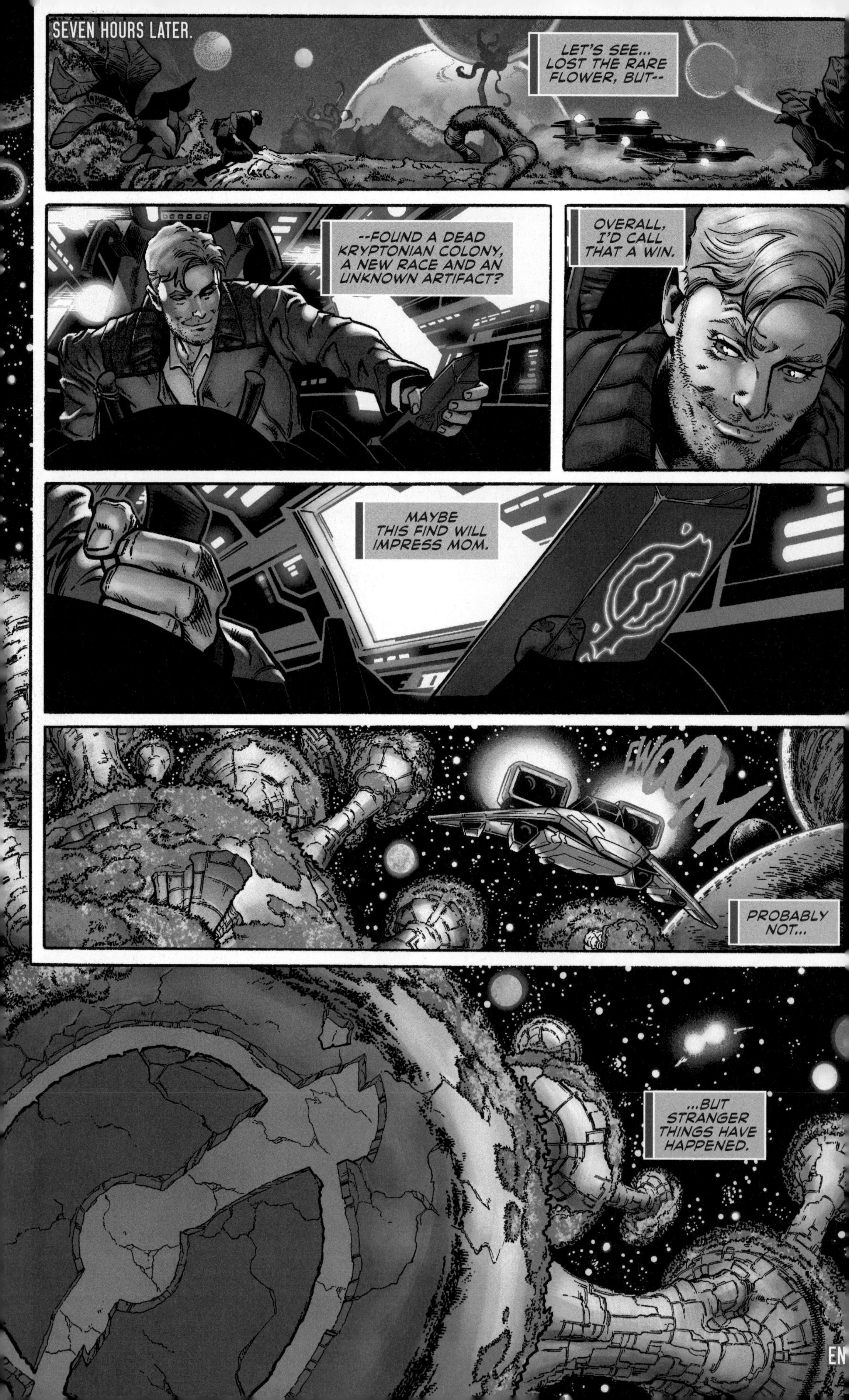
SEVEN HOURS LATER.
LET'S SEE... LOST THE RARE FLOWER, BUT--
--FOUND A DEAD KRYPTONIAN COLONY, A NEW RACE AND AN UNKNOWN ARTIFACT?
OVERALL, I'D CALL THAT A WIN.
MAYBE THIS FIND WILL IMPRESS MOM.
FWOOM
PROBABLY NOT...
...BUT STRANGER THINGS HAVE HAPPENED.
EN

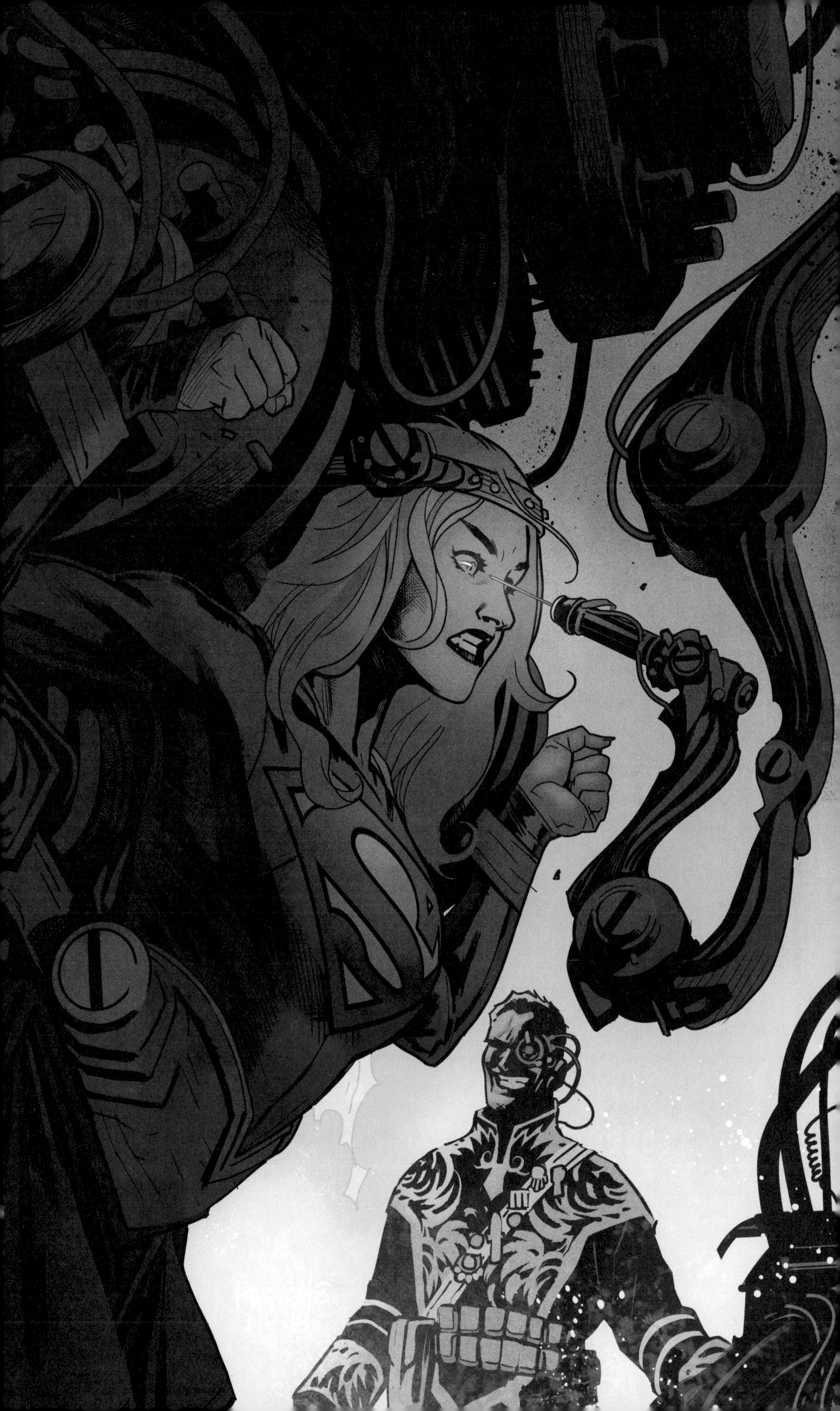

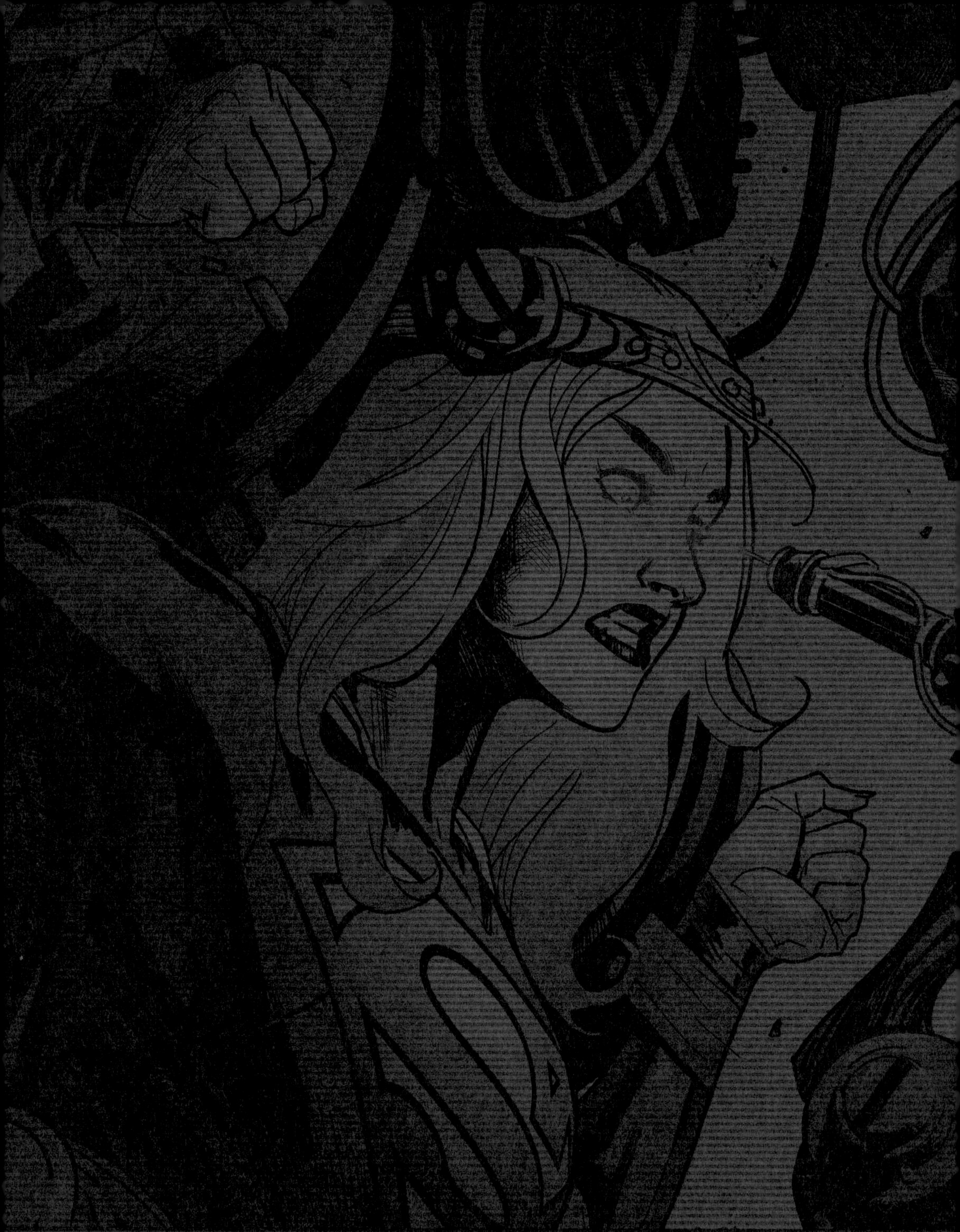

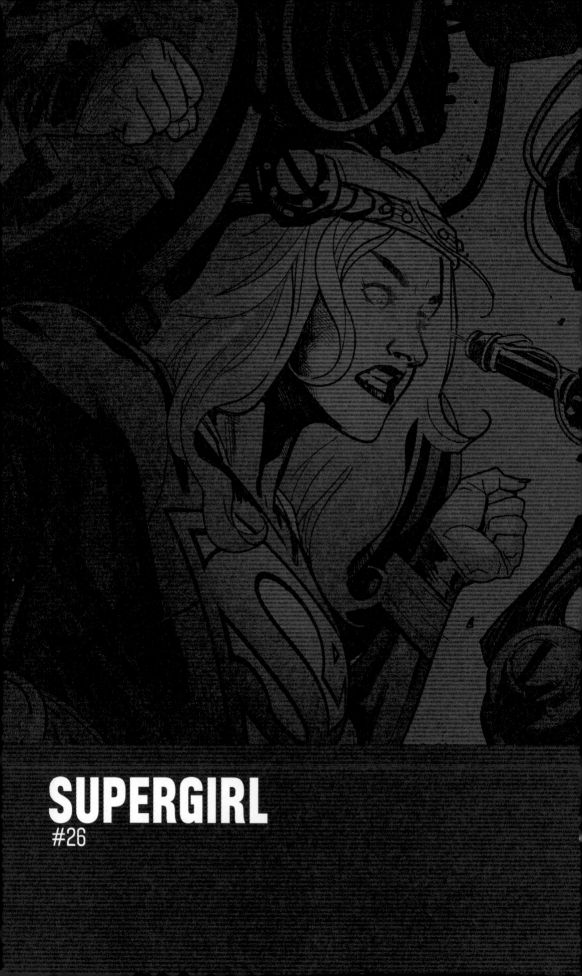

SUPERGIRL

#26

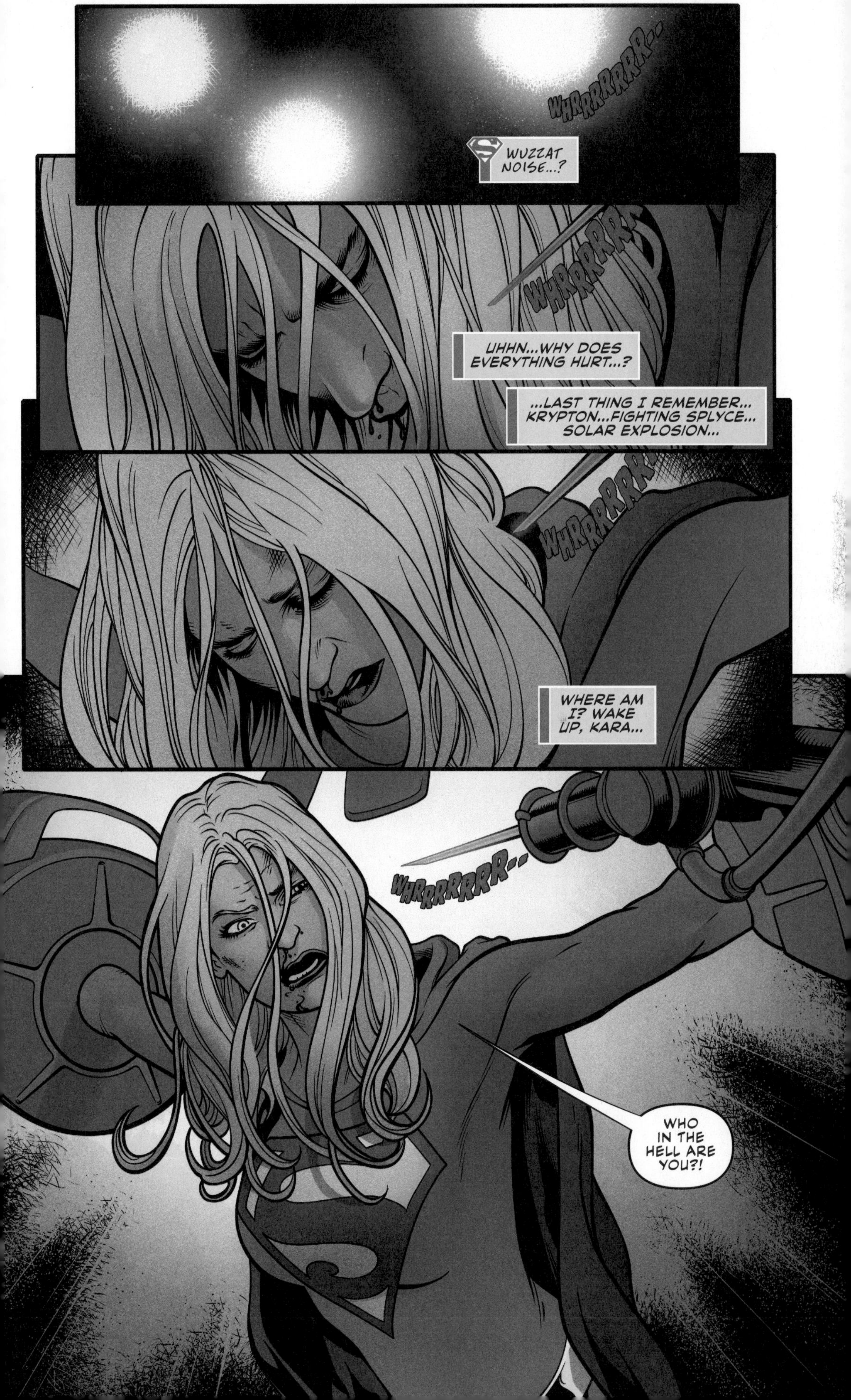
WHRRRRRRR--
WUZZAT NOISE...?
WHRRRRRR--
UHHN...WHY DOES EVERYTHING HURT...?
...LAST THING I REMEMBER... KRYPTON...FIGHTING SPLYCE... SOLAR EXPLOSION...
WHRRRRRRR--
WHERE AM I? WAKE UP, KARA...
WHRRRRRRR--
WHO IN THE HELL ARE YOU?!

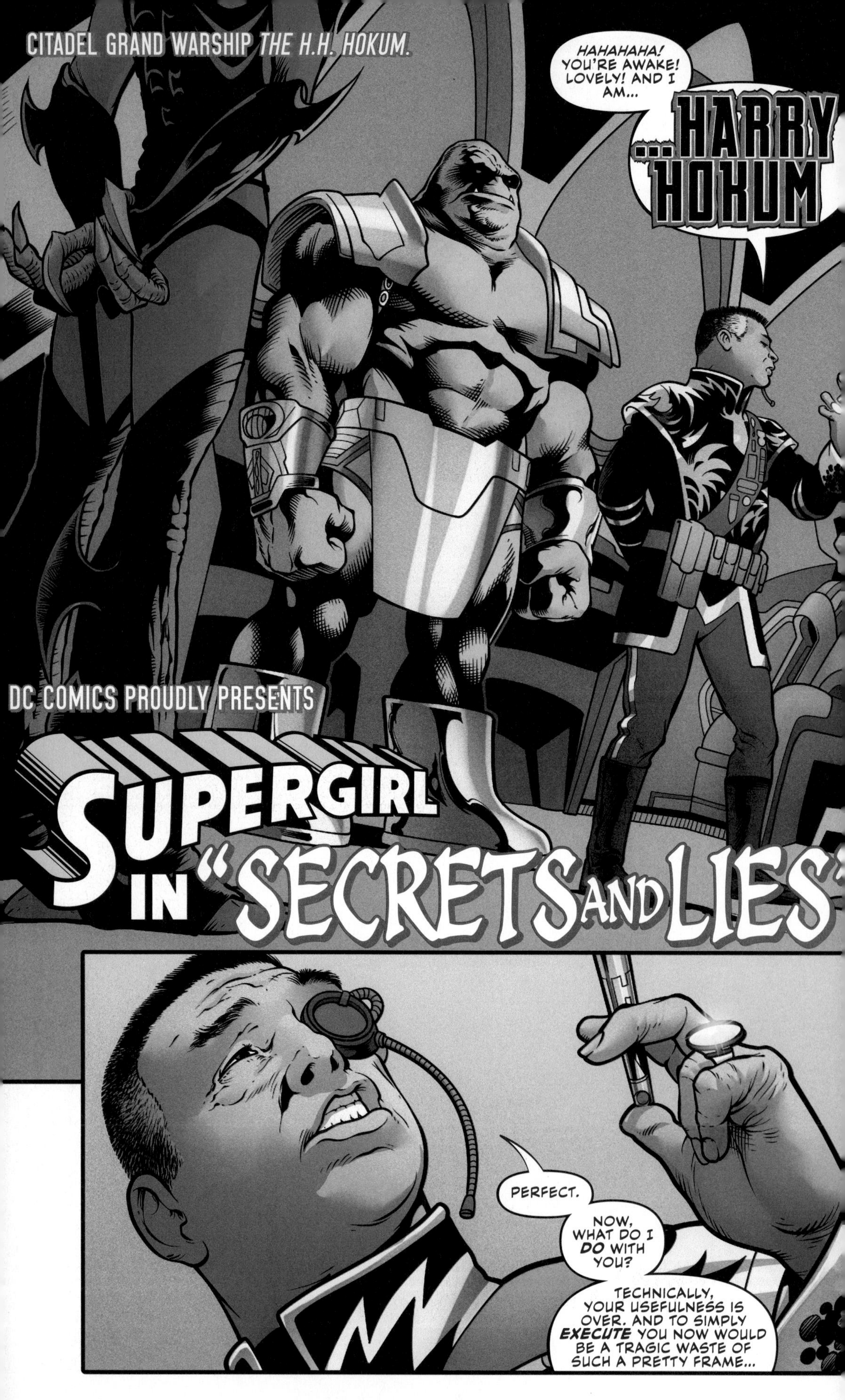
CITADEL GRAND WARSHIP *THE H.H. HOKUM.*
HAHAHAHA! YOU'RE AWAKE! LOVELY! AND I AM...
...HARRY HOKUM
DC COMICS PROUDLY PRESENTS
SUPERGIRL IN "SECRETS AND LIES"
PERFECT.
NOW, WHAT DO I *DO* WITH YOU?
TECHNICALLY, YOUR USEFULNESS IS OVER. AND TO SIMPLY *EXECUTE* YOU NOW WOULD BE A TRAGIC WASTE OF SUCH A PRETTY FRAME...

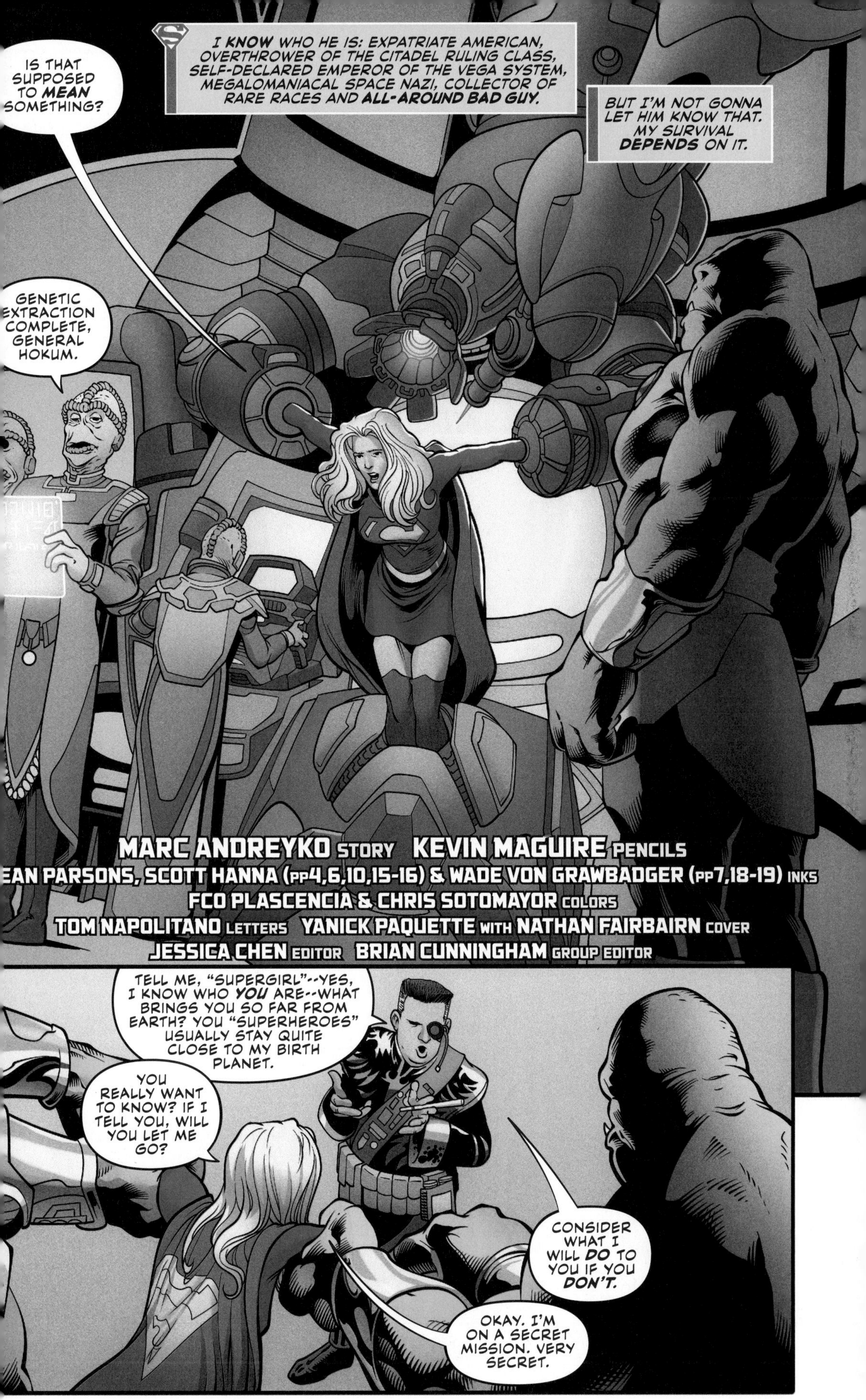
I KNOW WHO HE IS: EXPATRIATE AMERICAN, OVERTHROWER OF THE CITADEL RULING CLASS, SELF-DECLARED EMPEROR OF THE VEGA SYSTEM, MEGALOMANIACAL SPACE NAZI, COLLECTOR OF RARE RACES AND ALL-AROUND BAD GUY.
IS THAT SUPPOSED TO MEAN SOMETHING?
BUT I'M NOT GONNA LET HIM KNOW THAT. MY SURVIVAL DEPENDS ON IT.
GENETIC EXTRACTION COMPLETE, GENERAL HOKUM.
MARC ANDREYKO STORY KEVIN MAGUIRE PENCILS
EAN PARSONS, SCOTT HANNA (PP4,6,10,15-16) & WADE VON GRAWBADGER (PP7,18-19) INKS
FCO PLASCENCIA & CHRIS SOTOMAYOR COLORS
TOM NAPOLITANO LETTERS YANICK PAQUETTE WITH NATHAN FAIRBAIRN COVER
JESSICA CHEN EDITOR BRIAN CUNNINGHAM GROUP EDITOR
TELL ME, "SUPERGIRL"--YES, I KNOW WHO YOU ARE--WHAT BRINGS YOU SO FAR FROM EARTH? YOU "SUPERHEROES" USUALLY STAY QUITE CLOSE TO MY BIRTH PLANET.
YOU REALLY WANT TO KNOW? IF I TELL YOU, WILL YOU LET ME GO?
CONSIDER WHAT I WILL DO TO YOU IF YOU DON'T.
OKAY. I'M ON A SECRET MISSION. VERY SECRET.

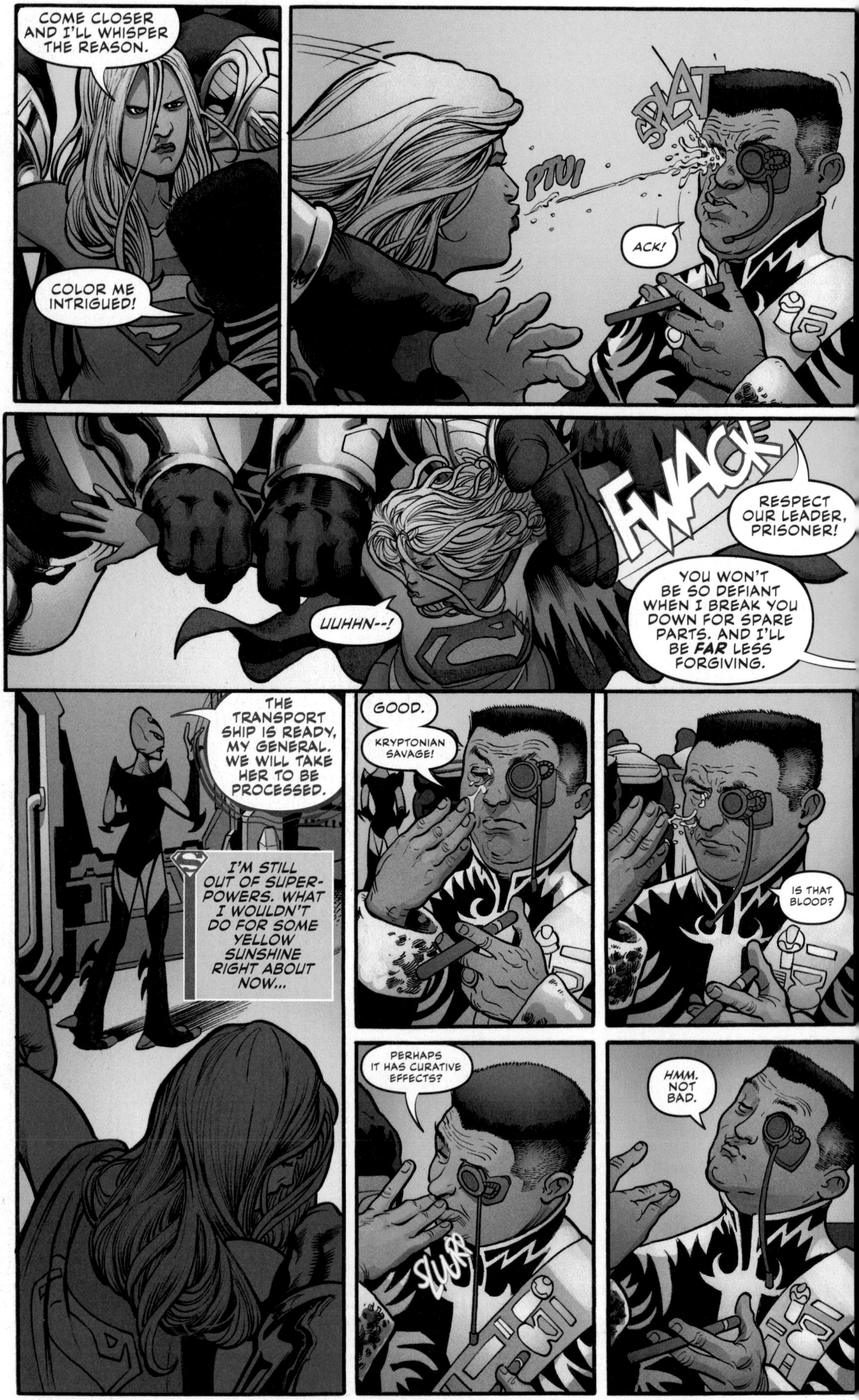
COME CLOSER AND I'LL WHISPER THE REASON.
COLOR ME INTRIGUED!
SPLAT
PTUI
ACK!
FWACK
RESPECT OUR LEADER, PRISONER!
UUHHN--!
YOU WON'T BE SO DEFIANT WHEN I BREAK YOU DOWN FOR SPARE PARTS. AND I'LL BE FAR LESS FORGIVING.
THE TRANSPORT SHIP IS READY, MY GENERAL. WE WILL TAKE HER TO BE PROCESSED.
I'M STILL OUT OF SUPER-POWERS. WHAT I WOULDN'T DO FOR SOME YELLOW SUNSHINE RIGHT ABOUT NOW...
GOOD.
KRYPTONIAN SAVAGE!
IS THAT BLOOD?
PERHAPS IT HAS CURATIVE EFFECTS?
SLURR
HMM. NOT BAD.

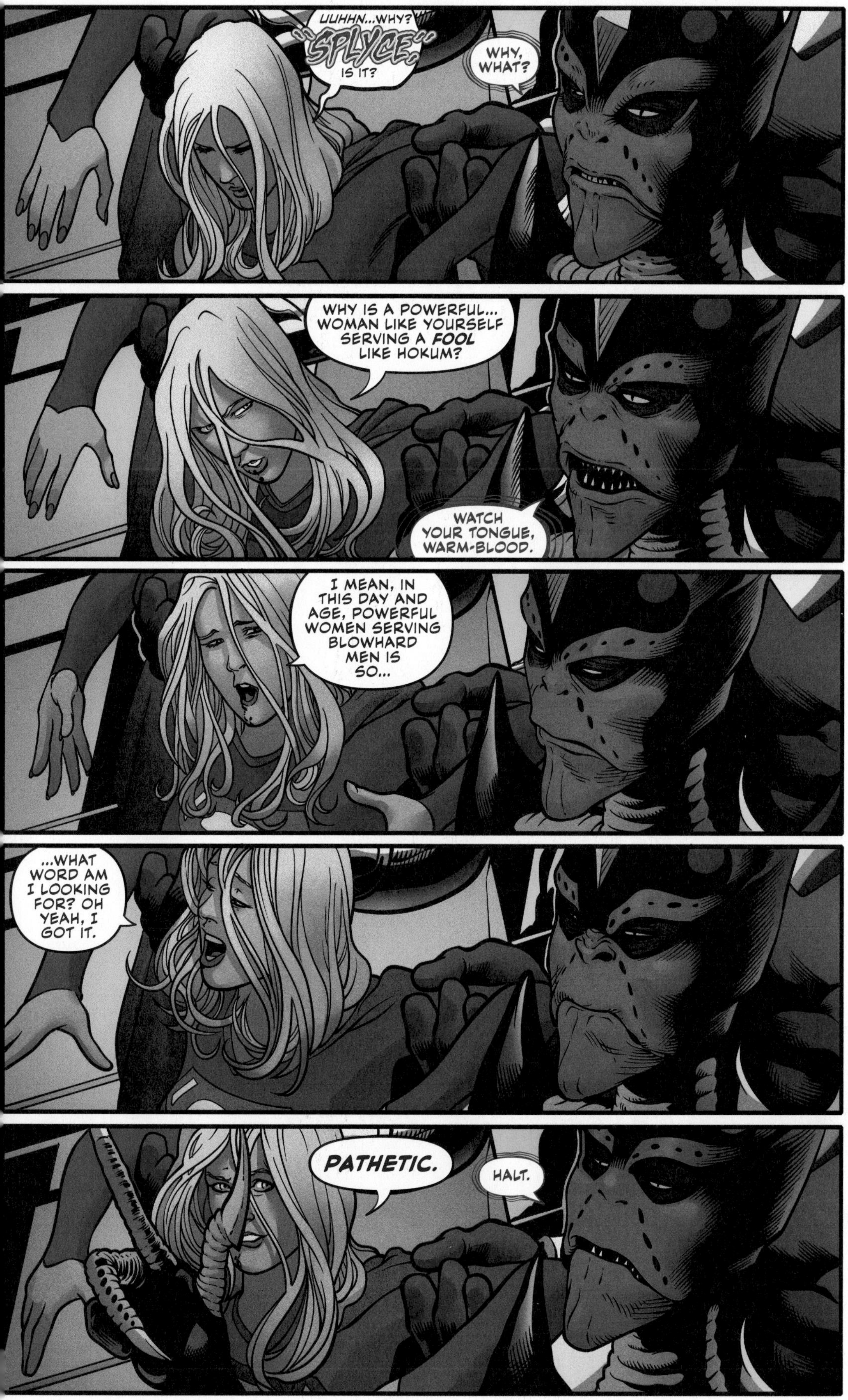
UUHHN...WHY? "SPLYCE," IS IT?
WHY, WHAT?
WHY IS A POWERFUL... WOMAN LIKE YOURSELF SERVING A FOOL LIKE HOKUM?
WATCH YOUR TONGUE, WARM-BLOOD.
I MEAN, IN THIS DAY AND AGE, POWERFUL WOMEN SERVING BLOWHARD MEN IS SO...
...WHAT WORD AM I LOOKING FOR? OH YEAH, I GOT IT.
PATHETIC.
HALT.

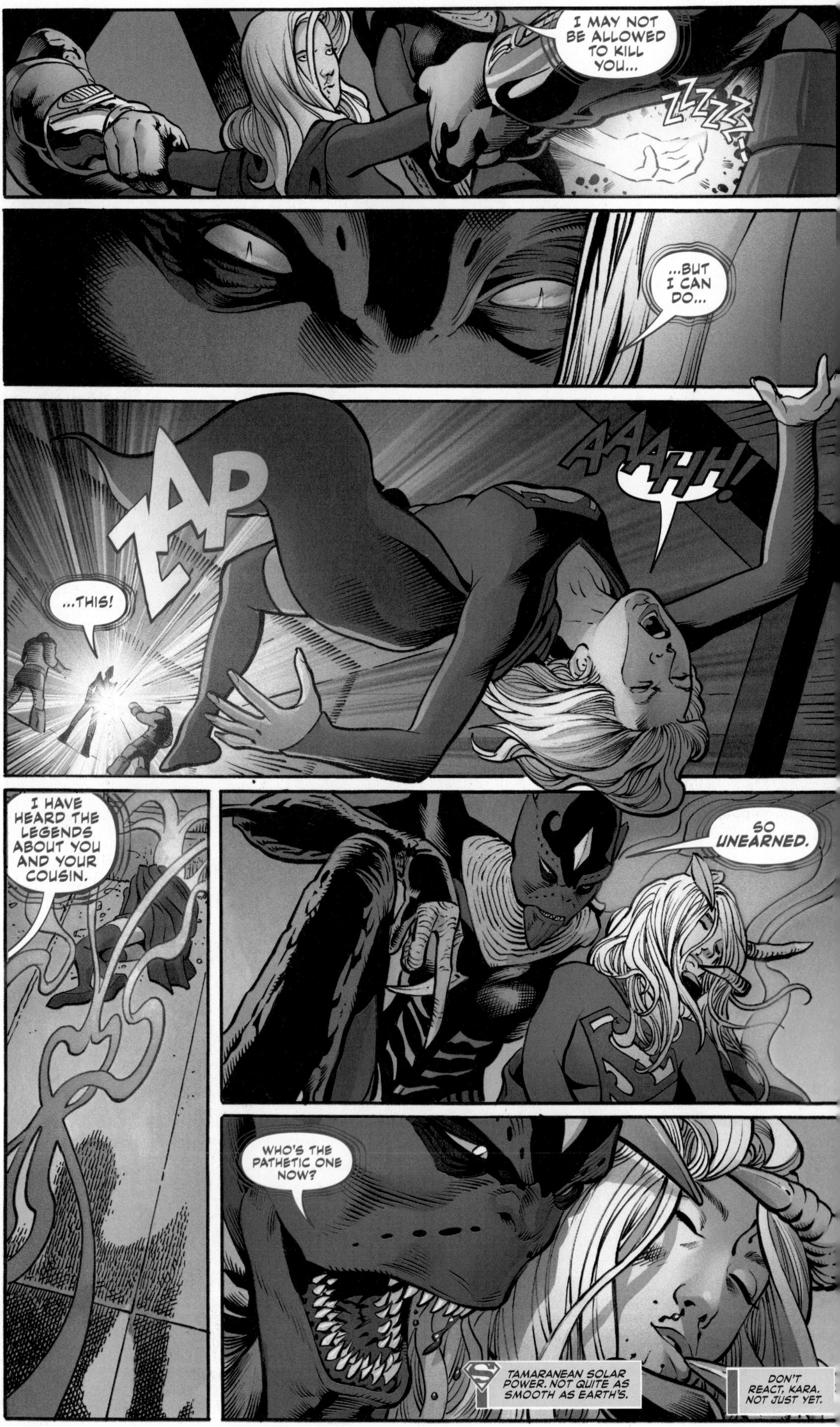

I MAY NOT BE ALLOWED TO KILL YOU...
ZZZZZZZ
...BUT I CAN DO...
ZAP
AAAHH!
...THIS!
I HAVE HEARD THE LEGENDS ABOUT YOU AND YOUR COUSIN.
SO UNEARNED.
WHO'S THE PATHETIC ONE NOW?
TAMARANEAN SOLAR POWER. NOT QUITE AS SMOOTH AS EARTH'S.
DON'T REACT, KARA. NOT JUST YET.

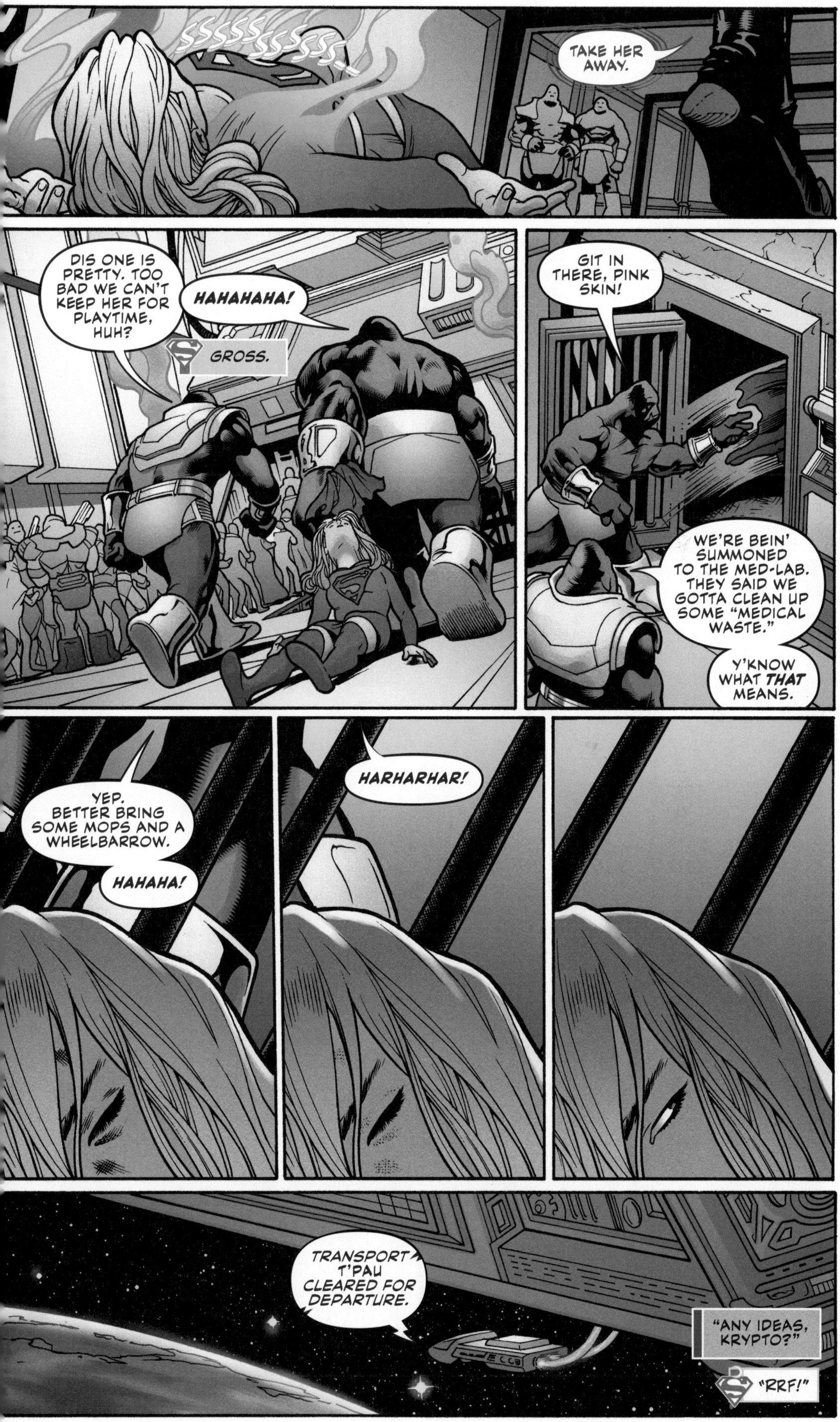
SSSSSSSSSSSS...
TAKE HER AWAY.
DIS ONE IS PRETTY. TOO BAD WE CAN'T KEEP HER FOR PLAYTIME, HUH?
HAHAHAHA!
GROSS.
GIT IN THERE, PINK SKIN!
WE'RE BEIN' SUMMONED TO THE MED-LAB. THEY SAID WE GOTTA CLEAN UP SOME "MEDICAL WASTE."
Y'KNOW WHAT THAT MEANS.
YEP. BETTER BRING SOME MOPS AND A WHEELBARROW.
HAHAHA!
HARHARHAR!
TRANSPORT T'PAU CLEARED FOR DEPARTURE.
"ANY IDEAS, KRYPTO?"
"RRF!"

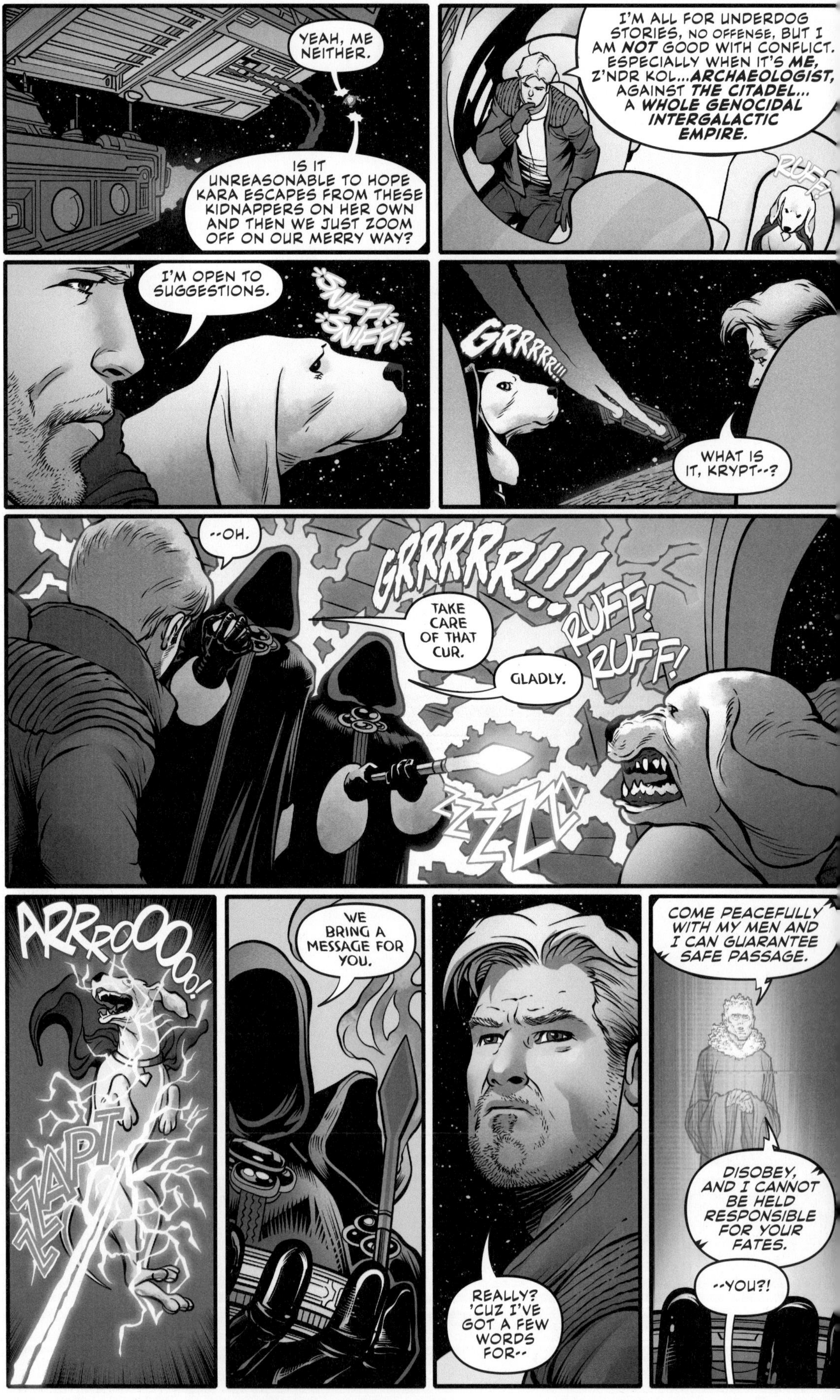
YEAH, ME NEITHER.
IS IT UNREASONABLE TO HOPE KARA ESCAPES FROM THESE KIDNAPPERS ON HER OWN AND THEN WE JUST ZOOM OFF ON OUR MERRY WAY?
I'M ALL FOR UNDERDOG STORIES, NO OFFENSE, BUT I AM NOT GOOD WITH CONFLICT. ESPECIALLY WHEN IT'S ME, Z'NDR KOL...ARCHAEOLOGIST, AGAINST THE CITADEL... A WHOLE GENOCIDAL INTERGALACTIC EMPIRE.
RUFF?
I'M OPEN TO SUGGESTIONS.
SNIFF! *SNIFF!*
GRRRRR!!!
WHAT IS IT, KRYPT--?
--OH.
GRRRRR!!!!
TAKE CARE OF THAT CUR.
RUFF! RUFF!
GLADLY.
ZZZZK!
ARRROOOOooo!
ZZAPT
WE BRING A MESSAGE FOR YOU.
REALLY? 'CUZ I'VE GOT A FEW WORDS FOR--
COME PEACEFULLY WITH MY MEN AND I CAN GUARANTEE SAFE PASSAGE.
DISOBEY, AND I CANNOT BE HELD RESPONSIBLE FOR YOUR FATES.
--YOU?!

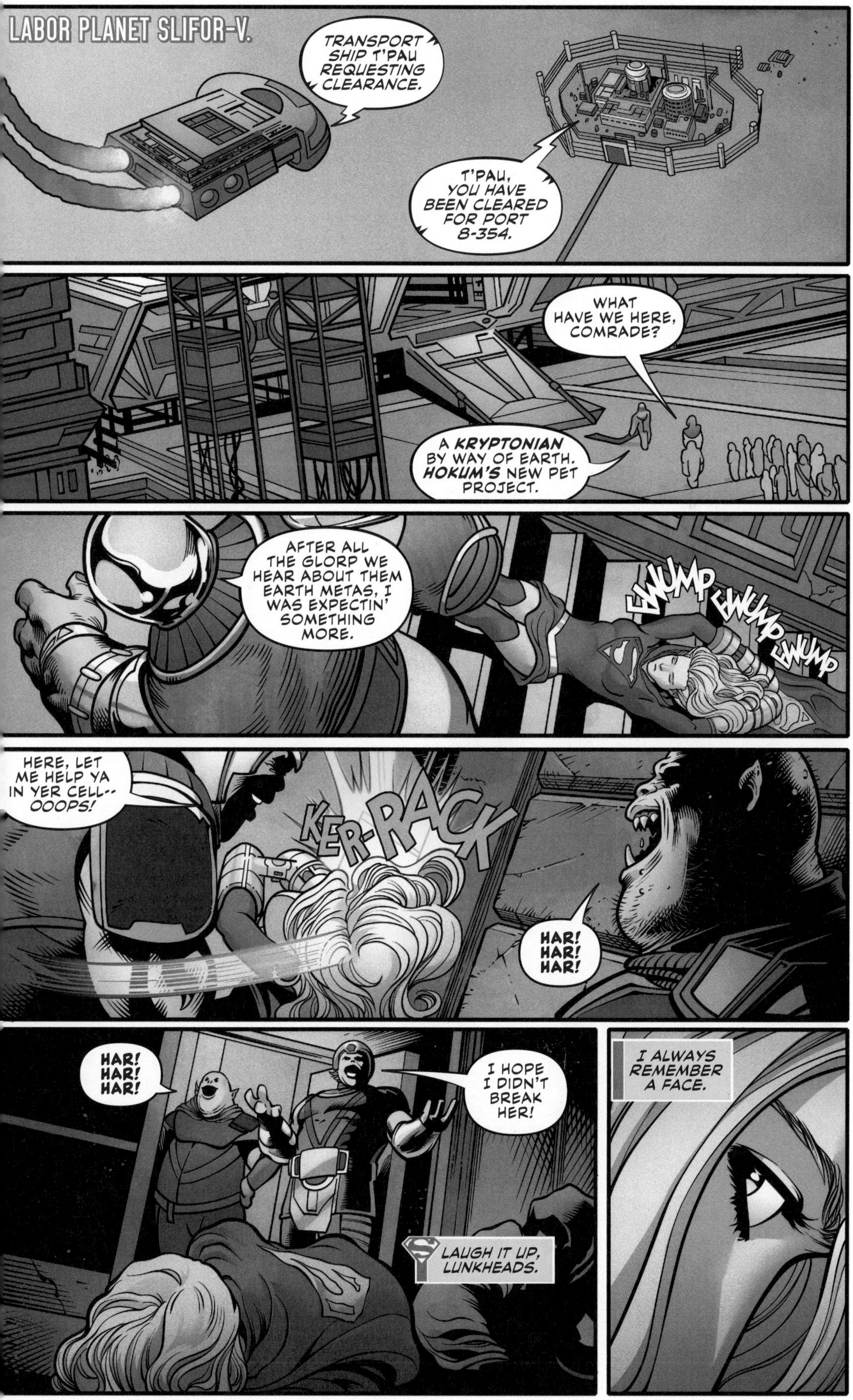
LABOR PLANET SLIFOR-V.
TRANSPORT SHIP T'PAU REQUESTING CLEARANCE.
T'PAU, YOU HAVE BEEN CLEARED FOR PORT 8-354.
WHAT HAVE WE HERE, COMRADE?
A KRYPTONIAN BY WAY OF EARTH. HOKUM'S NEW PET PROJECT.
AFTER ALL THE GLORP WE HEAR ABOUT THEM EARTH METAS, I WAS EXPECTIN' SOMETHING MORE.
FWUMP FWUMP FWUMP
HERE, LET ME HELP YA IN YER CELL-- OOOPS!
KER-RACK
HAR! HAR! HAR!
HAR! HAR! HAR!
I HOPE I DIDN'T BREAK HER!
LAUGH IT UP, LUNKHEADS.
I ALWAYS REMEMBER A FACE.

=COUGH= =COUGH= TELL US, DID YOU SEE OUR MEN? OUR HUSBANDS, OUR SONS, THEY TOOK THEM FROM US!

UM, HELLO.

MY NAME IS KARA...

KA-RA?

YES. AND I'M HERE TO HELP YOU.

MISS, THEY STOPPED GIVING US FOOD THREE DAYS AGO.

DEY KILLED MY PAPA...

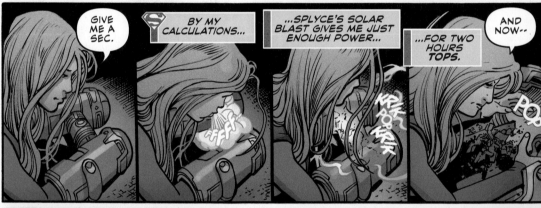

GIVE ME A SEC.

BY MY CALCULATIONS...

...SPLYCE'S SOLAR BLAST GIVES ME JUST ENOUGH POWER...

...FOR TWO HOURS TOPS.

AND NOW--

FFFFFT

KR/K POK KRK

POP

--WHO'S READY TO GET OUT OF HERE?

OOOOOHHHH!

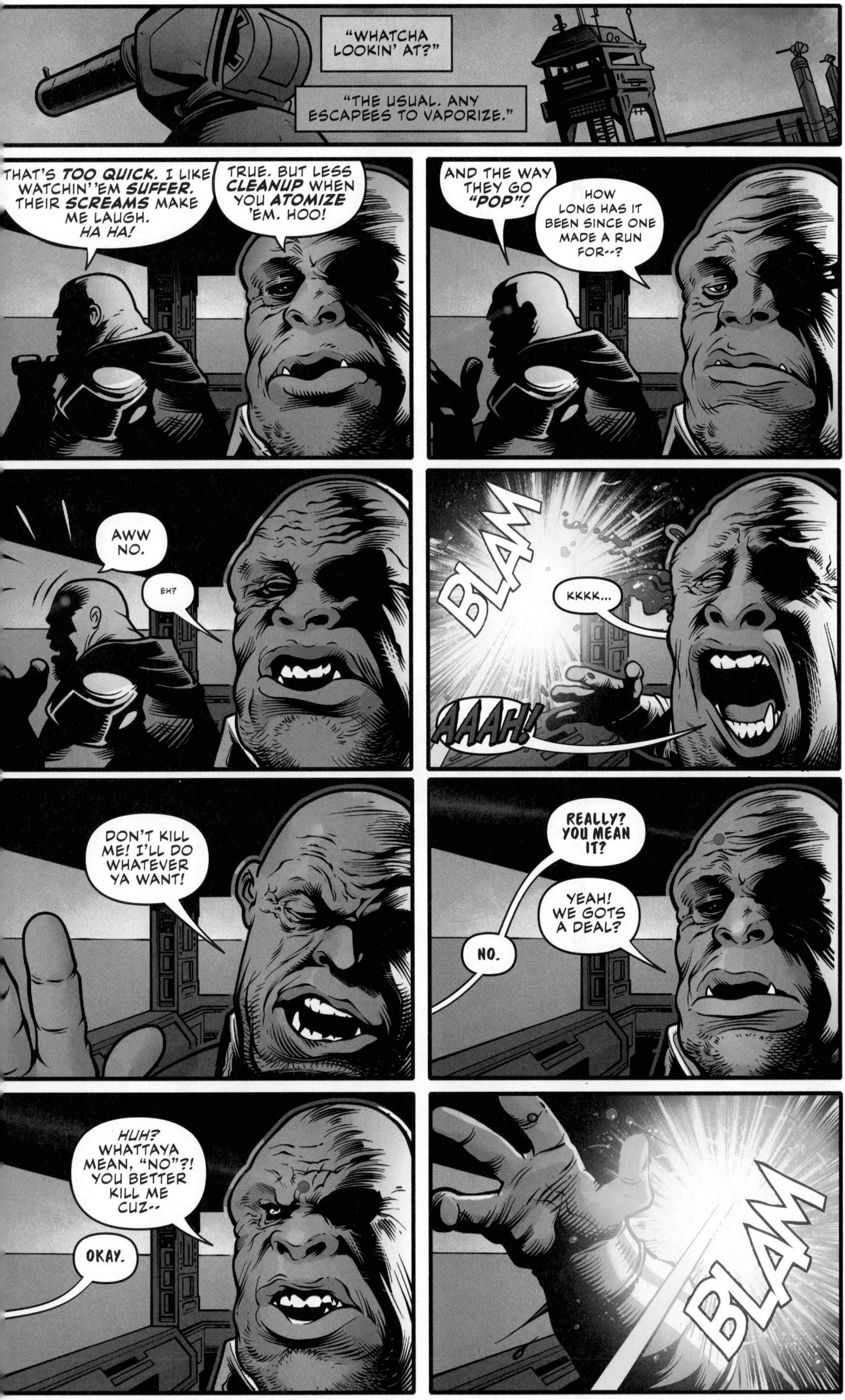

"WHATCHA LOOKIN' AT?"
"THE USUAL. ANY ESCAPEES TO VAPORIZE."
THAT'S TOO QUICK. I LIKE WATCHIN' 'EM SUFFER. THEIR SCREAMS MAKE ME LAUGH. HA HA!
TRUE. BUT LESS CLEANUP WHEN YOU ATOMIZE 'EM. HOO!
AND THE WAY THEY GO "POP"!
HOW LONG HAS IT BEEN SINCE ONE MADE A RUN FOR--?
AWW NO.
EH?
BLAM
KKKK...
AAAH!
DON'T KILL ME! I'LL DO WHATEVER YA WANT!
REALLY? YOU MEAN IT?
YEAH! WE GOTS A DEAL?
NO.
HUH? WHATTAYA MEAN, "NO"?! YOU BETTER KILL ME CUZ--
OKAY.
BLAM

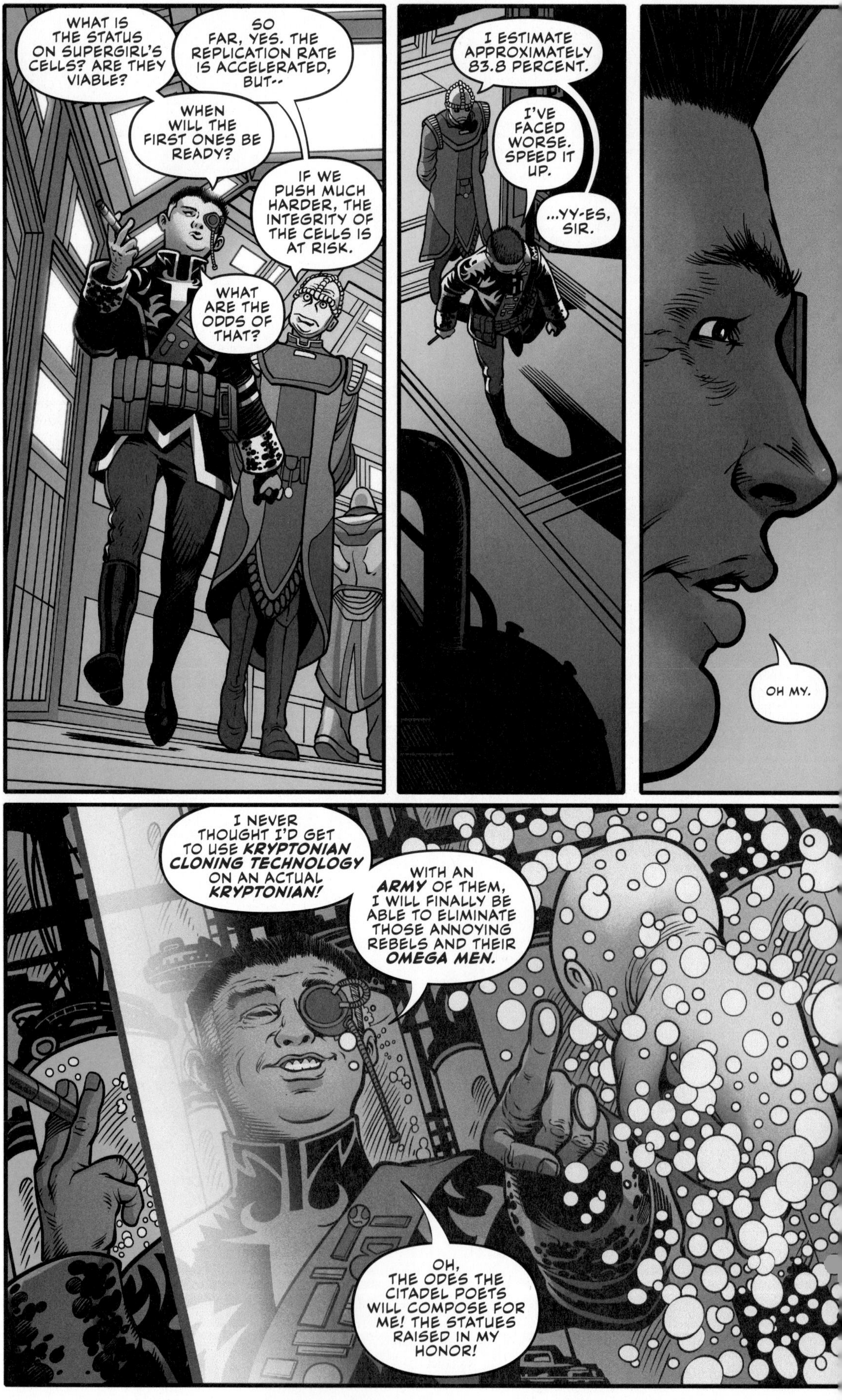
WHAT IS THE STATUS ON SUPERGIRL'S CELLS? ARE THEY VIABLE?
SO FAR, YES. THE REPLICATION RATE IS ACCELERATED, BUT--
WHEN WILL THE FIRST ONES BE READY?
IF WE PUSH MUCH HARDER, THE INTEGRITY OF THE CELLS IS AT RISK.
WHAT ARE THE ODDS OF THAT?
I ESTIMATE APPROXIMATELY 83.8 PERCENT.
I'VE FACED WORSE. SPEED IT UP.
...YY-ES, SIR.
OH MY.
I NEVER THOUGHT I'D GET TO USE ***KRYPTONIAN CLONING TECHNOLOGY*** ON AN ACTUAL ***KRYPTONIAN!***
WITH AN ***ARMY*** OF THEM, I WILL FINALLY BE ABLE TO ELIMINATE THOSE ANNOYING REBELS AND THEIR ***OMEGA MEN.***
OH, THE ODES THE CITADEL POETS WILL COMPOSE FOR ME! THE STATUES RAISED IN MY HONOR!

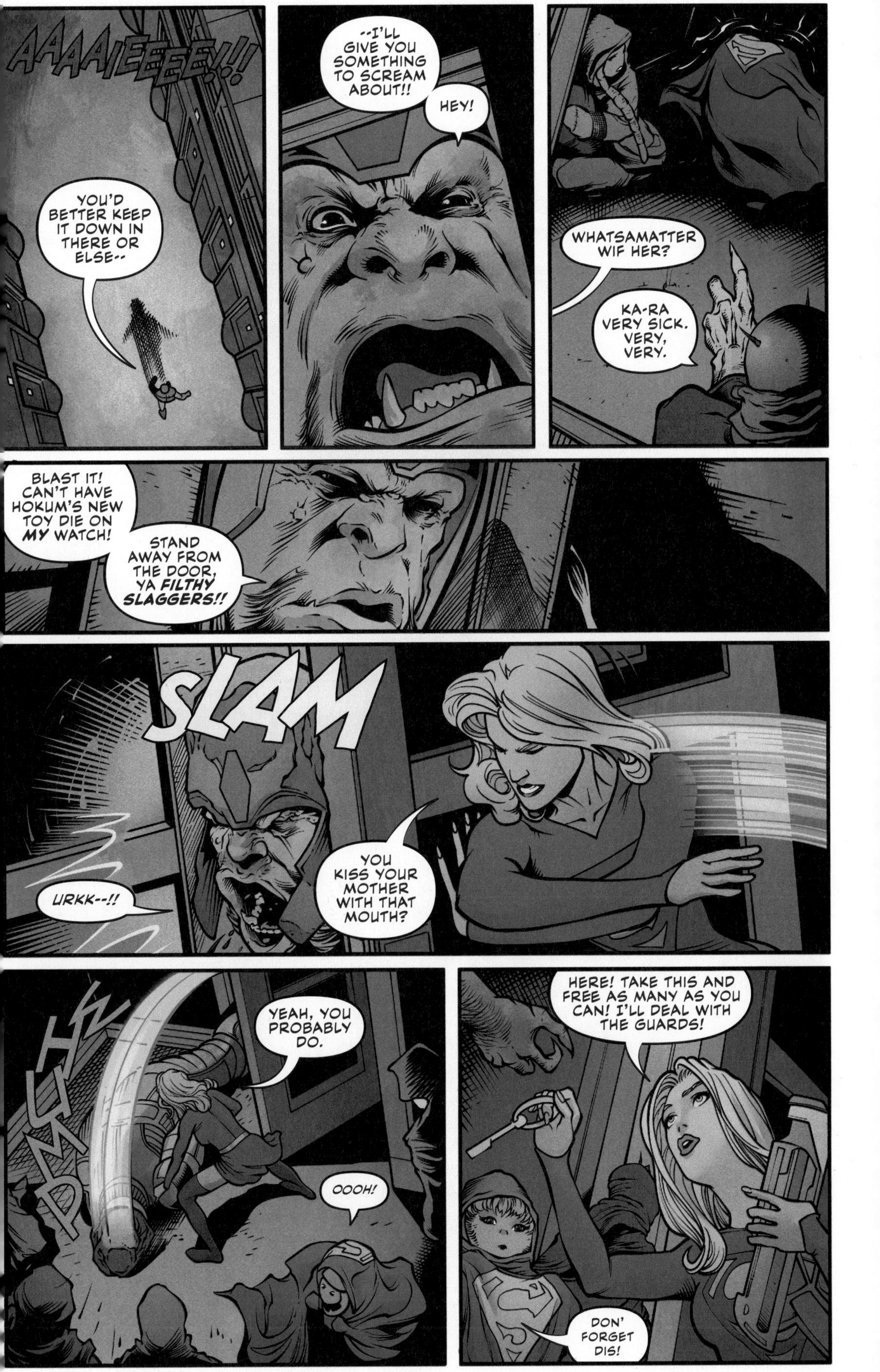
AAAAIEEEE!!!
YOU'D BETTER KEEP IT DOWN IN THERE OR ELSE--
--I'LL GIVE YOU SOMETHING TO SCREAM ABOUT!!
HEY!
WHATSAMATTER WIF HER?
KA-RA VERY SICK. VERY, VERY.
BLAST IT! CAN'T HAVE HOKUM'S NEW TOY DIE ON MY WATCH!
STAND AWAY FROM THE DOOR, YA FILTHY SLAGGERS!!
SLAM
URKK--!!
YOU KISS YOUR MOTHER WITH THAT MOUTH?
WHUMP
YEAH, YOU PROBABLY DO.
OOOH!
HERE! TAKE THIS AND FREE AS MANY AS YOU CAN! I'LL DEAL WITH THE GUARDS!
DON' FORGET DIS!

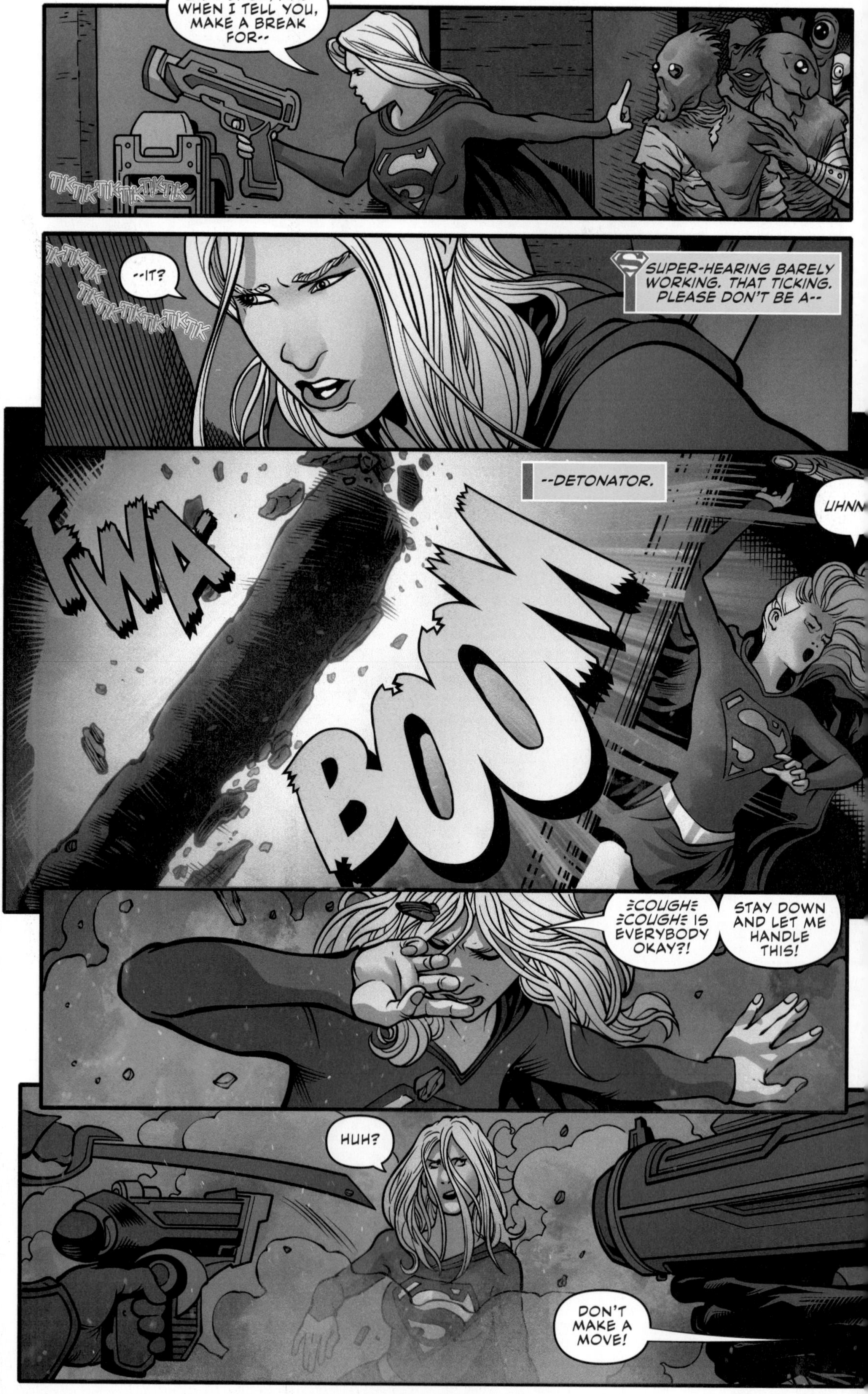
OKAY, STAY BACK, AND WHEN I TELL YOU, MAKE A BREAK FOR--
TIKTIKTIKTIKTIKTIK
TIKTIKTIK
--IT?
TIKTIKTIKTIKTIKTIK
SUPER-HEARING BARELY WORKING. THAT TICKING. PLEASE DON'T BE A--
--DETONATOR.
FWA
BOOM
UHNN
COUGH COUGH IS EVERYBODY OKAY?!
STAY DOWN AND LET ME HANDLE THIS!
HUH?
DON'T MAKE A MOVE!

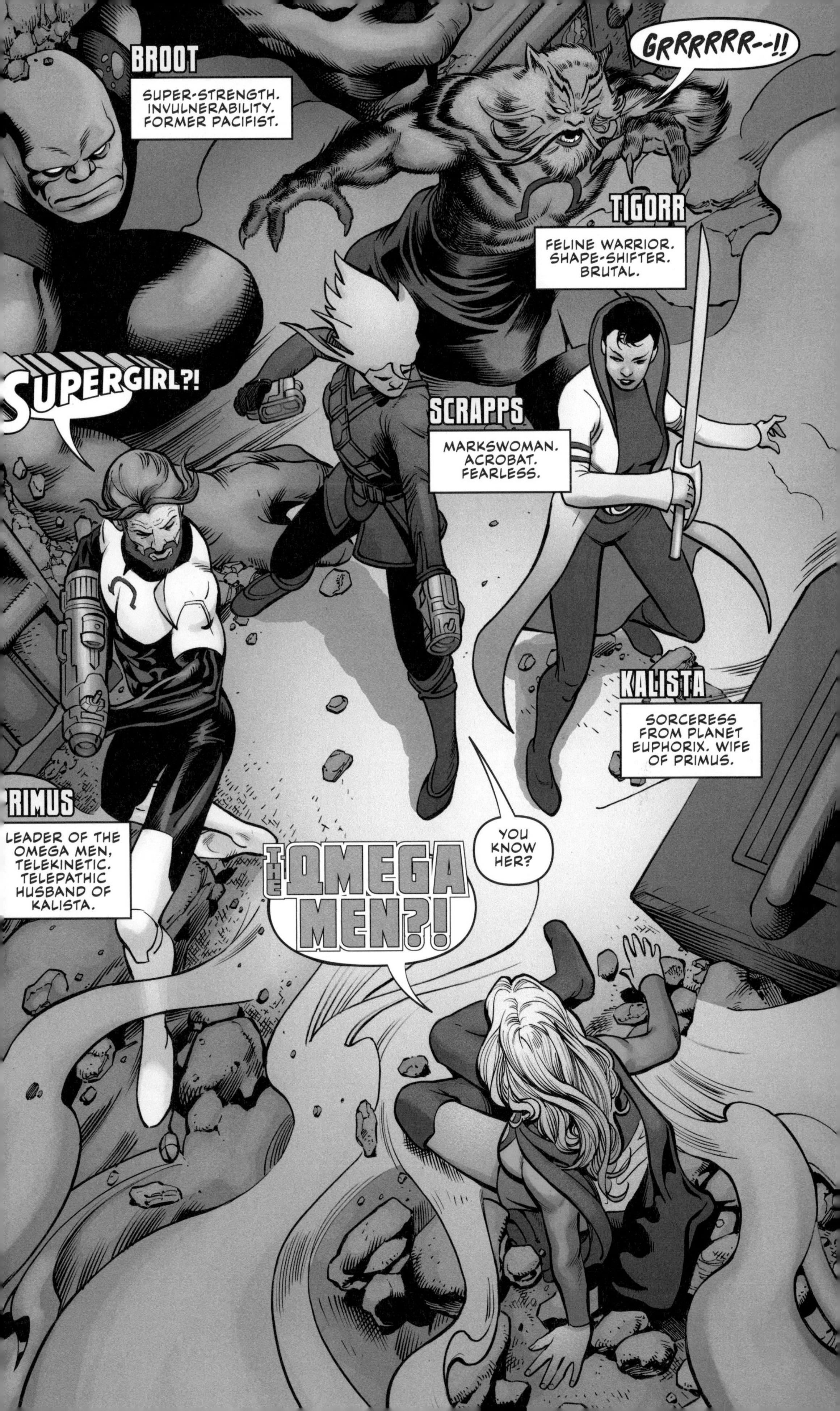
BROOT
SUPER-STRENGTH. INVULNERABILITY. FORMER PACIFIST.
GRRRRRR--!!
TIGORR
FELINE WARRIOR. SHAPE-SHIFTER. BRUTAL.
SUPERGIRL?!
SCRAPPS
MARKSWOMAN. ACROBAT. FEARLESS.
KALISTA
SORCERESS FROM PLANET EUPHORIX. WIFE OF PRIMUS.
RIMUS
LEADER OF THE OMEGA MEN, TELEKINETIC. TELEPATHIC HUSBAND OF KALISTA.
YOU KNOW HER?
THE OMEGA MEN?!

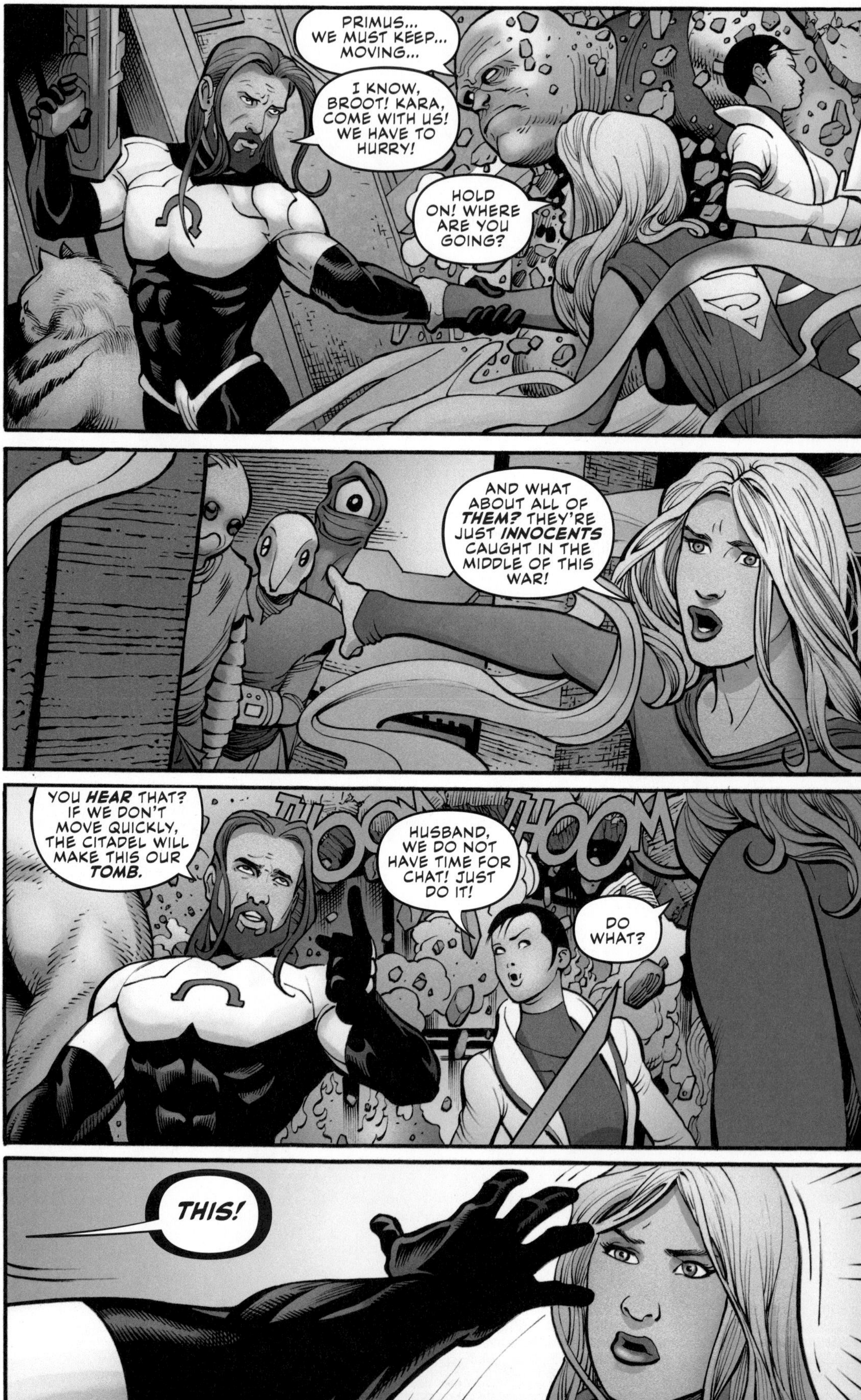
PRIMUS... WE MUST KEEP... MOVING...
I KNOW, BROOT! KARA, COME WITH US! WE HAVE TO HURRY!
HOLD ON! WHERE ARE YOU GOING?
AND WHAT ABOUT ALL OF ***THEM?*** THEY'RE JUST ***INNOCENTS*** CAUGHT IN THE MIDDLE OF THIS WAR!
THOOM THOOM
YOU ***HEAR*** THAT? IF WE DON'T MOVE QUICKLY, THE CITADEL WILL MAKE THIS OUR ***TOMB.***
HUSBAND, WE DO NOT HAVE TIME FOR CHAT! JUST DO IT!
DO WHAT?
THIS!

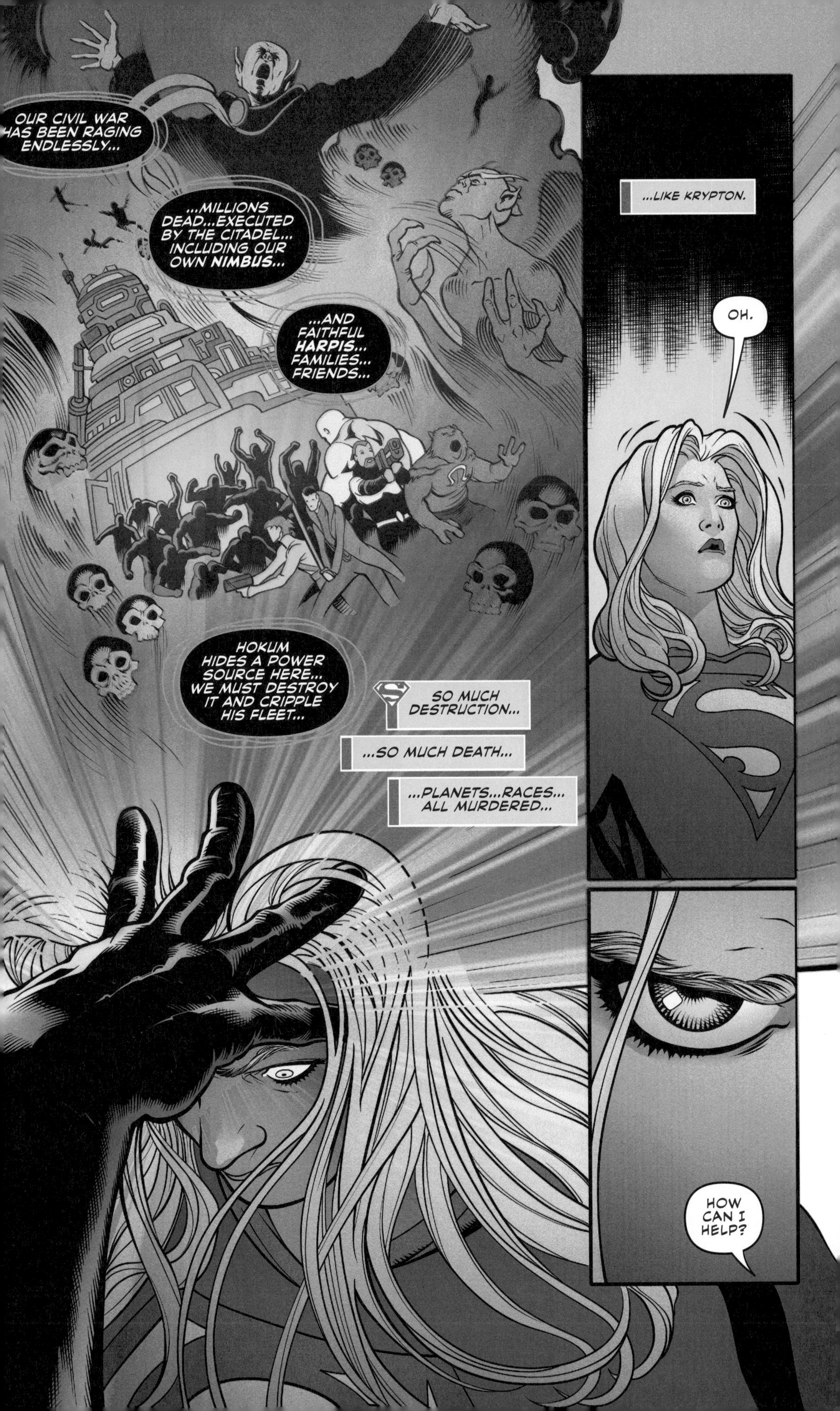
OUR CIVIL WAR HAS BEEN RAGING ENDLESSLY...
...MILLIONS DEAD...EXECUTED BY THE CITADEL... INCLUDING OUR OWN NIMBUS...
...AND FAITHFUL HARPIS... FAMILIES... FRIENDS...
HOKUM HIDES A POWER SOURCE HERE... WE MUST DESTROY IT AND CRIPPLE HIS FLEET...
SO MUCH DESTRUCTION...
...SO MUCH DEATH...
...PLANETS...RACES... ALL MURDERED...
...LIKE KRYPTON.
OH.
HOW CAN I HELP?

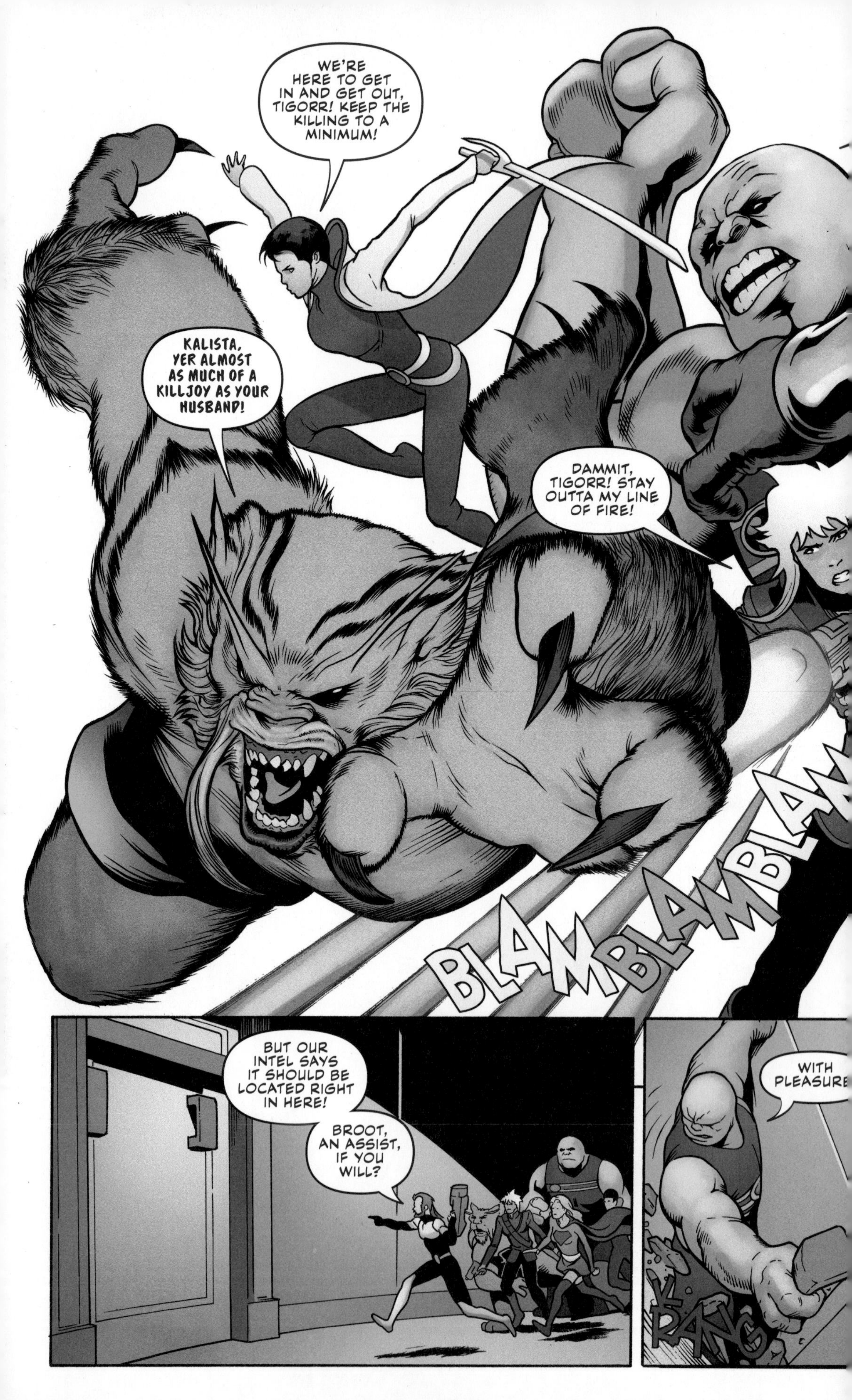
WE'RE HERE TO GET IN AND GET OUT, TIGORR! KEEP THE KILLING TO A MINIMUM!
KALISTA, YER ALMOST AS MUCH OF A KILLJOY AS YOUR HUSBAND!
DAMMIT, TIGORR! STAY OUTTA MY LINE OF FIRE!
BLAMBLAMBLAM
BUT OUR INTEL SAYS IT SHOULD BE LOCATED RIGHT IN HERE!
BROOT, AN ASSIST, IF YOU WILL?
WITH PLEASURE

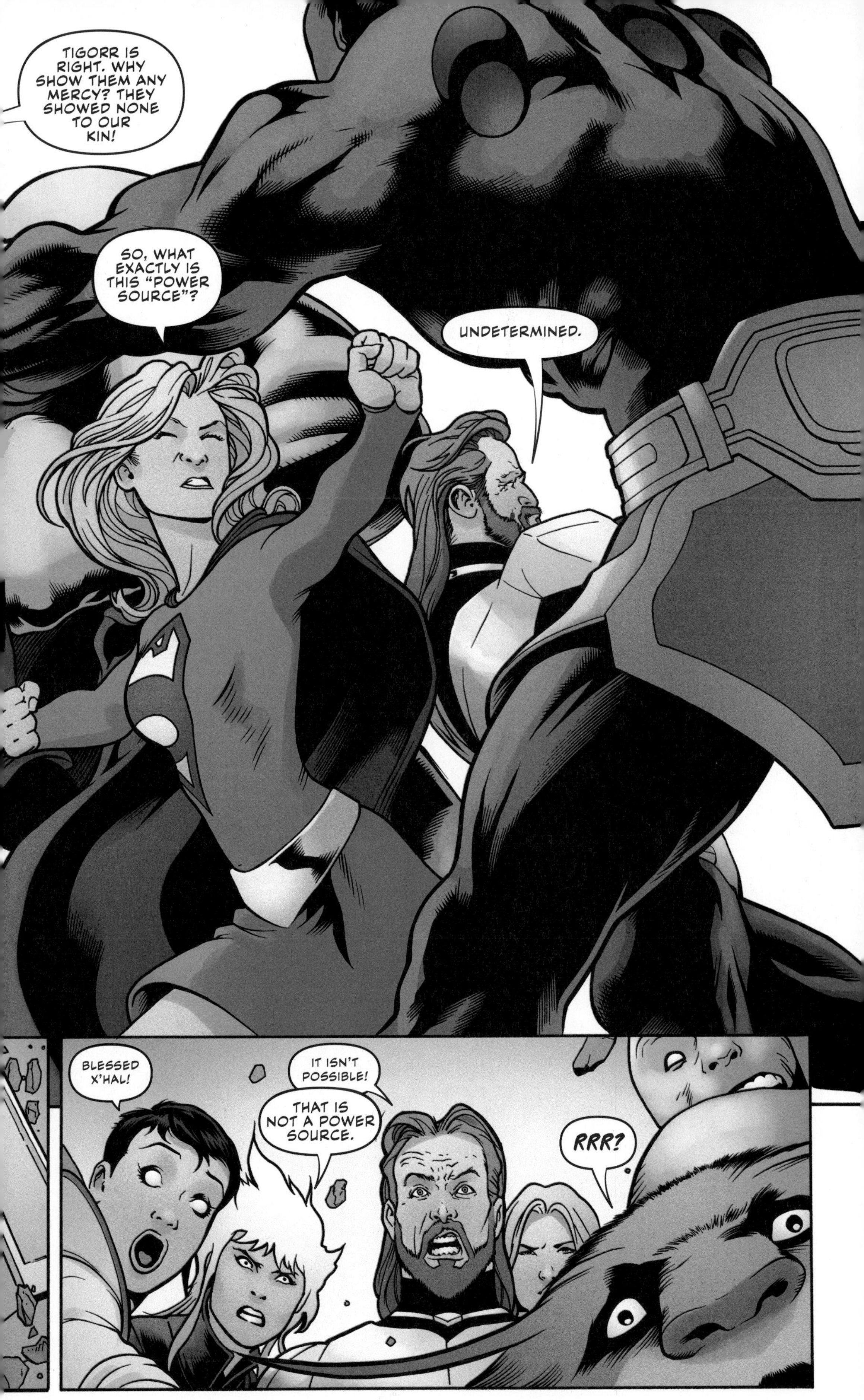
TIGORR IS RIGHT. WHY SHOW THEM ANY MERCY? THEY SHOWED NONE TO OUR KIN!
SO, WHAT EXACTLY IS THIS "POWER SOURCE"?
UNDETERMINED.
BLESSED X'HAL!
IT ISN'T POSSIBLE!
THAT IS NOT A POWER SOURCE.
RRR?

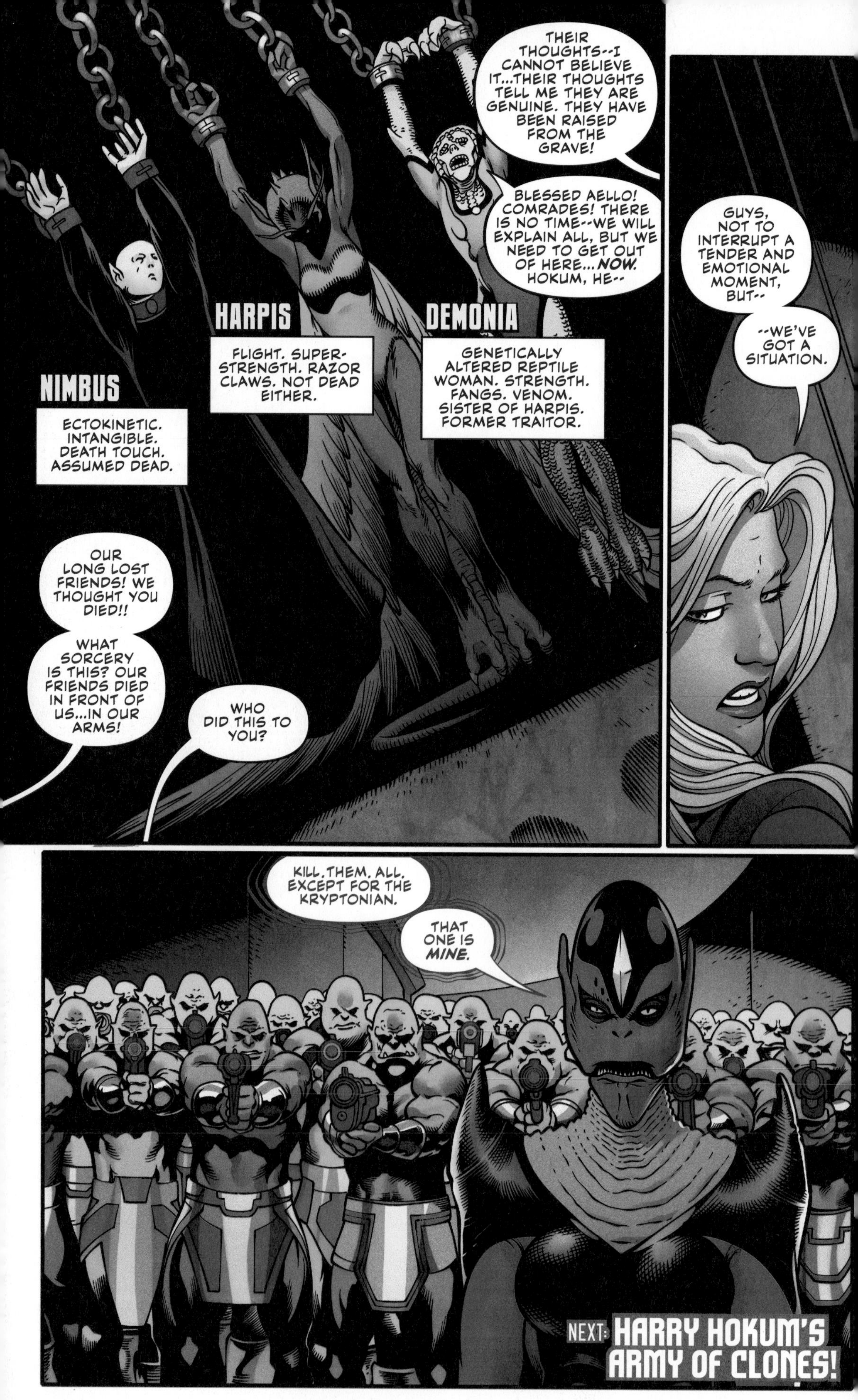
THEIR THOUGHTS--I CANNOT BELIEVE IT...THEIR THOUGHTS TELL ME THEY ARE GENUINE. THEY HAVE BEEN RAISED FROM THE GRAVE!
BLESSED AELLO! COMRADES! THERE IS NO TIME--WE WILL EXPLAIN ALL, BUT WE NEED TO GET OUT OF HERE...NOW. HOKUM, HE--
HARPIS
FLIGHT. SUPER-STRENGTH. RAZOR CLAWS. NOT DEAD EITHER.
DEMONIA
GENETICALLY ALTERED REPTILE WOMAN. STRENGTH. FANGS. VENOM. SISTER OF HARPIS. FORMER TRAITOR.
NIMBUS
ECTOKINETIC. INTANGIBLE. DEATH TOUCH. ASSUMED DEAD.
OUR LONG LOST FRIENDS! WE THOUGHT YOU DIED!!
WHAT SORCERY IS THIS? OUR FRIENDS DIED IN FRONT OF US...IN OUR ARMS!
WHO DID THIS TO YOU?
GUYS, NOT TO INTERRUPT A TENDER AND EMOTIONAL MOMENT, BUT--
--WE'VE GOT A SITUATION.
KILL. THEM. ALL. EXCEPT FOR THE KRYPTONIAN.
THAT ONE IS MINE.
NEXT: HARRY HOKUM'S ARMY OF CLONES!

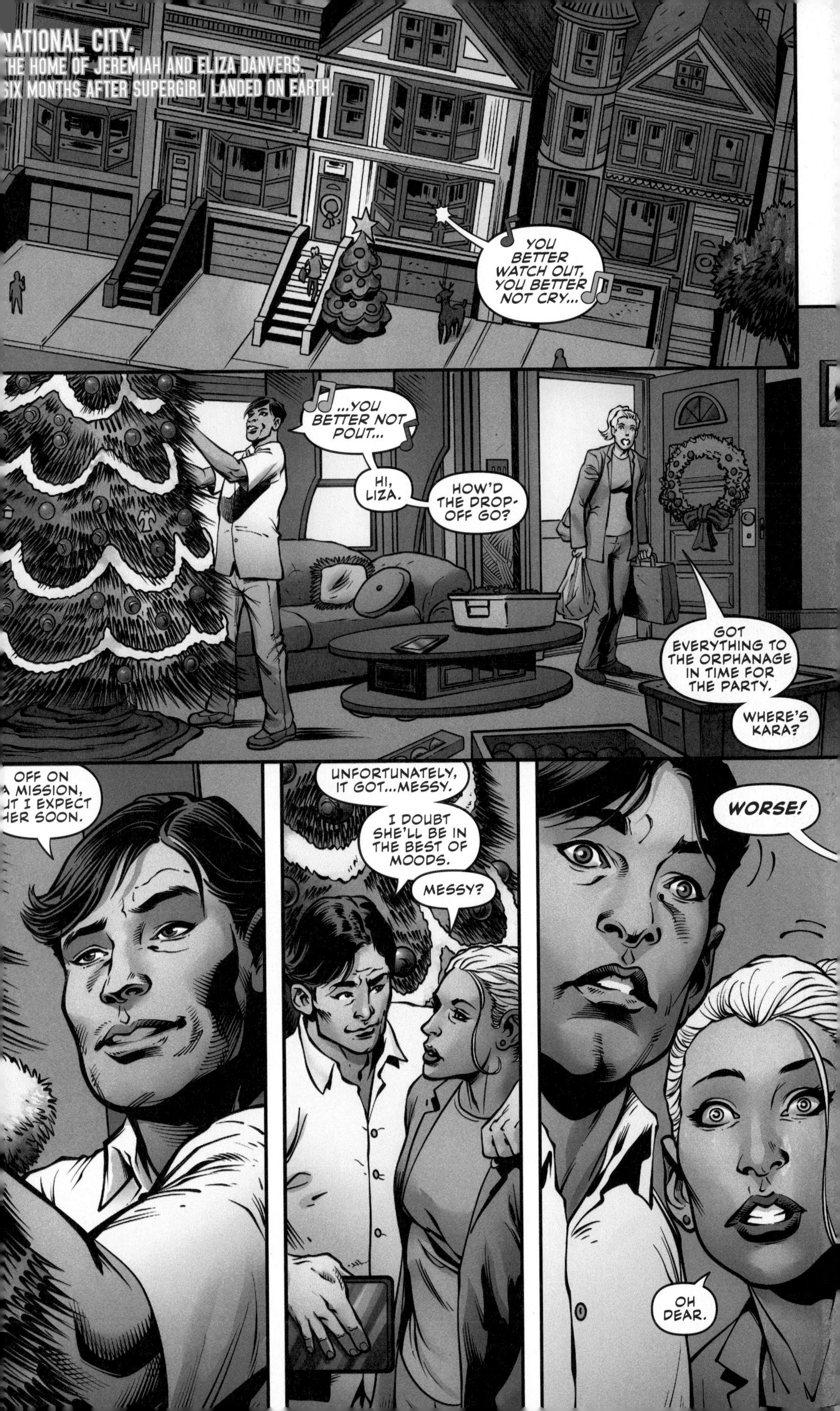
NATIONAL CITY.
THE HOME OF JEREMIAH AND ELIZA DANVERS.
SIX MONTHS AFTER SUPERGIRL LANDED ON EARTH.
YOU BETTER WATCH OUT, YOU BETTER NOT CRY...
...YOU BETTER NOT POUT...
HI, LIZA.
HOW'D THE DROP-OFF GO?
GOT EVERYTHING TO THE ORPHANAGE IN TIME FOR THE PARTY.
WHERE'S KARA?
OFF ON A MISSION, BUT I EXPECT HER SOON.
UNFORTUNATELY, IT GOT...MESSY.
I DOUBT SHE'LL BE IN THE BEST OF MOODS.
MESSY?
WORSE!
OH DEAR.

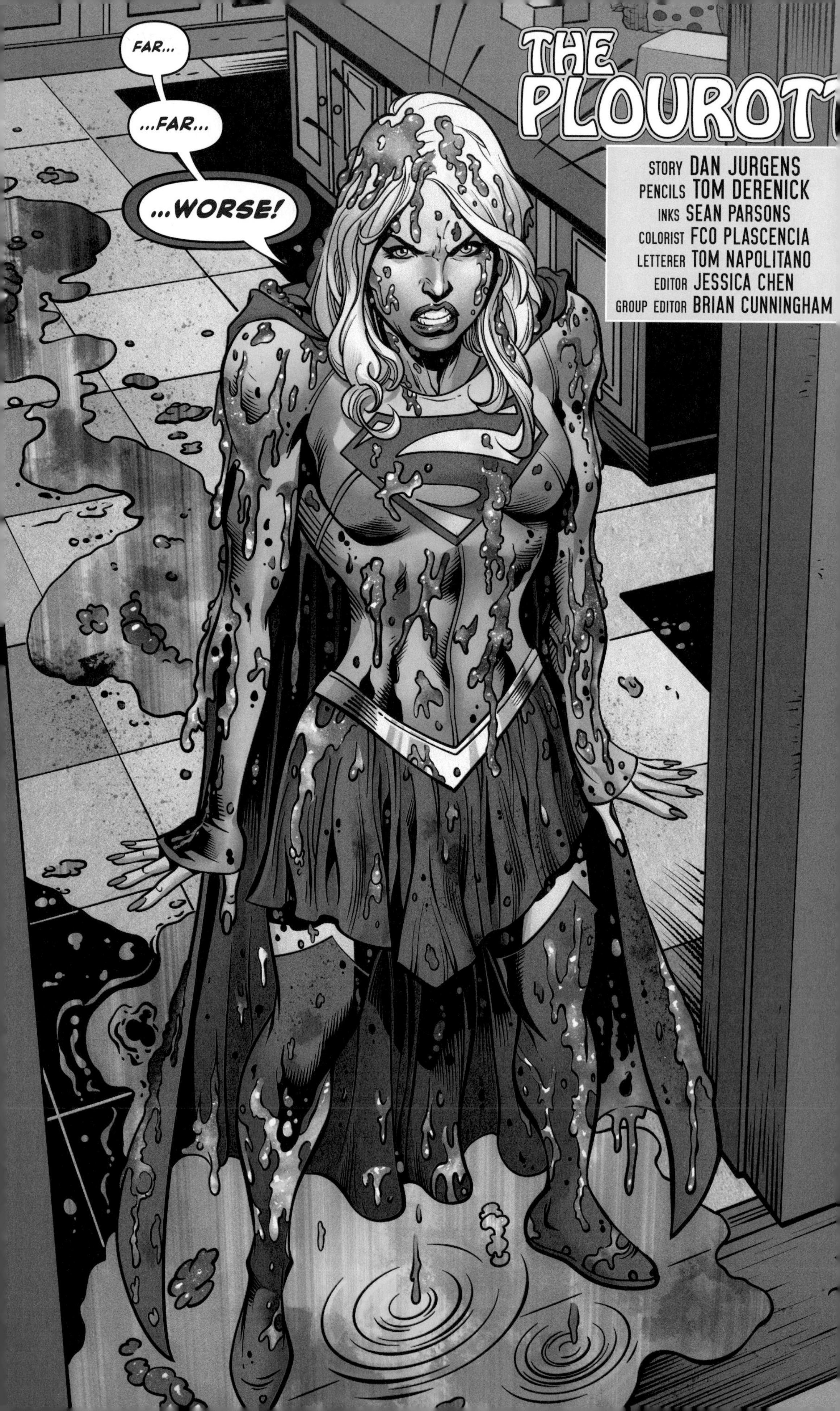

FAR...
...FAR...
...WORSE!
THE PLOUROT
STORY DAN JURGENS
PENCILS TOM DERENICK
INKS SEAN PARSONS
COLORIST FCO PLASCENCIA
LETTERER TOM NAPOLITANO
EDITOR JESSICA CHEN
GROUP EDITOR BRIAN CUNNINGHAM

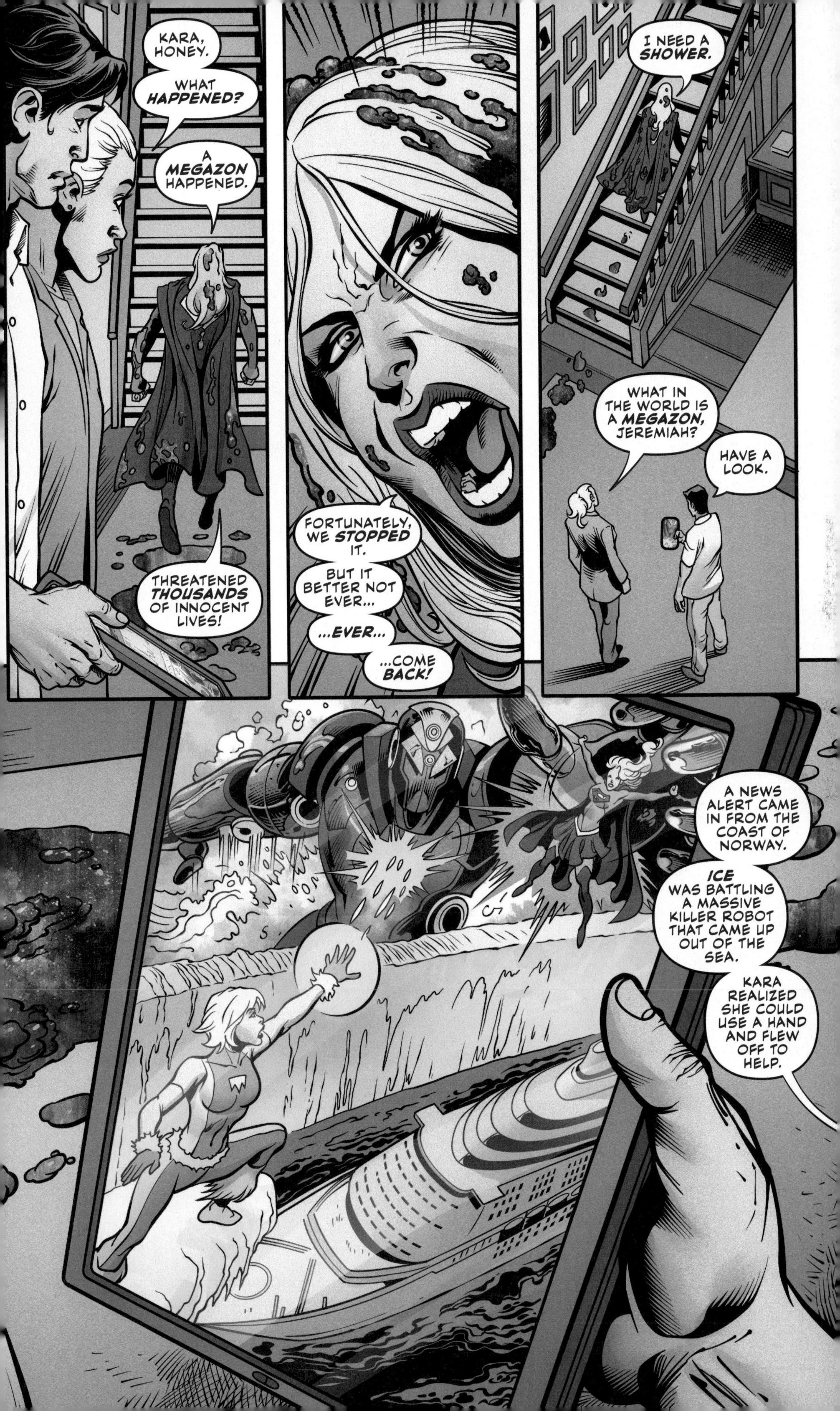

KARA, HONEY.
WHAT HAPPENED?
A MEGAZON HAPPENED.
THREATENED THOUSANDS OF INNOCENT LIVES!
FORTUNATELY, WE STOPPED IT.
BUT IT BETTER NOT EVER...
...EVER...
...COME BACK!
I NEED A SHOWER.
WHAT IN THE WORLD IS A MEGAZON, JEREMIAH?
HAVE A LOOK.
A NEWS ALERT CAME IN FROM THE COAST OF NORWAY.
ICE WAS BATTLING A MASSIVE KILLER ROBOT THAT CAME UP OUT OF THE SEA.
KARA REALIZED SHE COULD USE A HAND AND FLEW OFF TO HELP.

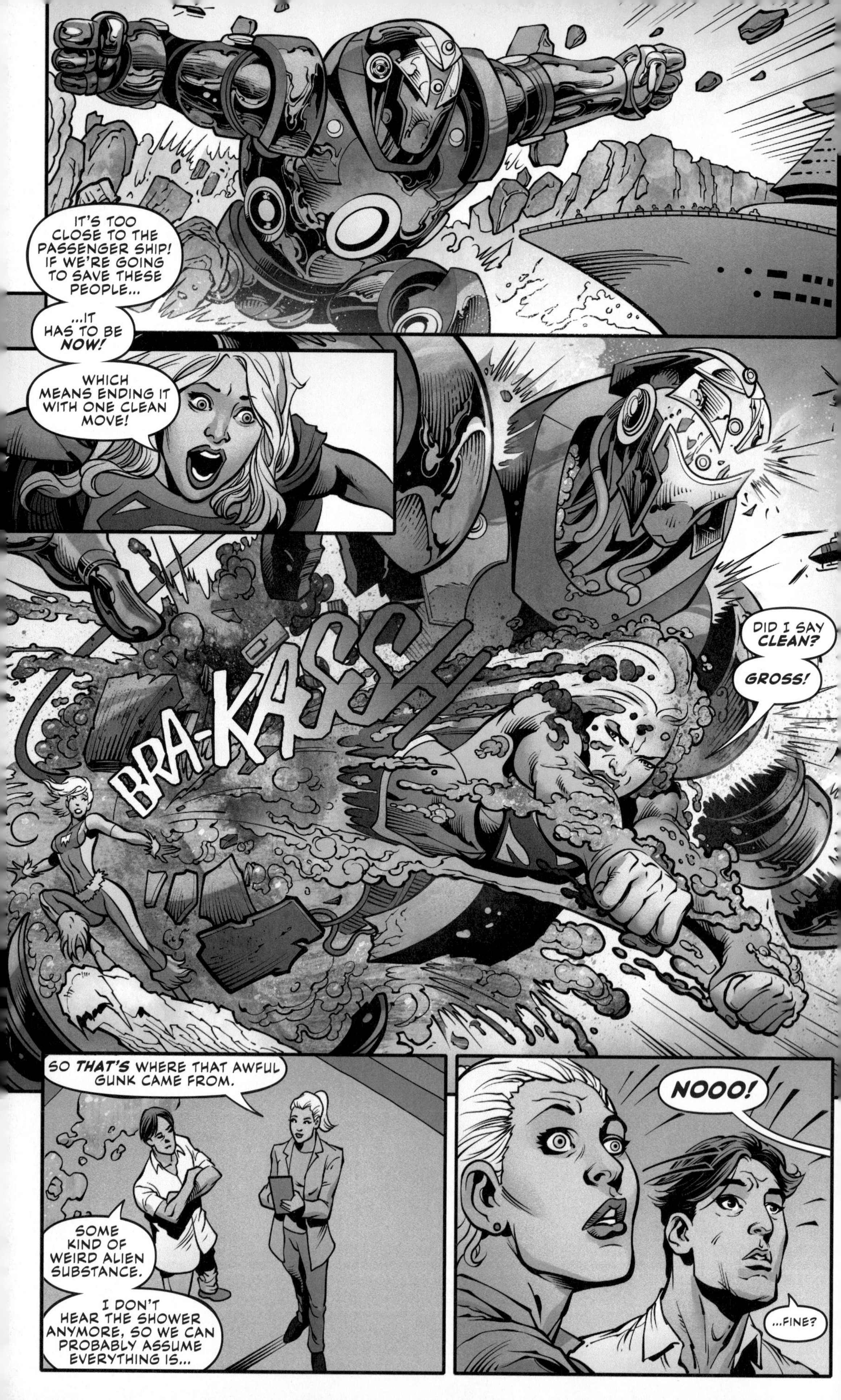
IT'S TOO CLOSE TO THE PASSENGER SHIP! IF WE'RE GOING TO SAVE THESE PEOPLE...
...IT HAS TO BE NOW!
WHICH MEANS ENDING IT WITH ONE CLEAN MOVE!
BRA-KASSH
DID I SAY CLEAN?
GROSS!
SO THAT'S WHERE THAT AWFUL GUNK CAME FROM.
SOME KIND OF WEIRD ALIEN SUBSTANCE.
I DON'T HEAR THE SHOWER ANYMORE, SO WE CAN PROBABLY ASSUME EVERYTHING IS...
NOOO!
...FINE?

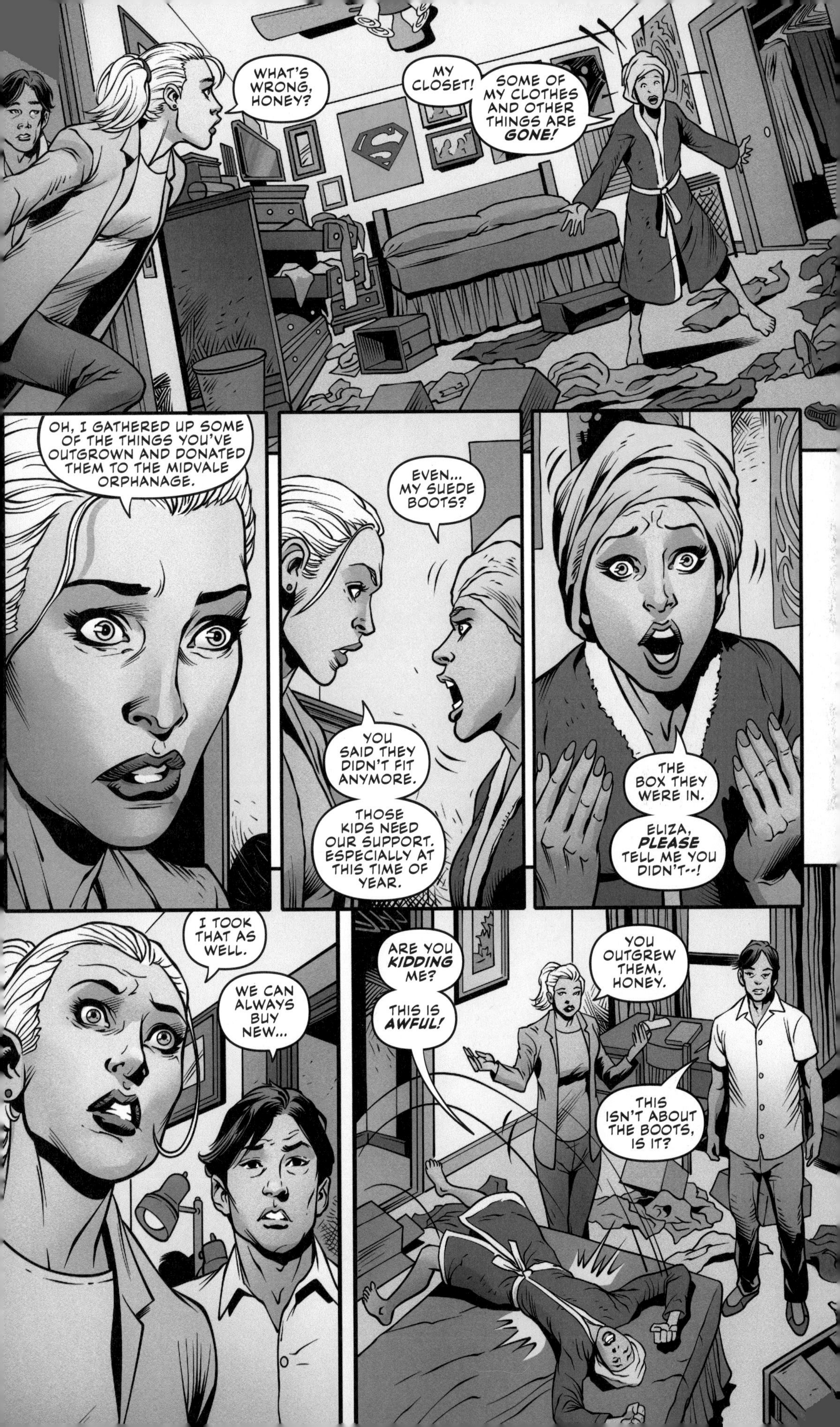
WHAT'S WRONG, HONEY?
MY CLOSET!
SOME OF MY CLOTHES AND OTHER THINGS ARE *GONE!*
OH, I GATHERED UP SOME OF THE THINGS YOU'VE OUTGROWN AND DONATED THEM TO THE MIDVALE ORPHANAGE.
EVEN... MY SUEDE BOOTS?
YOU SAID THEY DIDN'T FIT ANYMORE.
THOSE KIDS NEED OUR SUPPORT. ESPECIALLY AT THIS TIME OF YEAR.
THE BOX THEY WERE IN.
ELIZA, *PLEASE* TELL ME YOU DIDN'T--!
I TOOK THAT AS WELL.
WE CAN ALWAYS BUY NEW...
ARE YOU *KIDDING* ME?
THIS IS *AWFUL!*
YOU OUTGREW THEM, HONEY.
THIS ISN'T ABOUT THE BOOTS, IS IT?

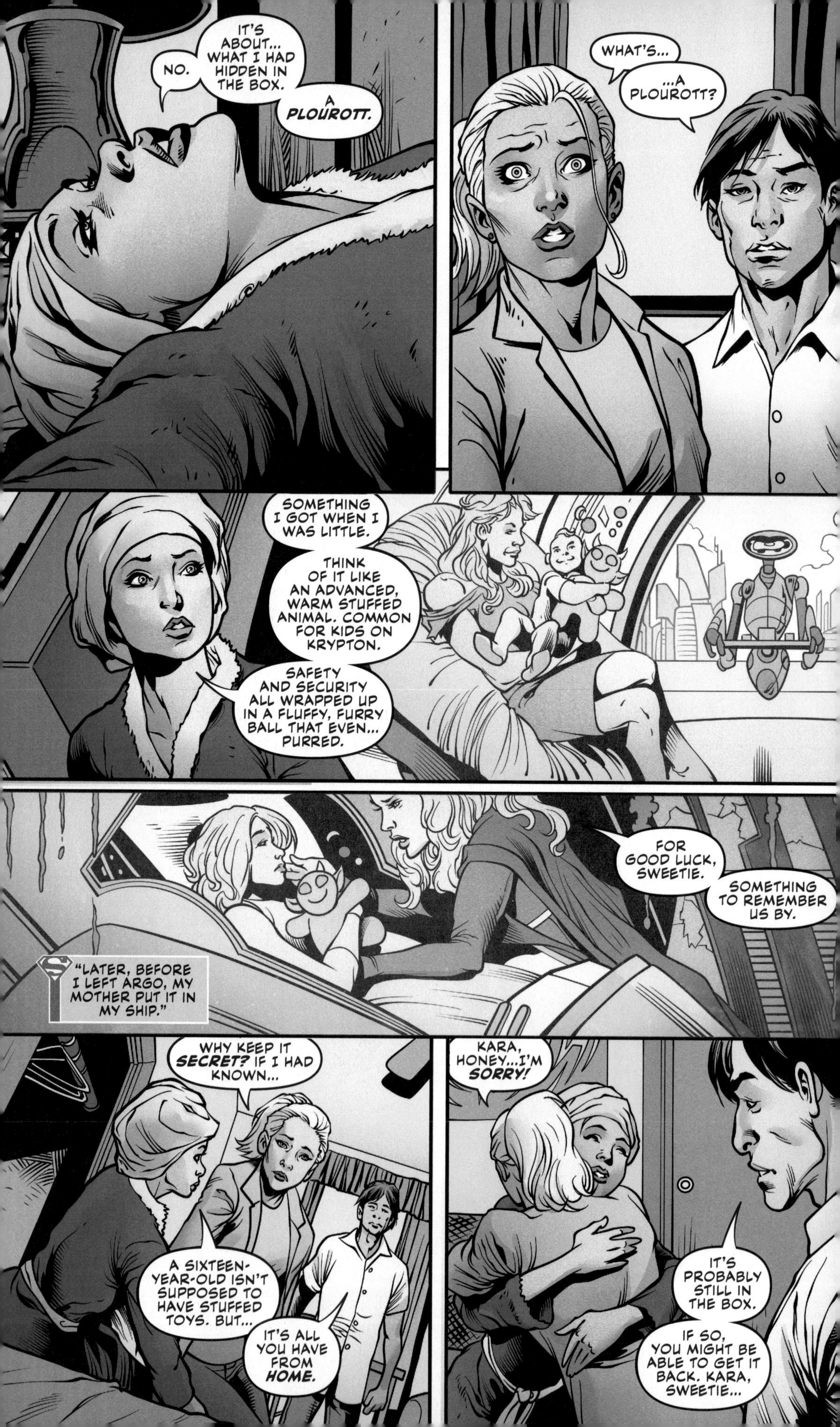
NO.
IT'S ABOUT... WHAT I HAD HIDDEN IN THE BOX.
A *PLOUROTT.*
WHAT'S...
...A PLOUROTT?
SOMETHING I GOT WHEN I WAS LITTLE.
THINK OF IT LIKE AN ADVANCED, WARM STUFFED ANIMAL. COMMON FOR KIDS ON KRYPTON.
SAFETY AND SECURITY ALL WRAPPED UP IN A FLUFFY, FURRY BALL THAT EVEN... PURRED.
FOR GOOD LUCK, SWEETIE.
SOMETHING TO REMEMBER US BY.
"LATER, BEFORE I LEFT ARGO, MY MOTHER PUT IT IN MY SHIP."
WHY KEEP IT *SECRET?* IF I HAD KNOWN...
A SIXTEEN-YEAR-OLD ISN'T SUPPOSED TO HAVE STUFFED TOYS. BUT...
IT'S ALL YOU HAVE FROM *HOME.*
KARA, HONEY...I'M *SORRY!*
IT'S PROBABLY STILL IN THE BOX.
IF SO, YOU MIGHT BE ABLE TO GET IT BACK. KARA, SWEETIE...

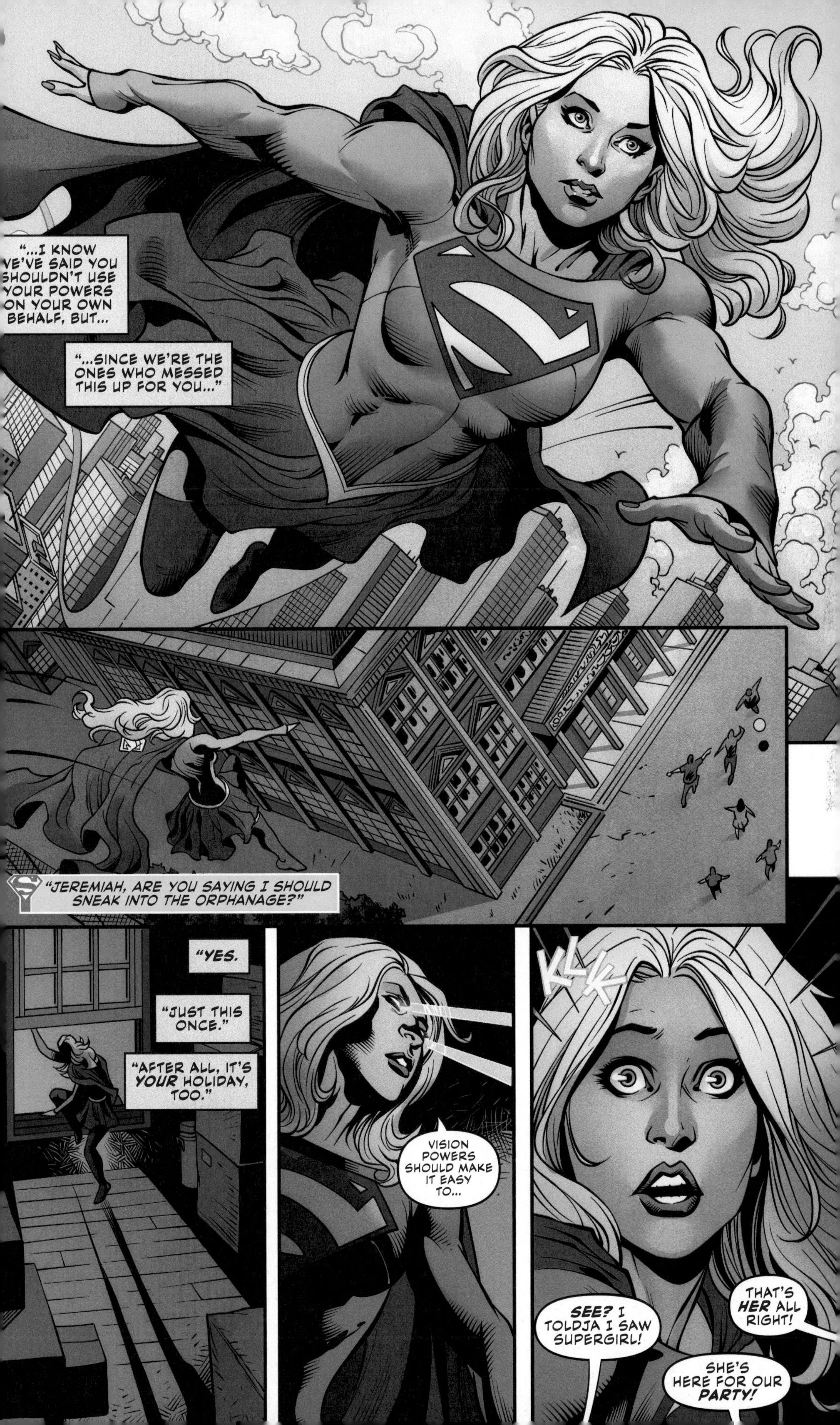
"...I KNOW VE'VE SAID YOU SHOULDN'T USE YOUR POWERS ON YOUR OWN BEHALF, BUT...
"...SINCE WE'RE THE ONES WHO MESSED THIS UP FOR YOU..."
"JEREMIAH, ARE YOU SAYING I SHOULD SNEAK INTO THE ORPHANAGE?"
"YES.
"JUST THIS ONCE."
"AFTER ALL, IT'S YOUR HOLIDAY, TOO."
VISION POWERS SHOULD MAKE IT EASY TO...
KLIK
SEE? I TOLDJA I SAW SUPERGIRL!
THAT'S HER ALL RIGHT!
SHE'S HERE FOR OUR PARTY!

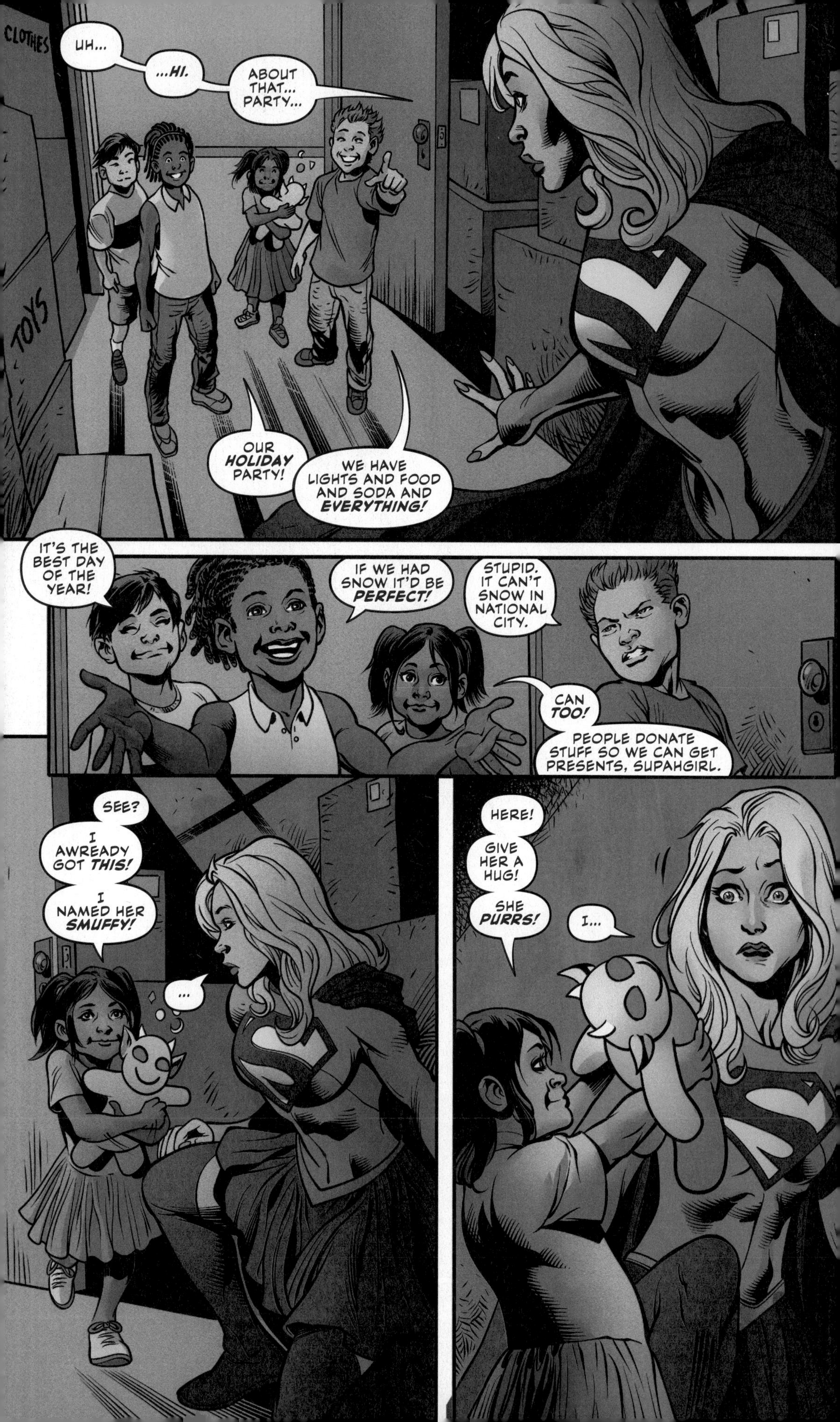
CLOTHES
UH...
...HI.
ABOUT THAT... PARTY...
TOYS
OUR HOLIDAY PARTY!
WE HAVE LIGHTS AND FOOD AND SODA AND EVERYTHING!
IT'S THE BEST DAY OF THE YEAR!
IF WE HAD SNOW IT'D BE PERFECT!
STUPID. IT CAN'T SNOW IN NATIONAL CITY.
CAN TOO!
PEOPLE DONATE STUFF SO WE CAN GET PRESENTS, SUPAHGIRL.
SEE?
I AWREADY GOT THIS!
I NAMED HER SMUFFY!
...
HERE!
GIVE HER A HUG!
SHE PURRS!
I...

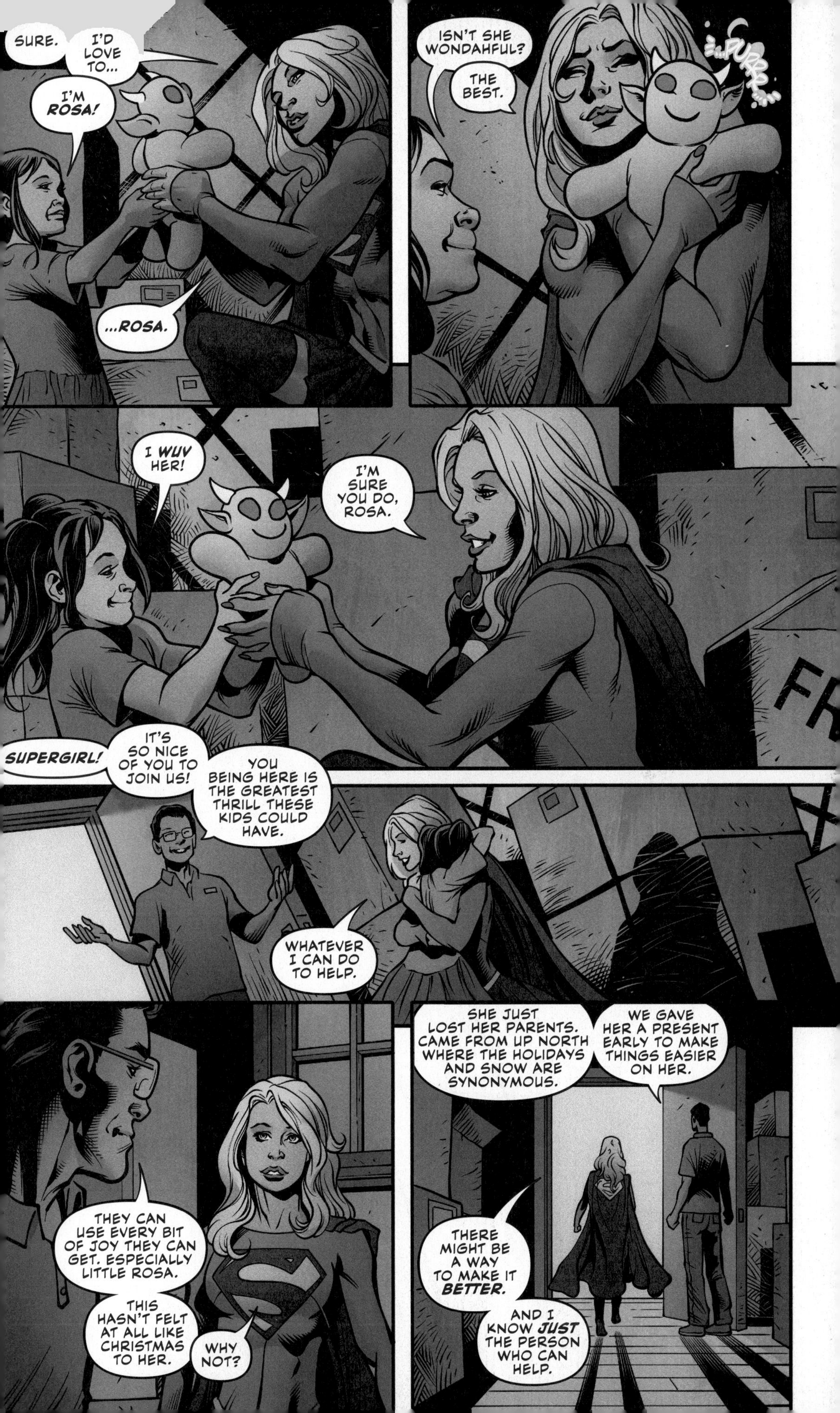

SURE.
I'D LOVE TO...
I'M ROSA!
...ROSA.
ISN'T SHE WONDAHFUL?
THE BEST.
PURRR
I WUV HER!
I'M SURE YOU DO, ROSA.
FR
SUPERGIRL!
IT'S SO NICE OF YOU TO JOIN US!
YOU BEING HERE IS THE GREATEST THRILL THESE KIDS COULD HAVE.
WHATEVER I CAN DO TO HELP.
THEY CAN USE EVERY BIT OF JOY THEY CAN GET. ESPECIALLY LITTLE ROSA.
THIS HASN'T FELT AT ALL LIKE CHRISTMAS TO HER.
WHY NOT?
SHE JUST LOST HER PARENTS. CAME FROM UP NORTH WHERE THE HOLIDAYS AND SNOW ARE SYNONYMOUS.
WE GAVE HER A PRESENT EARLY TO MAKE THINGS EASIER ON HER.
THERE MIGHT BE A WAY TO MAKE IT BETTER.
AND I KNOW JUST THE PERSON WHO CAN HELP.

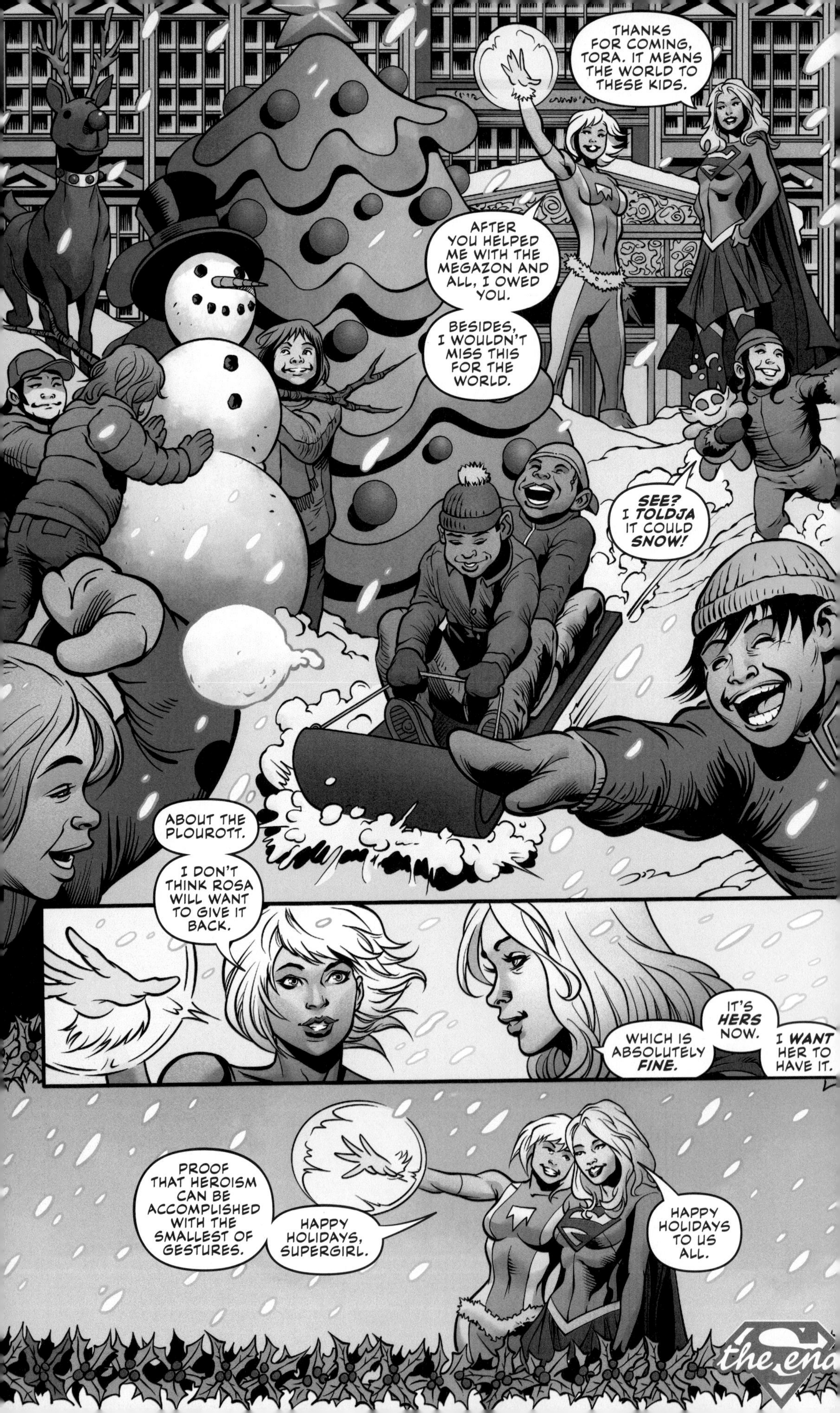
THANKS FOR COMING, TORA. IT MEANS THE WORLD TO THESE KIDS.
AFTER YOU HELPED ME WITH THE MEGAZON AND ALL, I OWED YOU.
BESIDES, I WOULDN'T MISS THIS FOR THE WORLD.
SEE? I TOLDJA IT COULD SNOW!
ABOUT THE PLOUROTT.
I DON'T THINK ROSA WILL WANT TO GIVE IT BACK.
WHICH IS ABSOLUTELY FINE.
IT'S HERS NOW.
I WANT HER TO HAVE IT.
PROOF THAT HEROISM CAN BE ACCOMPLISHED WITH THE SMALLEST OF GESTURES.
HAPPY HOLIDAYS, SUPERGIRL.
HAPPY HOLIDAYS TO US ALL.
the end

SUPERGIRL #21 variant cover
by AMANDA CONNER with PAUL MOUNTS

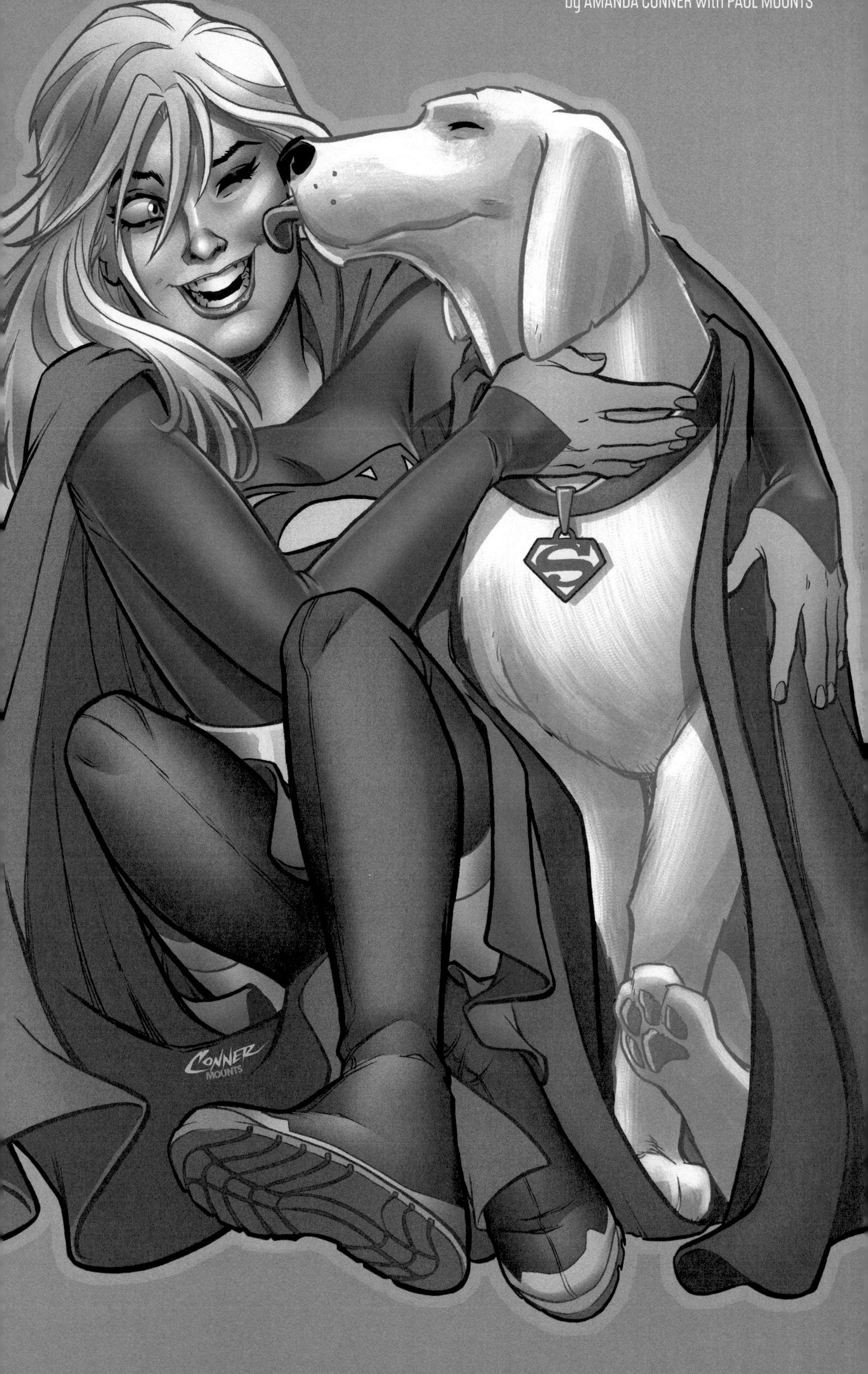
CONNER
MOUNTS

SUPERGIRL #22 variant cover
by AMANDA CONNER with PAUL MOUNTS

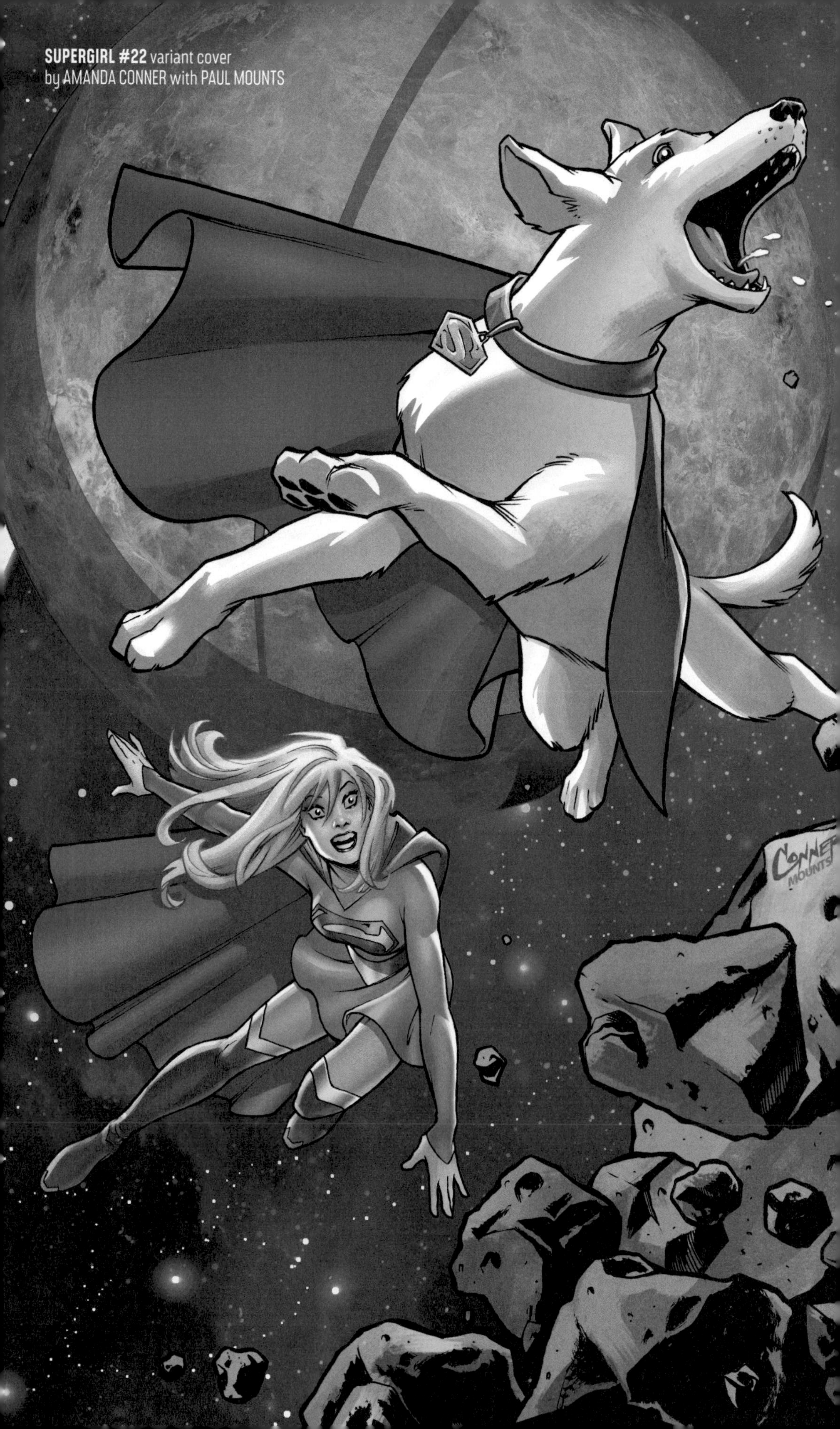
CONNER
MOUNTS

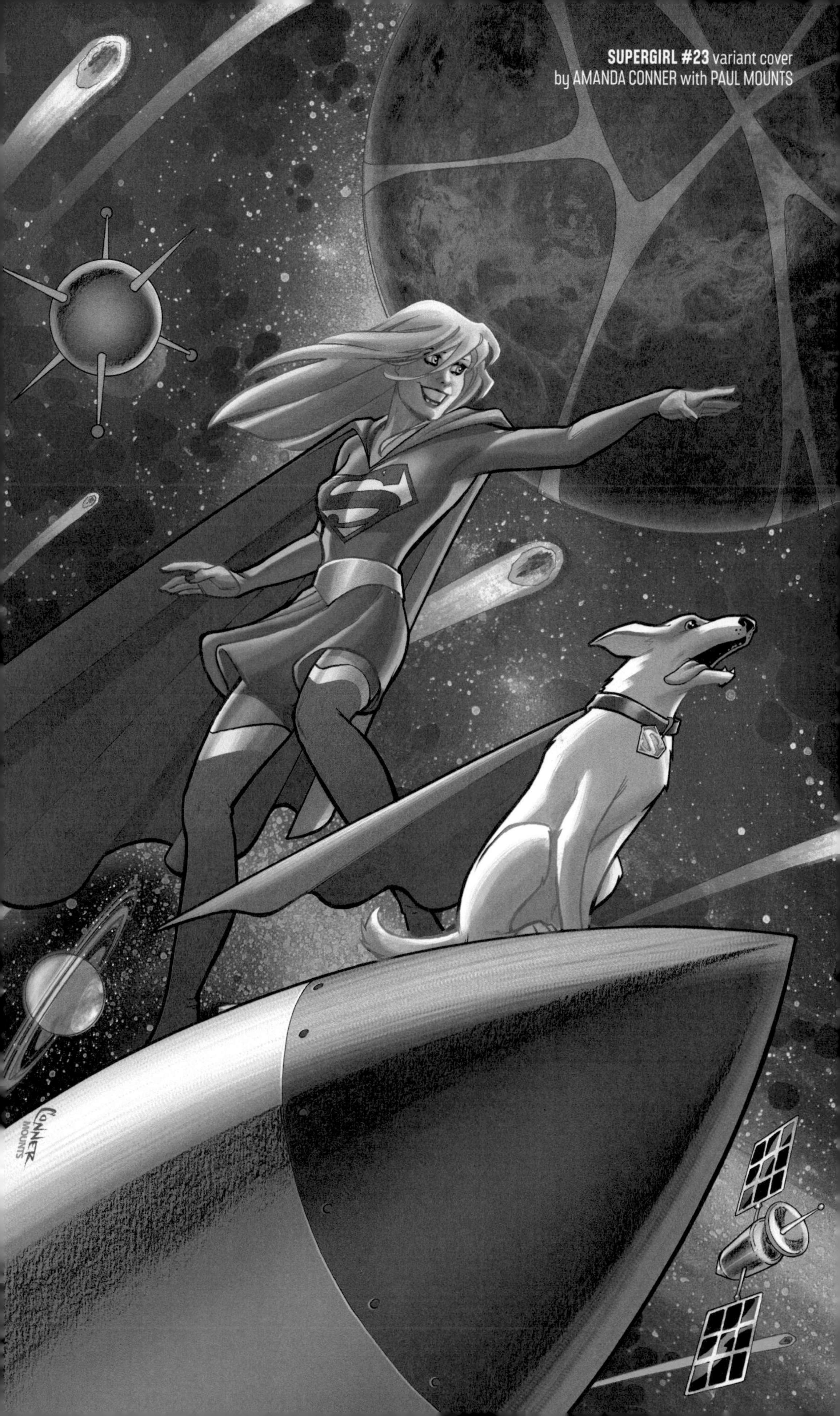
CONNER
MOUNTS

SUPERGIRL #23 variant cover
by AMANDA CONNER with PAUL MOUNTS

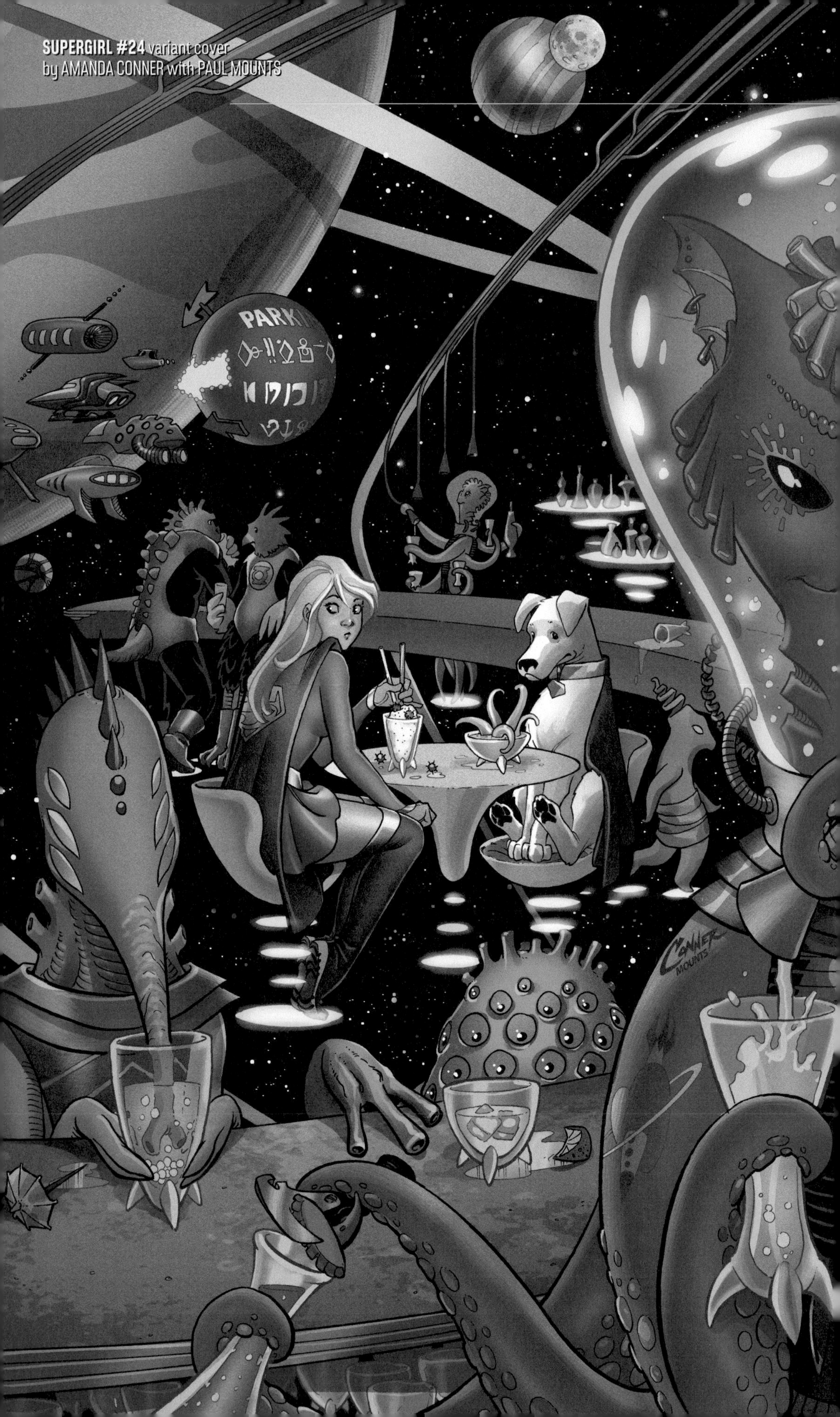
CONNER
MOUNTS
SUPERGIRL #24 variant cover
by AMANDA CONNER with PAUL MOUNTS

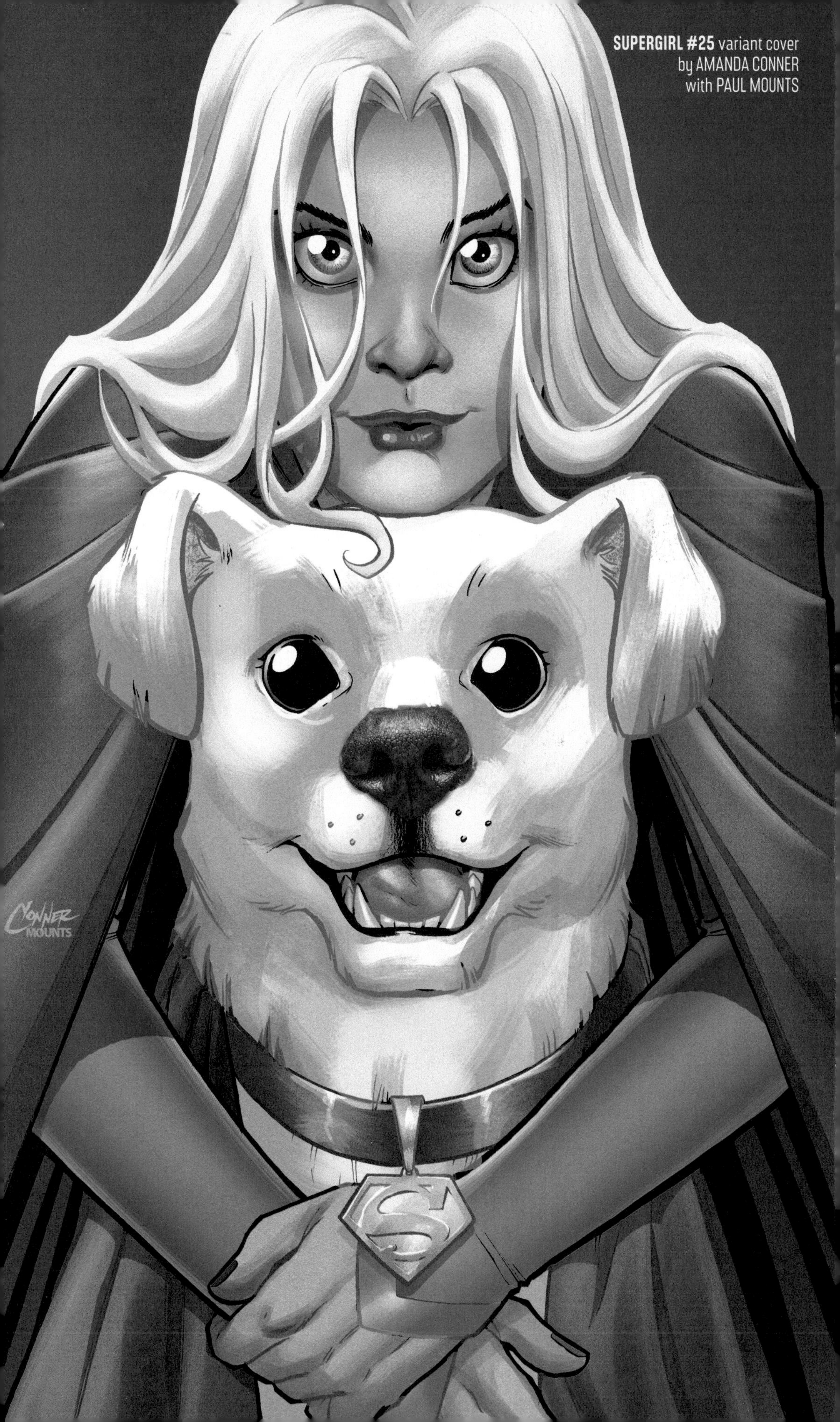
CONNER
MOUNTS

SUPERGIRL #25 variant cover
by AMANDA CONNER
with PAUL MOUNTS

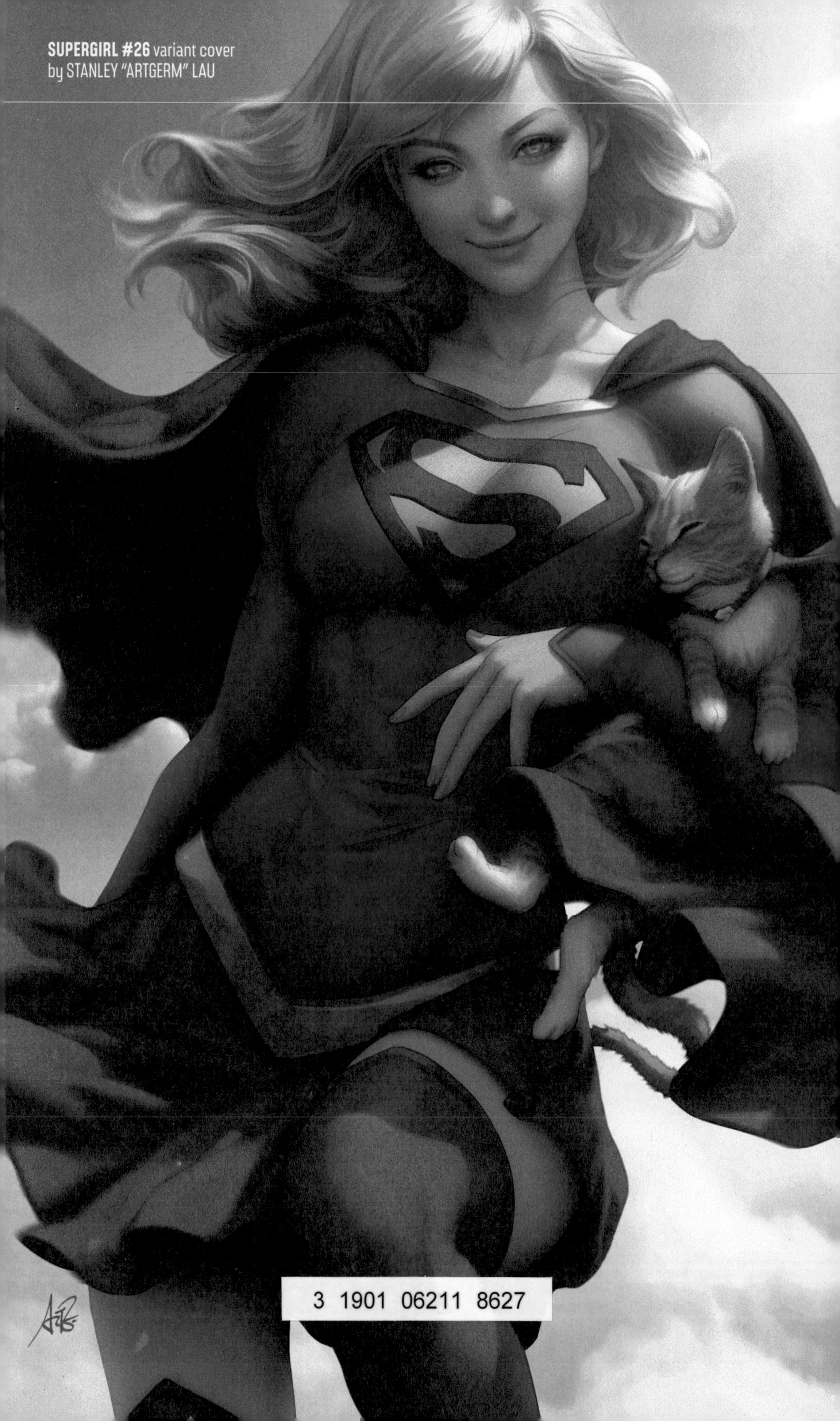

SUPERGIRL #26 variant cover
by STANLEY "ARTGERM" LAU